the PARIS
REVIEW
Interviews, II

*the*PARIS REVIEW
Interviews, II

WITH AN INTRODUCTION BY
ORHAN PAMUK

PICADOR • NEW YORK

www.picadorusa.com

Picador® is a U.S. registered trademark and is used by St. Martin's Press under license from Pan Books Limited.

For information on Picador Reading Group Guides, please contact Picador.
Phone: 646-307-5259
Fax: 212-253-9627
E-mail: readinggroupguides@picadorusa.com

Library of Congress Cataloging-in-Publication Data

The Paris Review Interviews, II / with an introduction by Orhan Pamuk.—1st ed.
    p. cm.
  ISBN-13: 978-0-312-36314-7 (v. 2)
  ISBN-10: 0-312-36314-1 (v. 2)
  1. Authors, American—20th century—Interviews. 2. Authors, English—20th century—Interviews. 3. American literature—20th century—History and criticism. 4. English literature—20th century—History and criticism. 5. Authorship. I. Gourevitch, Philip, 1961– II. Paris review.
  PS225.P26 2006
  823'.9109—dc22

2006051097

First Edition: November 2007

10 9 8 7 6 5 4 3 2 1

Contents

Introduction

by Orhan Pamuk

translated by Maureen Freely

When I first read Faulkner in *The Paris Review*, in Istanbul, in 1977, I felt as elated as if I had stumbled on a sacred text. I was twenty-five years old, living with my mother in an apartment overlooking the Bosphorus, sitting in a backroom, surrounded by books, chain-smoking, and struggling to finish my first novel. To write one's first novel is not just to learn how to tell one's own story as if it were someone else's. It is at the same time to become a person who can imagine a novel from start to finish in a balanced way, who can express this dream in words and sentences. . . . To become a novelist, I had dropped out of architectural school and shut myself up in a house. What sort of person should I now become?

INTERVIEWER

How does a writer become a serious novelist?

FAULKNER

Ninety-nine percent talent . . . ninety-nine percent discipline . . . ninety-nine percent work. He must never be satisfied with what he does. It never is as good as it can be done. Always dream and shoot higher than you know you can do. Don't bother just to be better than your contemporaries or predecessors. Try to be better than yourself. An artist is a creature driven by demons. He doesn't know why they choose him and he's usually too busy to wonder why. He is completely amoral in that he will rob, borrow, beg, or steal from anybody and everybody to get the work done. . . . The writer's only responsibility is to his art.

It was consoling to read these words in a country where the demands of the community came before all else. I arranged for all the *Paris Review* interviews published by Penguin under separate volumes to be sent to me in Istanbul: I read them with concentration and enjoyment. Day by day I was imposing on myself the discipline of working on a table all day, enjoying the smell of paper and pen in a lonely room—habits that I will never ever lose. I was writing my first novel, *Cevdet Bey and Sons*—a six-hundred-page volume that would take me four years to complete—and whenever I was stuck, I would instinctively rise from the desk; hopelessly throwing myself onto the divan in the same smoky room, I would again read these interviews with Faulkner, Nabokov, Dos Passos, Hemingway, or Updike, struggling to regain my faith in writing, and to find my own way. In the beginning I read these interviews because I loved these writers' books, because I wished to learn their secrets, to understand how they created their fictive worlds. But I also enjoyed reading interviews with novelists and poets whose names I hardly knew, and whose books I had not read. Let me try to unravel some of the sentiments that visited me as I read and reread these interviews:

- The *Paris Review* interviews were not tied to a particular book or work that the authors were obliged to promote. These were writers who were already established and world famous, and in these interviews they talked about their writing habits, the secrets of their trade, their ways of writing, their fragile moments, and the ways in which they overcame the difficulties they encountered. I needed to learn from their experience, as quickly as I could.

- Just as I took their books as examples, I drew upon these writers' varied habits, bugbears, eccentricities, and little quirks (such as insisting that there always be coffee on the table). For thirty-three years now, I have been writing longhand on graph paper. Sometimes I think this is because graph paper suits my way of writing. . . . Sometimes I think it is because I learned in those days that two of my favorite writers, Thomas Mann and Jean-Paul Sartre, wrote on graph paper. . . .

- I was not friends with any Turkish writers my age and my isolation increased my anxieties about my future. Every time I sat down to read these interviews, my loneliness faded away. By reading these authors' interviews, I discovered that there were many others who shared my passion, that the distance between what I desired and what I achieved was normal, that my loathing for normal everyday life was not a sign of sickness but of intelligence, and that I should embrace most of the little eccentric habits that fired up my imagination and helped me write.

- I feel as if I learned a great deal about the craft of writing novels—how the first germ formed in the writer's mind, how lovingly it was grown, and how carefully plotted, or not plotted at all. Sometimes it was by reacting with fury against a certain idea of the novel suggested in these interviews that I developed my own ideas on the novel as well.

- As a young man I had, after reading Flaubert's letters and the life stories of those writers I most admired, embraced the ethic of literary modernism that no serious writer can escape: to dedicate myself to art without expecting anything in return, to shun fame, success, and cheaply won popularity, to love literature for its own beauty. But when I read how Faulkner and other authors express their commitment to these same ideals, their unmediated frankness would lift my spirits even higher. During my early days as a writer, when I lacked confidence and had doubts about my future as a writer, I would return to these interviews to bolster my resolve.

To read these interviews again after so many years—and after I have myself appeared in the magazine's pages—is to recall the hopes and

anxieties of my early writing days. Thirty years later, I can read them
with the same enthusiasm, knowing that I was in no way misled: these
interviews speak to me of literature's joys and vexations more
strongly than ever before.

the PARIS REVIEW
REVIEW
Interviews, II

Graham Greene

The Art of Fiction

The eighteenth century succeeds to the twentieth on the ground floors at the bottom of St. James's Street. The gloss and the cellophane of oyster bars and travel agencies are wrapped incongruously round the legs of the dignified houses. Graham Greene lives here at the commercial end of this thoroughfare in a flat on the first floor of a narrow house sandwiched between the clubs of the aristocracy and St. James's Palace. Above him, General Auchinleck, the soldier who was beaten by Rommel; below him, the smartest oyster bar in Europe; opposite, the second smartest.

Readers of *Cakes and Ale* will remember that it was near here that Maugham met Hugh Walpole, but it is not the sort of area in which one expects to find a novelist, even a successful novelist. It's an area black with smartness; the Rolls-Royces and the bowler hats of the men are black, the court shoes and the correct suits of the women are black, and in the most august flats even the bathing pools set into the floors of the bathrooms are paved with black marble. Nearby are the courtyard and sundial of Pickering Place, where only the very rich penetrate to eat and wine in Carolinean isolation.

Isolation, the isolation of anonymity rather than that of wealth, is probably the lure for Greene, for he is, or was until recently, a man shy of the contacts that congeal to fame. Brown-suited, brown-shoed, browned face, he opened the door when we rang and ushered us up above the oyster bar to the large room. It was cold for April and a large number of electric fires were burning in various corners of the room. A many-lamped standard of Scandinavian design stood by the window; a couple of bulbs were lit, they made as much difference to the watery April light as a pair of afterburners to a flagging jet engine. They revealed a book-lined room with a desk, a dictaphone and a typewriter, great padded armchairs, and a furry rug. A painting by Jack Yeats overstood the mantle; sombre, Celtic, yet delicate, it had something in common with the red pastel drawings by Henry Moore, whose sad classicism against the wall was in keeping with the brownness that dominated the whole room. Brown as the headmaster's study or the little office in Lagos where he once said he might willingly have spent forty dreary years, brown as his collection of books was blue—blue with the blueness that the bindings of English academic publishers give to the shelves and studies of dons and scholarly men of letters. It was a shock; subconsciously we had expected the black and purple of a Catholic bookshop, a violence to match Mexico, Brighton, and West Africa—what we had found was a snuggery, a den such as might be found in any vicarage or small country house in England. The only suggestion of an obsession, or of anything out of the ordinary (for so many people have Henry Moores these days) was a collection of seventy-four different miniature whiskey bottles, ranged on top of a bookcase, bizarre as an international convention of Salesian novices.

In the retreat of the man within the novelist, the man whom we had come to besiege, they were a welcome discovery.

—*Martin Shuttleworth, Simon Raven, 1953*

INTERVIEWER

Mr. Greene, we thought that we could make the best use of our time here if we brought along a few focal questions and let the conversation eddy round them. We felt that any formal questionnaire that we might make out would be based only on a knowledge of your written work and that a portion of the answers would be contained in the assumptions that allowed us to formulate the questions; we wanted to get beyond this and so we have come prepared to let the conversation lead us and to try to find out, so far as you will let us, the unknown things about you.

GRAHAM GREENE

Very frank. What will you have to drink?

INTERVIEWER

Shall we begin by working backward from your latest production, your play *The Living Room*? It has not been seen in America yet so you will excuse us if we go into it in some detail.

GREENE

Have you seen this play yourselves?

INTERVIEWER

No, a percipient girl saw it for us—she went down to Portsmouth and came back with a review, a synopsis, and a great admiration for it.

GREENE

I am glad; it's my first play. I've been a film man to date and I was rather afraid that I had written it in such filmic terms that it might not have succeeded as a play.

INTERVIEWER

She enjoyed it well enough. She felt that you had conveyed the tense, haunted atmosphere of a house in which a family was decaying because of its ill-conceived gentility and religion; that you had made a drama out of the situation of the girl who was lost in the desert between the unhappiness, truth, and family that lay in the background and the lover and mirage of happiness that lay in the foreground. Her main criticism, and this perhaps has something to do with what you were saying just now about the difference between film and theatrical technique, was that you had made the drama depend too much on dialogue and not enough on action.

GREENE

There I disagree. I obeyed the unities. I confined myself to one set and I made my characters act, one upon the other. What other sort of action can you have? I get fed up with all this nonsense of ringing people up and lighting cigarettes and answering the doorbell that passes for action in so many modern plays. No, what I meant about filmic terms was that I was so used to the dissolve that I had forgotten about the curtain, and so used to the camera, which is only turned on when it is wanted, that I had forgotten that actors and actresses are on the stage all the time and I had left out many functional lines. Still, most of that has been put right now.

INTERVIEWER

Then the criticism, if it stands, means that the dialogue fell short in some other way; perhaps it was too closely related to the dialogue of your novels which doesn't often carry the burden of the action.

GREENE

I think that is nearer the mark: I tried to fuse everything and put it into the dialogue but I did not quite succeed. I will next time.

INTERVIEWER

The particular thing that impressed this critic of ours was your attitude toward the girl's suicide. This is what she writes: "The central point of much of Greene's writing has been suicide, in Catholic doctrine the most deadly sin. But in this play at least his interpretation of it is not a doctrinal one. We are left quite definitely feeling that her soul is saved, if anyone's is, and the message of the play, for it does not pretend not to have a message, is not mere Catholic propaganda but of far wider appeal. It is a plea to believe in a God who Father Browne, the girl's confessor, admits may not exist, but belief can only do good not ill and without it we cannot help ourselves . . . the girl's suicide will probably be the only answer visible to most people but Father Browne's own unshaken faith, his calm acceptance of her death, implies that there is another, but that the struggle for it must be unceasing."

GREENE

Yes, I would say that that is roughly true but the message is still Catholic.

INTERVIEWER

How do you make that out?

GREENE

The church is compassionate, you know . . .

INTERVIEWER

Sorry to interrupt you but could we ask a correlative question now to save going back later?

GREENE

Go ahead.

INTERVIEWER

Scobie in *The Heart of the Matter* committed suicide too. Was it your purpose when you wrote *The Living Room* to show a similar predicament and to show that suicide in certain circumstances can almost amount to an act of redemption?

GREENE

Steady, steady. Let's put it this way. I write about situations that are common, universal might be more correct, in which my characters are involved and from which only faith can redeem them, though often the actual manner of the redemption is not immediately clear. They sin, but there is no limit to God's mercy and because this is important, there is a difference between not confessing in fact, and the complacent and the pious may not realize it.

INTERVIEWER

In this sense Scobie, Rose (the girl in *The Living Room*), the boy Pinkie in *Brighton Rock*, and the whiskey priest of *The Power and the Glory* are all redeemed?

GREENE

Yes, though redemption is not the exact word. We must be careful of our language. They have all understood in the end. This is perhaps the religious sense.

INTERVIEWER

So we have touched the nerve of the theme, the theme that gives, as you have said somewhere yourself, to a shelf of novels the unity of a system?

GREENE

Yes, or rather it explains the unity of a group of my novels, which is now, I think, finished.

INTERVIEWER

Which group?

GREENE

Brighton Rock, The Power and the Glory, The Heart of the Matter, and *The End of the Affair*. My next novel will not deal explicitly with Catholic themes at all.

INTERVIEWER

So the *New Statesman* gibe that *The End of the Affair* is the last novel that a layman will be able to read is about to be disproved?

GREENE

Yes, I think so, as far as one can tell oneself. I think that I know what the next novel is about, but one never really knows, of course, until it's finished.

INTERVIEWER

Was that so of the earlier books?

GREENE

The very earliest ones particularly . . .

INTERVIEWER

Yes, what about them? How did you find their subjects? Their historical romanticism is so different from what came later, even from the "entertainments."

GREENE

How does one find one's subjects?—gradually, I suppose. My first three, *The Man Within*, *The Name of Action*, *Rumour at Nightfall*— as far as one is influenced by anybody and I don't think that one is consciously influenced—were influenced by Stevenson and Conrad and they are what they are because at the time those were the subjects that I wanted to write about. The entertainments (*Stamboul Train*, written a year after *Rumour at Nightfall*, is the first of them; then A *Gun for Sale*, *The Confidential Agent*, *The Ministry of Fear*, and *The Third Man* and *The Fallen Idol*) are distinct from the novels because as the name implies they do not carry a message (horrible word).

INTERVIEWER

They show traces though of the same obsession; they are written from the same point of view . . .

GREENE

Yes, I wrote them. They are not all that different.

INTERVIEWER

There is a great break between *Rumour at Nightfall* and *England Made Me*, our favorite novel of yours. What caused the historical novelist to turn into the contemporary one?

GREENE

I have a particularly soft spot for *England Made Me* too. The book came about when I began *Stamboul Train*. I had to write a potboiler, a modern adventure story, and I suddenly discovered that I liked the form, that the writing came easily, that I was beginning to find my world. In *England Made Me* I let myself go in it for the first time.

INTERVIEWER

You had begun to read James and Mauriac?

GREENE

Yes, I had begun to change. I had found that what I wanted to express, my fixations if you like, could best be expressed in the melodramatic, the contemporary, and later the Catholic novel.

INTERVIEWER

What influence has Mauriac had over you?

GREENE

Again, very little, I think.

INTERVIEWER

But you told Kenneth Allott, who quotes it in his book about you, that Mauriac had a distinct influence.

GREENE

Did I? That is the sort of thing that one says under pressure. I read *Thérèse* in 1930 and was turned up inside but, as I have said, I don't think that he had any influence on me unless it was an unconscious one. Our Catholicism is very different: I don't see the resemblance that people talk about.

INTERVIEWER

Where do the differences in your Catholicism lie?

GREENE

Mauriac's sinners sin against God whereas mine, however hard they try, can never quite manage to . . .

INTERVIEWER

Then Mauriac is almost a Manichee whereas you—

[*The telephone rang and when, after a brief conversation, Greene came back to his long low seat between the electric fires and topped up the glasses, the conversation was not resumed, for the point, we thought, if not implied, was difficult for him to discuss.*]

INTERVIEWER

Can we now discuss this fresh period that you mentioned just now?

GREENE

We can but I don't think that you'll find out much, for it has not begun yet. All that I can tell you is that I do know that my next novel is to be about an entirely different set of people with entirely different roots.

INTERVIEWER

Perhaps then it would be more profitable to talk about the roots of your previous sets of characters? If we leave the historical romantic novels and the entertainments out of it for the moment and concentrate on the contemporary ones, it is obvious that there is a relationship between the characters which is a product in part of your absorption with failure, pursuit, and poverty, and in part with interest in a particular type of person.

GREENE

I agree with you, of course, when you say that there is a relationship between, let us say, Anthony Farrant in *England Made Me* and Pinkie, or Scobie, even—but they are not the same sort of person even if they are the expressions of what critics are pleased to call my fixations. I don't know exactly where they came from but I think that I have now got rid of them.

INTERVIEWER

Ah, now, these fixations—they are what really matter, aren't they? We don't quite understand why you consider that it is so important for a novelist to be dominated in this way.

GREENE

Because if he is not he has to rely on his talent, and talent, even of a very high order, cannot sustain an achievement, whereas a ruling passion gives, as I have said, to a shelf of novels the unity of a system.

INTERVIEWER

Mr. Greene, if a novelist did not have this ruling passion, might it be possible to fabricate it?

GREENE

How do you mean?

INTERVIEWER

Well, put it this way, and I hope we won't seem to be impertinent: the contrast between the Nelson Places and the Mexicos of the novels and this flat in St. James's is marked. Urbanity, not tragedy, seems to reign in this room. Do you find, in your own life, that it is difficult to live at the high pitch of perception that you require of your characters?

GREENE

Well, this is rather difficult to answer. Could you perhaps qualify the question a bit?

INTERVIEWER

You made Scobie say in *The Heart of the Matter*: "Point me out the happy man and I will show you either egotism, selfishness, evil or else an absolute ignorance." What worries us is that you yourself seem to be so much happier than we had expected. Perhaps we are being rather naïve but the seventy-four miniature whiskey bottles, the expression on your face, so different from the fixed, set look of your photograph, the whole atmosphere, seem to be the products of something much more positive than that very limited optimum of happiness that you described in *The Power and the Glory* in this passage: "The world is all much of a piece: it is engaged everywhere in the same subterranean struggle . . . there is no peace anywhere where there is life; but there are quiet and active sectors of the line."

GREENE

Oh yes, I see what troubles you. I think that you have misjudged me and my consistency. This flat, my way of life—these are simply my hole in the ground.

INTERVIEWER

A moderately comfortable hole.

GREENE

Shall we leave it at that?

INTERVIEWER

Of course. There are just one or two other questions on a similar tack: Many of your most memorable characters, Raven for instance, are from low life. Have you ever had any experience of low life?

GREENE

No, very little.

INTERVIEWER

What did you know about poverty?

GREENE

I have never known it. I was "short," yes, in the sense that I had to be careful for the first eight years of my adult life but I have never been any closer.

INTERVIEWER

Then you don't draw your characters from life?

GREENE

No, one never knows enough about characters in real life to put them into novels. One gets started and then, suddenly, one cannot remember what toothpaste they use, what are their views on interior decoration, and one is stuck utterly. No, major characters emerge; minor ones may be photographed.

INTERVIEWER

Well now, how do you work? Do you work at regular hours?

GREENE

I used to; now I set myself a number of words.

INTERVIEWER

How many?

GREENE

Five hundred, stepped up to seven fifty as the book gets on. I reread the same day, again the next morning and again and again until the passage has got too far behind to matter to the bit that I am writing. Correct in type, final correction in proof.

INTERVIEWER

Do you correct much?

GREENE

Not overmuch.

INTERVIEWER

Did you always want to be a writer?

GREENE

No, I wanted to be a businessman and all sorts of other things; I wanted to prove to myself that I could do something else.

INTERVIEWER

Then the thing that you could always do was write?

GREENE

Yes, I suppose it was.

INTERVIEWER

What happened to your business career?

GREENE

Initially it lasted for a fortnight. They were a firm, I remember, of tobacco merchants. I was to go up to Leeds to learn the business and then go abroad. I couldn't stand my companion. He was an insufferable bore. We would play double noughts and crosses and he always won. What finally got me was when he said, We'll be able to play this on the way out, won't we? I resigned immediately.

INTERVIEWER

Then you became a journalist?

GREENE

Yes, for the same reason—that I wanted to prove I could do something else.

INTERVIEWER

But after *The Man Within* you gave it up?

GREENE

Then I became a professional author.

INTERVIEWER

So that is what you meant when you said, "I am an author who is a Catholic"?

GREENE

Indeed it is. I don't believe that anyone had ever realized that I was a Catholic until 1936 when I began to review for the *Tablet* and, for fun, or rather to give system to a series of reviews of unrelated books, I started to review from a Catholic standpoint. If it had not been for that . . .

INTERVIEWER

But surely a person would have to be very obtuse who reads any novel from *Brighton Rock* onwards and does not realize it?

GREENE

Some people still manage to. In fact, a Dutch priest wrote to me the other day, discussing *The Power and the Glory*, and concluded his letter: Well I suppose that even if you aren't a Catholic, you are not too hostile to us.

INTERVIEWER

Oh well, internal criticism.

GREENE

All the same, you see what I mean.

INTERVIEWER

Yes, you are "a writer who is a Catholic"; we seem to have cleared up that, but there are still a few gaps to be filled before we can know why you are a writer. Do you remember that you once said on the wireless that when you were fourteen or so and read Marjorie Bowen's *Viper of Milan* you immediately began to scribble imitation after imitation: "From that moment I began to write. All the other possible futures slid away . . ."

GREENE

Yes, that was so; I am very grateful to Marjorie Bowen. In that talk I was engaged on a little mild baiting of the intellectuals. Pritchett had said that Turgenev had influenced him most; somebody else, somebody else. I chose Marjorie Bowen because, as I have told you, I don't think that the books that one reads as an adult influence one as a writer. For example, of the many, many books on the art of the novel, only Percy Lubbock's *The Craft of Fiction* has interested me at all. But books such as Marjorie Bowen's, read at a young age, do influence one considerably. It is a very fine book, you know. I reread it again recently.

INTERVIEWER

We haven't read it, but from your description in the broadcast it seems that the book has many features in common with your writing as well as with your philosophy. You said that *The Viper of Milan* gave you your pattern of life, that "religion later might explain it to me in other terms, but the pattern was already there—perfect evil walking the world where perfect good can never walk again, and only the pendulum ensures that after all in the end justice is done." That explains a great deal about your philosophy, and it seems that the heightened colors and the violence of the Renaissance, as it is depicted by Miss Bowen and also as it is shown in the plays of Webster, also have their counterpart in your writing. As Edwin Muir has said of you: "Everything is shown up in a harsh light and casts fantastic colors."

GREENE

Yes, there is a lot to that. It is true, to a certain extent, about the earlier books, but I don't think that it does justice to the later ones. Melodrama is one of my working tools and it enables me to obtain effects that would be unobtainable otherwise; on the other hand, I am not deliberately melodramatic; don't get too annoyed if I say that I write in the way that I do because I am what I am.

INTERVIEWER

Do you ever need the stimulus of drink to write?

GREENE

No, on the contrary, I can only write when I am absolutely sober.

INTERVIEWER

Do you find collaboration easy, in particular collaboration with directors and producers?

GREENE

Well, I have been exceptionally lucky both with Carol Reed and recently with Peter Glenville. I like film work, even the impersonality of it. I have managed to retain a certain amount of control over my own stories so I have not suffered as badly as some people seem to have; all the same, filmmaking can be a distressing business for, when all is said and done, a writer's part in making a film is relatively small.

INTERVIEWER

Did it take you long to learn?

GREENE

I learned a lot on some not-very-good films before the war, so I was into my stride by the time that *The Fallen Idol* and *The Third Man* came along.

INTERVIEWER

Do you see much of your fellow authors?

GREENE

Not much, they are not one's material. A few of them are very dear friends of mine, but for a writer to spend much of his time in the company of authors is, you know, a form of masturbation.

INTERVIEWER

What was the nature of your friendship with Norman Douglas?

GREENE

We were so different that we could be friends. He was very tolerant in his last years, and if he thought me odd he never said so.

INTERVIEWER

Is there, in fact, any relationship between his paganism and your Catholicism?

GREENE

Not really, but his work, for which I have the very greatest admiration, was so remote from mine that I was able to enjoy it completely; to me it was like a great block of stone, which not being a sculptor myself I had no temptation to tamper with, yet could admire wholeheartedly for its beauty and strength.

INTERVIEWER

Yes, of course, there couldn't be any real connection between your writing and his—or between yours and Mauriac's. For as you have said, your sinners can never sin against God no matter how hard they try, but—

[*The telephone rang. Mr. Greene smiled in a faint deprecatory way as if to signify he'd said all he wished to say, picked up the instrument, and spoke into it.*]

GREENE

Hello? Hello Peter! How is Andrea? Oh, it's the other Peter. How is Maria? No, I can't do it this evening. I've got Mario Soldati on my hands—we're doing a film in Italy this summer. I'm coproducing. How about Sunday? Battersea? Oh, they're not open? Well, then, we'll go to my pleasant little Negro night club round the corner . . .

James Thurber

The Art of Fiction

The Hôtel Continental, just down from the Place Vendôme on the Rue Castiglione. It is from here that Janet Flanner (Genêt) sends her Paris letter to *The New Yorker*, and it is here that the Thurbers usually stay while in Paris. "We like it because the service is first-rate without being snobbish."

Thurber was standing to greet us in a small salon whose cold European formality had been somewhat softened and warmed by well-placed vases of flowers, by stacks and portable shelves of American novels in bright dust jackets, and by pads of yellow paper and bouquets of yellow pencils on the desk. Thurber impresses one immediately by his physical size. After years of delighting in the shy, trapped little man in the Thurber cartoons and the confused and bewildered man who has fumbled in and out of some of the funniest books written in this century, we, perhaps like many readers, were expecting to find the frightened little man in person. Not at all. Thurber, by his firm handgrip and confident voice, and by the way he lowered himself into his chair, gave the impression of outward calmness and assurance. Though his eyesight has almost failed him, it is not a disability one is aware of for more than the opening minute, and if Thurber seems to be the most nervous person in the room, it is because he has learned to put his visitors so completely at ease.

He talks in a surprisingly boyish voice, which is flat with the accents of the Midwest where he was raised and, though slow in tempo, never dull. He is not an easy man to pin down with questions. He once upon a time

How once an elf who

lived with his ilk,

in a Kensington rubety
on top

An example, considerably reduced, of a Thurber manusript page.

prefers to sidestep them and, rather than instructing, he entertains with a vivid series of anecdotes and reminiscences.

Opening the interview with a long history of the bloodhound, Thurber was only with some difficulty persuaded to shift to a discussion of his craft. Here again his manner was typical—the anecdotes, the reminiscences punctuated with direct quotes and factual data. His powers of memory are astounding. In quoting anyone—perhaps a conversation of a dozen years before—Thurber pauses slightly, his voice changes in tone, and you know what you're hearing is exactly as it was said.

—*George Plimpton, Max Steele, 1955*

JAMES THURBER

Well, you know it's a nuisance—to have memory like mine—as well as an advantage. It's . . . well . . . like a whore's top drawer. There's so much else in there that's junk—costume jewelry, unnecessary telephone numbers whose exchanges no longer exist. For instance, I can remember the birthday of anybody who's ever told me his birthday. Dorothy Parker—August 22, Lewis Gannett—October 3, Andy White—July 9, Mrs. White—September 17. I can go on with about two hundred. So can my mother. She can tell you the birthday of the girl I was in love with in the third grade, in 1903. Offhand, just like that. I got my powers of memory from her. Sometimes it helps out in the most extraordinary way. You remember Robert M. Coates? Bob Coates? He is the author of *The Eater of Darkness*, which Ford Madox Ford called the first true Dadaist novel. Well, the week after Stephen Vincent Benét died—Coates and I had both known him—we were talking about Benét. Coates was trying to remember an argument he had had with Benét some fifteen years before. He couldn't remember. I said, I can. Coates told me that was impossible since I hadn't been there. Well, I said, you happened to mention it in passing about twelve years ago. You were arguing about a play called *Swords*. I was right, and Coates was able to take it up from there. But it's strange to reach a position where your friends have to be supplied with their own memories. It's bad enough dealing with your own.

INTERVIEWER

Still, it must be a great advantage for the writer. I don't suppose you have to take notes.

THURBER

No. I don't have to do the sort of thing Fitzgerald did with *The Last Tycoon*—the voluminous, the tiny and meticulous notes, the long descriptions of character. I can keep all these things in my mind. I wouldn't have to write down "three roses in a vase" or something, or a man's middle name. Henry James dictated notes just the way that I write. His note writing was part of the creative act, which is why his prefaces are so good. He dictated notes to see what it was they might come to.

INTERVIEWER

Then you don't spend much time prefiguring your work?

THURBER

No. I don't bother with charts and so forth. Elliott Nugent, on the other hand, is a careful constructor. When we were working on *The Male Animal* together, he was constantly concerned with plotting the play. He could plot the thing from back to front—what was going to happen here, what sort of situation would end the first-act curtain, and so forth. I can't work that way. Nugent would say, Well, Thurber, we've got our problem, we've got all these people in the living room. Now what are we going to do with them? I'd say that I didn't know and couldn't tell him until I'd sat down at the typewriter and found out. I don't believe the writer should know too much where he's going. If he does, he runs into old man blueprint—old man propaganda.

INTERVIEWER

Is the act of writing easy for you?

THURBER

For me it's mostly a question of rewriting. It's part of a constant attempt on my part to make the finished version smooth, to make it seem effortless. A story I've been working on—"The Train on Track Six," it's called—was rewritten fifteen complete times. There must have been close to two hundred and forty thousand words in all the manuscripts put together, and I must have spent two thousand hours working at it. Yet the finished version can't be more than twenty thousand words.

INTERVIEWER

Then it's rare that your work comes out right the first time?

THURBER

Well, my wife took a look at the first version of something I was doing not long ago and said, God damn it, Thurber, that's high-school stuff. I have to tell her to wait until the seventh draft, it'll work out all right. I don't know why that should be so, that the first or second draft of everything I write reads as if it was turned out by a charwoman. I've only written one piece quickly. I wrote a thing called "File and Forget" in one afternoon—but only because it was a series of letters just as one would ordinarily dictate. And I'd have to admit that the last letter of the series, after doing all the others that one afternoon, took me a week. It was the end of the piece and I had to fuss over it.

INTERVIEWER

Does the fact that you're dealing with humor slow down the production?

THURBER

It's possible. With humor you have to look out for traps. You're likely to be very gleeful with what you've first put down, and you think it's fine, very funny. One reason you go over and over it is to make the piece sound less as if you were having a lot of fun with it yourself. You try to play it down. In fact, if there's such a thing as a New Yorker style, that would be it—playing it down.

INTERVIEWER

Do you envy those who write at high speed, as against your method of constant revision?

THURBER

Oh, no, I don't, though I do admire their luck. Hervey Allen, you know, the author of the big bestseller *Anthony Adverse*, seriously told a friend of mine who was working on a biographical piece on Allen that he could close his eyes, lie down on a bed, and hear the voices of his ancestors. Furthermore there was some sort of angel-like creature that danced along his pen while he was writing. He wasn't balmy by any means. He just felt he was in communication with some sort of metaphysical recorder. So you see the novelists have all the luck. I never knew a humorist who got any help from his ancestors. Still, the act of writing is either something the writer dreads or actually likes, and I actually like it. Even rewriting's fun. You're getting somewhere, whether it seems to move or not. I remember Elliot Paul and I used to argue about rewriting back in 1925 when we both worked for the *Chicago Tribune* in Paris. It was his conviction you should leave the story as it came out of the typewriter, no changes. Naturally, he worked fast. Three novels he could turn out, each written in three weeks' time. I remember once he came into the office and said that a sixty-thousand-word manuscript had been stolen. No carbons existed, no notes. We were all horrified. But it didn't bother him at all. He'd just get back to the typewriter and bat away again. But for me—writing as fast as that would seem too facile. Like my drawings, which I do very quickly, sometimes so quickly that the result is an accident, something I hadn't intended at all. People in the arts I've run into in France are constantly indignant when I say I'm a writer and not an artist. They tell me I mustn't run down my drawings. I try to explain that I do them for relaxation, and that I do them too fast for them to be called art.

INTERVIEWER

You say that your drawings often don't come out the way you intended?

THURBER

Well, once I did a drawing for *The New Yorker* of a naked woman on all fours up on top of a bookcase—a big bookcase. She's up there near the ceiling, and in the room are her husband and two other women. The husband is saying to one of the women, obviously a guest, "This is the present Mrs. Harris. That's my first wife up there." Well, when I did the cartoon originally I meant the naked woman to be at the top of a flight of stairs, but I lost the sense of perspective and instead of getting in the stairs when I drew my line down, there she was stuck up there, naked, on a bookcase.

Incidentally, that cartoon really threw the *New Yorker* editor, Harold Ross. He approached any humorous piece of writing, or more particularly a drawing, not only grimly but realistically. He called me on the phone and asked if the woman up on the bookcase was supposed to be alive, stuffed, or dead. I said, I don't know, but I'll let you know in a couple of hours. After a while I called him back and told him I'd just talked to my taxidermist, who said you can't stuff a woman, that my doctor had told me a dead woman couldn't support herself on all fours. So, Ross, I said, she must be alive. Well then, he said, what's she doing up there naked in the home of her husband's second wife? I told him he had me there.

INTERVIEWER

But he published it.

THURBER

Yes, he published it, growling a bit. He had a fine understanding of humor, Ross, though he couldn't have told you about it. When I introduced Ross to the work of Peter de Vries, he first said, He won't be good; he won't be funny; he won't know English. (He was the only successful editor I've known who approached everything like a ship going on the rocks.) But when Ross had looked at the work he said, How can you get this guy on the phone? He couldn't have said why, but he had that bloodhound instinct. The same with editing. He was a wonderful man at detecting something wrong with a story without knowing why.

INTERVIEWER

Could he develop a writer?

THURBER

Not really. It wasn't true what they often said of him—that he broke up writers like matches—but still he wasn't the man to develop a writer. He was an unread man. Well, he'd read Mark Twain's *Life on the Mississippi* and several other books he told me about—medical books—and he took the *Encyclopaedia Britannica* to the bathroom with him. I think he was about up to *H* when he died. But still his effect on writers was considerable. When you first met him you couldn't believe he was the editor of *The New Yorker* and afterward you couldn't believe that anyone else could have been. The main thing he was interested in was clarity. Someone once said of *The New Yorker* that it never contained a sentence that would puzzle an intelligent fourteen-year-old or in any way affect her morals badly. Ross didn't like that, but nevertheless he was a purist and a perfectionist and it had a tremendous effect on all of us: it kept us from being sloppy. When I first met him he asked me if I knew English. I thought he meant French or a foreign language. But he repeated, Do you know English? When I said I did he replied, God damn it, nobody knows English. As Andy White mentioned in his obituary, Ross approached the English sentence as though it was an enemy, something that was going to throw him. He used to fuss for an hour over a comma. He'd call me in for lengthy discussions about the Thurber colon. And as for poetic license, he'd say, Damn any license to get things wrong. In fact, Ross read so carefully that often he didn't get the sense of your story. I once said, I wish you'd read my stories for pleasure, Ross. He replied he hadn't time for that.

INTERVIEWER

It's strange that one of the main ingredients of humor—low comedy—has never been accepted for *The New Yorker*.

THURBER

Ross had a neighbor woman's attitude about it. He never got over his Midwestern provincialism. His idea was that sex is an incident. If you can prove it, I said, we can get it in a box on the front page of *The*

New York Times. Now I don't want to say that in private life Ross was a prude. But as regards the theater or the printed page he certainly was. For example, he once sent an office memorandum to us in a sealed envelope. It was an order: When you send me a memorandum with four-letter words in it, *seal it*. There are women in this office. I said, Yeah, Ross, and they know a lot more of these words than you do. When women were around he was very conscious of them. Once my wife and I were in his office and Ross was discussing a man and woman he knew much better than we did. Ross told us, I have every reason to believe that they're *s-l-e-e-p-i-n-g* together. My wife replied, Why, Harold Ross, what words you do spell out. But honest to goodness, that was genuine. Women are either good or bad, he once told me, and the good ones must not hear these things.

Incidentally, I'm telling these things to refresh my memory. I'm doing a short book on him called "Ross in Charcoal." I'm putting a lot of this stuff in. People may object, but after all it's a portrait of the man and I see no reason for not putting it in.

INTERVIEWER

Did he have much direct influence on your own work?

THURBER

After the seven years I spent in newspaper writing, it was more E B. White who taught me about writing, how to clear up sloppy journalese. He was a strong influence, and for a long time in the beginning I thought he might be too much of one. But at least he got me away from a rather curious style I was starting to perfect—tight journalese laced with heavy doses of Henry James.

INTERVIEWER

Henry James was a strong influence, then?

THURBER

I have the reputation for having read all of Henry James. Which would argue a misspent youth *and* middle age.

INTERVIEWER

But there were things to be learned from him?

THURBER

Yes, but again he was an influence you had to get over. Especially if you wrote for *The New Yorker*. Harold Ross wouldn't have understood it. I once wrote a piece called "The Beast in the Dingle" which everybody took as a parody. Actually it was a conscious attempt to write the story as James would have written it. Ross looked at it and said, God damn it, this is too literary; I got only fifteen percent of the allusions. My wife and I often tried to figure out which were the fifteen percent he could have got.

You know, I've occasionally wondered what James would have done with our world. I've just written a piece—"Preface to Old Friends," it's called—in which James at the age of a hundred and four writes a preface to a novel about our age in which he summarizes the trends and complications, but at the end is so completely lost he doesn't really care enough to read it over to find his way out again.

That's the trouble with James. You get bored with him finally. He lived in the time of four-wheelers, and no bombs, and the problems then seemed a bit special and separate. That's one reason you feel restless reading him. James is like—well, I had a bulldog once who used to drag rails around, enormous ones—six-, eight-, twelve-foot rails. He loved to get them in the middle and you'd hear him growling out there, trying to bring the thing home. Once he brought home a chest of drawers—without the drawers in it. Found it on an ash heap. Well, he'd start to get these things in the garden gate, everything finely balanced, you see, and then *crash*, he'd come up against the gateposts. He'd get it through finally, but I had that feeling in some of the James novels: that he was trying to get that rail through a gate not wide enough for it.

INTERVIEWER

How about Mark Twain? Pretty much everybody believes him to have been the major influence on American humorists.

THURBER

Everybody wants to know if I've learned from Mark Twain. Actually I've never read much of him. I did buy *Tom Sawyer*, but dammit, I'm sorry, I've not got around to reading it all the way through. I told H. L. Mencken that, and he was shocked. He said America had produced only two fine novels: *Huck Finn* and *Babbitt*. Of course it's always a matter of personal opinion—these lists of the great novels. I can remember calling on Frank Harris—he was about seventy then—when I was on the *Chicago Tribune*'s edition in Nice. In his house he had three portraits on the wall—Mark Twain, Frank Harris, and I think it was Hawthorne. Harris was in the middle. Harris would point up to them and say, Those three are the best American writers. The one in the middle is the best. Harris really thought he was wonderful. Once he told me he was going to live to be a hundred. When I asked him what the formula was, he told me it was very simple. He said, I've bought myself a stomach pump and one half hour after dinner I pump myself out. Can you imagine that? Well, it didn't work. It's a wonder it didn't kill him sooner.

INTERVIEWER

Could we ask you why you've never attempted a long work?

THURBER

I've never wanted to write a long work. Many writers feel a sense of frustration or something if they haven't, but I don't.

INTERVIEWER

Perhaps the fact that you're writing humor imposes a limit on the length of a work.

THURBER

Possibly. But brevity in any case—whether the work is supposed to be humorous or not—would seem to me to be desirable. Most of the books I like are short books: *The Red Badge of Courage*, *The Turn of the Screw*, Conrad's short stories, *A Lost Lady*, Joseph Hergesheimer's

Wild Oranges, Victoria Lincoln's *February Hill*, *The Great Gatsby* . . . You know Fitzgerald once wrote Thomas Wolfe: "You're a putter-inner and I'm a taker-outer." I stick with Fitzgerald. I don't believe, as Wolfe did, that you have to turn out a massive work before being judged a writer. Wolfe once told me at a cocktail party that I didn't know what it was to be a writer. My wife, standing next to me, complained about that. But my husband is a writer, she said. Wolfe was genuinely surprised. He is? he asked. Why, all I ever see is that stuff of his in *The New Yorker*. In other words, he felt that prose under five thousand words was certainly not the work of a writer . . . it was some kind of doodling in words. If you said you were a writer, he wanted to know where the books were, the great big long books. He was really genuine about that.

I was interested to see William Faulkner's list not so long ago of the five most important American authors of this century. According to him Wolfe was first, Faulkner second—let's see, now that Wolfe's dead that puts Faulkner up there in the lead, doesn't it?—Dos Passos third, then Hemingway, and finally Steinbeck. It's interesting that the first three are putter-inners. They write expansive novels.

INTERVIEWER

Wasn't Faulkner's criterion whether or not the author dared to go out on a limb?

THURBER

It seems to me you're going out on a limb these days to keep a book short.

INTERVIEWER

Though you've never done a long serious work you have written stories—"The Cane in the Corridor" and "The Whippoorwill" in particular—in which the mood is far from humorous.

THURBER

In anything funny you write that isn't close to serious you've missed something along the line. But in those stories of which you speak there was an element of anger—something I wanted to get off my chest. I wrote "The Whippoorwill" after five eye operations. It came somewhere out of a grim fear in the back of my mind. I've never been able to trace it.

INTERVIEWER

Some critics think that much of your work can be traced to the depicting of trivia as a basis for humor. In fact, there's been some criticism—

THURBER

Which is trivia—the diamond or the elephant? Any humorist must be interested in trivia, in every little thing that occurs in a household. It's what Robert Benchley did so well—in fact so well that one of the greatest fears of the humorous writer is that he has spent three weeks writing something done faster and better by Benchley in 1919. Incidentally, you never got very far talking to Benchley about humor. He'd do a takeoff of Max Eastman's *Enjoyment of Laughter*. We must understand, he'd say, that all sentences which begin with *W* are funny.

INTERVIEWER

Would you care to define humor in terms of your own work?

THURBER

Well, someone once wrote a definition of the difference between English and American humor. I wish I could remember his name. I thought his definition very good. He said that the English treat the commonplace as if it were remarkable and the Americans treat the remarkable as if it were commonplace. I believe that's true of humorous writing. Years ago we did a parody of *Punch* in which Benchley did a short piece depicting a wife bursting into a room and shouting, "The primroses are in bloom!"—treating the commonplace as remarkable, you see. In "The Secret Life of Walter Mitty" I tried to treat the remarkable as commonplace.

INTERVIEWER

Does it bother you to talk about the stories on which you're working? It bothers many writers, though it would seem that particularly the humorous story is polished through retelling.

THURBER

Oh yes. I often tell them at parties and places. And I write them there too.

INTERVIEWER

You write them?

THURBER

I never quite know when I'm not writing. Sometimes my wife comes up to me at a party and says, Dammit, Thurber, stop writing. She usually catches me in the middle of a paragraph. Or my daughter will look up from the dinner table and ask, Is he sick? No, my wife says, he's writing something. I have to do it that way on account of my eyes. I still write occasionally—in the proper sense of the word—using black crayon on yellow paper and getting perhaps twenty words to the page. My usual method, though, is to spend the mornings turning over the text in my mind. Then in the afternoon, between two and five, I call in a secretary and dictate to her. I can do about two thousand words. It took me about ten years to learn.

INTERVIEWER

How about the new crop of writers? Do you note any good humorists coming along with them?

THURBER

There don't seem to be many coming up. I once had a psychoanalyst tell me that the Depression had a considerable effect—much worse than Hitler and the war. It's a tradition for a child to see his father in uniform as something glamorous—not his father coming home from Wall Street in a three-button sack suit saying, We're ruined, and the mother bursting into tears—a catastrophe that to a child's mind is unexplainable. There's been a great change since the thirties. In those days students used to ask me what Peter Arno did at night. And about Dorothy Parker. Now they want to know what my artistic credo is. An element of interest seems to have gone out of them.

INTERVIEWER

Has the shift in the mood of the times had any effect on your own work?

THURBER

Well, *The Thurber Album* was written at a time when in America there was a feeling of fear and suspicion. It's quite different from *My Life and Hard Times*, which was written earlier and is a funnier and better book. The *Album* was kind of an escape—going back to the Middle West of the last century and the beginning of this, when there wasn't this fear and hysteria. I wanted to write the story of some solid American characters, more or less as an example of how Americans started out and what they should go back to—to sanity and soundness and away from this jumpiness. It's hard to write humor in the mental weather we've had, and that's likely to take you into reminiscence. Your heart isn't in it to write anything funny. In the years 1950 to 1953 I did very few things, nor did they appear in *The New Yorker*. Now, actually, I think the situation is beginning to change for the better.

INTERVIEWER

No matter what the mental climate, though, you would continue writing?

THURBER

Well, the characteristic fear of the American writer is not so much that as it is the process of aging. The writer looks in the mirror and examines his hair and teeth to see if they're still with him. Oh my God, he says, I wonder how my writing is. I bet I can't write today. The only time I met Faulkner he told me he wanted to live long enough to do three more novels. He was fifty-three then, and I think he *has* done them. Then Hemingway says, you know, that he doesn't expect to be alive after sixty. But he doesn't look forward *not* to being. When I met Hemingway with John O'Hara in Costello's Bar five or six years ago we sat around and talked about how *old* we were getting. You see it's constantly on the minds of American writers. I've never known a woman who could weep about her age the way the men I know can.

Coupled with this fear of aging is the curious idea that the writer's inventiveness and ability will end in his fifties. And of course it often does. Carl Van Vechten stopped writing. The prolific Joseph Herge-sheimer suddenly couldn't write any more. Over here in Europe that's never been the case—Hardy, for instance, who started late and kept going. Of course Keats had good reason to write, "When I have fears that I may cease to be / Before my pen has glean'd my teeming brain." That's the great classic statement. But in America the writer is more likely to fear that his brain may cease to teem. I once did a draw-ing of a man at his typewriter, you see, and all this crumpled paper is on the floor, and he's staring down in discouragement. "What's the matter," his wife is saying, "has your pen gleaned your teeming brain?"

INTERVIEWER

In your case there wouldn't be much chance of this?

THURBER

No. I write basically because it's so much fun—even though I can't see. When I'm not writing, as my wife knows, I'm miserable. I don't have that fear that suddenly it will all stop. I have enough outlined to last me as long as I live.

William Faulkner

The Art of Fiction

William Faulkner was born in 1897 in New Albany, Mississippi, where his father worked as a conductor on the railroad that was built by the novelist's great-grandfather, Colonel William Falkner (without the *u*), author of *The White Rose of Memphis*. The family soon moved to Oxford, thirty-five miles away, where young Faulkner, although a voracious reader, failed to earn enough credits to graduate from the local high school. In 1918 he enlisted as a student flyer in the Royal Canadian Air Force. He spent a little more than a year as a special student at the state university, Ole Miss, and later worked as postmaster at the university station until he was fired for reading on the job.

Encouraged by Sherwood Anderson, he wrote *Soldier's Pay* (1926). His first widely read book was *Sanctuary* (1931), a sensational novel that he claims he wrote for money after his previous books—including *Mosquitoes* (1927), *Sartoris* (1929), *The Sound and the Fury* (1929), and *As I Lay Dying* (1930)—failed to earn enough royalties to support his family.

A steady succession of novels followed, most of them related to what is now known as the Yoknapatawpha saga: *Light in August* (1932), *Pylon* (1935), *Absalom, Absalom!* (1936), *The Unvanquished* (1938), *The Wild Palms [If I Forget Thee, Jerusalem]* (1939), *The Hamlet* (1940), and *Go Down, Moses, and Other Stories* (1941). Since World War II his principal works have been *Intruder in the Dust* (1948), *A Fable* (1954), and *The Town* (1957). His *Collected Stories* received the National Book Award in 1951, as did *A Fable* in 1955. In 1949 Faulkner was awarded the Nobel Prize in Literature.

Although shy and retiring, Faulkner has recently begun to travel widely, giving talks under the auspices of the United States Information Service.

This conversation took place in New York City, early in 1956.

—*Jean Stein, 1956*

INTERVIEWER

Mr. Faulkner, you were saying a while ago that you don't like being interviewed.

WILLIAM FAULKNER

The reason I don't like interviews is that I seem to react violently to personal questions. If the questions are about the work, I try to answer them. When they are about me, I may answer or I may not, but even if I do, if the same question is asked tomorrow, the answer may be different.

INTERVIEWER

How about yourself as a writer?

FAULKNER

If I had not existed, someone else would have written me, Hemingway, Dostoyevsky, all of us. Proof of that is that there are about three candidates for the authorship of Shakespeare's plays. But what is important is *Hamlet* and *A Midsummer Night's Dream*—not who wrote them, but that somebody did. The artist is of no importance. Only what he creates is important, since there is nothing new to be said. Shakespeare, Balzac, Homer have all written about the same things, and if they had lived one thousand or two thousand years longer, the publishers wouldn't have needed anyone since.

INTERVIEWER

But even if there seems nothing more to be said, isn't perhaps the individuality of the writer important?

FAULKNER

Very important to himself. Everybody else should be too busy with the work to care about the individuality.

INTERVIEWER

And your contemporaries?

FAULKNER

All of us failed to match our dream of perfection. So I rate us on the basis of our splendid failure to do the impossible. In my opinion, if I could write all my work again, I am convinced that I would do it better, which is the healthiest condition for an artist. That's why he keeps on working, trying again; he believes each time that this time he will do it, bring it off. Of course he won't, which is why this condition is healthy. Once he did it, once he matched the work to the image, the dream, nothing would remain but to cut his throat, jump off the other side of that pinnacle of perfection into suicide. I'm a failed poet. Maybe every novelist wants to write poetry first, finds he can't, and then tries the short story, which is the most demanding form after poetry. And, failing at that, only then does he take up novel writing.

INTERVIEWER

How does a writer become a serious novelist?

FAULKNER

Ninety-nine percent talent . . . ninety-nine percent discipline . . . ninety-nine percent work. He must never be satisfied with what he does. It never is as good as it can be done. Always dream and shoot higher than you know you can do. Don't bother just to be better than your contemporaries or predecessors. Try to be better than yourself. An artist is a creature driven by demons. He doesn't know why they choose him and he's usually too busy to wonder why. He is completely amoral in that he will rob, borrow, beg, or steal from anybody and everybody to get the work done.

INTERVIEWER

Do you mean the writer should be completely ruthless?

FAULKNER

The writer's only responsibility is to his art. He will be completely ruthless if he is a good one. He has a dream. It anguishes him so much he must get rid of it. He has no peace until then. Everything goes by the board: honor, pride, decency, security, happiness, all, to get the book written. If a writer has to rob his mother, he will not hesitate; the "Ode on a Grecian Urn" is worth any number of old ladies.

INTERVIEWER

Then could the *lack* of security, happiness, honor, be an important factor for the artist's work?

FAULKNER

No. They are important only to his peace and contentment, and art has no concern with peace and contentment.

INTERVIEWER

Then what would be the best environment for a writer?

FAULKNER

Art is not concerned with environment either; it doesn't care where it is. If you mean me, the best job that was ever offered to me was to become a landlord in a brothel. In my opinion it's the perfect milieu for an artist to work in. It gives him perfect economic freedom; he's free of fear and hunger; he has a roof over his head and nothing whatever to do except keep a few simple accounts and go once every month and pay off the local police. The place is quiet during the morning hours, which is the best time of the day to work. There's enough social life in the evening, if he wishes to participate, to keep him from being bored; it gives him a certain standing in his society; he has nothing to do because the madam keeps the books; all the inmates of the house are females and would defer to him and call him "sir."

All the bootleggers in the neighborhood would call him "sir." And he could call the police by their first names.

So the only environment the artist needs is whatever peace, whatever solitude, and whatever pleasure he can get at not too high a cost. All the wrong environment will do is run his blood pressure up; he will spend more time being frustrated or outraged. My own experience has been that the tools I need for my trade are paper, tobacco, food, and a little whiskey.

INTERVIEWER

Bourbon, you mean?

FAULKNER

No, I ain't that particular. Between scotch and nothing, I'll take scotch.

INTERVIEWER

You mentioned economic freedom. Does the writer need it?

FAULKNER

No. The writer doesn't need economic freedom. All he needs is a pencil and some paper. I've never known anything good in writing to come from having accepted any free gift of money. The good writer never applies to a foundation. He's too busy writing something. If he isn't first-rate he fools himself by saying he hasn't got time or economic freedom. Good art can come out of thieves, bootleggers, or horse swipes. People really are afraid to find out just how much hardship and poverty they can stand. They are afraid to find out how tough they are. Nothing can destroy the good writer. The only thing that can alter the good writer is death. Good ones don't have time to bother with success or getting rich. Success is feminine and like a woman; if you cringe before her, she will override you. So the way to treat her is to show her the back of your hand. Then maybe she will do the crawling.

INTERVIEWER

Can writing for the movies hurt your work?

FAULKNER

Nothing can injure a man's writing if he's a first-rate writer. If a man is not a first-rate writer, there's not anything can help it much. The problem does not apply if he is not first-rate because he has already sold his soul for a swimming pool.

INTERVIEWER

Does a writer have to compromise when writing for the movies?

FAULKNER

Always, because a moving picture is by its nature a collaboration, and any collaboration is compromise because that is what the word means—to give and to take.

INTERVIEWER

Which actors do you like to work with most?

FAULKNER

Humphrey Bogart is the one I've worked with best. He and I worked together in *To Have and Have Not* and *The Big Sleep*.

INTERVIEWER

Would you like to make another movie?

FAULKNER

Yes, I would like to make one of George Orwell's *1984*. I have an idea for an ending that would prove the thesis I'm always hammering at: that man is indestructible because of his simple will to freedom.

INTERVIEWER

How do you get the best results when working for the movies?

FAULKNER

The moving-picture work of my own which seemed best to me was done by the actors and the writer throwing the script away and inventing the scene in actual rehearsal just before the camera turned on. If I didn't take, or feel I was capable of taking, motion-picture work seriously, out of simple honesty to motion pictures and myself too, I would not have tried. But I know now that I will never be a good motion-picture writer; so that work will never have the urgency for me which my own medium has.

INTERVIEWER

Would you comment on the legendary Hollywood experience you were involved in?

FAULKNER

I had just completed a contract at MGM and was about to return home. The director I had worked with said, If you would like another job here, just let me know and I will speak to the studio about a new contract. I thanked him and came home. About six months later I wired my director friend that I would like another job. Shortly after that I received a letter from my Hollywood agent enclosing my first week's paycheck. I was surprised because I had expected first to get an official notice or recall and a contract from the studio. I thought to myself, the contract is delayed and will arrive in the next mail. Instead, a week later I got another letter from the agent, enclosing my second week's paycheck. That began in November 1932 and continued until May 1933. Then I received a telegram from the studio. It said: "William Faulkner, Oxford, Miss. Where are you? MGM Studio."

I wrote out a telegram: "MGM Studio, Culver City, California. William Faulkner."

The young lady operator said, Where is the message, Mr. Faulkner? It said, That's it. She said, The rule book says that I can't send it without a message, you have to say something. So we went through her samples and selected I forget which one—one of the canned anniversary-greeting messages. I sent that. Next was a long-distance telephone call from the studio directing me to get on the first airplane, go to New Orleans, and report to Director Browning. I could have got on a train in Oxford and been in New Orleans eight hours later. But I obeyed the studio and went to Memphis, where an airplane did occasionally go to New Orleans. Three days later, one did.

I arrived at Mr. Browning's hotel about six P.M. and reported to him. A party was going on. He told me to get a good night's sleep and be ready for an early start in the morning. I asked him about the story. He said, Oh, yes. Go to room so-and-so. That's the continuity writer. He'll tell you what the story is.

I went to the room as directed. The continuity writer was sitting in there alone. I told him who I was and asked him about the story. He said, When you have written the dialogue I'll let you see the story. I went back to Browning's room and told him what had happened. Go back, he said, and tell that so-and-so—. Never mind, you get a good night's sleep so we can get an early start in the morning.

So the next morning in a very smart rented launch all of us except the continuity writer sailed down to Grand Isle, about a hundred miles away, where the picture was to be shot, reaching there just in time to eat lunch and have time to run the hundred miles back to New Orleans before dark.

That went on for three weeks. Now and then I would worry a little about the story, but Browning always said, Stop worrying. Get a good night's sleep so we can get an early start tomorrow morning.

One evening on our return I had barely entered my room when the telephone rang. It was Browning. He told me to come to his room at once. I did so. He had a telegram. It said: FAULKNER IS FIRED. MGM STUDIO. Don't worry, Browning said. I'll call that so-and-so up this minute and not only make him put you back on the payroll but send you a written apology. There was a knock on the door. It was a page with another telegram. This one said: BROWNING IS FIRED. MGM STUDIO. So I came back home. I presume Browning went somewhere too. I imagine that continuity writer is still sitting in a room somewhere with his weekly salary check clutched tightly in his hand. They never did finish the film. But they did build a shrimp village—a long platform on piles in the water with sheds built on it—something like a wharf. The studio could have bought dozens of them for forty or fifty dollars apiece. Instead, they built one of their own, a false one. That is, a platform with a single wall on it, so that when you opened the door and stepped through it, you stepped right off onto the ocean itself. As they built it, on the first day, a Cajun fisherman paddled up in his narrow, tricky pirogue made out of a hollow log. He would sit in it all day long in the broiling sun watching the strange white folks building this strange imitation platform. The next day he was back in the pirogue with his whole family, his wife nursing the baby, the other children, and the mother-in-law, all to sit all that day in the broiling sun to watch this foolish and incomprehensible activity. I was in New Orleans two or three years later and heard that the Cajun people were still coming in for miles to look at that imitation shrimp platform that a lot of white people had rushed in and built and then abandoned.

INTERVIEWER

You say that the writer must compromise while working for the motion pictures. What about his books? Is he under any obligation to his reader?

FAULKNER

His obligation is to get the work done the best he can do it; whatever obligation he has left over after that he can spend any way he likes. I myself am too busy to care about the public. I have no time to wonder who is reading me. I don't care about John Doe's opinion on my work or anyone else's. Mine is the standard which has to be met, which is when the work makes me feel the way I do when I read *La Tentation de Saint Antoine* or the Old Testament. They make me feel good. So does watching a bird make me feel good. You know that if I were reincarnated, I'd want to come back a buzzard. Nothing hates him or envies him or wants him or needs him. He is never bothered or in danger, and he can eat anything.

INTERVIEWER
What techniques do you use to arrive at your standard?

FAULKNER
Let the writer take up surgery or bricklaying if he is interested in technique. There is no mechanical way to get the writing done, no

shortcut. The young writer would be a fool to follow a theory. Teach yourself by your own mistakes; people learn only by error. The good artist believes that nobody is good enough to give him advice. He has supreme vanity. No matter how much he admires the old writer, he wants to beat him.

INTERVIEWER

Then would you deny the validity of technique?

FAULKNER

By no means. Sometimes technique charges in and takes command of the dream before the writer himself can get his hands on it. That is tour de force and the finished work is simply a matter of fitting bricks neatly together, since the writer knows probably every single word right to the end before he puts the first one down. This happened with *As I Lay Dying*. It was not easy. No honest work is. It was simple in that all the material was already at hand. It took me just about six weeks in the spare time from a twelve-hour-a-day job at manual labor. I simply imagined a group of people and subjected them to the simple universal natural catastrophes, which are flood and fire, with a simple natural motive to give direction to their progress. But then, when technique does not intervene, in another sense writing is easier too. Because with me there is always a point in the book where the characters themselves rise up and take charge and finish the job—say somewhere about page 275. Of course I don't know what would happen if I finished the book on page 274. The quality an artist must have is objectivity in judging his work, plus the honesty and courage not to kid himself about it. Since none of my work has met my own standards, I must judge it on the basis of that one which caused me the most grief and anguish, as the mother loves the child who became the thief or murderer more than the one who became the priest.

INTERVIEWER

Which work is that?

FAULKNER

The Sound and the Fury. I wrote it five separate times, trying to tell the story, to rid myself of the dream which would continue to anguish me until I did. It's a tragedy of two lost women: Caddy and her daughter, Quentin. Dilsey is one of my own favorite characters, because she is brave, courageous, generous, gentle, and honest. She's much more brave and honest and generous than me.

INTERVIEWER

What were the origins of *The Sound and the Fury*?

FAULKNER

It began with a mental picture. I didn't realize at the time it was symbolical. The picture was of the muddy seat of a little girl's drawers in a pear tree, where she could see through a window where her grandmother's funeral was taking place and report what was happening to her brothers on the ground below. By the time I explained who they were and what they were doing and how her pants got muddy, I realized it would be impossible to get all of it into a short story and that it would have to be a book. And then I realized the symbolism of the soiled pants, and that image was replaced by the one of the fatherless and motherless girl climbing down the drainpipe to escape from the only home she had, where she had never been offered love or affection or understanding.

I had already begun to tell the story through the eyes of the idiot child, since I felt that it would be more effective as told by someone capable only of knowing what happened but not why. I saw that I had not told the story that time. I tried to tell it again, the same story through the eyes of another brother. That was still not it. I told it for the third time through the eyes of the third brother. That was still not it. I tried to gather the pieces together and fill in the gaps by making myself the spokesman. It was still not complete, not until fifteen years after the book was published, when I wrote as an appendix to another book the final effort to get the story told and off my mind, so that I myself could have some peace from it. It's the book I feel tenderest toward. I couldn't leave it alone, and I never could tell it right, though I tried hard and would like to try again, though I'd probably fail again.

INTERVIEWER

What emotion does Benjy arouse in you?

FAULKNER

The only emotion I can have for Benjy is grief and pity for all mankind. You can't feel anything for Benjy because he doesn't feel anything. The only thing I can feel about him personally is concern as to whether he is believable as I created him. He was a prologue, like the gravedigger in the Elizabethan dramas. He serves his purpose and is gone. Benjy is incapable of good and evil because he had no knowledge of good and evil.

INTERVIEWER

Could Benjy feel love?

FAULKNER

Benjy wasn't rational enough even to be selfish. He was an animal. He recognized tenderness and love though he could not have named them, and it was the threat to tenderness and love that caused him to bellow when he felt the change in Caddy. He no longer had Caddy; being an idiot he was not even aware that Caddy was missing. He knew only that something was wrong, which left a vacuum in which he grieved. He tried to fill that vacuum. The only thing he had was one of Caddy's discarded slippers. The slipper was his tenderness and love, which he could not have named, but he knew only that it was missing. He was dirty because he couldn't coordinate and because dirt meant nothing to him. He could no more distinguish between dirt and cleanliness than between good and evil. The slipper gave him comfort even though he no longer remembered the person to whom it had once belonged, any more than he could remember why he grieved. If Caddy had reappeared he probably would not have known her.

INTERVIEWER

Does the narcissus given to Benjy have some significance?

FAULKNER

The narcissus was given to Benjy to distract his attention. It was simply a flower which happened to be handy that fifth of April. It was not deliberate.

INTERVIEWER

What were the advantages of casting *A Fable* as an allegory?

FAULKNER

Same advantage the carpenter finds in building square corners in order to build a square house. In *A Fable*, the Christian allegory was the right allegory to use in that particular story, like an oblong, square corner is the right corner with which to build an oblong, rectangular house.

INTERVIEWER

Does that mean an artist can use Christianity simply as another tool, as a carpenter would borrow a hammer?

FAULKNER

The carpenter we are speaking of never lacks that hammer. No one is without Christianity, if we agree on what we mean by the word. It is every individual's individual code of behavior, by means of which he makes himself a better human being than his nature wants to be, if he followed his nature only. Whatever its symbol—cross or crescent or whatever—that symbol is man's reminder of his duty inside the human race. Its various allegories are the charts against which he measures himself and learns to know what he is. It cannot teach man to be good as the textbook teaches him mathematics. It shows him how to discover himself, evolve for himself a moral code and standard within his capacities and aspirations, by giving him a matchless example of suffering and sacrifice and the promise of hope. Writers have always drawn, and always will draw, upon the allegories of moral consciousness, for the reason that the allegories are matchless—the three men in *Moby-Dick*, who represent the trinity of conscience: knowing nothing, knowing but not caring, knowing and caring. The same trinity is represented in *A Fable* by the young Jewish pilot officer, who said, This is terrible. I refuse to accept it, even if I must refuse life to do so; the old French Quartermaster General, who said, This is terrible, but we can weep and bear it; and the English battalion runner, who said, This is terrible, I'm going to do something about it.

INTERVIEWER

Are the two unrelated themes in *The Wild Palms* brought together in one book for any symbolic purpose? Is it, as certain critics intimate, a kind of aesthetic counterpoint, or is it merely haphazard?

FAULKNER

No, no. That was one story—the story of Charlotte Rittenmeyer and Harry Wilbourne, who sacrificed everything for love and then lost that. I did not know it would be two separate stories until after I had started the book. When I reached the end of what is now the first section of *The Wild Palms*, I realized suddenly that something was missing, it needed emphasis, something to lift it like counterpoint in music. So I wrote on the "Old Man" story until "The Wild Palms" story rose back to pitch. Then I stopped the "Old Man" story at what is now its first section and took up "The Wild Palms" story until it began again to sag. Then I raised it to pitch again with another section of its antithesis, which is the story of a man who got his love and spent the rest of the book fleeing from it, even to the extent of voluntarily going back to jail where he would be safe. They are only two stories by chance, perhaps necessity. The story is that of Charlotte and Wilbourne.

INTERVIEWER

How much of your writing is based on personal experience?

FAULKNER

I can't say. I never counted up. Because "how much" is not important. A writer needs three things: experience, observation, and imagination, any two of which—at times any one of which—can supply the lack of the others. With me, a story usually begins with a single idea or memory or mental picture. The writing of the story is simply a matter of working up to that moment, to explain why it happened or what it caused to follow. A writer is trying to create believable people in credible moving situations in the most moving way he can. Obviously he must use as one of his tools the environment that he knows. I would say that music is the easiest means in which to express oneself, since it came first in man's experience and history. But since words are my talent, I must try to express clumsily in words what the pure music would have done better. That is, music would express better and simpler, but I prefer to use words, as I prefer to read rather than listen. I prefer silence to sound, and the image produced by words occurs in silence. That is, the thunder and the music of the prose take place in silence.

INTERVIEWER

Some people say they can't understand your writing, even after they have read it two or three times. What approach would you suggest for them?

FAULKNER

Read it four times.

INTERVIEWER

You mentioned experience, observation, and imagination as being important for the writer. You did not include inspiration.

FAULKNER

I don't know anything about inspiration because I don't know what inspiration is—I've heard about it, but I never saw it.

INTERVIEWER

Some critics say you are obsessed with violence.

FAULKNER

That's like saying the carpenter is obsessed with his hammer. Violence is simply one of the carpenter's tools. The writer can no more build with one tool than the carpenter can.

INTERVIEWER

How did you start writing?

FAULKNER

I was living in New Orleans, doing whatever kind of work was necessary to earn a little money now and then. I met Sherwood Anderson. We would walk about the city in the afternoon and talk to people. In the evenings we would meet again and sit over a bottle or two while he talked and I listened. In the forenoon I would never see him. He was secluded, working. I decided that if that was the life of a writer, then becoming a writer was the thing for me. So I began to write my first book. At once I found that writing was fun. I even forgot that I hadn't seen Mr. Anderson for three weeks until he walked in my door, the first time he ever came to see me, and said, What's wrong? Are you mad at me? I told him I was writing a book. He said, My God, and walked out. When I finished the book—it was *Soldier's Pay*—I met Mrs. Anderson on the street. She asked how the book was going, and I said I'd finished it. She said, Sherwood says that he will make a trade with you. If he doesn't have to read your manuscript he will tell his publisher to accept it. I said, Done, and that's how I became a writer.

INTERVIEWER

What kind of work were you doing to earn that "little money now and then"?

FAULKNER

Whatever came up. I could do a little of almost anything—run boats, paint houses, fly airplanes. I never needed much money because living was cheap in New Orleans then, and all I wanted was a place to sleep, a little food, tobacco, and whiskey. There were many things I could do for two or three days and earn enough money to live on for the rest of the month. By temperament I'm a vagabond and a tramp. I don't want money badly enough to work for it. In my opinion it's a shame that there is so much work in the world. One of the saddest things is that the only thing a man can do for eight hours a day, day after day, is work. You can't eat eight hours a day nor drink for eight hours a day nor make love for eight hours—all you can do for eight hours is work. Which is the reason why man makes himself and everybody else so miserable and unhappy.

INTERVIEWER

You must feel indebted to Sherwood Anderson, but how do you regard him as a writer?

FAULKNER

He was the father of my generation of American writers and the tradition of American writing that our successors will carry on. He has never received his proper evaluation. Dreiser is his older brother and Mark Twain the father of them both.

INTERVIEWER

What about the European writers of that period?

FAULKNER

The two great men in my time were Mann and Joyce. You should approach Joyce's *Ulysses* as the illiterate Baptist preacher approaches the Old Testament: with faith.

INTERVIEWER

How did you come to be so familiar with the Bible?

FAULKNER

My Great-Grandfather Murry was a kind and gentle man, to us children anyway. That is, although he was a Scot, he was to us neither especially pious nor stern either: he was simply a man of inflexible principles. One of them was everybody, children on up through all adults present, had to have a verse from the Bible ready and glib at tongue-tip when we gathered at the table for breakfast each morning. If you didn't have your scripture verse ready, you didn't have any breakfast; you would be excused long enough to leave the room and swot one up. There was a maiden aunt, a kind of sergeant major for this duty, who retired with the culprit and gave him a brisk breezing which carried him over the jump next time.

It had to be an authentic, correct verse. While we were little, it could be the same one, once you had it down good, morning after morning, until you got a little older and bigger, when one morning— by this time you would be pretty glib at it, galloping through without even listening to yourself since you were already five or ten minutes ahead, already among the ham and steak and fried chicken and grits and sweet potatoes and two or three kinds of hot bread—you would suddenly find his eyes on you, very blue, very kind and gentle, and even then not stern so much as inflexible, and next morning you had a new verse. In a way, that was when you discovered that your child-hood was over; you had outgrown it and entered the world.

INTERVIEWER

Do you read your contemporaries?

FAULKNER

No, the books I read are the ones I knew and loved when I was a young man and to which I return as you do to old friends: the Old Testament, Dickens, Conrad, Cervantes, *Don Quixote*—I read that every year, as some do the Bible. Flaubert, Balzac—he created an in-tact world of his own, a bloodstream running through twenty books—Dostoyevsky, Tolstoy, Shakespeare. I read Melville occasion-ally and, of the poets, Marlowe, Campion, Jonson, Herrick, Donne, Keats, and Shelley. I still read Housman. I've read these books so of-ten that I don't always begin at page one and read on to the end. I just read one scene, or about one character, just as you'd meet and talk to a friend for a few minutes.

INTERVIEWER

Many contemporary writers cite Freud as an influence. Would you?

FAULKNER

Everybody talked about Freud when I lived in New Orleans, but I have never read him. Neither did Shakespeare. I doubt if Melville did either, and I'm sure Moby Dick didn't.

INTERVIEWER

Do you ever read mystery stories?

FAULKNER

I read Simenon because he reminds me somewhat of Chekhov.

INTERVIEWER

Do you have favorite characters?

FAULKNER

My favorite characters are Sarah Gamp—a cruel, ruthless woman, a drunkard, opportunist, unreliable, most of her character was bad, but at least it was character; Mrs. Harris, Falstaff, Prince Hal, Don Quixote, and Sancho of course. Lady Macbeth I always admired. And Bottom, Ophelia, and Mercutio—both he and Mrs. Gamp coped with life, didn't ask any favors, never whined. Huck Finn, of course, and Jim. Tom Sawyer I never liked much—an awful prig. And then I like Sut Lovingood, from a book written by George Harris about 1840 or 1850 in the Tennessee mountains. He had no illusions about himself, did the best he could; at certain times he was a coward and knew it and wasn't ashamed; he never blamed his misfortunes on anyone and never cursed God for them.

INTERVIEWER

Would you comment on the future of the novel?

FAULKNER

I imagine as long as people will continue to read novels, people will continue to write them, or vice versa, unless of course the pictorial magazines and comic strips finally atrophy man's capacity to read, and literature really is on its way back to the picture writing in the Neanderthal cave.

INTERVIEWER

What is the function of the critic?

FAULKNER

The artist doesn't have time to listen to the critics. The ones who want to be writers read the reviews, the ones who want to write don't have the time to read reviews. The critic too is trying to say, "Kilroy was here." His function is not directed toward the artist himself. The artist is a cut above the critic, for the artist is writing something that will move the critic. The critic is writing something that will move everybody but the artist.

INTERVIEWER

So you never feel the need to discuss your work with anyone?

FAULKNER

No, I am too busy writing it. It has got to please me and if it does I don't need to talk about it. If it doesn't please me, talking about it won't improve it, since the only thing to improve it is to work on it some more. I am not a literary man but only a writer. I don't get any pleasure from talking shop.

INTERVIEWER

Critics claim that blood relationships are central in your novels.

FAULKNER

That is an opinion and, as I have said, I don't read critics. I doubt that a man trying to write about people is any more interested in blood relationships than in the shape of their noses, unless they are necessary to help the story move. If the writer concentrates on what he does need to be interested in, which is the truth and the human heart, he won't have much time left for anything else, such as ideas and facts like the shape of noses or blood relationships, since in my opinion ideas and facts have very little connection with truth.

INTERVIEWER

Critics also suggest that your characters never consciously choose between good and evil.

FAULKNER

Life is not interested in good and evil. Don Quixote was constantly choosing between good and evil, but then he was choosing in his dream state. He was mad. He entered reality only when he was so busy trying to cope with people that he had no time to distinguish between good and evil. Since people exist only in life, they must devote their time simply to being alive. Life is motion, and motion is concerned with what makes man move—which is ambition, power, pleasure. What time a man can devote to morality, he must take by force from the motion of which he is a part. He is compelled to make choices between good and evil sooner or later, because moral conscience demands that from him in order that he can live with himself tomorrow. His moral conscience is the curse he had to accept from the gods in order to gain from them the right to dream.

INTERVIEWER

Could you explain more what you mean by motion in relation to the artist?

FAULKNER

The aim of every artist is to arrest motion, which is life, by artificial means and hold it fixed so that a hundred years later, when a stranger looks at it, it moves again since it is life. Since man is mortal, the only immortality possible for him is to leave something behind him that is immortal since it will always move. This is the artist's way of scribbling "Kilroy was here" on the wall of the final and irrevocable oblivion through which he must someday pass.

It has been said by Malcolm Cowley that your characters carry a sense of submission to their fate.

That is his opinion. I would say that some of them do and some of them don't, like everybody else's characters. I would say that Lena Grove in *Light in August* coped pretty well with hers. It didn't really matter to her in her destiny whether her man was Lucas Burch or not. It was her destiny to have a husband and children and she knew it, and so she went out and attended to it without asking help from anyone. She was the captain of her soul. One of the calmest, sanest speeches I ever heard was when she said to Byron Bunch at the very instant of repulsing his final desperate and despairing attempt at rape, "Aint you ashamed? You might have woke the baby." She was never for one moment confused, frightened, alarmed. She did not even know that she didn't need pity. Her last speech for example: "My, my. A body does get around. Here aint we been coming from Alabama but two months, and now it's already Tennessee."

The Bundren family in *As I Lay Dying* pretty well coped with theirs. The father having lost his wife would naturally need another one, so he got one. At one blow he not only replaced the family cook, he acquired a gramophone to give them all pleasure while they were resting. The pregnant daughter failed this time to undo her condition, but she was not discouraged. She intended to try again, and even if they all failed right up to the last, it wasn't anything but just another baby.

And Mr. Cowley claims you find it hard to create sympathetic characters between the ages of twenty and forty.

FAULKNER

People between twenty and forty are not sympathetic. The child has the capacity to do but it can't know. It only knows when it is no longer able to do—after forty. Between twenty and forty the will of the child to do gets stronger, more dangerous, but it has not begun to learn to know yet. Since his capacity to do is forced into channels of evil through environment and pressures, man is strong before he is moral. The world's anguish is caused by people between twenty and forty. The people around my home who have caused all the interracial tension—the Milams and the Bryants (in the Emmett Till murder) and the gangs of Negroes who grab a white woman and rape her in revenge, the Hitlers, Napoleons, Lenins—all these people are symbols of human suffering and anguish, all of them between twenty and forty.

INTERVIEWER

You gave a statement to the papers at the time of the Emmett Till killing. Have you anything to add?

FAULKNER

No, only to repeat what I said before: that if we Americans are to survive it will have to be because we choose and elect and defend to be first of all Americans; to present to the world one homogeneous and unbroken front, whether of white Americans or black ones or purple or blue or green. Maybe the purpose of this sorry and tragic error committed in my native Mississippi by two white adults on an afflicted Negro child is to prove to us whether or not we deserve to survive. Because if we in America have reached that point in our desperate culture when we must murder children, no matter for what reason or what color, we don't deserve to survive and probably won't.

INTERVIEWER

What happened to you between *Soldier's Pay* and *Sartoris*—that is, what caused you to begin the Yoknapatawpha saga?

FAULKNER

With *Soldier's Pay* I found out writing was fun. But I found out afterward not only that each book had to have a design but the whole output or sum of an artist's work had to have a design. With *Soldier's Pay* and *Mosquitoes* I wrote for the sake of writing because it was fun. Beginning with *Sartoris* I discovered that my own little postage stamp of native soil was worth writing about and that I would never live long enough to exhaust it, and that by sublimating the actual into the apocryphal I would have complete liberty to use whatever talent I might have to its absolute top. It opened up a gold mine of other people, so I created a cosmos of my own. I can move these people around like God, not only in space but in time too. The fact that I have moved my characters around in time successfully, at least in my own estimation, proves to me my own theory that time is a fluid condition which has no existence except in the momentary avatars of individual people. There is no such thing as "was"—only "is." If "was" existed, there would be no grief or sorrow. I like to think of the world I created as being a kind of keystone in the universe; that, small as that keystone is, if it were ever taken away the universe itself would collapse. My last book will be the Doomsday Book, the Golden Book, of Yoknapatawpha County. Then I shall break the pencil and I'll have to stop.

Issue 12, 1956

Robert Lowell

The Art of Poetry

On one wall of Mr. Lowell's study was a large portrait of Ezra Pound, the tired, haughty outlines of the face concentrated as in the raised outlines of a ring seal in an enlargement. Also bearded, but on another wall, over the desk, James Russell Lowell looked down from a gray old-fashioned photograph on the apex of the triangle thus formed, where his great-grandnephew sat and answered questions.

Mr. Lowell had been talking about the classes he teaches at Boston University.

Four floors below the study window, cars whined through the early spring rain on Marlborough Street toward the Boston Public Garden.

—Frederick Seidel, 1961

INTERVIEWER

What are you teaching now?

ROBERT LOWELL

I'm teaching one of these poetry-writing classes and a course in the novel. The course in the novel is called Practical Criticism. It's a course I teach every year, but the material changes. It could be anything from Russian short stories to Baudelaire, a study of the New Critics, or just fiction. I do whatever I happen to be working on myself.

THE VOYAGE

I

For the child playing with its globe and stamps,
the planet 'equals its rapacity--
how grand the world in the light of the lamps,
how small in the blue day of maturity!

One morning we set sail, giddy with brave
predjudices, judgements, ingenuity--
we swing with the velvet swell of the wave,
our infinite is rocked by the fixed sea.

Some wish to fly a cheapness they detest,
others their crades' terror--others stand
sky-watching the great arc of a woman's breast,
reptilian Circe with her junk and wand.

Not to be changed to reptiles, such men craze
themselves with spaces, light, the burning sky;
cold toughens them, they bronze in the sun's blaze,
and dry the sores of their debauchery.

But the true voyagers are those who move
simply to move--balloons; their heart
is a sick motor thumping in one groove,
their irrational scream is, "Let's depart!"

Oh conscripts lusting for the first fire of the guns,
our sciences have never learned to tag
your dreams--unfathomable, enormous, vague
hopes grease the gears of these automatons.

A manuscript page from Robert Lowell's translation
of Baudelaire's "Le Voyage."

INTERVIEWER

Has your teaching over the last few years meant anything to you as a writer?

LOWELL

It's meant a lot to me as a human being, I think. But my teaching is part-time and has neither the merits nor the burdens of real teaching. Teaching is entirely different from writing. You're always up to it, or more or less up to it; there's no question of its clogging, of its not coming. It's much less subjective, and it's a very pleasant pursuit in itself. In the kind of teaching I do, conversational classes, seminars, if the students are good, which they've been most of the time, it's extremely entertaining. Now, I don't know what it has to do with writing. You review a lot of things that you like, and you read things that you haven't read or haven't read closely, and read them aloud, go into them much more carefully than you would otherwise; and that must teach you a good deal. But there's such a jump from teaching to writing.

INTERVIEWER

Well, do you think the academic life is liable to block up the writer-professor's sensitivity to his own intuitions?

LOWELL

I think it's impossible to give a general answer. Almost all the poets of my generation, all the best ones, teach. I only know one, Elizabeth Bishop, who doesn't. They do it for a livelihood, but they also do it because you can't write poetry all the time. They do it to extend themselves, and I think it's undoubtedly been a gain to them. Now the question is whether something else might be more of a gain. Certainly the danger of teaching is that it's much too close to what you're doing—close and not close. You can get expert at teaching and be crude in practice. The revision, the consciousness that tinkers with the poem—that has something to do with teaching and criticism. But the impulse that starts a poem and makes it of any importance is distinct from teaching.

INTERVIEWER

And protected, you think, from whatever you bring to bear in the scrutiny of parts of poems and aspects of novels?

LOWELL

I think you have to tear it apart from that. Teaching may make the poetry even more different, less academic than it would be otherwise. I'm sure that writing isn't a craft, that is, something for which you learn the skills and go on turning out. It must come from some deep impulse, deep inspiration. That can't be taught; it can't be what you use in teaching. And you may go further afield looking for that than you would if you didn't teach. I don't know, really; the teaching probably makes you more cautious, more self-conscious, makes you write less. It may make you bolder when you do write.

INTERVIEWER

You think the last may be so?

LOWELL

The boldness is ambiguous. It's not only teaching, it's growing up in this age of criticism which we're all so conscious of, whether we like it or don't like it, or practice it or don't practice it. You think three times before you put a word down and ten times about taking it out. And that's related to boldness; if you put words down they must do something, you're not going to put clichés. But then it's related to caution; you write much less.

INTERVIEWER

You yourself have written very little criticism, haven't you? You did once contribute to a study of Hopkins.

LOWELL

Yes, and I've done a few omnibus reviews. I do a review or two a year.

INTERVIEWER

You did a wonderful one of Richards's poems.

LOWELL

I felt there was an occasion for that, and I had something to say about it. Sometimes I wish I did more, but I'm very anxious in criticism not to do the standard analytical essay. I'd like my essay to be much sloppier and more intuitive. But my friends are critics, and most of them poet-critics. When I was twenty and learning to write, Allen Tate, Eliot, Blackmur, and Winters, and all those people were very much news. You waited for their essays, and when a good critical essay came out it had the excitement of a new imaginative work.

INTERVIEWER

Which is really not the case with any of the critics writing today, do you think?

LOWELL

The good critics are almost all the old ones. The most brilliant critic of my generation, I think, was Jarrell, and he in a way connects with that older generation. But he's writing less criticism now than he used to.

INTERVIEWER

In your schooling at St. Mark's and Harvard—we can talk about Kenyon in a minute—were there teachers or friends who had an influence on your writing, not so much by the example of their own writing as by personal supervision or direction, by suggesting certain reading, for instance?

LOWELL

Well, my school had been given a Carnegie set of art books, and I had a friend, Frank Parker, who had great talent as a painter but who'd never done it systematically. We began reading the books and histories of art, looking at reproductions, tracing the *Last Supper* on tracing paper, studying dynamic symmetry, learning about Cézanne, and so on. I had no practical interest in painting, but that study seemed rather close to poetry. And from there I began. I think I read Elizabeth Drew or some such book on modern poetry. It had free verse in it, and that seemed very simple to do.

INTERVIEWER

What class were you in then?

LOWELL

It was my last year. I'd wanted to be a football player very much and got my letter but didn't make the team. Well, that was satisfying but crushing too. I read a good deal but had never written. So this was a recoil from that. Then I had some luck in that Richard Eberhart was teaching there.

INTERVIEWER

I'd thought he'd been a student there with you.

LOWELL

No, he was a young man about thirty. I never had him in class, but I used to go to him. He'd read aloud and we'd talk; he was very pleasant that way. He'd smoke honey-scented tobacco, and read Baudelaire and Shakespeare and Hopkins—it made the thing living—and he'd read his own poems. I wrote very badly at first, but he was encouraging and enthusiastic. That probably was decisive, that there was someone there whom I admired who was engaged in writing poetry.

INTERVIEWER

I heard that a very early draft of "The Drunken Fisherman" appeared in the St. Mark's magazine.

LOWELL

No, it was the Kenyon college magazine that published it. The poem was very different then. I'd been reading Winters, whose model was Robert Bridges, and what I wanted was a rather distant, quiet, classical poem without any symbolism. It was in four-foot couplets as smooth as I could write them. *The Kenyon Review* had published a poem of mine and then they'd stopped. This was the one time they said, if you'd submitted this we'd have taken it.

INTERVIEWER

Then you were submitting other poems to the *Review*?

LOWELL

Yes, and that poem was rather different from anything else I did. I was also reading Hart Crane and Thomas and Tate and Empson's *Seven Types of Ambiguity*; and each poem was more difficult than the one before, and had more ambiguities. Ransom, editing *The Kenyon Review*, was impressed but didn't want to publish them. He felt they were forbidding and clotted.

INTERVIEWER

But finally he did come through.

LOWELL

Well, after I'd graduated. I published when I was a junior, then for about three years no magazine would take anything I did. I'd get sort of pleasant letters: One poem in this group interests us, if you can get seven more. At that time it took me about a year to do two or three poems. Gradually I just stopped, and really sort of gave it up. I seemed to have reached a great impasse. The kind of poem I thought was interesting and would work on became so cluttered and overdone that it wasn't really poetry.

INTERVIEWER

I was struck on reading *Land of Unlikeness* by the difference between the poems you rejected for *Lord Weary's Castle* and the few poems and passages that you took over into the new book.

LOWELL

I think I took almost a third, but almost all of what I took was rewritten. But I wonder what struck you.

INTERVIEWER

One thing was that almost all the rejected poems seemed to me to be those that Tate, who in his introduction spoke about two kinds of poetry in the book, said were the more strictly religious and strictly symbolic poems, as against the poems he said were perhaps more powerful because more experienced or relying more on your sense of history. What you took seemed really superior to what you left behind.

LOWELL

Yes, I took out several that were paraphrases of early Christian poems, and I rejected one rather dry abstraction, then whatever seemed to me to have a messy violence. All the poems have religious imagery, I think, but the ones I took were more concrete. That's what the book was moving toward: less symbolic imagery. And as I say, I tried to take some of the less fierce poems. There seemed to be too much twisting and disgust in the first book.

INTERVIEWER

I wondered how wide your reading had been at the time. I wondered, when I read in Tate's introduction that the stanza in one of your poems was based on the stanza in "The Virginian Voyage," whether someone had pointed out Drayton's poem to you.

LOWELL

Tate and I started to make an anthology together. It was a very interesting year I spent with Tate and his wife. He's a poet who writes in spurts, and he had about a third of a book. I was going to do a biography of Jonathan Edwards and he was going to write a novel, and our wives were going to write novels. Well, the wives just went humming away. I've just finished three pages, they'd say at the end of the day; and their books mounted up. But ours never did, though one morning Allen wrote four pages to his novel, very brilliant. We were in a little study together separated by a screen. I was heaping up books on Jonathan Edwards and taking notes, and getting more and more numb on the subject, looking at old leather-bound volumes on freedom of the will and so on, and feeling less and less a calling. And there we stuck. And then we decided to make an anthology together. We both liked rather formal, difficult poems, and we were reading particularly the sixteenth and seventeenth centuries. In the evening we'd read aloud, and we started a card catalog of what we'd make for the anthology. And then we started writing. It seems to me we took old models like Drayton's Ode—Tate wrote a poem called "The Young Proconsuls of the Air" in that stanza. I think there's a trick to formal poetry. Most poetry is very formal, but when a modern poet is formal he gets more attention for it than old poets did. Somehow we've tried to make it look difficult. For example, Shelley can just rattle off terza rima by the page, and it's very smooth, doesn't seem an obstruction to him— you sometimes wish it were more difficult. Well, someone does that today and in modern style it looks as though he's wrestling with every line and may be pushed into confusion, as though he's having a real struggle with form and content. Marks of that are in the finished poem. And I think both Tate and I felt that we wanted our formal patterns to seem a hardship and something that we couldn't rattle off easily.

INTERVIEWER

But in *Lord Weary's Castle* there were poems moving toward a sort of narrative calm, almost a prose calm—"Katherine's Dream," for example, or the two poems on texts by Edwards, or "The Ghost"—and then, on the other hand, poems in which the form was insisted upon and maybe shown off, and where the things that were characteristic of your poetry at that time—the kind of enjambments, the rhyming, the meters, of course—seem willed and forced, so that you have a terrific logjam of stresses, meanings, strains.

LOWELL

I know one contrast I've felt, and it takes different forms at different times. The ideal modern form seems to be the novel and certain short stories. Maybe Tolstoy would be the perfect example—his work is imagistic, it deals with all experience, and there seems to be no conflict of the form and content. So one thing is to get into poetry that kind of human richness in rather simple descriptive language. Then there's another side of poetry: compression, something highly rhythmical and perhaps wrenched into a small space. I've always been fascinated by both these things. But getting it all on one page in a few stanzas, getting it all done in as little space as possible, revising and revising so that each word and rhythm though not perfect is pondered and wrestled with—you can't do that in prose very well; you'd never get your book written. "Katherine's Dream" was a real dream. I found that I shaped it a bit, and cut it, and allegorized it, but still it was a dream someone had had. It was material that ordinarily, I think, would go into prose, yet it would have had to be much longer or part of something much longer.

INTERVIEWER

I think you can either look for forms, you can do specific reading for them, or the forms can be demanded by what you want to say. And when the material in poetry seems under almost unbearable pressure you wonder whether the form hasn't cookie-cut what the poet wanted to say. But you chose the couplet, didn't you, and some of your freest passages are in couplets.

LOWELL

The couplet I've used is very much like the couplet Browning uses in "My Last Duchess," run-on with its rhymes buried. I've always, when I've used it, tried to give the impression that I had as much freedom in choosing the rhyme word as I had in any of the other words. Yet they were almost all true rhymes, and maybe half the time there'd be a pause after the rhyme. I wanted something as fluid as prose; you wouldn't notice the form, yet looking back you'd find that great obstacles had been climbed. And the couplet is pleasant in this way—once you've got your two lines to rhyme, then that's done and you can go on to the next. You're not stuck with the whole stanza to round out and build to a climax. A couplet can be a couplet or can be split and left as one line, or it can go on for a hundred lines; any sort of compression or expansion is possible. And that's not so in a stanza. I think a couplet's much less lyrical than a stanza, closer to prose. Yet it's an honest form, its difficulties are in the open. It really is pretty hard to rhyme each line with the one that follows it.

INTERVIEWER

Did the change of style in *Life Studies* have something to do with working away from that compression and pressure by way of, say, the kind of prose clarity of "Katherine's Dream"?

LOWELL

Yes. By the time I came to *Life Studies* I'd been writing my autobiography and also writing poems that broke meter. I'd been doing a lot of reading aloud. I went on a trip to the West Coast and read at least once a day and sometimes twice for fourteen days, and more and more I found that I was simplifying my poems. If I had a Latin quotation I'd translate it into English. If adding a couple of syllables in a line made it clearer I'd add them, and I'd make little changes just impromptu as I read. That seemed to improve the reading.

INTERVIEWER

Can you think of a place where you added a syllable or two to an otherwise regular line?

LOWELL

It was usually articles and prepositions that I added, very slight little changes, and I didn't change the printed text. It was just done for the moment.

INTERVIEWER

Why did you do this? Just because you thought the most important thing was to get the poem over?

LOWELL

To get it over, yes. And I began to have a certain disrespect for the tight forms. If you could make it easier by adding syllables, why not? And then when I was writing *Life Studies*, a good number of the poems were started in very strict meter, and I found that, more than the rhymes, the regular beat was what I didn't want. I have a long poem in there about my father, called "Commander Lowell," which actually is largely in couplets, but I originally wrote perfectly strict four-foot couplets. Well, with that form it's hard not to have echoes of Marvell. That regularity just seemed to ruin the honesty of sentiment, and became rhetorical; it said, "I'm a poem"—though it was a great help when I was revising having this original skeleton. I could keep the couplets where I wanted them and drop them where I didn't; there'd be a form to come back to.

INTERVIEWER

Had you originally intended to handle all that material in prose?

LOWELL

Yes. I found it got awfully tedious working out transitions and putting in things that didn't seem very important but were necessary to the prose continuity. Also, I found it hard to revise. Cutting it down into small bits, I could work on it much more carefully and make fast transitions. But there's another point about this mysterious business of prose and poetry, form and content, and the reasons for breaking forms. I don't think there's any very satisfactory answer. I seesaw back and forth between something highly metrical and something highly free; there isn't any one way to write. But it seems to me we've gotten into a sort of Alexandrian age. Poets of my generation and particularly younger ones have gotten terribly proficient at these forms. They write a very musical, difficult poem with tremendous skill, perhaps there's never been such skill. Yet the writing seems divorced from culture somehow. It's become too much something specialized that can't handle much experience. It's become a craft, purely a craft, and there must be some breakthrough back into life. Prose is in many ways better off than poetry. It's quite hard to think of a young poet who has the vitality, say, of Salinger or Saul Bellow. Yet prose tends to be very diffuse. The novel is really a much more difficult form than it seems; few people have the wind to write anything that long. Even a short story demands almost poetic perfection. Yet on the whole prose is less cut off from life than poetry is. Now, some of this Alexandrian poetry is very brilliant, you would not have it changed at all. But I thought it was getting increasingly stifling. I couldn't get my experience into tight metrical forms.

INTERVIEWER

So you felt this about your own poetry, your own technique, not just about the general condition of poetry?

LOWELL

Yes, I felt that the meter plastered difficulties and mannerisms on what I was trying to say to such an extent that it terribly hampered me.

INTERVIEWER

This then explains—in part, anyway—your admiration for Elizabeth Bishop's poetry. I know that you've said the qualities and the abundance of its descriptive language reminded you of the Russian novel more than anything else.

LOWELL

Any number of people are guilty of writing a complicated poem that has a certain amount of symbolism in it and a really difficult meaning, a wonderful poem to teach. Then you unwind it and you feel that the intelligence, the experience, whatever goes into it, is skin-deep. In Elizabeth Bishop's "Man-Moth" a whole new world is gotten out and you don't know what will come after any one line. It's exploring. And it's as original as Kafka. She's gotten a world, not just a way of writing. She seldom writes a poem that doesn't have that exploratory quality; yet it's very firm, it's not like beat poetry, it's all controlled.

INTERVIEWER

What about Snodgrass? What you were trying to do in *Life Studies* must have something to do with your admiration for his work.

LOWELL

He did these things before I did, though he's younger than I am and had been my student. He may have influenced me, though people have suggested the opposite. He spent ten years at the University of Iowa, going to writing classes, being an instructor; rather unworldly, making little money, and specializing in talking to other people writing poetry; obsessed, you might say, with minute technical problems and rather provincial experience—and then he wrote about just that. I mean, the poems are about his child, his divorce, and Iowa City, and his child is a Dr. Spock child—all handled in expert little stanzas. I believe that's a new kind of poetry. Other poems that are direct that way are slack and have no vibrance. His experience wouldn't be so interesting and valid if it weren't for the whimsy, the music, the balance, everything revised and placed and pondered. All that gives light to those poems on agonizing subjects comes from the craft.

INTERVIEWER

And yet his best poems are all on the verge of being slight and even sentimental.

LOWELL

I think a lot of the best poetry is. Laforgue—it's hard to think of a more delightful poet, and his prose is wonderful too. Well, it's on the verge of being sentimental, and if he hadn't dared to be sentimental he wouldn't have been a poet. I mean, his inspiration was that. There's some way of distinguishing between false sentimentality, which is blowing up a subject and giving emotions that you don't feel, and using whimsical, minute, tender, small emotions that most people don't feel but which Laforgue and Snodgrass do. So that I'd say he had pathos and fragility—but then that's a large subject too. He has fragility along the edges and a main artery of power going through the center.

INTERVIEWER

Some people were disappointed with *Life Studies* just because earlier you had written a kind of heroic poetry, an American version of heroic poetry, of which there had been none recently except your own. Is there any chance that you will go back to that?

LOWELL

I don't think that a personal history can go on forever, unless you're Walt Whitman and have a way with you. I feel I've done enough personal poetry. That doesn't mean I won't do more of it, but I don't want to do more now. I feel I haven't gotten down all my experience, or perhaps even the most important part, but I've said all I really have much inspiration to say, and more would just dilute. So that you need something more impersonal, and other things being equal it's better to get your emotions out in a Macbeth than in a confession. Macbeth must have tons of Shakespeare in him. We don't know where, nothing in Shakespeare's life was remotely like Macbeth, yet he somehow gives the feeling of going to the core of Shakespeare. You have much more freedom that way than you do when you write an autobiographical poem.

INTERVIEWER

These poems, I gather from what you said earlier, did take as much working over as the earlier ones.

LOWELL

They were just as hard to write. They're not always factually true. There's a good deal of tinkering with fact. You leave out a lot, and emphasize this and not that. Your actual experience is a complete flux. I've invented facts and changed things, and the whole balance of the poem was something invented. So there's a lot of artistry, I hope, in the poems. Yet there's this thing: if a poem is autobiographical— and this is true of any kind of autobiographical writing and of historical writing—you want the reader to say, this is true. In something like Macaulay's *History of England* you think you're really getting

William III. That's as good as a good plot in a novel. And so there was always that standard of truth which you wouldn't ordinarily have in poetry—the reader was to believe he was getting the real Robert Lowell.

I wanted to ask you about this business of taking over passages from earlier poems and rewriting them and putting them in new contexts. I'm thinking of the passage at the end of the "Cistercians in Germany," in *Land of Unlikeness*, which you rewrote into those wonderful lines that end "At the Indian Killer's Grave." I know that Hart Crane rewrote early scraps a great deal and used most of the rewrites. But doesn't doing this imply a theory of poetry that would talk much more about craft than about experience?

I don't know. It's such a miracle if you get lines that are halfway right; it's not just a technical problem. The lines must mean a good deal to you. All your poems are in a sense one poem, and there's always the struggle of getting something that balances and comes out right, in which all parts are good, and that has experience that you value. And so if you have a few lines that shine in a poem or are beginning to shine, and they fail and get covered over and drowned, maybe their real form is in another poem. Maybe you've mistaken the real inspiration in the original poem and they belong in something else entirely. I don't think that violates experience. The "Cistercians" wasn't very close to me, but the last lines seemed felt; I dropped the Cistercians and put a Boston graveyard in.

But in Crane's "Praise for an Urn," a poem about a personal friend, there are lines that originally applied to something very different, and therefore, in one version or the other, at least can't be called personal.

LOWELL

I think we always bring over some unexplained obscurities by shifting lines. Something that was clear in the original just seems odd and unexplained in the final poem. That can be quite bad, of course; but you always want—and I think Chekhov talks about this—the detail that you can't explain. It's just there. It seems right to you, but you don't have to have it; you could have something else entirely. Now if everything's like that you'd just have chaos, but a few unexplained difficult things—they seem to be the lifeblood of variety—they may work. What may have seemed a little odd, a little difficult in the original poem, gets a little more difficult in a new way in the new poem. And that's purely accidental, yet you may gain more than you lose—a new suggestiveness and magic.

INTERVIEWER

Do you revise a very great deal?

LOWELL

Endlessly.

INTERVIEWER

You often use an idiom or a very common phrase either for the sake of irony or to bear more meaning than it's customarily asked to bear—do these come late in the game; do you have to look around for them?

LOWELL

They come later because they don't prove much in themselves, and they often replace something that's much more formal and worked up. Some of my later poetry does have this quality that the earlier doesn't: several lines can be almost what you'd say in conversation. And maybe talking with a friend or with my wife I'd say, This doesn't sound quite right, and sort of reach in the air as I talked and change a few words. In that way the new style is easier to write; I sometimes fumble out a natural sequence of lines that will work. But a whole poem won't come that way; my seemingly relaxed poems are just about as hard as the very-worked-up ones.

That rightness and familiarity, though, is in "Between the Porch and the Altar" in several passages which are in couplets.

When I am writing in meter I find the simple lines never come right away. Nothing does. I don't believe I've ever written a poem in meter where I've kept a single one of the original lines. Usually when I was writing my old poems I'd write them out in blank verse and then put in the rhymes. And of course I'd change the rhymes a lot. The most I could hope for at first was that the rhymed version wouldn't be much inferior to the blank verse. Then the real work would begin, to make it something much better than the original out of the difficulties of the meter.

Have you ever gone as far as Yeats and written out a prose argument and then set down the rhymes?

With some of the later poems I've written out prose versions, then cut the prose down and abbreviated it. A rapidly written prose draft of the poem doesn't seem to do much good, too little pain has gone into it; but one really worked on is bound to have phrases that are invaluable. And it's a nice technical problem: how can you keep phrases and get them into meter?

Do you usually send off your work to friends before publishing it?

I do it less now. I always used to do it, to Jarrell and one or two other people. Last year I did a lot of reading with Stanley Kunitz.

INTERVIEWER

At the time you were writing the poems for *Lord Weary's Castle*, did it make a difference to you whether the poet to whom you were sending your work was Catholic?

LOWELL

I don't think I ever sent any poems to a Catholic. The person I was closest to then was Allen Tate, who wasn't a Catholic at the time; and then later it became Jarrell, who wasn't at all Catholic. My two close Catholic writer friends are prose writers, J. F. Powers and Flannery O'Connor, and they weren't interested in the technical problems of poems.

INTERVIEWER

So you feel that the religion is the business of the poem that it's in and not at all the business of the Church or the religious person.

LOWELL

It shouldn't be. I mean, a religion ought to have objective validity. But by the time it gets into a poem it's so mixed up with technical and imaginative problems that the theologian, the priest, the serious religious person isn't of too much use. The poem is too strange for him to feel at home and make any suggestions.

INTERVIEWER

What does this make of the religious poem as a religious exercise?

LOWELL

Well, it at least makes this: that the poem tries to be a poem and not a piece of artless religious testimony. There is a drawback. It seems to me that with any poem, but maybe particularly a religious one where there are common interests, the opinion of intelligent people who are not poets ought to be useful. There's an independence to this not getting advice from religious people and outsiders, but also there's a narrowness. Then there is a question whether my poems are religious or whether they just use religious imagery. I haven't really any idea. My last poems don't use religious imagery, they don't use symbolism. In many ways they seem to me more religious than the early ones, which are full of symbols and references to Christ and God. I'm sure the symbols and the Catholic framework didn't make the poems religious experiences. Yet I don't feel my experience changed very much. It seems to me it's clearer to me now than it was then, but it's very much the same sort of thing that went into the religious poems—the same sort of struggle, light and darkness, the flux of experience. The morality seems much the same. But the symbolism is gone; you couldn't possibly say what creed I believed in. I've wondered myself often. Yet what made the earlier poems valuable seems to be some recording of experience, and that seems to be what makes the later ones.

INTERVIEWER

So you end up saying that the poem does have some integrity and can have some beauty apart from the beliefs expressed in the poem.

LOWELL

I think it can only have integrity apart from the beliefs; that no political position, religious position, position of generosity, or what have you, can make a poem good. It's all to the good if a poem *can* use politics, or theology, or gardening, or anything that has its own validity aside from poetry. But these things will never per se make a poem.

INTERVIEWER

The difficult question is whether when the beliefs expressed in a poem are obnoxious the poem as a whole can be considered to be beautiful—the problem of the *Pisan Cantos*.

LOWELL

The *Pisan Cantos* are very uneven, aren't they? If you took what most people would agree are maybe the best hundred passages, would the beliefs in those passages be obnoxious? I think you'd get a very mixed answer. You could make quite a good case for Pound's good humor about his imprisonment, his absence of self-pity, his observant eye, his memories of literary friends, for all kinds of generous qualities and open qualities and lyrical qualities that anyone would think were good. And even when he does something like the death of Mussolini, in the passage that opens the *Pisan Cantos*, people debate about it. I've talked to Italians who were partisans, and who said that this is the only poem on Mussolini that's any good. Pound's quite wily often: Mussolini hung up like an ox—his brutal appearance. I don't know whether you could say the beliefs there are wrong or not. And there are other poems that come to mind: in Eliot, the Jew spelled with a small *j* in "Gerontion," is that anti-Semitism or not? Eliot's not anti-Semitic in any sense, but there's certainly a dislike of Jews in those early poems. Does he gain in the fierceness of writing his Jew with a small *j*? He says you write what you have to write and in criticism you can say what you think you should believe in. Very ugly emotions perhaps make a poem.

INTERVIEWER

You were on the Bollingen Committee at the time the award was made to Pound. What did you think of the great ruckus?

LOWELL

I thought it was a very simple problem of voting for the best book of the year; and it seemed to me Pound's was. I thought the *Pisan Cantos* was the best writing Pound had ever done, though it included some of his worst. It is a very mixed book: that was the question. But the consequences of not giving the best book of the year a prize for extraneous reasons, even terrible ones in a sense—I think that's the death of art. Then you have Pasternak suppressed and everything becomes stifling. Particularly in a strong country like ours you've got to award things objectively and not let the beliefs you'd like a man to have govern your choice. It was very close after the war, and anyone must feel that the poetry award was a trifling thing compared with the concentration camps. I actually think they were very distant from Pound. He had no political effect whatsoever and was quite eccentric and impractical. Pound's social credit, his fascism, all these various things, were a tremendous gain to him; he'd be a very Parnassian poet without them. Even if they're bad beliefs—and some were bad, some weren't, and some were just terrible, of course—they made him more human and more to do with life, more to do with the times. They served him. Taking what interested him in these things gave a kind of realism and life to his poetry that it wouldn't have had otherwise.

INTERVIEWER

Did you become a translator to suit your own needs or because you wanted to get certain poems, most of them not before translated, into English? Or was it a matter of both, as I suppose it usually is, and as it was for Pound?

LOWELL

I think both. It always seemed to me that nothing very close to the poems I've translated existed in English; and on the other hand, there was some kind of closeness. I felt a kinship. I felt some sort of closeness to the Rilke and Rimbaud poems I've translated, yet they were doing things I couldn't do. They were both a continuation of my own bias and a release from myself.

INTERVIEWER

How did you come to translate Propertius—in fact, how did you come to have such a great interest in Roman history and Latin literature?

LOWELL

At Harvard my second year I took almost entirely English courses—the easiest sort of path. I think that would have been a disaster. But before going to Kenyon I talked to Ford Madox Ford and Ransom, and Ransom said you've just got to take philosophy and logic, which I did. The other thing he suggested was classics. Ford was rather flippant about it, said of course you've got to learn classics, you'll just cut yourself off from humanity if you don't. I think it's always given me some sort of yardstick for English. And then the literature was amazing, particularly the Greek; there's nothing like Greek in English at all. Our plays aren't formally at all like Aeschylus and Sophocles. Their whole inspiration was unbelievably different, and so different that you could hardly think of even the attempt to imitate them, great as their prestige was. That something like *Antigone* or *Oedipus* or the great Achilles moments in *The Iliad* would be at the core of a literature is incredible for anyone brought up in an English culture—Greek wildness and sophistication all different, the women different, everything. Latin's of course much closer. English is a half-Latin language, and we've done our best to absorb the Latin literature. But a Roman poet is much less intellectual than the Englishman, much less abstract. He's nearer nature somehow—somewhat what we feel about a Frenchman but more so still. And yet he's very sophisticated. He has his way of doing things, though the number of forms he explored is quite limited. The amount he could take from the Greeks and yet change is an extraordinary piece of firm discipline. Also, you take almost any really good Roman poet—Juvenal, or Virgil, or Propertius, Catullus—he's much more raw and direct than anything in English, and yet he has this blocklike formality. The Roman frankness interests me. Until recently our literature hasn't been as raw as the Roman, translations had to have stars. And their history has a terrible human frankness that isn't customary with us—corrosive attacks on the establishment, comments on politics and the decay of morals, all felt terribly strongly, by poets as well as historians. The English writer who reads the classics is working at one thing, and his eye is on something else that can't be done. We will always have the Latin and Greek classics, and they'll never be absorbed. There's something very restful about that.

INTERVIEWER

But, more specifically, how did Latin poetry—your study of it, your translations—affect your measure of English poetry?

LOWELL

My favorite English poetry was the difficult Elizabethan plays and the Metaphysicals, then the nineteenth century, which I was aquiver about and disliked but which was closer to my writing than anything else. The Latin seemed very different from either of these. I immediately saw how Shelley wasn't like Horace and Virgil or Aeschylus—and the Latin was a mature poetry, a realistic poetry, which didn't have the contortions of the Metaphysicals. What a frail, bony, electric person Marvell is compared with Horace!

INTERVIEWER

What about your adaptation of Propertius?

LOWELL

I got him through Pound. When I read him in Latin I found a kind of Propertius you don't get in Pound at all. Pound's Propertius is a rather Ovidian figure with a great deal of Pound's fluency and humor and irony. The actual Propertius is a very excited, tense poet, rather desperate; his line is much more like parts of Marlowe's *Faustus*. And he's of all the Roman poets the most like a desperate Christian. His experiences, his love affair with Cynthia, are absolutely rending, destroying. He's like a fallen Christian.

INTERVIEWER

Have you done any other translations of Latin poems?

LOWELL

I did a monologue that started as a translation of Virgil and then was completely rewritten, and there are buried translations in several other poems. There's a poem called "To Speak of Woe That Is in Marriage" in my last book that started as a translation of Catullus. I don't know what traces are left, but it couldn't have been written without the Catullus.

INTERVIEWER

You've translated Pasternak. Do you know Russian?

LOWELL

No, I have rewritten other English translations, and seldom even checked with Russian experts. I want to get a book of translations together. I read in the originals, except for Russian, but I have felt quite free to alter things, and I don't know that Pasternak would look less close than the Italian, which I have studied closely. Before I publish, I want to check with a Russian expert.

INTERVIEWER

Can I get you back to Harvard for a minute? Is it true you tried out for the Harvard *Advocate*, did all the dirty work for your candidacy, and then were turned down?

LOWELL

I nailed a carpet down. I forget who the editor was then, but he was a man who wrote on Frost. At that time people who wrote on Frost were quite different from the ones who write on him now; they tended to be conservative, out of touch. I wasn't a very good writer then, perhaps I should have been turned down. I was trying to write like William Carlos Williams, very simple, free verse, imagistic poems. I had a little group I was very proud of which was set up in galleys; when I left Harvard it was turned down.

INTERVIEWER

Did you know any poets at the time?

LOWELL

I had a friend, Harry Brown, who writes dialogue for movies and has been in Hollywood for years. He was a terribly promising poet. He came to Harvard with a long correspondence with Harriet Monroe and was much more advanced than anyone else. He could write in the style of Auden or Webster or Eliot or Crane. He'd never graduated from high school, and wasn't a student, but he was the person I felt closest to. My other friends weren't writers.

INTERVIEWER

Had you met any older poets—Frost, for instance, who must have been around?

LOWELL

I'd gone to call on Frost with a huge epic on the First Crusade, all written out in clumsy longhand on lined paper. He read a page of that and said, You have no compression. Then he read me a very short poem of Collins, "How Sleep the Brave," and said, That's not a great poem, but it's not too long. He was very kindly about it. You know his point about the voice coming into poetry: he took a very unusual example of that, the opening of *Hyperion*—the line about the Naiad, something about her pressing a cold finger to her cold lips, which wouldn't seem like a voice passage at all. And he said, Now Keats comes alive here. That was a revelation to me; what had impressed me was the big Miltonic imitation in *Hyperion*. I don't know what I did with that, but I recoiled and realized that I was diffuse and monotonous.

INTERVIEWER

What decided you to leave Harvard and go to Kenyon?

LOWELL

I'd made the acquaintance of Merrill Moore, who'd been at Vanderbilt and a Fugitive. He said that I ought to study with a man who was a poet. He was very close to Ransom, and the plan was that I'd go to Vanderbilt; and I would have, but Ransom changed to Kenyon.

INTERVIEWER

I understand you left much against the wishes of your family.

LOWELL

Well, I was getting quite morose and solitary, and they sort of settled for this move. They'd rather have had me a genial social Harvard student, but at least I'd be working hard this way. It seemed to them a queer but orderly step.

INTERVIEWER

Did it help you that you had had intellectual and literary figures in your family?

LOWELL

I really didn't know I'd had them till I went to the South. To my family, James Russell Lowell was the ambassador to England, not a writer. Amy seemed a bit peculiar to them. When I began writing I think it would have been unimaginable to take either Amy or James Russell Lowell as models.

INTERVIEWER

Was it through Ransom that you met Tate?

LOWELL

I met them at more or less the same time, but actually stayed with Tate before I knew Ransom very well.

INTERVIEWER

And Ford Madox Ford was there at some time, wasn't he?

LOWELL

I met Ford at a cocktail party in Boston and went to dinner with him at the Athens Olympia. He was going to visit the Tates, and said, Come and see me down there, we're all going to Tennessee. So I drove down. He hadn't arrived, so I got to know the Tates quite well before his appearance.

INTERVIEWER

Staying in a pup tent.

LOWELL

It's a terrible piece of youthful callousness. They had one Negro woman who came in and helped, but Mrs. Tate was doing all the housekeeping. She had three guests and her own family, and was doing the cooking and writing a novel. And this young man arrived, quite ardent and eccentric. I think I suggested that maybe I'd stay with them. And they said, We really haven't any room, you'd have to pitch a tent on the lawn. So I went to Sears, Roebuck and got a tent and rigged it on their lawn. The Tates were too polite to tell me that what they'd said had been just a figure of speech. I stayed two months in my tent and ate with the Tates.

INTERVIEWER

And you were showing him your work all the while.

LOWELL

Oh, I became converted to formalism and changed my style from brilliant free verse, all in two months. And everything was in rhyme, and it still wasn't any good. But that was a great incentive. I poured out poems and went to writers' conferences.

INTERVIEWER

What about Ford?

LOWELL

I saw him out there and took dictation from him for a while. That was hell, because I didn't know how to type. I'd take the dictation down in longhand, and he rather mumbled. I'd ask him what he'd said, and he'd say, Oh, you have no sense of prose rhythm, and mumble some more. I'd get most of his words, then I'd have to improvise on the typewriter.

INTERVIEWER

So for part of Ford's opus we're indebted to you.

LOWELL

A handful of phrases in *The March of Literature*, on the Provençal poets.

INTERVIEWER

That was the summer before you entered Kenyon, but most of the poems in *Land of Unlikeness* were written after you'd graduated, weren't they?

LOWELL

Yes, they were almost all written in a year I spent with the Tates, though some of them were earlier poems rewritten. I think becoming a Catholic convert had a good deal to do with writing again. I was much more interested in being a Catholic than in being a writer. I read Catholic writers but had no intention of writing myself. But somehow, when I started again, I won't say the Catholicism gave me subject matter, but it gave me some kind of form, and I could begin a poem and build it to a climax. It was quite different from what I'd been doing earlier.

INTERVIEWER

Why, then, did you choose to print your work in the small liberal magazines whose religious and political positions were very different from yours? Have you ever submitted to *The New Yorker* or *The Atlantic Monthly*?

LOWELL

I think I may have given something to *The Atlantic* on Santayana; *The New Yorker* I haven't given anything. I think *The New Yorker* does some of the best prose in the country, in many ways much more interesting than the quarterlies and little magazines. But poems are lost in it; there's no table of contents, and some of their poetry is light verse. There's no particular continuity of excellence. There just seems no point in printing there. For a while the little magazines, whose religious-political positions *were* very different from mine, were the only magazines that would publish me, and I feel like staying with them. I like magazines like *The New Statesman*, *The Nation*, *The New Republic*—something a little bit off the track.

INTERVIEWER

Just because they are off the track?

LOWELL

I think so. A political position I don't necessarily agree with which is a little bit adverse seems to me just more attractive than a time-serving, conventional position. And they tend to have good reviews, those magazines. I think you write for a small audience, an ardent critical audience. And you know Graves says that poets ought to take in each other's washing because they're the only responsible audience. There's a danger to that—you get too specialized—but I pretty much agree that's the audience you do write for. If it gets further, that's all fine.

INTERVIEWER

There is, though, a certain inbred, in-group anemia to those magazines, at least to the literary quarterlies. For instance, it would have been almost inconceivable for *Partisan Review*, which is the best of them, I think, to give your last book a bad review or even a sharp review.

LOWELL

I think no magazine likes to slam one of its old contributors. *Partisan* has sometimes just not reviewed a book by someone they liked very much and their reviewer didn't. I know Shapiro has been attacked in *Partisan* and then published there, and other people have been unfavorably reviewed and made rather a point of sending them something afterward. You want to feel there's a certain degree of poorer writing that wouldn't get published in the magazine your work appears in. The good small magazine may publish a lot of rather dry stuff, but at least it's serious, and if it's bad it's not bad by trying to be popular and put something over on the public. It's a wrenched personal ineptitude that will get published rather than a public slickness. I think that has something to do with good reviews coming out in the magazine. We were talking about *Partisan*'s not slamming one of its contributors, but *Partisan* has a pretty harsh, hard standard of reviewing, and they certainly wouldn't praise one of their contributors who'd gone to pot.

INTERVIEWER

What poets among your contemporaries do you most admire?

LOWELL

The two I've been closest to are Elizabeth Bishop—I spoke about her earlier—and Jarrell, and they're different. Jarrell's a great man of letters, a very informed man, and the best critic of my generation, the best professional poet. He's written the best war poems, and those poems are a tremendous product of our culture, I feel. Elizabeth Bishop's poems, as I said, are more personal, more something she did herself, and she's not a critic but has her own tastes, which may be very idiosyncratic. I enjoy her poems more than anybody else's. I like some of Shapiro very much, some of Roethke and Stanley Kunitz.

INTERVIEWER

What about Roethke, who tries to do just about everything you don't try to do?

LOWELL

We've read to each other and argued, and may be rather alike in temperament actually, but he wants a very musical poem and always would quarrel with my ear as I'd quarrel with his eye. He has love poems and childhood poems and startling surrealistic poems, rather simple experience done with a blaze of power. He rejoices in the rhetoric and the metrics, but there's something very disorderly working there. Sometimes it will smash a poem and sometimes it will make it. The things he knows about I feel I know nothing about, flowers and so on. What we share, I think, is the exultant moment, the blazing out. Whenever I've tried to do anything like his poems, I've felt helpless and realized his mastery.

INTERVIEWER

You were apparently a very close friend of Delmore Schwartz's.

LOWELL

Yes, and I think that I've never met anyone who has somehow as much seeped into me. It's a complicated personal thing to talk about. His reading was very varied, Marx and Freud and Russell, very Catholic and not from a conservative position at all. He sort of grew up knowing those things and has a wonderful penetrating humorous way of talking about them. If he met T. S. Eliot his impressions of Eliot would be mixed up with his impressions of Freud and what he'd read about Eliot; all these things flowed back and forth in him. Most of my writer friends were more specialized and limited than Schwartz, most of them took against-the-grain positions that were also narrow. Schwartz was a revelation. He felt the poet who had experience was very much better than the poet with polish. Wordsworth would interest him much more than Keats—he wanted openness to direct experience. He said that if you got people talking in a poem you could do anything. And his own writing, *Coriolanus* and *Shenandoah*, is interesting for that.

INTERVIEWER

Isn't this much what you were saying about your own hopes for *Life Studies*?

LOWELL

Yes, but technically I think that Delmore and I are quite different. There have been very few poets I've been able to get very much from technically. Tate has been one of the closest to me. My early poems I think grew out of my admiration for his poems.

INTERVIEWER

What about poets in the past?

LOWELL

It's hard for me to imitate someone; I'm very self-conscious about it. That's an advantage, perhaps—you don't become too imitative— but it's also a limitation. I tremble when I feel I'm being like someone else. If it's Rilke or Rimbaud or Propertius, you know the language is a big bar and that if you imitate you're doing something else. I've felt greater freedom that way. I think I've tried to write like some of the Elizabethans.

INTERVIEWER

And Crane? You said you had read a good deal of Crane.

LOWELL

Yes, but his difficult style is one I've never been able to do much with. He can be very obscure and yet write a much more inspired poem than I could by being obscure. There's a relationship between Crane and Tate, and for some reason Tate was much easier for me. I could see how Tate was done, though Tate has a rhythm that I've never been able to imitate. He's much more irregular than I am, and I don't know where the rhythm comes from, but I admire it very much. Crane said somewhere that he could write five or six good lines but Tate could write twelve that would hang together, and you'd see how the twelve were built. Tate was somehow more of a model: he had a lot of wildness and he had a lot of construction. And of course I knew him and never knew Crane. I think Crane is the great poet of that generation. He got out more than anybody else. Not only is it the tremendous power there, but he somehow got New York City; he was at the center of things in the way that no other poet was. All the chaos of his life missed getting sidetracked the way other poets did, and he was less limited than any other poet of his generation. There was a fullness of experience; and without that, if you just had his mannerisms and not his rather simple writing— which if done badly would be sentimental merely—or just his obscure writing, the whole thing would be merely verbal. It isn't with Crane. The push of the whole man is there. But his style never worked for me.

INTERVIEWER

But something of Crane does seem to have gotten into your work— or maybe it's just that sense of power thrashing about. I thought it had come from a close admiring reading of Crane.

LOWELL

Yes, some kind of wildness and power that appeals to me, I guess. But when I wrote difficult poems they weren't meant to be difficult, though I don't know that Crane meant his to be. I wanted to be loaded and rich, but I thought the poems were all perfectly logical. You can have a wonderful time explaining a great poem like "Voyages II," and it all can be explained, but in the end it's just a love poem with a great confusion of images that are emotionally clear; a prose paraphrase wouldn't give you any impression whatever of the poem. I couldn't do that kind of poem, I don't think; at least I've never been able to.

INTERVIEWER

You said that most of the writers you've known have been against the grain. What did you mean?

LOWELL

When I began writing most of the great writers were quite unpopular. They hadn't reached the universities yet, and their circulation was small. Even Eliot wasn't very popular then. But life seemed to be there. It seemed to be one of those periods when the lid was still being blown. The great period of blowing the lid was the time of Schoenberg and Picasso and Joyce and the early Eliot, where a power came into the arts that we perhaps haven't had since. These people were all rather traditional, yet they were stifled by what was being done, and they almost wrecked things to do their great works—even rather minor but very good writers such as Williams or Marianne Moore. Their kind of protest and queerness has hardly been repeated. They're wonderful writers. You wouldn't see anyone as strange as Marianne Moore again, not for a long while. Conservative and Jamesian as she is, it was a terrible, private, and strange revolutionary poetry. There isn't the motive to do that now. Yet those were the classics, and it seems to me they were all against the grain, Marianne Moore as much as Crane. That's where life was for the small audience. It would be a tremendous subject to say whether the feelings were against the grain too, and whether they were purifying, nihilistic, or both.

INTERVIEWER

Have you had much contact with Eliot?

LOWELL

I may have seen him a score of times in my life, and he's always been very kind. Long before he published me he had some of my poems in his files. There's some kind of New England connection.

INTERVIEWER

Has he helpfully criticized your work?

LOWELL

Just very general criticism. With the first book of mine Faber did he had a lot of little questions about punctuation, but he never said he liked this or disliked that. Then he said something about the last book—These are first-rate, I mean it—something like that that was very understated and gratifying. I feel Eliot's less tied to form than a lot of people he's influenced, and there's a freedom of the twenties in his work that I find very sympathetic. Certainly he and Frost are the great New England poets. You hardly think of Stevens as New England, but you have to think of Eliot and Frost as deeply New England and puritanical. They're a continuation and a criticism of the tradition, and they're probably equally great poets. Frost somehow put life into a dead tradition. His kind of poetry must have seemed almost unpublishable, it was so strange and fresh when it was first written. But still it was old-fashioned poetry and really had nothing to do with modern writing—except that he is one of the greatest modern writers. Eliot was violently modern and unacceptable to the traditionalist. Now he's spoken of as a literary dictator, but he's handled his position with wonderful sharpness and grace, it seems to me. It's a narrow position and it's not one I hold particularly, but I think it's been held with extraordinary honesty and finish and development. Eliot has done what he said Shakespeare had done: all his poems are one poem, a form of continuity that has grown and snowballed.

INTERVIEWER

I remember Jarrell in reviewing *Mills of the Kavanaughs* said that Frost had been doing narrative poems with ease for years, and that nobody else had been able to catch up.

LOWELL

And what Jarrell said is true: nobody except Frost can do a sort of Chaucerian narrative poem that's organized and clear. Well, a lot of people do them, but the texture of their verse is so limp and unin-spired. Frost does them with great power. Most of them were done early, in that *North of Boston* period. That was a miracle, because except for Robinson—and I think Frost is a very much greater poet than Robinson—no one was doing that in England or America.

But you hadn't simply wanted to tell a story in *Mills of the Kavanaughs*.

No, I was writing an obscure, rather Elizabethan, dramatic and melodramatic poem. I don't know quite how to describe this business of direct experience. With Browning, for instance, for all his gifts—and there is almost nothing Browning couldn't use—you feel there's a glaze between what he writes and what really happened, you feel the people are made up. In Frost you feel that's just what the farmers and so on were like. It has the virtue of a photograph but all the finish of art. That's an extraordinary thing; almost no other poet can do that now.

What do you suppose are the qualities that go into that ability?

I don't know. Prose writers have it much more, and quite a few prose writers have it. It's some kind of sympathy and observation of people. It's the deep, rather tragic poems that I value most. Perhaps it's been overdone with Frost, but there's an abundance and geniality about those poems that isn't tragic. With this sense of rhythm and words and composition, and getting into his lines language that is very much like the language he speaks—which is also a work of art, much better than other people's ordinary speech and yet natural to him; he has that continuity with his ordinary self and his poetic self—he's made what with anyone else would be just flat. A very good prose writer can do this and make something of it. You get it quite often in

Faulkner. Though he's an Elizabethan sort of character, rather unlike Frost, he can get this amazing immediacy and simplicity. When it comes to verse the form is so hard that all of that gets drained out. In a very conventional old-fashioned writer, or someone who's trying to be realistic but also dramatic and inspired, though he may remain a good poet, most of that directness and realism goes. It's hard for Eliot to be direct that way, though you get it in bits of *The Waste Land*, that marvelous Cockney section. And he can be himself; I feel Eliot's real all through the *Quartets*. He can be very intelligent or very simple there, and *he's* there, but there are no other people in the *Quartets*.

INTERVIEWER

Have many of your poems been taken from real people and real events?

LOWELL

I think, except when I've used myself or occasionally named actual people in poems, the characters are purely imaginary. I've tried to buttress them by putting images I've actually seen and in indirect ways getting things I've actually experienced into the poem. If I'm writing about a Canadian nun the poem may have a hundred little bits of things I've looked at, but she's not remotely anyone I've ever known. And I don't believe anybody would think my nun was quite a real person. She has a heart and she's alive, I hope, and she has a lot of color to her and drama, and has some things that Frost's characters don't, but she doesn't have their wonderful quality of life. His Witch of Coös is absolutely there. I've gathered from talking to him that most of the *North of Boston* poems came from actual people he knew shuffled and put together. But then it's all-important that Frost's plots are so extraordinary, so carefully worked out though it almost seems that they're not there. Like some things in Chekhov, the art is very well hidden.

INTERVIEWER

Don't you think a large part of it is getting the right details, symbolic or not, around which to wind the poem tight and tighter?

LOWELL

Some bit of scenery or something you've felt. Almost the whole problem of writing poetry is to bring it back to what you really feel, and that takes an awful lot of maneuvering. You may feel the doorknob more strongly than some big personal event, and the doorknob will open into something that you can use as your own. A lot of poetry seems to me very good in the tradition but just doesn't move me very much because it doesn't have personal vibrance to it. I probably exaggerate the value of it, but it's precious to me. Some little image, some detail you've noticed—you're writing about a little country shop, just describing it, and your poem ends up with an existentialist account of your experience. But it's the shop that started it off. You didn't know why it meant a lot to you. Often images and often the sense of the beginning and end of a poem are all you have—some journey to be gone through between those things; you know that, but you don't know the details. And that's marvelous; then you feel the poem will come out. It's a terrible struggle, because what you really feel hasn't got the form, it's not what you can put down in a poem. And the poem you're equipped to write concerns nothing that you care very much about or have much to say on. Then the great moment comes when there's enough resolution of your technical equipment, your way of constructing things, and what you can make a poem out of, to hit something you really want to say. You may not know you have it to say.

Issue 25, 1961

Isaac Bashevis Singer

The Art of Fiction

Isaac Bashevis Singer lives with his second wife in a large, sunny five-room apartment in an Upper Broadway apartment house. In addition to hundreds of books and a large television set, it is furnished with the kind of pseudo-Victorian furniture typical of the comfortable homes of Brooklyn and the Bronx in the 1930s.

Singer works at a small, cluttered desk in the living room. He writes every day, but without special hours—in between interviews, visits, and phone calls. His name is still listed in the Manhattan telephone directory, and hardly a day goes by without his receiving several calls from strangers who have read something he has written and want to talk to him about it. Until recently, he would invite anyone who called for lunch, or at least coffee.

Singer writes his stories and novels in lined notebooks, in longhand, in Yiddish. Most of what he writes still appears first in the *Jewish Daily Forward*, America's largest Yiddish-language daily, published in New York City. Getting translators to put his work into English has always been a major problem. He insists on working very closely with his translators, going over each word with them many times.

Singer always wears dark suits, white shirts, and dark ties. His voice is high but pleasant, and never raised. He is of medium height, thin, and has an unnaturally pale complexion. For many years he has followed a strict vegetarian diet.

The first impression Singer gives is that he is a fragile, weak man

A manuscript page from "The Professor's Wife" by Isaac Bashevis Singer.

who would find it an effort to walk a block. Actually, he walks fifty to sixty blocks a day, a trip that invariably includes a stop to feed pigeons from a brown paper bag. He loves birds and has two pet parakeets who fly about his apartment uncaged.

—*Harold Flender*, *1968*

INTERVIEWER

Many writers when they start out have other writers they use as models.

ISAAC BASHEVIS SINGER

Well, my model was my brother, I. J. Singer, who wrote *The Brothers Ashkenazi*. I couldn't have had a better model than my brother. I saw him struggle with my parents and I saw how he began to write and how he slowly developed and began to publish. So naturally he was an influence. Not only this, but in the later years before I began to publish, my brother gave me a number of rules about writing that seem to me sacred. Not that these rules cannot be broken once in a while, but it's good to remember them. One of his rules was that while facts never become obsolete or stale, commentaries *always* do. When a writer tries to explain too much, to psychologize, he's already out of time when he begins. Imagine Homer explaining the deeds of his heroes according to the old Greek philosophy or the psychology of his time. Why, nobody would read Homer! Fortunately, Homer just gave us the images and the facts, and because of this *The Iliad* and *The Odyssey* are fresh in our time. And I think this is true about all writing. Once a writer tries to explain what the hero's motives are from a psychological point of view, he has already lost. This doesn't mean that I am against the psychological novel. There are some masters who have done it well. But I don't think it is a good thing for a writer, especially a young writer, to imitate them. Dostoyevsky, for example—if you can call him a writer of the psychological school. I'm not sure I do. He had his digressions and he tried to explain things in his own way, but even with him his basic power is in giving the facts.

INTERVIEWER

What do you think of psychoanalysis and writing? Many writers have been psychoanalyzed and feel this has helped them to understand not only themselves but the characters they write about.

SINGER

If the writer is psychoanalyzed in a doctor's office, that is his business. But if he tries to put the psychoanalysis into the writing, it's just terrible. The best example is the one who wrote *Point Counter Point*. What was his name?

INTERVIEWER

Aldous Huxley.

SINGER

Aldous Huxley. He tried to write a novel according to Freudian psychoanalysis. And I think he failed in a bad way. This particular novel is now so old and so stale that even in school it cannot be read anymore. So, I think that when a writer sits down and he psychoanalyzes, he's ruining his work.

INTERVIEWER

You once told me that the first piece of fiction you ever read was the *Adventures of Sherlock Holmes*.

SINGER

Well, I read these things when I was a boy of ten or eleven, and to me they looked so sublime, so wonderful, that even today I don't dare to read Sherlock Holmes again because I am afraid that I may be disappointed.

INTERVIEWER

Do you think A. Conan Doyle influenced you in any way?

SINGER

Well, I don't think that the stories of Sherlock Holmes had any real influence on me. But I will say one thing—from my childhood I have always loved tension in a story. I liked that a story should be a story. That there should be a beginning and an end, and there should be some feeling of what will happen at the end. And to this rule I keep today. I think that storytelling has become in this age almost a forgotten art. But I try my best not to suffer from this kind of amnesia. To me a story is still a story where the reader listens and wants to know what happens. If the reader knows everything from the very beginning, even if the description is good, I think the story is not a story.

INTERVIEWER

What do you think about the Nobel Prize for literature going to S. Y. Agnon and Nelly Sachs?

SINGER

About Nelly Sachs, I know nothing, but I know Agnon. Since I began to read. And I think he's a good writer. I wouldn't call him a genius, but where do you get so many geniuses nowadays? He's a solid writer of the old school, a school that loses a lot in translation. But as far as Hebrew is concerned, his style is just wonderful. Every work of his is associated with the Talmud and the Bible and the Midrash. Everything he writes has many levels, especially to those who know Hebrew. In translation, all of these other levels disappear and there is only the pure writing, but then that is also good.

INTERVIEWER

The prize committee said that they were giving the Nobel Prize to two Jewish writers who reflected the voice of Israel. That leads me to wonder how you would define a Jewish writer as opposed to a writer who happens to be Jewish?

SINGER

To me there are only Yiddish writers, Hebrew writers, English writers, Spanish writers. The whole idea of a Jewish writer, or a Catholic writer, is kind of far-fetched to me. But if you forced me to admit that there is such a thing as a Jewish writer, I would say that he would have to be a man really immersed in Jewishness, who knows Hebrew, Yiddish, the Talmud, the Midrash, the Hasidic literature, the Cabbala, and so forth. And then if in addition he writes about Jews and Jewish life, perhaps then we can call him a Jewish writer, whatever language he writes in. Of course, we can also call him just a writer.

INTERVIEWER

You write in Yiddish, which is a language very few people can read today. Your books have been translated into fifty-eight different languages, but you have said you are bothered by the fact that most of your readers—the vast majority of your readers—have to read you in translation, whether it's English or French, that very few writers can read you in Yiddish. Do you feel that a lot is lost in translation?

SINGER

The fact that I don't have as many readers in Yiddish as I would have liked to have bothers me. It's not good that a language is going downhill instead of up. I would like Yiddish to bloom and flower just as the Yiddishists say it *does* bloom and flower. But as far as translation is concerned, naturally every writer loses in translation, particularly poets and humorists. Also writers whose writing is tightly connected to folklore are heavy losers. In my own case, I think I am a heavy loser. But then lately I have assisted in the translating of my works, and knowing the problem, I take care that I don't lose too much. The problem is that it's very hard to find a perfect equivalent for an idiom in another language. But then it's also a fact that we all learned our literature through translation. Most people have studied the Bible only in translation, have read Homer in translation, and all the classics. Translation, although it does do damage to an author, it cannot kill him: if he's really good, he will come out even in translation. And I have seen it in my own case. Also, translation helps me in a way. Because I go through my writings again and again while I edit the translation and work with the translator, and while I am doing this I see all the defects of my writing. Translation has helped me avoid pitfalls that I might not have avoided if I had written the work in Yiddish and published it and not been forced because of the translation to read it again.

INTERVIEWER

Is it true that for five years you stopped writing entirely because you felt there was nobody to write for?

SINGER

It is true that when I came to this country I stopped writing for a number of years. I don't know exactly if it was because I thought there were no readers. There were many readers. Coming from one country to another, immigrating, is a kind of a crisis. I had a feeling that my language was so lost. My images were not anymore. Things— I saw thousands of objects for which I had no name in Yiddish in Poland. Take such a thing as the subway—we didn't have a subway in Poland. And we didn't have a name for it in Yiddish. Suddenly I had to do with a subway and with a shuttle train and a local, and my feeling was that I lost my language and also my feeling about the things that surrounded me. Then, of course, there was the trouble of making a living and adjusting myself to the new surroundings—all of this worked so that for a number of years I couldn't write.

INTERVIEWER

Do you think that Yiddish has any future at all, or do you think that very soon it will be a dead language completely?

SINGER

It won't be a dead language because Yiddish is connected with five or six hundred years of Jewish history—important Jewish history. And whoever will want to study this history will have to study Yiddish. In a joke I say that I have a special comfort for Yiddish and this is that now we are having as a world population only about 3.5 billion people, but one hundred years from now we will have most probably one hundred billion people, and every one of them will need a topic for a Ph.D. Imagine how useful Yiddish will be for all these students looking for a topic. They will bring out everything that was connected with Yiddish and analyze it and write things about it, articles and these things that you write for universities—theses. So, I don't think it will be forgotten. Take such a language as Aramaic. It's already two thousand years that the Jews didn't use Aramaic, and the language is still here. It has become now a part of Hebrew. Aramaic is used now in certificates and in divorce papers. Jews never forget really anything, especially a language that has created so much and has played such a part like Yiddish.

INTERVIEWER

When one thinks of contemporary writers writing in Yiddish, one thinks immediately of you. But then it is hard to come up with any other names. Are there any other writers writing in Yiddish whom you consider highly?

SINGER

There is one writer whom I consider highly. Really, he is a great writer. He's a poet. His name is Aaron Zeitlin. This man, he is my friend, but I don't praise him because he's my friend. He's really a great poet. I consider his writing of the same value as the poetry of Thomas Hardy, and I have a high opinion of Thomas Hardy. The others—there are a number of other Yiddish writers, some of them are well known, like Sholem Asch. There was David Bergelson. There was one very strong prose writer called A. M. Fuchs who is really a strong writer, but he wrote always on the same topic. He had only one story to tell with a million variations. But I would say that there is something about Yiddish writing that is very effective and yet very old-fashioned—because the modern Yiddish writer does not write about real Jewish things, though it happens he is the product of enlightenment. He was brought up with the idea that one should get out of Jewishness and become universal. And because he tried so hard to become universal, he became very provincial. This is the tragedy. Not with the whole of Yiddish writings but with a lot of it. And thank God when I began to write I avoided this misfortune. Even though I was discouraged all the time. They told me, Why do you write about devils and imps? Why don't you write about the situation of the Jews, about Zionism, about socialism, about the unions, and about how the tailors must get a raise, and so on and so on? But something in me refused to do this. They complained to me that I am obsolete. That I go back to the generations which have already vanished. That I'm almost a reactionary. But young writers are sometimes very stubborn. I refused to go their way and I was later glad that I had the character not to do what they wanted me to do. This type of writing has become so obsolete and so stale that it's not a question of getting translators in Yiddish, but really that we have very little to translate.

INTERVIEWER

When you say "this type of writing," you mean writing about unions and—

SINGER

About unions, about immigration, about progress, about anti-Semitism. This kind of journalistic writing in which one had the desire to create what they call a better world. To make the world better, to make the Jewish situation better. This kind of writing was very much in fashion in the twenties and I would say that the Yiddish writers never got out of it really.

INTERVIEWER

Don't you believe in a better world?

SINGER

I believe in a better world, but I don't think that a fiction writer who sits down to write a novel to make a better world can achieve anything.

The better world will be done by many people, by the politicians, by the statesmen, by the sociologists. I don't know who is going to create it or if there will ever be a better world. One thing I am sure is that the novelists will not do it.

INTERVIEWER

The supernatural keeps cropping up in practically everything you write, particularly your short stories. Why this strong concern with the supernatural? Do you personally believe in the supernatural?

SINGER

Absolutely. The reason why it always comes up is because it is always on my mind. I don't know if I should call myself a mystic, but I feel always that we are surrounded by powers, by mysterious powers, which play a great part in everything we are doing. I would say that telepathy and clairvoyance play a part in every love story. Even in business. In everything human beings are doing. For thousands of years people used to wear woolen clothes and when they took them off at night they saw sparks. I wonder what these people thought thousands of years ago of these sparks they saw when they took off their woolen clothes? I am sure that they ignored them and the children asked them, Mother, what are these sparks? And I am sure the mother said, You imagine them! People must have been afraid to talk about the sparks so they would not be suspected of being sorcerers and witches. Anyhow, they were ignored, and we know now that they were not hallucinations, that they were real, and that what was behind these sparks was the same power that today drives our industry. And I say that we too in each generation see such sparks that we ignore just because they don't fit into our picture of science or knowledge. And I think that it is the writer's duty, and also pleasure and function, to bring out these sparks. To me, clairvoyance and telepathy and devils and imps—all of these things . . .

INTERVIEWER

Ghosts?

SINGER

Ghosts and all these things that people call today superstition are the very sparks that we are ignoring in our day.

INTERVIEWER

Do you think they will be able to be explained scientifically, just as sparks can be explained today as electricity?

SINGER

I think the notion of science—what is scientific and what is not—will change in time. There are many facts that cannot be worked out in a laboratory, and still they are facts. You cannot show in a laboratory that there has ever been a Napoleon, you can't prove it as clearly as you can an electric current, but we know there *was* a Napoleon. What we call today ghosts and spirits and clairvoyance is also the sort of fact that you cannot just prepare and cannot make experiments with. But this doesn't mean that the fact is not true.

INTERVIEWER

How about the devil? In many of your writings the devil is the main character.

SINGER

Naturally, I use the devil and the imps as literary symbols. True, but the reason I use them as symbols is because I have a feeling for them. If I didn't have a feeling for these entities I would not use them. I still live with this idea that we are surrounded by all kinds of powers and I've been brought up with it and I still cling to it. Not that I try to, but they cling to me. If you extinguish the light at night and I am in a dark room, I am afraid. Just as I was when I was seven or eight years old. I have spoken to many rationalists who say how illogical that is, but when I ask them if they would consent to sleep a winter's night in a room with a corpse, they shiver. The fear of the supernatural is in everybody. And since we are all afraid of the supernatural, there is no reason why we shouldn't make use of it. Because if you are afraid of something, the very fact that you are afraid means that you have admitted that it exists. We aren't afraid of something which doesn't exist.

INTERVIEWER

You are the only Jewish writer who writes about the devil. Even Hebrew literature avoids the theme of the diabolical.

SINGER

It is true that Yiddish and Hebrew literature are both under the influence of the Enlightenment. They are both in a way modern kinds of literature. Writers were brought up with the idea that they had been sunk in the Middle Ages long enough, and that since modern literature should be rational and logical, they should deal with the real world. To them, when I began to write, I seemed a most reactionary writer, a writer who went back to the dark ages. But, as I was saying, young writers are sometimes very stubborn. What is to you *dark* is to me *real*. They all condemned me for it. But today, since this kind of writing has had a certain degree of success, they began somehow to make peace with it. Because you know how it is in this world: if something works it works. In fact, I didn't expect that anybody would be interested in my kind of writing. I was interested, and this was for me enough.

INTERVIEWER

Being as interested as you are in ritual and superstition, do you have any about yourself—in particular connected with your work and work habits?

SINGER

It is true that I believe in miracles, or, rather, grace from heaven. But I believe in miracles in every area of life *except* writing. Experience has shown me that there are no miracles in writing. The only thing that produces good writing is hard work. It's impossible to write a good story by carrying a rabbit's foot in your pocket.

INTERVIEWER

How do you come to write a story? Do you observe all the time, like a reporter? Do you take notes?

SINGER

I never go out to look for a story. I take notes, but never like a reporter. My stories are all based on things that have come to me in life without my going out to look for them. The only notes I take are notes on an idea for a story. But it must be a story with a climax. I am not a slice-of-life writer. When such an idea comes to me, I put it down in a little notebook I always carry around. Finally the story demands to be written, and then I write it.

INTERVIEWER

In addition to writing stories and novels, you spent many years of your life in journalism. You still work as a journalist for the *Forward*.

SINGER

Yes. I am a journalist. Every week I write two or three journalistic articles. Journalism in Yiddish is quite different from journalism in other languages, especially in English. In America, a journalist is a man who either deals completely with facts, or he is a commentator on the political situation. In a Yiddish newspaper, even if it's a daily, it's actually a daily *magazine*. I can write articles in the *Forward* about life making sense or not, or that you shouldn't commit suicide, or a treatise on imps or devils being in everything. Our readers are accustomed to get the news mostly from the radio and television or from the English newspaper that comes out in the evening. When he buys the newspaper in the morning, he is not after the news; he wants to read articles. So if I am a journalist, I am not exactly the same kind of journalist who works for, let's say, *The New York Times*.

INTERVIEWER

Do you think working as a journalist for such a paper as the *Times* is a good background for somebody who wants to write novels and stories?

SINGER

I think that any information a human being gets, especially a writer, is good for him. I don't think that being a journalist can do any damage to a writer.

INTERVIEWER

Do you know any other writers?

SINGER

Very few, because here in America I find there is no place to meet them. When I lived in Poland, I used to hang out at the writers' club. I'd be there every day. But there is nothing quite like that in America. I know practically no other writers. Once in a while I meet some writers at a cocktail party, and I like them; they are very fine people. But somehow it never goes beyond a superficial meeting. I am sorry about this. I would like to be friendly with more writers.

INTERVIEWER

Many contemporary writers are affiliated with the universities. What do you think of teaching as a way of making a living while writing?

SINGER

I think that journalism is a healthier occupation for a writer than teaching, especially if he teaches literature. By teaching literature, the writer gets accustomed to analyzing literature all the time. One man, a critic, said to me, I could never write anything because the moment I write the first line I am already writing an essay about it. I am already criticizing my own writing.

It's not good when the writer is both a critic and a writer. It doesn't matter if he writes a review once in a while or even an essay about criticism. But if this kind of analyzing goes on all the time and it becomes his daily bread, it may one day become a part of his writing: it is very bad when the writer is half writer and half critic. He writes essays about his heroes instead of telling a story.

INTERVIEWER

Could you tell me something about the way you work? Do you work every day, seven days a week?

SINGER

Well, when I get up in the morning, I always have the desire to sit down to write. And most of the days I *do* write something. But then I get telephone calls, and sometimes I have to write an article for the *Forward*. And once in a while I have to write a review, and I am interviewed, and I am all the time interrupted. Somehow I manage to keep on writing. I don't have to run away. Some writers say that they can only write if they go to a far island. They would go to the moon to write not to be disturbed. I think that being disturbed is a part of human life and sometimes it's useful to be disturbed because you interrupt your writing and while you rest, while you are busy with something else, your perspective changes or the horizon widens. All I can say about myself is that I have never really written in peace, as some writers say that they have. But whatever I had to say I kept on saying no matter what the disturbances were.

INTERVIEWER

What do you consider the most difficult aspect of writing?

SINGER

Story construction. This is the most difficult part for me. How to construct the story so that it will be interesting. Easiest for me is the actual writing. Once I have the construction set, the writing itself— the description and dialogue—simply flows along.

INTERVIEWER

The hero of most Western writing is the Superman, the Prometheus character. The hero of Yiddish fiction, Jewish writing, seems to be the little man. He's a poor but proud man always struggling. And your own classic example of the little man would be Gimpel the Fool. How do

you account for the fact that in so much of Yiddish fiction the hero is
the little man?

SINGER

Well, the Yiddish writer was really not brought up with the idea of
heroes. I mean there were very few heroes in the Jewish ghettos—very
few knights and counts and people who fought duels and so on. In my
own case, I don't think I write in the tradition of the Yiddish writers'
little man, because their little man is actually a *victim*—a man who is a
victim of anti-Semitism, the economic situation, and so on. My characters, though they are not big men in the sense that they play a big
part in the world, still they are not little, because in their own fashion
they are men of character, men of thinking, men of great suffering. It
is true that Gimpel the Fool is a little man, but he's not the same kind
of little man as Sholom Aleichem's Tevye. Tevye is a little man with
little desires, and with little prejudice. All he needed was to make a living. If Tevye could have made a living, he wouldn't have been driven
out of his village. If he could have married off his daughters, he would
have been a happy man. In my case, most of my heroes could not be
satisfied with just a few rubles or with the permission to live in Russia
or somewhere else. Their tragedies are different. Gimpel was not a little man. He was a fool, but he wasn't little. The tradition of the little
man is something which I avoid in my writing.

INTERVIEWER

If most of your writing deals with a people without power, without
land, without statehood, political organization, or even a choice of
occupation, and who yet have a great moral response and an intensity
of faith, are you in effect suggesting that the Jews were better off when
they were restricted and discriminated against?

SINGER

I think there is no question that power is a great temptation and
those who have power will sooner or later stumble into injustice. It
was the good fortune of the Jewish people that for two thousand years

they didn't have any power. The little bit of power that they did have they have certainly misused like anyone else who has power. But we were blessed for almost two thousand years with a complete lack of power, so because of this our sins were never as great as those who really had power over the life and death of other people. But I bring this up not to preach. I never really knew people who had a lot of power. Except when I describe Poles or when I describe once in a while a rich man whose power was in his money. But even so, these people were not really rich enough to wield much power.

INTERVIEWER

I can't help but get the feeling from your writing that you have grave doubts about the sufficiency of knowledge or even wisdom.

SINGER

Well, in a way it is true. Yiddish writing was all built on the ideas of the Enlightenment. Enlightenment, no matter how far it will go, will not bring the redemption. I have never believed that socialism or any other *ism* is going to redeem humanity and create what they call the "new man." I have had many discussions with writers about this. When I was young, when I began to write, people really believed that once the means of production belonged to the government, the new man would result. I was clever enough or maybe foolish enough and skeptical enough to know that was a lot of nonsense; no matter who owns the railroads or the factories, men will remain the same.

INTERVIEWER

Is there anything that you think will save humanity?

SINGER

Nothing will save us. We will make a lot of progress, but we will keep on suffering, and there will never be an end to it. We will always invent new sources of pain. The idea that man is going to be saved is a completely religious idea, and even the religious leaders never suggest that we will be saved on this earth. They believe that the soul is going to be saved in another world, that if we behave here well, there is a hope that our soul will go to paradise. The idea of creating a paradise here on this earth is not Jewish and certainly not Christian, but a completely Greek or pagan idea. As the Jews say, from a pig's tail you cannot make a silk purse. You cannot take life and suddenly turn it into one great delight, one ocean of pleasure. I never believed in it, and whenever people speak about a better world, while I admit that conditions can be made better and I hope that we can do away with wars, still there will be enough sickness and enough tragedy so that humanity will keep on suffering more or less in the same way as it always has. Being a pessimist to me means to be a realist.

I feel that in spite of all our sufferings, in spite of the fact that life will never bring the paradise we want it to bring, there is something to live for. The greatest gift that humanity has received is free choice. It is true that we are limited in our use of free choice. But the little free choice we have is such a great gift and is potentially worth so much that for this itself life is worthwhile living. While I am in one way a fatalist, I also know that what we have reached up until now is largely because of free will, not because conditions have changed, as the Marxists believe.

INTERVIEWER

Many readers look upon you as a master storyteller. Others feel that you have a far more significant purpose in your writing than merely to tell stories.

SINGER

Well, I think that to write a story *well* is the duty of a storyteller. To try with all his might that a story should come out right. What I call right is that the construction should be right, the description right, that there should be equilibrium between form and content, and so on. But this is not everything. In each story, I try to say something, and what I try to say is more or less connected with my ideas that this world and this kind of life is not everything, that there is a soul and there is a God and there may be life after death. I always come back to these religious truths although I am not religious in the sense of dogma. I don't keep to all the rules of organized religion. But the basic truths of religion are near to me and I always contemplate them. I would consider myself more of a Jewish writer than most of the Yiddish writers because I am more a believer in the Jewish truths than they. Most of them believe in progress. Progress has become their idol. They believe that people will progress to such a degree that the Jews will be treated well, they will be able to assimilate, mix with the Gentiles, get good jobs, and perhaps be president one day. To me all these hopes are very little and very obsolete and very petty. I feel that our real great hope lies in the soul and not in the body. In this way I consider myself a religious writer.

INTERVIEWER

Sometimes reading you I think of certain Far Eastern philosophers, such as the Indian philosopher Krishnamurti. Were you at all influenced by Buddhist or Hindu writings?

SINGER

I read these writers too late to have been really influenced by them. But when I read them in my later years, a short time ago, I said to myself, I have thought these same thoughts without having read them. When I read the Bhagavad Gita, it looked to me so very near, and I almost wondered if I had read this in a former life. This is true also about the sayings of Buddha and other Far Eastern writings. The so-called eternal truths are really eternal. They are in our blood and in our very essence.

INTERVIEWER

Some commentators on the current scene, notably Marshall McLuhan, feel that literature as we have known it for hundreds of years is an anachronism, that it's on the way out. The reading of stories and novels, they feel, is soon to be a thing of the past, because of electronic entertainments, radio, television, film, stereophonic records, magnetic tapes, and other mechanical means of communication yet to be invented. Do you believe this to be true?

SINGER

It will be true if our writers will not be good writers. But if we have people with the power to tell a story, there will always be readers. I don't think that human nature is going to change to such a degree that people will stop being interested in a work of imagination. Certainly, the true facts, the real facts, are always interesting. Today nonfiction plays a very big part—to hear stories about what happened. If people get to the moon, journalists will tell us, or films will tell us, what happened there, and these will be more interesting stories than anything a fiction writer can produce. But still there will be a place for the good fiction writer. There is no machine and no kind of reporting and no kind of film that can do what a Tolstoy or a Dostoyevsky or Gogol did. It is true that poetry has suffered a great blow in our times. But not because of television or because of other things, but because poetry itself became bad. If we are going to have numbers of bad novels, and bad novelists imitate each other, what they write will be neither interesting nor understood. Naturally, this may kill the novel, at least for a time. But I don't think that literature, good literature, has anything to fear from technology. The very opposite. The more technology, the more people will be interested in what the human mind can produce *without* the help of electronics.

INTERVIEWER

So you would encourage young people today to think of serious writing as a way of life?

SINGER

When it comes to business, to the finances of writing, I really don't know. It may be that a time will come when the novelist will get such small royalties that he will not be able to make a living. I just cannot tell you about this. But if a young man would come to me and I can see that he has talent and he asks me if he should write, I would say go on and write and don't be afraid of any inventions and of any kind of progress. Progress can never kill literature, any more than it can kill religion.

It's hard to keep from noticing that among the most widely read and respected authors in the United States today there is a large percentage of Jewish authors—yourself, Saul Bellow, Philip Roth, Henry Roth, Bernard Malamud. Even non-Jewish writers are writing on Jewish themes and producing bestsellers, as, for example, James Michener with his novel *The Source*. How do you account for the post–World War II popularity of Jewish writers and Jewish themes?

SINGER

I think that for many centuries the Jew was completely ignored in literature. They wrote about the Jew always in the way of a cliché. Either the Jew was a usurer, a bad man, a Shylock, or he was a poor man, a victim of anti-Semitism. In other words, they either scolded him or they pitied him. And because of this the Jew's way of life, his way of love, was a secret to humanity. It's only a short time ago that Jewish writers began to write about Jews the same way as Americans write about Americans and English writers about Englishmen. They tell everything about them, the good and the evil. They don't try to apologize for them. They don't try to scold them. And I would say that since there was a lot of curiosity about Jewish life, I am not astonished that Jewish literature is now in vogue. This doesn't mean that it is always going to be so. I believe that sooner or later things will even out. How many Jews are good writers or bad writers I don't know. I don't think that we are producing as many good writers as people think. We have a lot of able, gifted writers, and able people, but I see as few great writers among us as there are few great writers among other people! There are a very few great writers anywhere.

Eudora Welty

The Art of Fiction

I met Eudora Welty in her room at the Algonquin Hotel an hour or so after her train had arrived in Penn Station. She had given me the wrong room number, so I first saw her peering out of her door as the elevator opened. A tall, large-boned, gray-haired woman greeted me apologetically. She was admittedly nervous about being interviewed, particularly on a tape recorder. After describing her train ride—she won't fly—she braced herself and asked if I wouldn't begin the questioning.

Once the interview got underway, she grew more at ease. As she herself might say, she was "not unforthcoming." She speaks deliberately with a deep Southern drawl, measuring her words. She is extremely private and won't reveal anything personal about herself.

—*Linda Kuehl, 1972*

INTERVIEWER

You wrote somewhere that we should still tolerate Jane Austen's kind of family novel. Is Austen a kindred spirit?

EUDORA WELTY

Tolerate? I should just think so! I love and admire all she does, and profoundly, but I don't read her or anyone else for "kindredness." The piece you're referring to was written on assignment for *Brief Lives*, an anthology Louis Kronenberger was editing. He did offer me

"Bywy River, my father killed his last bear. Blessed old
now Laid her adross the doorstep."

Dragged her Home,

"Granny! Did you ever have a father? And mother?" cried

Elvie.

"Mama said, 'Take that back where you found it, Mr. Blaikie.
You're nothing but bragging now,'" said Granny.

"Was you born?" Elvie pleaded to know. "Granny!
Like Lady May?"

"Granny'd like her picture taken!" Aunt Beck divined. "Ninety
today!"

"With all of us!" cried Aunt Birdie. "A picture with Granny
in the middle. Haul her out here in the broil, see what you can
get, Sister Cleo!"

Miss Beulah was summoned, and stood at center back, the
wives lined up at her sides. Granny sat composed in the center, and for the only time that day drew the pipe from her pocket,
in order to pose with it cooked in her mouth. The aunts as
one dropped their hands before them, as if called to the door in
their aprons.

How close a
Hook or an
Tony my factory?

The men squatted or reclined on the ground,

A manuscript page from Losing Battles by Eudora Welty.

either Jane Austen or Chekhov, and Chekhov I do dare to think is more kindred. I feel closer to him in spirit, but I couldn't read Russian, which I felt whoever wrote about him should be able to do. Chekhov is one of us—so close to today's world, to my mind, and very close to the South—which Stark Young pointed out a long time ago.

INTERVIEWER

Why is Chekhov close to today's South?

WELTY

He loved the singularity in people, the individuality. He took for granted the sense of family. He had the sense of fate overtaking a way of life, and his Russian humor seems to me kin to the humor of a Southerner. It's the kind that lies mostly in character. You know, in *Uncle Vanya* and *The Cherry Orchard*, how people are always gathered together and talking and talking, no one's really listening. Yet there's a great love and understanding that prevails through it, and a knowledge and acceptance of each other's idiosyncrasies, a tolerance of them, and also an acute enjoyment of the dramatic. Like in *The Three Sisters*, when the fire is going on, how they talk right on through their exhaustion, and Vershinin says, "I feel a strange excitement in the air," and laughs and sings and talks about the future. That kind of responsiveness to the world, to whatever happens, out of their own deeps of character seems very Southern to me. Anyway, I took a temperamental delight in Chekhov, and gradually the connection was borne in upon me.

INTERVIEWER

Do you ever return to Virginia Woolf?

WELTY

Yes. She was the one who opened the door. When I read *To the Lighthouse*, I felt, Heavens, what is this? I was so excited by the experience I couldn't sleep or eat. I've read it many times since, though more often these days I go back to her diary. Any day you open it to will be tragic, and yet all the marvelous things she says about her work, about working, leave you filled with joy that's stronger than your misery for her. Remember—"I'm not very far along, but I think I have my statues against the sky"?* Isn't that beautiful?

INTERVIEWER

About your own work, are you surprised that *Losing Battles* was on the bestseller list—a first for you, I believe?

WELTY

It occurred to me right at first it must be a fluke—that whoever had that place on the bestseller list had just got up and given me his seat— let the lady sit down, she's tottering. Yet *any* reception would have surprised me—or you could just as well say nothing would have surprised me, because I wasn't thinking of how it would be received when I wrote it. I thought about the opinion of a handful of friends I would love to have love that book, but not about the public.

INTERVIEWER

Do you write for your friends?

WELTY

At the time of writing, I don't write for my friends or myself, either; I write for *it*, for the pleasure of *it*. I believe if I stopped to wonder what so-and-so would think, or what I'd feel like if this were read by a stranger, I would be paralyzed. I care what my friends think, very deeply—and it's only after they've read the finished thing that I really can rest, deep down. But in the writing, I have to just keep going straight through with only the *thing* in mind and what it dictates.

It's so much an inward thing that reading the proofs later can be a real shock. When I received them for my first book—no, I guess it was for *Delta Wedding*—I thought, *I* didn't write this. It was a page

*The exact quote reads: "It is bound to be imperfect. But I think it possible that I have got my statues against the sky."

of dialogue—I might as well have never seen it before. I wrote to my editor, John Woodburn, and told him something had happened to that page in the typesetting. He was kind, not even surprised—maybe this happens to all writers. He called me up and read me from the manuscript, word for word what the proofs said. Proofs don't shock me any longer, yet there's still a strange moment with every book when I move from the position of writer to the position of reader, and I suddenly see my words with the eyes of the cold public. It gives me a terrible sense of exposure, as if I'd gotten sunburned.

INTERVIEWER

Do you make changes in galleys?

WELTY

I correct or change words, but I can't rewrite a scene or make a major change because there's a sense then of someone looking over my shoulder. It's necessary, anyway, to trust that moment when you were sure at last you had done all you could, done your best for that time. When it's finally in print, you're delivered—you don't ever have to look at it again. It's too late to worry about its failings. I'll have to apply any lessons this book has taught me toward writing the next one.

INTERVIEWER

Is *Losing Battles* a departure from your previous fiction?

WELTY

I wanted to see if I could do something that was new for me: translating every thought and feeling into action and speech—speech being another form of action—to bring the whole life of it off through the completed gesture, so to speak. I felt that I'd been writing too much by way of description, of introspection on the part of my characters. I tried to see if I could make everything shown, brought forth, without benefit of the author's telling any more about what was going on inside the characters' minds and hearts. For me, this makes almost certainly for comedy—which I love to write best of all. Now I see it might be a transition toward writing a play.

INTERVIEWER

Did you know what you were going to write before you put it on paper?

WELTY

Yes, it was there in my head, but events proliferated as I went along. For instance, I thought all the action in the novel would be contained in one day and night, but a folder started to fill up with things marked "Next A.M." I didn't foresee the stories that grew out of the stories—that was one of the joys of working the novel out. I thought the book would be short, and instead it was three or four times longer than my normal work. There's no way of estimating its original length because I had great chunks of things in paper clips that weren't numbered until they went to the printer. And I must have thrown away at least as much as I kept in the book.

INTERVIEWER

Did you learn anything new about writing dialogue?

WELTY

I believe so. In its beginning, dialogue's the easiest thing in the world to write when you have a good ear, which I think I have. But as it goes on, it's the most difficult, because it has so many ways to function. Sometimes I needed to make a speech do three or four or five things at once—reveal what the character said but also what he thought he said, what he hid, what others were going to think he meant, and what they misunderstood, and so forth—all in his single speech. And the speech would have to keep the essence of this one character, his whole particular outlook, in concentrated form. This isn't to say I succeeded. But I guess it explains why dialogue gives me my greatest pleasure in writing. I used to laugh out loud sometimes when I wrote it—the way P. G. Wodehouse is said to do. I'd think of some things my characters would say, and even if I couldn't use it, I would write the scene out just to let them loose on something—my private show.

INTERVIEWER

Where does the dialogue come from?

WELTY

Familiarity. Memory of the way things get said. Once you have heard certain expressions, sentences, you almost never forget them. It's like sending a bucket down the well and it always comes up full. You don't know you've remembered, but you have. And you listen for the right word, in the present, and you hear it. Once you're into a story everything seems to apply—what you overhear on a city bus is exactly what your character would say on the page you're writing. Wherever you go, you meet part of your story. I guess you're tuned in for it, and the right things are sort of magnetized—if you can think of your ears as magnets. I could hear someone saying—and I had to cut this out—"What, you never ate goat?" And someone answering, "Goat! Please don't say you serve *goat* at this reunion. I wasn't told it was *goat* I was served. I thought . . . ," and so on, and then the recipe, and then it ended up with—I can't remember exactly now—it ended with, "You can do a whole lot of things with vinegar." Well, all these things I would just laugh about and think about for so long and put them in. And then I'd think, that's just plain indulgence. Take it out! And I'd take it out.

INTERVIEWER

Are you an eavesdropper?

WELTY

I'm not as much as I used to be, or would like to be, because I don't hear as well as I used to, or there's too much other noise everywhere. But I've heard some wonderful remarks. Well, in the South, everybody stays busy talking all the time—they're not sorry for you to overhear their tales. I don't feel in helping myself I ever did anything underhanded. I was *helping out*.

INTERVIEWER

Do you think this oral tradition, so to speak, accounts for your vigorous use of dialogue?

WELTY

I think it accounts for the pleasure people take in a story told. It's a treasure I helped myself to. I took it for my ways and means, and that's proper and justified: Our people talk that way. They learn and teach and think and enjoy that way. Southerners do have—they've inherited—a narrative sense of human destiny. This may or may not come out in *Losing Battles*. A reunion is everybody remembering together—remembering and relating when their people were born and what happened in their lives, what that made happen to their children, and how it was that they died. There's someone to remember a man's whole life, every bit of the way along. I think that's a marvelous thing, and I'm glad I got to know something of it. In New York you may have the greatest and most congenial friends, but it's extraordinary if you ever know anything about them except that little wedge of their life that you meet with the little wedge of your life. You don't get that sense of a continuous narrative line. You never see the full circle. But in the South, where people don't move about as much, even now, and where they once hardly ever moved away at all, the pattern of life was always right there.

INTERVIEWER

Would you say that Southerners—Deep Southerners—are more open than Northerners?

WELTY

I think we have a sort of language we all understand and speak—a shorthand of some kind, based on familiarity—but I'm not sure we're more open. We may not tell as much as we think we do, and we may not hide as much as we think we do. We're just more used to talking—as you can see—and the subject doesn't especially cut us down.

INTERVIEWER

And that profoundly affects your fiction?

WELTY

I think that's what gives a pattern to it and a sense of its shape to me. I do want to say that I'm only speaking for myself when I speak of Southern qualities, because I don't know how other people work. It may be entirely different, especially with a genius like William Faulkner, who had such a comprehensive sense of the whole deep, deep past and more far-reaching, bred-in country knowledge than I have, which is so valuable, besides all the rest of his equipment that I don't need to tell you about.

INTERVIEWER

Did you know Faulkner?

WELTY

Slightly and over a long period of time, but not well. I liked him ever so much. We met at a dinner party in Oxford, just old friends of his and old friends of mine, which was the right way for it to happen, and it was just grand. We sang hymns, and we sang some old ballads—and the next day he invited me to go sailing. If we ever met in New York, we just talked about being in Oxford. He didn't bring up writing, and if *he* didn't, you know *I* wasn't going to bring it up! But when he was working in Hollywood, he once wrote me a two-line letter—this was long before we met—and told me he liked a little book of mine called *The Robber Bridegroom* and said would I let him know if he could ever do anything for me. It was on a little piece of note-book paper, written in that fine, neat, sort of unreadable hand, in pencil—and I've lost it.

INTERVIEWER

Did you feel at all influenced by his presence?

WELTY

I don't honestly think so. It is hard to be sure about such things. I was naturally in the deepest awe and reverence of him. But that's no help in your own writing. Nobody can help you but yourself. So often I'm asked how I could have written a word with William Faulkner living in Mississippi, and this question amazes me. It was like living near a big mountain, something majestic—it made me happy to know it was there, all that work of his life. But it wasn't a helping or hindering presence. Its magnitude, all by itself, made it something remote in my own working life. When I thought of Faulkner it was when I *read*.

On the other hand, he didn't seem remote to everybody in being our great writer. I know a story about him, though he never knew anybody knew of it, I'd bet. Mississippi is full of writers, and I heard this from the person it was told to. A lady had decided she'd write a novel and got along fine till she came to the love scene. So, she told my friend, I thought, there's William Faulkner, sitting right up there in Oxford. Why not send it to William Faulkner and ask him? So she sent it to him, and time went by, and she didn't ever hear from him, and so she called him up. Because there he was. She said, Mr. Faulkner, did you ever get that love scene I sent you? He said yes, he had got it. And she said, Well, what did you think of it? And he said, Well, honey, it's not the way I'd do it—but you go *right ahead*. Now, wasn't that gentle of him?

INTERVIEWER

Do people give you unpublished manuscripts to read? I mean, women especially tend to write voluminous historical novels, and I wonder if any of them are in Jackson.

WELTY

I wouldn't be surprised. I don't think there's any neck of the woods they're not in. Yes, I get sent manuscripts, but those historical and Gothic novels are really a subject on which I know nothing, and I say so. There is, in point of fact, a good deal of writing talent in general around our state now—a lot of good young ones, serious ones.

INTERVIEWER

Did you ever feel part of a literary community, along with people like Flannery O'Connor, Carson McCullers, Katherine Anne Porter, and Caroline Gordon?

WELTY

I'm not sure there's any dotted line connecting us up, though all of us knew about each other, and all of us, I think, respected and read each other's work and understood it. And some of us are friends of long standing. I don't think there was any passing about of influences, but there's a lot of pleasure in thinking in whose lifetimes your own lifetime has happened to come along. Of course, Katherine Anne Porter was wonderfully generous to me from the beginning. At the time I began sending my first stories to *The Southern Review*, she read them and wrote to me from Baton Rouge inviting me to come down to see her. It took me, I suppose, six months or a year to fully get up my nerve. Twice I got as far as Natchez and turned around and came back. But I finally did get there, and Katherine Anne couldn't have been more welcoming. Later on, she wrote the introduction to my first book of stories, and I owe her very much for that. We've been friends all these years.

INTERVIEWER

How would you feel about a biography about yourself?

WELTY

Shy, and discouraged at the very thought, because to me a writer's work should be everything. A writer's whole feeling, the force of his whole life, can go into a story—but what he's worked for is to get an objective piece down on paper. That should be read instead of some account of his life, with that understanding—here is something which now exists and was made by the hands of this person. Read it for what it is. It doesn't even matter too much whose hands they were. Well, of course it does—I was just exaggerating to prove my point. But your private life should be kept private. My own I don't think would particularly interest anybody, for that matter. But I'd guard it; I feel strongly about that. They'd have a hard time trying to find something about me. I think I'd better burn everything up. It's best to burn letters, but at least I've never kept diaries or journals. All my manuscripts I've given to the Department of Archives and History in Jackson as they came out because that's my hometown and the director is a lifelong friend. But I don't give them everything. I must have a trunk full of stuff that I didn't give because I didn't think it was anybody else's concern, or that anybody would even care to see my mistakes and false turns. Like about eating goat and all the million things that I left out.

INTERVIEWER

Why do *Losing Battles* and *Delta Wedding* take place back in the 1920s and 1930s?

WELTY

It was a matter of setting the stage and confining the story. These are both family stories, and I didn't want them inhibited by outward events I couldn't control. In the case of *Delta Wedding*, I remember I made a careful investigation to find the year in which nothing very terrible had happened in the Delta by way of floods or fires or wars that would have taken the men away. I settled it by the almanac. It was a little inconvenient for me because I myself was only a little girl during the era I was writing about—that's why I let a little girl be the observer of part of it. In the case of *Losing Battles*, I wanted to write about a family who had *nothing*. A bare stage. I chose the time that was the very hardest, when people had the least and the stage could be the barest—and that was the Depression, of course.

INTERVIEWER

Do you prefer working with a bare stage?

WELTY

In this case, it was in order to overcrowd it with people. I start with ideas about character and situation, and the technique grows out of these as I grow into the work. It's different, of course, for every story. In *Losing Battles* I wanted to write about people who had nothing at all and yet had all the resources of their own character and situation to do what they could about their lives.

INTERVIEWER

Were you familiar with plantation life when you wrote *Delta Wedding*?

WELTY

No, but I had some friends who came from there, and I used to hear their stories, and I'd be taken on picnics and visits there. Family visits. The Delta is very rich and visually striking, but completely flat. I would find it maddening after days with nothing but the horizon. Just before you reach it, there are high bluffs, and to get in you plunge down a deep hill, and from then on there's nothing but flatness. Some of the things I saw and heard began to stick. Some family tales and sayings are right in the book, though by now I can't remember which are true and which are made up.

INTERVIEWER

John Crowe Ransom wrote in a review that *Delta Wedding* might well be "one of the last novels in the tradition of the Old South."

WELTY

I revere Mr. Ransom, but his meaning here is not quite clear to me. I wasn't trying to write a novel of the Old South. I don't think of myself as writing out of any special tradition, and I'd hesitate to accept that sanction for *Delta Wedding*. I'd hesitate still more today because the term itself, "Old South," has a connotation of something unreal and not quite straightforward.

INTERVIEWER

Your parents weren't from the Deep South originally. Do you think that contributed to your ironic perspective?

WELTY

It may have given me balance. But other factors mattered more. My father's father owned a farm in southern Ohio, and my mother's father was a country lawyer and farmer in West Virginia, and both my mother's parents came from Virginia families made up mostly of teachers and preachers. Some of these wrote for newspapers or kept journals, though none wrote fiction. But the family influence I felt came from the important fact that they all loved to read and that I was brought up with books. Yet my parents would have been the people they were, people of character, no matter where they were from, and I would have been their child wherever I was born. I'm a native Southerner, but as a writer I think background matters most in how well it teaches you to look around and see clearly what's there and in how deeply it nourishes your imagination.

INTERVIEWER

"Where Is the Voice Coming From?" is about the Medgar Evers assassination and must be your only topical story.

WELTY

I'm certain it is. It pushed up through something else I was working on. I had been having a feeling of uneasiness over the things being written about the South at that time because most of them were done in other parts of the country, and I thought most were synthetic. They were perfectly well-intentioned stories but generalities written from a distance to illustrate generalities. When that murder was committed, it suddenly crossed my consciousness that I knew what was in that man's mind because I'd lived all my life where it happened. It was the strangest feeling of horror and compulsion all in one. I tried to write from the interior of my own South, and that's why I dared to put it in the first person. The title isn't very good; I'd like to get a better one. At the time I wrote it—it was overnight—no one knew who the murderer was, and I just meant by the title that whoever was speaking, I—the writer—knew, was in a position to know, what the murderer must be saying and why.

Do real events hinder you in writing?

WELTY

Well, if you write about an actual event, you can't shape it the way you can an imaginary one. In "The Voice" I was writing about the real thing, and at the point of its happening. I was like a real-life detective trying to discover who did it. I don't mean the name of the murderer but his *nature*. That's not really a short-story writer's prerogative, or is it? Anyway, as events went on to prove, I think I came close to pinpointing the mind, but I went a bit wide of the mark in placing the social background of the person arrested for it. As a friend of mine said, You thought it was a Snopes, and it was a Compson. However, in some ways, that isn't a very lasting distinction anymore.

INTERVIEWER

Do you see a difference between your early stories in *A Curtain of Green* and *The Wide Net*, where you deal more with the grotesque and grim than you do in *The Bride of the Innisfallen*?

WELTY

It's a difference not really in subject matter so much as in the ways I approached it. In those early stories I'm sure I needed the device of what you call the "grotesque." That is, I hoped to differentiate characters by their physical qualities as a way of showing what they were like inside—it seemed to me then the most direct way to do it. This is an afterthought, though. I don't suppose I did it as consciously as all that, and I didn't know it was the easiest way. But it is easier to show somebody as lonely if you make him deaf and dumb than if you go feeling your way into his mind. And there was another reason for making the boy in "First Love" a deaf character: one of the other characters—Aaron Burr—was a real person. I couldn't invent conversation for him as I could for an imaginary character, so I had him speak in front of a deaf boy who could report and interpret him in his own way—that is, to suit the story. It's instinctive for a writer to show acute feeling or intense states of emotion by translating it into something visible—red hair, if nothing else. But it's not necessary. I believe I'm writing about the same inward things now without resorting to such obvious devices. But all devices—and the use of symbols is another—must come about organically, out of the story. I feel emphatic about that.

INTERVIEWER

Are you also talking here about other early stories like "Lily Daw and the Three Ladies" and "Petrified Man"?

WELTY

Well, when I wrote my first stories, I wrote much faster, and it failed to occur to me that I could write them any other way, and perhaps better the second time. They show all the weaknesses of the headlong. I never rewrote, I just wrote. The plots in these stories are weak because I didn't know enough to worry about plots. In the dialogue stories, they came into being exactly as the dialogue led them along. I didn't realize their real weakness until I began reading stories in public—and my ear told me. They could have been made stronger so easily. Sometimes I fixed them up a little for my readings—cut, transposed—small things, just to see the difference.

INTERVIEWER

What inspired "Powerhouse"?

WELTY

I wrote it in one night after I'd been to a concert and dance in Jackson where Fats Waller played. I tried to write my idea of the life of the traveling artist and performer—not Fats Waller himself, but any artist—in the alien world and tried to put it in the words and plot suggested by the music I'd been listening to. It was a daring attempt for a writer like me—as daring as it was to write about the murderer of

Medgar Evers on *that* night—and I'm not qualified to write about music or performers. But trying it pleased me then, and it still does please me.

INTERVIEWER

Are there problems with ending a story?

WELTY

Not so far, but I could have made mistakes without knowing it yet. It's really part of plotting to know the exact moment you're through. I go by my ear, and this may trick me. When I read, I hear what's on the page. I don't know whose voice it is, but some voice is reading to me, and when I write my own stories, I hear it too. I have a visual mind, and I *see* everything I write, but I have to hear the words when they're put down. Oh, that sounds absurd. This is not the same as working with dialogue, which of course is another, specialized kind of hearing.

INTERVIEWER

Your first stories were about Paris.

WELTY

It's not worth remembering. That was when I was a college freshman, sixteen years old. Oh, you know, I was writing about the great world, of which I only knew Jackson, Mississippi. But part of it stemmed from my sense of mystery in people and places, and that's legitimate and lifelong. As for Paris, I remember a sentence I opened one story with, to show you how bad I was: "Monsieur Boule inserted a delicate dagger in Mademoiselle's left side and departed with a poised immediacy." I like to think I didn't take myself seriously then, but I did.

INTERVIEWER

When you sent out "Death of a Traveling Salesman," how did you know you had ended your apprenticeship?

WELTY

I was just beginning it! I was thrilled to find that out. I hadn't conceived of a story's actually being taken. A boy up the street, an old friend, Hubert Creekmore, who's dead now, knew all about sending stories out. He was a writer who started before I did and published many good novels and poems. I wouldn't let him read anything I wrote but just asked him, Hubert, do you know where I can send this? And he said send it to John Rood of *Manuscript*. So I sent it off, and John Rood took it, and of course I was flabbergasted. So was Hubert! I believe I've always been lucky—my work has always landed safely and among friends.

INTERVIEWER

You were lucky to escape the novel-first requirement that publishers seem to impose upon young writers. They're wary of short-story collections.

WELTY

I owe that to John Woodburn, my first editor, who was then at Doubleday, and to Diarmuid Russell, my agent and friend of many years now. I owe it to my nature too, because I never wrote anything that didn't spring naturally to mind and engage my imagination.

INTERVIEWER

Compared to your stories, I see your novels as looser, freer, happier works that enjoy reconciliations and a final sense of communion.

WELTY

My natural temperament is one of positive feelings, and I really do work for resolution in a story. I don't think we often see life resolving itself, not in any sort of perfect way, but I like the fiction writer's feeling of being able to confront an experience and resolve it as art, however imperfectly and briefly—to give it a form and try to embody it—to hold it and express it in a story's terms. You have more chance to try it in a novel. A short story is confined to one mood, to which everything in the story pertains. Characters, setting, time, events, are all subject to the mood. And you can try more ephemeral, more fleeting things in a story—you can work more by suggestion—than in a novel. Less is resolved, more is suggested, perhaps.

INTERVIEWER

You reserve the short story for the ephemeral and the novel for the resolution?

WELTY

I can only say such things after the fact. If I'd known I was going to finish *Losing Battles* as a long novel, I don't know that I'd have begun it. I'm a short-story writer who writes novels the hard way, and by accident. You see, all my work grows out of the work itself. It seems to set its form from the idea, which is complete from the start, and a sense of the form is like a vase into which you pour something and fill it up. I have that completely in mind from the beginning, and I don't realize how far I can wander and yet come back. The flexibility and freedom are exciting to me, not being used to them, and they are hard to come by. But no one could have enjoyed learning those lessons more than I did. There's no end to what can be tried, is there? So better luck next time.

INTERVIEWER

Do you think critics have made too much of you as a regional writer, taking off from your own essays on the subject?

WELTY

I don't mind being called a regional writer. It's the critic's job to place and judge. But the critic can't really have a say in what a writer chooses to write about—that's the writer's lone responsibility. I just think of myself as writing about human beings, and I happen to live in a region, as do we all, so I write about what I know—it's the same case for any writer living anywhere. I also happen to love my particular region. If this shows, I don't mind.

INTERVIEWER

Is place your source of inspiration?

WELTY

Not only that, it's my source of knowledge. It tells me the important things. It steers me and keeps me going straight, because place is
a definer and a confiner of what I'm doing. It helps me to identify, to
recognize and explain. It does so much for you of itself. It saves me.
Why, you couldn't write a story that happened nowhere. *I* couldn't,
anyway. I couldn't write anything that abstract. I wouldn't be interested in anything that abstract.

INTERVIEWER

How about the function of place in "No Place for You, My Love"?

WELTY

That story is the one that place did the most for. It really wrote
the story. I saw that setting only one time—the Delta of the Mississippi River itself, down below New Orleans where it winds toward
the Gulf—one time only. Which smote me. It started the story and
made it for me—and *was* the story, really. At its very least, place is essential, though. Time and place make the framework that any story's
built on. To my mind, a fiction writer's honesty begins right there, in
being true to those two facts of time and place. From there, imagination can take him anywhere at all.

You can equally well be true, I feel, to an *impression* of place. A
new place seen in a flash may have an impact almost as strong as the
place you've grown up in, one you're familiar with down to the bone
and know what it's like without having to think. I've written about
place from either one extreme or the other but not from partial familiarity or guessing—there's no solidity there.

INTERVIEWER

"Music from Spain" takes place in San Francisco.

WELTY

That's using impression of place. I was in San Francisco for only three or four months—that's seeing it in a flash. That story was all a response to a place, an act of love at first sight. It's written from the point of view of the stranger, of course—the only way to write about a strange place. On the other hand, I couldn't write a story laid in New York, where I've come so many times—because it's both familiar and unfamiliar, a no-man's-land.

INTERVIEWER

Where is Morgana, in *The Golden Apples*?

WELTY

It's a made-up Delta town. I was drawn to the name because I always loved the conception of fata morgana—the illusory shape, the mirage that comes over the sea. All Delta places have names after people, so it was suitable to call it Morgana after some Morgans. My population might not have known there was such a thing as fata morgana, but illusions weren't unknown to them all the same—coming in over the cottonfields.

INTERVIEWER

Do you see a similarity between Miss Eckhart in *The Golden Apples* and Julia Mortimer in *Losing Battles*, both being schoolteachers who were civilizing agents and therefore outsiders?

WELTY

It doesn't have to be "therefore"—though mine were indeed outsiders. I suppose they are kin, but teachers like those are all over the South and maybe everywhere else too—dedicated, and losing their battles, but not losing them every time. I went all through grammar school in Jackson under a principal all of us who went there still remember and talk about—Miss Lorena Duling. This isn't to say I based my character on her, but she gave me insight into what it meant to be a great teacher. And so was my mother one. All her teaching was done by the time I came along, but she told me stories about it. She taught in the little mountain schools in West Virginia, riding to her school on horseback and crossing the river in a boat, teaching children older than she was—she started at fifteen. I think it was my mother who made seventeen silver dollars the first month she taught, and after that they never could quite come up to that high a standard—which also happened to Miss Julia Mortimer. The shaping influence of teachers like that stays real for a lifetime.

INTERVIEWER

I see another group of characters forming a pattern in your work. Virgie Rainey in *The Golden Apples* is an individualist and outsider and similar in that respect to Robbie Reid of *Delta Wedding* and Gloria Short of *Losing Battles*.

WELTY

In looking back I can see the pattern. It's funny—when I'm writing, I never see a repeat I make in large or small degree. I learn about it later. In Jackson they were recently doing a play of *The Ponder Heart* when I had just finished writing *Losing Battles*. The new novel was so fresh in my mind, whereas I hadn't thought of *The Ponder Heart* for years. But when I sat in at rehearsals, I kept seeing bits and pieces come up that I thought I had invented for *Losing Battles*, and there they were in another version in *Ponder Heart*. So I thought, It's sort of dismaying, but there it is. Your mind works that way. Yet they occur to me as new every time.

INTERVIEWER

Do you write when you're away from home?

WELTY

I've found it possible to write almost anywhere I've happened to try. I like it at home better because it's much more convenient for an early riser, which I am. And it's the only place where you can really promise yourself time and keep out interruptions. My ideal way to write a short story is to write the whole first draft through in one sitting, then work as long as it takes on revisions, and then the final version all in one, so that in the end the whole thing amounts to one long sustained effort. That's not possible anywhere, but it comes nearest to being possible in your own home.

INTERVIEWER

Do you typewrite?

WELTY

Yes, and that's useful—it helps give me the feeling of making my work objective. I can correct better if I see it in typescript. After that, I revise with scissors and pins. Pasting is too slow, and you can't undo it, but with pins you can move things from anywhere to anywhere, and that's what I really love doing—putting things in their best and proper place, revealing things at the time when they matter most. Often I shift things from the very beginning to the very end. Small things—one fact, one word—but things important to me. It's possible I have a reverse mind and do things backwards, being a broken left-hander. Just so I've caught on to my weakness.

INTERVIEWER

You rewrite considerably?

WELTY

Yes, I do. Some things I let alone from first to last—the kernel of the story. You know enough not to touch something if it's right. The hardest thing for me is getting people in and out of rooms—the mechanics of a story. A simple act of putting on clothes is almost impossible for me to describe without many false starts. You have to be quick and specific in conveying that sort of action or fact, and also as neat and quiet about it as possible so that it doesn't obtrude. And I find that very challenging, especially to describe an action that I don't do very well myself, like sewing. I made Aunt Lexie in *Losing Battles* a poor sewer so that I wouldn't have to describe it too well. The easiest things to write about are emotions.

INTERVIEWER

And yet the most difficult thing would seem to be the hidden reaches of the human heart, the mystery, those impalpable emotions.

WELTY

For a writer those things are what you start with. You wouldn't have started a story without that awareness—that's what made you begin. That's what makes a character, projects the plot. Because you write from the inside. You can't start with how people look and speak and behave and come to know how they feel. You must know exactly what's in their hearts and minds before they ever set visible foot on the stage. You must know all, then not tell it all, or not tell too much at once: simply the right thing at the right moment. And the same character would be written about entirely differently in a novel as opposed to a short story. In a story you don't go into a character in order to develop him. He was born full grown, and he's present there to perform his part in the story. He's subservient to his function, and he doesn't exist outside it. But in a novel, he may. So you may have to allow for his growth and maybe hold him down and not tell everything you know, or else let him have his full sway—make room for a hero, even, in more spacious premises.

INTERVIEWER

Can you talk objectively about your language, perhaps about your use of metaphor?

WELTY

I don't know how to because I think of the actual writing as having existence only in the story. When I think of something, I put it into a narrative form, not in analytical form, and so anything I say would be artificial. Which reminds me of an Armenian friend of mine, an artist, who told me that his dreams all happened in the same place. When he went to bed, he'd imagine himself on a sled going down a steep hill. At the foot of the hill was a little town, and by the time he reached it, he was asleep, and his dreams happened right there. He didn't know why or how. And to go to the ridiculous and yet the sublime, there's W. C. Fields, who read an analysis of how he juggled. He couldn't juggle for six years afterward. He'd never known that was how it was done. He'd just thrown up the balls and juggled.

Issue 55, 1972

John Gardner

The Art of Fiction

The following interview incorporates three done with John Gardner over the last decade of his life. After interviewing him in 1971, Frank McConnell wrote of the thirty-nine-year-old author as one of the most original and promising younger American novelists. His first four novels—*The Resurrection* (1966), *The Wreckage of Agathon* (1970), *Grendel* (1971), and *The Sunlight Dialogues* (1972)— represented, in the eyes of many critics and reviewers, a new and exhilarating phase in the enterprise of modern writing, a consolidation of the resources of the contemporary novel and a leap forward—or backward—into a reestablished humanism. One finds in his books elements of the three major strains of current fiction: the elegant narrative gamesmanship of Barth or Pynchon, the hyperrealistic gothicism of Joyce Carol Oates and Stanley Elkin, and the cultural, intellectual history of Saul Bellow. Like so many characters in current fiction, Gardner's are men on the fringe, men shocked into the consciousness that they are living lives that seem to be determined not by their own will but by massive myths, cosmic fictions over which they have no control (e.g., Ebeneezer Cooke in Barth's *Sot-Weed Factor*, Tyrone Slothrop in Pynchon's *Gravity's Rainbow*); but Gardner's characters are philosophers on the fringe, heirs, all of them, to the great debates over authenticity and bad faith that characterize our era. In *Grendel*, for example, the hero-monster is initiated into the Sartrean vision of Nothingness by an ancient, obviously well-read dragon: a myth speaking of the emptiness of all myths—"Theory-makers . . . They'd

Days passed, and weeks, and Vlemk became so changed that often not even the
regulars at the tavern seemed to know him as he groped his way past them on his
way to the bathroom or ~~out~~ to the alley. He forgot about the Princess, or remembered
her only as one remembers certain moments from one's childhood. Sometimes if ~~someone~~
someone spoke of her, and it was early in the evening, when Vlemk was still relatively
sober, Vlemk would smile like a man who knows more than he's telling about something,
and it would cross people's minds, especially the barmaid's, that Vlemk and the
princess were closer than one might think. But since he was a mute and declined
to write notes, no one pressed him. Anyway, no one ~~cared~~ to get close to him; he
~~had~~ smell like an old sick bear. ~~Who's been lying in his moss.~~

Things went from bad to worse for Vlemk the box-painter. He no longer spoke
of life as "boxing him in," not only because the expression bored him but also, and
mainly, because the box ~~was~~ had become such ~~a~~ given of his existence that he no
longer noticed ~~it.~~ bleary-eyed

Then one ~~spring~~ May morning as he was lying in a gutter, squinting up/~~at~~
~~~~ and exploring a newly broken tooth with his tongue, a carriage of black
leather with golden studs drew up beside him and, at a command from the person
inside, ~~slowed down and~~ stopped.

"Driver," said ~~the person in the carriage, with a feathery sweet~~ voice
that seemed as near as Vlemk's heart, "who is that unfortunate creature in the
gutter?"

Vlemk turned his head ~~a little~~ and tried to focus his eyes, but it was
useless. The carriage was, ~~to Vlemk,~~ like a shadow ~~against the sun, or a~~
on a painted box-lid.

"I'm sorry, Princess," said the driver, "I have no idea."

When he heard it was the Princess, Vlemk thought briefly of raising ~~his~~ one
hand to hide his face, but his will remained inactive and he lay as he was.

"Throw the poor creature a coin," said the Princess. "I hope he's not
past using it."

After a moment something landed, plop, on Vlemk's belly, and the carriage
drove away. Slowly, Vlemk moved one hand toward the cool place--his shirt had
lost its buttons, and the coin lay flat on his pale, grimy skin-- where at last
his ~~stiff,~~ groping fingers found it and dragged it back down to the ~~sixth~~ ground
~~beside him,~~ where it would be safe while he ~~finished his~~ nap. Hours later
he sat up abruptly and realized what had happened. He looked down at his hand.
There lay the coin, real silver with a picture of the king on it.

"How strange!" thought Vlemk.

When he'd gotten to his feet and moved carefully to the streetcorner,
touching the walls of the buildings with one hand, he found that he had no idea
where he was, much less how he'd gotten there, and no idea which direction to
take to reach his house. When he waved to hurrying passers-by, silently moving
his loose, mute mouth, they ducked their heads, touching their hats, and hurried
around him as they would if he were Death. He ~~moved~~ on alone, hunting for some
landmark, but it was as if all the streets of the city had been ~~moved to new~~
~~locations, arranged in new patterns.~~ He shook his head, still moving his mouth,
unaware that he was doing it. In his right hand he clenched--so tightly that
the rim of it bit into his flesh--the coin with the picture of the king on it.

Three days later, having carefully ~~thought it over~~ from every point of
view, having bathed ~~himself~~ and trimmed his beard and washed his old black suit
in the sink in the studio, and having dried it on the railing of the balcony,
~~outside his window,~~ Vlemk the box-painter started up the ~~mountain~~ toward the
Royal Palace, ~~carrying~~ the box with the talking picture ~~of the Princess under his~~
~~arm.~~ In his pocket he had a note which he'd ~~carefully~~ lettered, and intended to
~~hand her~~ as he gave her the box. "Here is the gift I ~~promised~~ you," the note
read, "a picture ~~of you~~ so real it can speak. I release you from your promise
to talk with me, since ~~I have since then become~~ a mute, ~~who can't ask for~~
~~such impertinence.~~ Respectfully, Vlemk the Box-Painter."

He arrived at the palace, as he had planned to do, just at the time when
the Princess would be coming in from walking her dogs. The last of the sunset
was ~~just~~ fading from the clouds, ~~and~~ here and there pockets of fog were taking
shape, intruding on the smoothly mown slopes from ponds and woods. To Vlemk's
dismay, the outer gates of iron stood open, ~~when~~ the grayhounds saw him, ~~they~~
would tear him to bits?; But then he noticed that all around the front of the
palace ~~where were~~ carriages, and near the arched front door aristocrats stood talking
and laughing in their splendid dress. It ~~seemed to him~~ unlikely that they would
let the grayhounds kill him, though he had learned enough, ~~from the experience with~~
~~people had made to him,~~ to ~~know~~ that in these matters nothing is ever quite certain.
But the dogs, he thought the next instant, were the least of it. How could he
walk in, in the middle of a party of ~~aristocrats,~~ and give the Princess his ~~card~~
~~and present?~~ How would he even find her? As he drew nearer, moving more slowly
now, he saw that the ~~aristocrats'~~ clothes were all of ~~splendid~~ material, with clasps
and buckles, buttons, epaulettes, and swordhilts of gold and silver. He looked

A manuscript page from Vlemk the Box-Painter *by John Gardner.*

map out roads through Hell with their crackpot theories, their here-to-the-moon-and-back lists of paltry facts. Insanity—the simplest insanity ever devised!" His heroes—like all men—are philosophers who are going to die, and their characteristic discovery—the central creative energy of Gardner's fiction—is that the death of consciousness finally justifies consciousness itself. The myths, whose artificiality contemporary writers have been at such pains to point out, become in Gardner's work real and life giving once again without ever losing their modern character of fictiveness.

Gardner's work may well represent, then, the new "conservatism" that some observers have noted in the current scene. But it is a conservatism of high originality and, at least in Gardner's case, of deep authority in his life. When he guest-taught a course in Narrative Forms at Northwestern University, a number of his students were surprised to find a modern writer—and a hot property—not only enthusiastic about Homer, Virgil, Apollonius Rhodius, and Dante but deeply concerned with the critical controversies surrounding those writers and with mistakes in their English translations. As the interview following makes clear, Gardner's affection for ancient writing and the tradition of metaphysics is, if anything, greater than that for the explosions and involutions of modern fiction. He is, in the full sense of the word, a literary man.

"It's as if God put me on earth to write," Gardner observed once. And writing, or thinking about writing, takes up much of his day. He works, he says, usually on three or four books at the same time, allowing the plots to cross-pollinate, shape, and qualify each other.

Sara Matthiessen describes Gardner in the spring of 1978 (additional works published by then included *October Light*; *On Moral Fiction* was about to be published). Matthiessen arrived with a friend to interview him at the Breadloaf Writers' Colony in Vermont: "After we'd knocked a couple of times, he opened the door looking haggard and just wakened. Dressed in a purple sateen, bell-sleeved, turtleneck shirt, and jeans, he was an exotic figure: unnaturally white hair to below his shoulders, of medium height, he seemed an incarnation from the medieval era central to his study. 'Come in!' he said, as though there were no two people he'd rather have seen than Sally and me, and he led us into a cold, bright room sparsely equipped with wooden furniture. We were offered extra socks against the chill. John lit his pipe, and we sat down to talk."

—*Paul F. Ferguson, John R. Maier,*
Frank McConnell, Sara Matthiessen, 1979

INTERVIEWER

You've worked in several different areas: prose, fiction, verse, criticism, book reviews, scholarly books, children's books, radio plays; you wrote the libretto for a recently produced opera. Could you discuss the different genres? Which one have you most enjoyed doing?

JOHN GARDNER

The one that feels the most important is the novel. You create a whole world in a novel and you deal with values in a way that you can't possibly in a short story. The trouble is that since novels represent a whole world, you can't write them all the time. After you finish a novel, it takes a couple of years to get in enough life and enough thinking about things to have anything to say, any clear questions to work through. You have to keep busy, so it's fun to do the other things. I do book reviews when I'm hard up for money, which I am all the time. They don't pay much, but they keep you going. Book reviews are interesting because it's necessary to keep an eye on what's good and what's bad in the books of a society worked so heavily by advertising, public relations, and so on. Writing reviews isn't really analytical, it's for the most part quick reactions—joys and rages. I certainly never write a review about a book I don't think worth reviewing, a flat-out bad book, unless it's an enormously fashionable bad book. As for writing children's books, I've done them because when my kids were growing up I would now and then write them a story as a Christmas present, and then after I became sort of successful, people saw the stories and said they should be published. I like them, of course. I wouldn't give junk to my kids. I've also done scholarly books and articles. The reason I've done those is that I've been teaching things like *Beowulf* and Chaucer for a long time. As you teach a poem year after year, you realize, or anyway convince yourself, that you understand the poem and that most people have got it slightly wrong. That's natural with any poem, but during the years I taught lit courses, it was especially true of medieval and classical poetry. When the general critical view has a major poem or poet *badly* wrong, you feel like you ought to straighten it out. The studies of Chaucer since the fifties are very strange stuff: like the theory that Chaucer is a frosty Oxford-donnish guy shunning carnality and cupidity. Not true. So close analysis is useful. But writing novels—and maybe opera libretti— is the kind of writing that gives me the greatest satisfaction. The rest is more like entertainment.

INTERVIEWER

You have been called a philosophical novelist. What do you think of the label?

GARDNER

I'm not sure that being a philosophical novelist is better than being some other kind, but I guess that there's not much doubt that, in a way at least, that's what I am. A writer's material is what he cares about, and I like philosophy the way some people like politics, or football games, or unidentified flying objects. I read a man like Collingwood, or even Brand Blanchard or C. D. Broad, and I get excited—even anxious—filled with suspense. I read a man like Swinburne on time and space and it becomes a matter of deep concern to me whether the structure of space changes near large masses. It's as if I actually think philosophy will solve life's great questions—which sometimes, come to think of it, it does, at least for me. Probably not often, but I like the illusion. Blanchard's attempt at a logical demonstration that there re- ally *is* a universal human morality, or the recent flurry of theories by various majestical cranks that the universe is stabilizing itself instead of flying apart—those are lovely things to run into. Interesting and ar- resting, I mean, like talking frogs. I get a good deal more out of the philosophy section of a college bookstore than out of the fiction sec- tion, and I more often read philosophical books than I read novels. So sure, I'm "philosophical," though what I write is by no means straight philosophy. I make up stories. Meaning creeps in of necessity, to keep things clear, like paragraph breaks and punctuation. And, I might add, my friends are all artists and critics, not philosophers. Philosophers—except for the few who are my friends—drink beer and watch football games and defeat their wives and children by the fraudulent tyranny of logic.

INTERVIEWER

But insofar as you *are* a philosophical novelist, what is it that you do?

GARDNER

I write novels, books about people, and what I write is philosophical only in a limited way. The human dramas that interest me—stir me to excitement and, loosely, vision—are always rooted in serious philosophical questions. That is, I'm bored by plots that depend on the psychological or sociological quirks of the main characters— mere melodramas of healthy against sick—stories that, subtly or otherwise, merely preach. Art as the wisdom of Marcus Welby, M.D. Granted, most of fiction's great heroes are at least slightly crazy, from Achilles to Captain Ahab, but the problems that make great heroes act are the problems no sane man could have gotten around either. Achilles, in his nobler, saner moments, lays down the whole moral code of *The Iliad*. But the violence and anger triggered by war, the human passions that overwhelm Achilles's reason and make him the greatest criminal in all fiction—they're just as much a problem for lesser, more ordinary people. The same with Ahab's desire to pierce the Mask, smash through to absolute knowledge. Ahab's crazy, so he actually tries it, but the same Mask leers at all of us. So, when I write a piece of fiction I select my characters and settings and so on because they have a bearing, at least to me, on the old unanswerable philosophical questions. And as I spin out the action, I'm always very concerned with springing discoveries—actual philosophical discoveries. But at the same time I'm concerned—and finally *more* concerned— with what the discoveries do to the character who makes them, and to the people around him. It's that that makes me not really a philosopher, but a novelist.

INTERVIEWER

The novel *Grendel* is a retelling of the Beowulf story from the monster's point of view. Why does an American writer living in the twentieth century abandon the realistic approach and borrow such legendary material as the basis for a novel?

GARDNER

I've never been terribly fond of realism because of certain things that realism seems to commit me to. With realism you have to spend two hundred pages proving that somebody lives in Detroit so that something can happen and be absolutely convincing. But the value systems of the people involved is the important thing, not the fact that they live on Nine Mile Road. In my earlier fiction I went as far as I could from realism because the easy way to get to the heart of what you want to say is to take somebody else's story, particularly a nonrealistic story. When you tell the story of Grendel, or Jason and Medeia, you've got to end it the way the story ends—traditionally, but you can get to do it in your own way. The result is that the writer comes to understand things about the modern world in light of the history of human consciousness; he understands it a little more deeply and has a lot more fun writing it.

INTERVIEWER

But why specifically *Beowulf*?

GARDNER

Some stories are more interesting than others. *Beowulf* is a terribly interesting story. It gives you some really wonderful visual images, such as the dragon. It's got Swedes looking over the hills and scaring everybody. It's got mead halls. It's got Grendel and Grendel's mother. I really do believe that a novel has to be a feast of the senses, a delightful thing. One of the better things that has happened to the novel in recent years is that it has become rich. Think of a book like *Chimera* or *The Sot-Weed Factor*—they may not be very good books, but they are at least rich experiences. For me, writers like John

O'Hara are interesting only in the way that movies and TV plays are interesting. There is almost nothing in a John O'Hara novel that couldn't be in the movies just as easily. On the other hand, there is no way an animator, or anyone else, can create an image from *Grendel* as exciting as the image in the reader's mind: Grendel is a monster, and living in the first person, because we're all in some sense monsters, trapped in our own language and habits of emotion. Grendel expresses feelings we all feel—enormous hostility, frustration, disbelief, and so on, so that the reader, projecting his own monster, projects a monster that is, for him, the perfect horror show. There is no way you can do that in television or the movies, where you are always seeing the kind of realistic novel O'Hara wrote . . . Gregory Peck walking down the street. It's just the same old thing to me. There are other things that are interesting in O'Hara, and I don't mean to put him down excessively, but I go for another kind of fiction: I want the effect that a radio play gives you or that novels are always giving you at their best.

INTERVIEWER

You do something very interesting in *Grendel*. You never name Beowulf, and in the concluding scene you describe him in such a way as to give the impression that Grendel is really confronting not Beowulf or another human being but the dragon. That seems a significant change from the poem.

GARDNER

I didn't mean it to be a change. As a medievalist, one knows there are two great dragons in medieval art. There's Christ the dragon, and there's Satan the dragon. There's always a war between those two great dragons. In modern Christian symbolism a sweeter image of Jesus with the sheep in his arms has evolved, but I like the old image of the warring dragon. That's not to say Beowulf really is Christ but that he's Christ-like. Actually, he is many things. When Grendel first sees Beowulf coming, Grendel thinks of him as a sort of machine, and what comes to the reader's mind is a kind of computer, a spaceman, a complete alien, unknown. The inescapable mechanics of the universe.

At other times, Beowulf looks like a fish to Grendel. He comes in the season of Pisces when, among other things, you stab yourself in the back. On other occasions, Grendel sees other things, one after another, and for a brief flash, when he is probably hallucinating—he's fighting, losing blood very badly because he has his arm torn off— Grendel thinks he's fighting the dragon instead of Beowulf. At the end of the story, Grendel doesn't know *who* he's fighting. He's just fighting something big and horrible and sure to kill him, something that he could never have predicted in the universe as he understood it, because from the beginning of the novel, Grendel feels himself hopelessly determined, hopelessly struggling against—in the profoundest sense—the way things are. He feels there's no way out, that there's no hope for living consciousness, particularly *his* consciousness, since, for reasons inexplicable to him, he's on the wrong side, Cain's side instead of mankind's.

INTERVIEWER

It seems to me that determinism is an affliction imposed on him by the *scop*.

GARDNER

It's true, but only partly. In the novel, he's undeniably pushed around by the universe, but also pushed not to believe, not to have faith in life. What happens is, in the story, the shaper, the *scop*, the court poet comes to this horrible court that's made itself what it is by killing everybody, beating people, chopping them to death, and the poet looks at this havoc around him and makes up a story about what a wonderful court it is, what noble ideals it has. The courtiers are just dumb enough to believe it, just as Americans have believed the stories about Sam Adams and Ethan Allen and all those half-mythical heroes. George Washington once stood for thirty minutes stuttering in a rage before executing a private for a minor misdeed. Sam Adams was like a well-meaning Marxist agitator. Constantly lied. He told Boston that New York had fallen when it hadn't fallen. Or anyway so one of my characters claims. I no longer remember what the truth is.

INTERVIEWER

But that's an important moment in Grendel's development, isn't it, when he hears this story?

GARDNER

He hears the story and is tempted to believe it. And for certain reasons, partly because he is kicked out of the mead hall, he decides to reject the myth. That's Grendel's hard luck, because when he goes to the mead hall and wants to be a good monster and doesn't want to kill people anymore, Hrothgar's warriors don't know that, and they throw spears at him and hurt him.

INTERVIEWER

You don't see yourself, as a novelist, analogous to the *scop* in the telling of a story?

GARDNER

Oh, sure. Absolutely. I absolutely believe every artist is in the position of the *scop*. As I tried to make plain in *On Moral Fiction*, I think that the difference right now between good art and bad art is that the good artists are the people who are, in one way or another, creating, out of deep and honest concern, a vision of life in the twentieth century that is worth pursuing. And the bad artists, of whom there are many, are whining or moaning or staring, because it's fashionable, into the dark abyss. If you believe that life is fundamentally a volcano full of baby skulls, you've got two main choices as an artist: You can either stare into the volcano and count the skulls for the thousandth time and tell everybody, There are the skulls; that's your baby, Mrs. Miller. Or you can try to build walls so that fewer baby skulls go in. It seems to me that the artist ought to hunt for positive ways of surviving, of living. You shouldn't lie. If there aren't any so far as you can see, you should say so, like the *Merdistes*. But I don't think the *Merdistes* are right—except for Céline himself, by accident, because Céline (as character, not as author) is comic—a villain so outrageous, miserable, and inept that we laugh at him and at all he so earnestly stands for. I think the world is not all merde. I think it's possible to make walls around at least some of the smoking holes.

Won't this have the effect of transforming the modern writer into a didactic writer?

Not didactic. The didactic writer is anything but moral because he is always simplifying the argument, always narrowing away, getting rid of legitimate objections. *Mein Kampf* is a moralistic book—a stupid, ugly one. A truly moral book is one that is radically open to persuasion, but looks hard at a problem and keeps looking for answers. It gives you an absolutely clear vision, as if the poet, the writer, had nothing to do with it, had just done everything in his power to imagine how things are. It's the situation of Dostoyevsky and Nietzsche—an illusion I use in *On Moral Fiction*. Nietzsche sets up this abstract theory of the superman according to which a person can kill or do anything he wants because there is no basis of law except the herd. God doesn't speak—he's dead. So the people get together and vote to have a red light on Highway 61 where there's no traffic. It's three o'clock in the morning. You're traveling, there's a red light, and you decide to jump the light. A car pulls out of the weeds, a policeman, and he comes after you. If you're a superman, you politely and gently kill him, put him back in the weeds, and drive on. The theory of the superman is kind of interesting, abstractly. The question is, Is it right? Will it work? Can human beings live with it? So Dostoyevsky sets up the experiment imaginatively. Obviously he doesn't want to go out and actually kill somebody to see if it works, so he imagines a perfectly convincing St. Petersburg and a perfectly convincing person who would do this. (What student in all of St. Petersburg would commit a murder? What relatives would he have? What friends? What would his pattern be? What would he eat?) Dostoyevsky follows the experiment out and finds out what does happen.

I think all great art does this, and you don't have to do it realistically. Obviously Raskolnikov could have been a giant saurian as long as his character is consistent and convincing, tuned to what we know about actual feeling. The point is realism of imagination, convincingness of imagination. The novelist pursues questions and pursues them thoroughly. Not only when does it rain and when doesn't it rain, but can we tolerate rain? What can we be made to tolerate? What should we not allow ourselves to be made to tolerate? And so on. So that finally, what's moral in fiction is chiefly its way of looking. The premise of moral art is that life is better than death; art hunts for avenues to life. The book succeeds if we're powerfully persuaded that the focal characters, in their fight for life, have won honestly or, if they lose, are tragic in their loss, not just tiresome or pitiful.

INTERVIEWER

So you have a strong sense of mission, or of a goal, in modern fiction.

GARDNER

Yes, I do. In my own way, anyway. I want to push the novel in a new direction, or back to an old one—Homer's or the *Beowulf* poet's. Of course, a lot of other writers are trying to do something rather different—Barth and Pynchon, I grant them their right—grudgingly. But to paraphrase the Imagists, I want no ideas but in *energeia*—Aristotle's made-up word for, excuse the jazz, the actualization of the potential which exists in character and situation. Philosophy as plot. I think no novel can please for very long without plot as the center of its argument. We get too many books full of meaning by innuendo—the ingenious symbol, the allegorical overlay, stories in which *events* are of only the most trivial importance, just the thread on which the writer strings hints of his "real" meaning. This has been partly a fault of the way we've been studying and teaching literature, of course. Our talk of levels and all that. For instance, take John Updike's *Couples*. It's a fairly good book, it seems to me, but there's a good reason no one reads it anymore: contrived phrases bear all the burden. Symbolically constructed names; descriptions of a living room that slyly hint at the expansion of the universe; or Updike's whole cunning trick with Christian iconography, circles and straight lines—circles traditionally associated with reason, straight lines with faith. You work the whole symbolic structure out and you're impressed by Updike's intelligence—maybe, in this book, even wisdom—but you have difficulty telling the fornicators apart. Reading *Couples* is like studying science while watching pornographic movies put together from random scraps on the cutting-room floor.

INTERVIEWER

You want novels to be whole entertainments, then.

GARDNER

Sure! Look, it's impossible for us to read Dostoyevsky as a writer of thrillers anymore because of this whole weight of explanation and analysis we've loaded on the books. And yet *The Brothers Karamazov* is obviously, among other things, a thriller novel. It also contains, to my mind, some pretentious philosophizing. What I've wanted to do, in *The Sunlight Dialogues*, for example, is write a book—maybe not a novel—that you could read as entertainment. Where there's straight philosophizing, here as in *The Resurrection*, it's present because that's what the character would say—or so I thought at the time—present because that's what makes him behave as he does. No meaning but emotion-charged action and emotional reaction.

INTERVIEWER

The classical forms, like *Grendel*, are not your only models, nor do you always adhere to the superficial nature of the form you've chosen—for instance, there are parts in *The Sunlight Dialogues* that parody Faulkner.

GARDNER

Sure. In fact, the whole conception of the book is in a way parodic of Faulkner, among others—the whole idea of family and locale. A lot of times I've consciously taken a writer on. In the first novel I did, I used the title *The Resurrection* to give the reader a clue as to what's wrong with Tolstoy in his *Resurrection*. I don't think many readers notice, and of course it doesn't matter. In fact, a friend of mine who's

a very good critic asked me one time if I were aware that I'd used a title that Tolstoy had used. That's all right. If I sounded too much like
Tolstoy, then my novel would be a critical footnote.

INTERVIEWER

How about your contemporaries? Has any of their work influenced your writing?

GARDNER

Of course I'm aware of modern writers . . . and some writers have
changed my way of thinking. I don't always like what Bill Gass does—
though I do immensely like much of his fiction—but I certainly have
changed my writing style because of his emphasis on language—that
is, his brilliant use of it in books. It has always seemed to me that the
main thing you ought to be doing when you write a story is, as Robert
Louis Stevenson said, to set a "dream" going in the reader's mind . . .
so that he opens the page, reads about three words, and drops into a
sort of trance. He's seeing Russia instead of his living room. Not that
he's *passive*. The reader hopes and judges. I used to think that words
and style should be transparent, that no word should call attention to
itself in any way, that you could say the plainest thing possible to get
the dream going. After I read some early Gass—"The Pedersen Kid,"
I think—I realized that you don't really interfere with the dream by
saying things in an interesting way. Performance is an important part
of the show. But I don't, like Gass, think language is of value when
it's opaque, more decorative than communicative. Gass loves those
formalist arguments. He's said, for instance, that it's naïve to think of
characters as real—that it's absurd to cry for little Nell. It may be absurd to cry at that particular death, because in that case the writing is
lousy. But what happens in real fiction is identical to what happens in
a dream—as long as we have the right to wake up screaming from a
nightmare, we have the right to worry about a character. Gass has a
funny theory. But I have borrowed a great many elements from it—
I'm sure I owe more to him than to any other living writer. And I have
learned a few things from slightly contemporary writers. About symbols, for instance. If you stop with James Joyce, you may write a

slightly goofy kind of symbolic novel. Joyce's fondness for the "mannered" is the least of it. At the time Joyce was writing, people were less attuned than they are now to symbolic writing, so he sometimes let himself get away with bald, obvious symbols. Now, thanks largely to the New Criticism, any smart college freshman can catch every symbol that comes rolling along. The trouble is that if a reader starts watching the play of symbolism and missing what's happening to the characters, he gets an intellectual apprehension of the book, and that's pretty awful. He might as well read philosophy or meditations on the wounds of Christ. But you still need resonance, deep effect. You have to build into the novel the movement from particular to general. The question is, how do you get a symbolic structure without tipping your hand? A number of modern writers have shown ways of doing it. The red herring symbols of Pynchon, the structural distractions of Barth, the machine-gun energy of Gaddis. Above all, Gass's verbal glory.

INTERVIEWER

Do you, like Joyce, play to the reader subliminally through symbolism, or do you make fairly overt statements by demonstrating what certain values can lead to?

GARDNER

I try to be as overt as possible. Plot, character, and action first. I try to say everything with absolute directness so that the reader sees the characters moving around, sees the house they're moving through, the landscape, the weather, and so on. I try to be absolutely direct about moral values and dilemmas. Read it to the charwoman, Richardson said. I say, make it plain to her dog. But when you write fiction such as mine, fantastic or quasi-realistic fiction, it happens inevitably that as you're going over it, thinking about it, you recognize unconscious symbols bubbling up to the surface, and you begin to revise to give them room, sort of nudge them into sight. Though ideally the reader should never catch you shaking a symbol at him. Intellect is the chief distracter of the mind. The process of writing becomes more and more mysterious as you go over the draft more and more times—finally everything is symbolic. Even then you keep pushing it, making sure that it's as coherent and self-contained as a grapefruit. Frequently, when you write a novel you start out feeling pretty clear about your position, what side you're on. As you revise, you find your unconscious pushing up associations that modify that position, force you to reconsider.

INTERVIEWER

You began *October Light*, you've said, with the idea that "the traditional New England values are the values we should live by: good workmanship, independence, unswerving honesty—," but these proved oversimple. Is the process of fiction always the process of discovery for you? In other words, do you often find that the idea that prompted the fiction turns out to be too simple, or even wrong?

GARDNER

I always start out with a position I later discover to be too simple. That's the nature of things—what physicists call complementarity. What's interesting is that my ideas prove too simple in ways I could never have anticipated. In everything I've written I've come to the realization that I was missing something, telling myself lies. That's one of the main pleasures of writing. What I do is follow the drama where it goes, the potential of the characters in their given situation. I let them go where they have to go and analyze as I'm going along what's involved, what the implications are. When I don't like the implications, I think hard about it. Chasing implications to the wall is my one real skill. I think of ways of dramatically setting up contrasts so that my position on a thing is clear to me, and then I hound the thing till it rolls over. I certainly wouldn't ever fake the actions, or the characters, or make people say what they wouldn't say. I never use sleight of wits like Stanley Elkin—though no one can fail to admire a really good sophist's skill.

INTERVIEWER

How important is setting?

GARDNER

Setting is one of the most powerful symbols you have, but mainly it serves characterization. The first thing that makes a reader read a book is the characters. Say you're standing in a train station, or an airport, and you're leafing through books; what you're hoping for is a book where you'll like the characters, where the characters are interesting. To establish powerful characters, a writer needs a landscape to help define them, so setting becomes important. Setting is also a powerful vehicle of thematic concerns; in fact, it's one of the most powerful. If you're going to talk about the decline of Western civilization or at least the possibility of that decline, you take an old place that's sort of worn out and run-down. For instance, Batavia, New York, where the Holland Land Office was . . . the beginning of a civilization . . . selling the land in this country. It was, in the beginning, a wonderful, beautiful place with the smartest Indians in America around. Now it's this old, run-down town that has been urban-renewalized just about out of existence. The factories have stopped and the people are poor and sometimes crabby; the elm trees are all dead, and so are the oaks and maples. So it's a good symbol. If you're writing the kind of book I was writing in *Sunlight Dialogues* or *The Resurrection*, both of them books about death, both spiritual death and the death of civilization, you choose a place like that. I couldn't have found, in my experience, a better setting. It's just not a feeling you have in San Francisco. If I was going to write a book about southern Illinois, which in fact I did in *King's Indian*, that's another, completely different feeling. There it's as if human beings had never landed; the human beings—the natives, anyway—seem more like gnomes. You choose the setting that suits and illuminates your material.

INTERVIEWER

The Resurrection, *Sunlight Dialogues*, *Nickel Mountain*, and *October Light* all take place in your native surroundings, more or less. Do you find that you need distance on a place before you can write about it? Would you have been able to get a proper perspective on these places in the East, and the type of people who live there, if you'd not spent a good deal of your time in the West and Midwest?

GARDNER

I don't really think so. It's true that *The Resurrection* and *Sunlight Dialogues* take place in Batavia. I wrote one of them in California, the other partly in California and partly in southern Illinois. So I was using memories from my childhood. Every once in a while, I'd go back and see my parents and go over and see the Brumsteds and the characters who show up in the story, and I'd look the streets over and think, that'd be funny to put in a novel, or whatever. But *Nickel Mountain* is set in the Catskills, which I'd only passed through once or twice, and when I did *October Light*, which came out of a very direct and immediate experience in the East, I'd just moved back to the East after years away. I'd never been in Vermont, and the landscape and the feeling of the people is not at all like western New York. I had never seen anything like it; I certainly didn't have any distance on it. It may be that ten years from now when I look the book over I'll see that I didn't do it very well, but now it feels just as authentic to me as the other books I've written. So I don't think you necessarily do need distance. It is certainly true though that memory selects well. What you keep in your memory is psychologically symbolic, hence powerful, so that when you write about things that you knew a long time ago, you're going to get a fairly powerful evocation of place. I think one sees that in Bernard Malamud's work. When he writes about his childhood, his early memories of New York, you get a very powerful sense of the place. But I think in *A New Life*, written out of immediate experience, you get a more superficial sense of place.

It's different. Nobody could deny that the landscapes in *A New Life* are vivid, it's just that they don't have that *lived* feeling that the earlier cityscapes have. You have to write about what's useful and that's the problem—you can't just write about the place that's the most digested for you. In a really good writer's work you'll see that a writer doesn't have to have been around a place very long at all. John Fowles's novel *Daniel Martin* has got some long sections on Los Angeles that seem to be absolutely incredible. You'd swear he grew up there. Most people writing about Los Angeles can only see the phoniness, the greenery, and the gilt. Fowles sees everything, and he gets in it.

INTERVIEWER

Your *belief* in literature, your affection for it as a living force, goes back pretty far in your childhood. Did you read mostly the classics when you were a boy?

GARDNER

Not mostly—we had a lot of books. My mother was a school-teacher, and my father was a farmer who loved to read: classics, Shakespeare, and of course, the Bible. They were great reciters of literature, too. I've had visitors—sophisticated people—who've heard my father recite things and have been amazed at how powerfully he does it. It's an old country tradition, but my father was and is the best. We'd be put to bed with a recital of poetry, things like that. At Grange meetings, for instance, my mother and father would do recitations as part of the evening's entertainment. Or while my father was milking the cows my mother would come out and read something to him— *Lear*, say—leaving out the part of whomever my father felt like being that day, and he'd answer his lines from the cow.

INTERVIEWER

He actually had the whole thing memorized?

GARDNER

Oh, sure. Lots of plays. And he'd write things—lay sermons, stories—while he was driving his tractor: compose them in his head, rather like Ben Hodge in *Sunlight*. Not that Ben Hodge is exactly like my father. My father isn't weak willed. My father knows hundreds of poems, including some very long ones. Beautiful to listen to. A lot of people that we dismiss as terrible poets, like Longfellow, are changed entirely when you say their poems out loud—as they were intended to be. It's like singing. A song can't be very complex—the tune takes up part of the energy so that the words are kind of silly on the page—but when you sing it, it may be wonderful. The same thing happens with oral poetry—lots of stuff that's thin, even goofy on the page can be recited beautifully. That's one of the reasons I write the way I do. Oral stuff written. I hope that comes through.

INTERVIEWER

Did you do any writing as a child?

GARDNER

I started writing stories when I was five or so—making these books I'd send to relatives every Christmas. By around eight I was writing longer things . . . I wrote in ledger books given to me by my grandmother the lawyer. I really enjoyed writing on ledger paper: There's something nice about a page with a red line down the middle.

INTERVIEWER

Do you still use them?

GARDNER

No, I own my own typewriter now. Very professional.

INTERVIEWER

Is there an advantage to growing up on a farm?

GARDNER

Farm boys have some advantages; it depends on the family. I learned to love the land at least partly because my parents did—working it, watching things grow. Farm boys spend a lot of time with animals of all kinds. I liked it. Some don't. Also, sometimes on the happiest farms, the hunger comes to get away from all that work, and so they may see New York with more excited eyes than some New Yorkers do, or Chicago, or Los Angeles. I love all those places, even the ones that everybody else hates. I have a little trouble with Cleveland, but parts of it are nice. But except for short stints in San Francisco, Chicago, and Detroit, my whole life has been spent in the country, working with plants and animals, reading and writing. It's

nice to live in the country when you grew up there and worked yourself to death in the old days and now you don't have to; you just have
a few horses and you play.

INTERVIEWER

What did you study at college?

GARDNER

The usual things—wanted to major in chemistry for a while. In
graduate school I studied creative writing and medieval literature
mostly. It was useful. I learned a lot of things about an older kind of
literature that I thought would be handy in writing my own works, if
only because I wouldn't be doing the same thing as everybody else.

INTERVIEWER

Is your fiction at all autobiographical? Do you write about people
you know specifically, do you write about yourself?

GARDNER

Sometimes. My fiction is usually autobiographical, but in a distant,
almost unrecognizable way. Once in a while, as in the story "Redemption," I write pretty close to what happened. But I fictionalized
that too—which worries me, in fact. When you get to an event that
close to real life and you change the characters, you run the risk of
your sister, or your mother or father, thinking, You don't understand
me. That wasn't what I was thinking. I *know* that's not what they were
thinking, but I need searchlights on a piece, so I have to change characters, make them more appropriate to the fictional idea, the *real* subject, which isn't just history. Usually, though, I'm not interested—as
Updike and Malamud are—in celebrating my own life. I use feelings
that I have myself—the only feelings I know, directly—and I deal
them out to a group of characters and let the characters fight out the
problems that I've been fighting out. Characteristically there's a battle
in my fiction between the hunger for roots, stability, law, and another element in my character that is anarchic. I hate to obey speed laws. I hate
to park where it says you have to park. I hate to have to be someplace on

time. And in fact I often don't do those things I know I should do, which of course fills me with uneasiness and guilt. Every time you break the law you pay, and every time you obey the law you pay. That compulsion not to do what people tell me, to avoid tic repetitions, makes me constantly keep pushing the edges. It makes me change places of living or change my life in one way or another, which often makes me very unhappy. I wish I could just settle down. I keep promising myself that really soon now I'm going to get this little farm or maybe house and take care of it, never move again. But I'll probably never do it. Anyway, the autobiographical element is more emotional than anything else.

INTERVIEWER

How do you name your characters?

GARDNER

Sometimes I use characters from real life and sometimes I use their real names—when I do, it's always in celebration of people that I like. Once or twice, as in *October Light*, I've borrowed other people's fictional characters. Naming is only a problem, of course, when you make the character up. It seems to me that every character—every person—is an embodiment of a very complicated, philosophical way of looking at the world, whether conscious or not. Names can be strong clues to the character's system. Names are magic. If you name a kid John, he'll grow up a different kid than if you named him Rudolph. I've used real characters in every single novel, except in *Grendel*, where it's impossible—they didn't have our kinds of names in those days—but even in *Grendel* I used jokes and puns that give you clues to who I'm talking about. For instance, there's a guy named Red Horse, which is really a sorrel, which is really George Sorel. And so on. Sometimes I put real, live characters into books under fictional names—to protect the real person from what the fiction makes of him—and thus I get the pleasure of thinking, for example, what my cousin Bill would do if he were confronted with a particular problem. I get to understand my cousin Bill, whom I love, in a way I never understood him before. I get to see him in a situation perhaps more grave, certainly more compromising, than any he's ever been in. Besides using real people, as I've said, I get great pleasure out of stealing other people's writings. Actually, I do that at least partly because of a peculiar and unfortunate quality of my mind: I remember things. Word for word. I'm not always aware of it. Once, in college, I wrote a paragraph of a novel that was word for word out of Joyce's "The Dead," and I wasn't aware of it at all. I absolutely wasn't. My teacher at the time said, Why did you do this? He wasn't accusing me of plagiarism, he was just saying it was a very odd thing to do. I realized then that I had a problem. Of course, it was a big help when I was a teacher, because I could quote long passages of *Beowulf* and things like that. Once I realized that I also accidentally quote, that I'm constantly alluding to things I'm not consciously aware of, I began to develop this allusive technique—at least when it's fiction—so that nobody could accuse me of plagiarism, since it's so obvious that I'm alluding. In fact, sometimes I have great fun with it. Particularly in *Jason and Medeia*, where I took long sections of writing by Bill Gass, whom I'm enormously fond of, and with whom I completely disagree on almost everything unimportant, and altered a few words to mess up his argument. And in *The Wreckage of Agathon* I took long sections out of Jean-Paul Sartre, changed all the images, but kept the rest directly translated. So I use everything.

INTERVIEWER

How do your victims react? Is Sartre aware? Or Gass?

GARDNER

I'm sure Sartre has never heard of me. I hope he'd be amused. As for Gass, he knows why I do it: partly from impishness, partly for a comically noble reason that has to do with Gass's present and future fame.

INTERVIEWER

How do you react to Peter Prescott's insinuation in *Newsweek* that you plagiarized in your *Life and Times of Chaucer*?

GARDNER

With a sigh.

INTERVIEWER

How about the charge that you're, excuse the expression, a male chauvinist?

GARDNER

Consciously, I'm a feminist; but neither the best things we do or the worst are fully conscious. That's why the effect of art is so important. One does not consciously make oneself more bestial by reading pornographic books, and I think only the worst sort of people become consciously "better" people by reading the Bible. When I'm accused of male chauvinism, as I was in one review of *Nickel Mountain*, I'm indignant and hurt, but I watch myself more closely to see if it's true. I've also been accused of being antihomosexual. I'm glad I was accused, because although I wasn't aware of that bigotry, the accusation was just. I don't want to hurt people.

INTERVIEWER

What about the influences of being a teacher?

GARDNER

My academic career has, of course, had considerable influence on my writing of fiction and poetry, though I hope my writing has had no effect on my scholarship and teaching—except to boost my university salary, attract students I might otherwise not meet, and get me invited to visit now and then at other universities. When I first began teaching my main job was in creative writing, and I discovered very quickly that it's fairly easy to transform an eager, intelligent student to a publishing creative writer. Silly as it sounds, that discovery was a shock to my ego and changed my whole approach to writing fiction. I was twenty-four, twenty-five at the time. Since I found out that anyone has stories he can tell and, once you've shown him a little technique, can tell them relatively well, I was determined to set myself apart from the herd—I was reading that devil Nietzsche then—by writing as other people couldn't. I became a mildly fanatic stylist and an experimenter with form, and so on. Also, I quit teaching creative writing, maybe partly from annoyance that my students were as good as I was, but mainly in hopes of learning the things I had to know to become a good writer. I began teaching history of criticism courses, which turned out to be one of the most valuable experiences in my life.

INTERVIEWER

I don't mean to dwell on this, but it's obviously a subject you've thought about a lot. Any more specific effects of your teaching on your writing?

GARDNER

Two more, at least. One is, it's given me material—a lot of it—with which to give a modern story line resonance. For instance, though I don't mention it in the novel, Chief Fred Clumly in *Sunlight* once read Dante on a ship, though he no longer remembers it. It sank deep into the swamp of his mind and now throws strange light on his modern-seeming problems. The narrator of the novel has obviously read and pondered hard on Malory's *Morte D'Arthur*, which presents a medieval worldview totally opposed to Dante's. I mention this not because I care how readers read the novel but because it shows, more clearly than anything else I can say, the usefulness of my scholarly work in my writing. Nobody but Blake—except possibly Stanley Elkin—can churn up ideas and images with the genius of Blake. But stealing the ideas and images of brilliant men like Dante and Malory and of course many others, forcing them into confrontation, trying to find some sane resolution to the opposition of such minds and values, a writer can not only get new insights but get, far more important, rich texture and an energy of language beyond the energy of mere conflict in plot. Which is to say, my subject really is, as one critic once mentioned, human history—the conflict of ideas and emotions through the ages. The other important effect of my teaching on my writing is that, working with intelligent undergraduate and graduate students— and working alongside intelligent teachers—I have a clear idea of my audience, or anyway of a hypothetical audience. I don't think a writer can write well without some such notions. One may claim one writes for oneself, but it's a paltry claim.

One more word on all this: I'm obviously convinced that my scholarly career has made me a better writer than I would have been without it, but I'm no longer concerned—as I was in my tempestuous, ego-maddened youth—with proving myself the greatest writer of all time. What I notice now is that all around me there are first-rate writers, and in nearly every case it seems to me that what makes them first-rate is their similar involvement in teaching and scholarship. There are exceptions—maybe William Gaddis, I'm not sure. A brilliant writer, though I disapprove of him. Perhaps the most important exception is John Updike, who, unlike John Hawkes, Bill Gass, Stanley Elkin, and Saul Bellow and so on, is not a teacher. But the exception means nothing, because, teacher or not, he's the most academic of all.

INTERVIEWER

What about the teaching of creative writing?

GARDNER

When you teach creative writing, you discover a great deal. For instance, if a student's story is really wonderful but thin, you have to analyze to figure out why it's thin, how you could beef it up. Every discovery of that kind is important. When you're reading only classical and medieval literature, all the bad stuff has been filtered out. There are no bad works in either Greek or Anglo-Saxon. Even the ones that are minor are the very best of the minor, because everything else has been lost or burned or thrown away. When you read this kind of literature, you never really learn how a piece can go wrong, but when you teach creative writing, you see a thousand ways that a piece can go wrong. So it's helpful to me. The other thing that's helpful when you're teaching creative writing is that there are an awful lot of people who at the age of seventeen or eighteen can write as well as you do. That's a frightening discovery. So you ask yourself, What am I doing? Here I've decided that what I'm going to be in life is to be this literary artist, at best; I'm going to stand with Tolstoy, Melville, and all the boys. And there's this kid, nineteen, who's writing just as well. The characters are vividly perceived, the rhythm in the story is wonderful. What have I got that he hasn't got? You begin to think harder and harder about what makes great fiction. That can lead you to straining and overblowing your own fiction, which I've done sometimes, but it's useful to think about.

INTERVIEWER

What are some specific things you can teach in creative writing?

GARDNER

When you teach creative writing, you teach people, among other things, how to plot. You explain the principles, how it is that fiction *thinks*. And to give the kids a sense of how a plot works, you just spin out plot after plot after plot. In an hour session, you may spin out forty possible plots, one adhering to the real laws of *energeia*, each one a balance of the particular and general—and not one of them a story that you'd really want to write. Then one time, you hit one that *catches* you for some reason—you hit on the story that expresses your unrest. When I was teaching creative writing at Chico State, for instance, one of many plots I spun out was *The Resurrection*.

INTERVIEWER

How does this work?

GARDNER

One plot will just sort of rise above all the others for reasons that you don't fully understand. All of them are interesting, all of them have interesting characters, all of them talk about things that you could talk about, but one of them catches you like a nightmare. Then you have no choice but to write it—you can't forget it. It's a weird thing. If it's the kind of plot you really don't want to do because it involves your mother too closely, or whatever, you can try to do something else. But the typewriter keeps hissing at you and shooting sparks, and the paper keeps wrinkling and the lamp goes off and nothing else works, so finally you do the one that God said you've got to do. And once you do it, you're grounded. It's an amazing thing. For instance, before I wrote the story about the kid who runs over his younger brother ("Redemption"), always, regularly, every day I used to have four or five flashes of that accident. I'd be driving down the highway and I couldn't see what was coming because I'd have a memory flash. I haven't had it once since I wrote the story. You really do ground your nightmares, you name them. When you write a story, you have to play that image, no matter how painful, over and over until you've got all the sharp details so you know exactly how to put it down on paper. By the time you've run your mind through it a hundred times, relentlessly worked every tic of your terror, it's lost its power over you. That's what bibliotherapy is all about, I guess. You take crazy people and have them write their story, better and better, and soon it's just a story on a page, or, more precisely, everybody's story on a page. It's a wonderful thing. Which isn't to say that I think writing is done for the health of the writer, though it certainly does incidentally have that effect.

INTERVIEWER

Do you feel that literary techniques can really be taught? Some people feel that technique is an artifice or even a hindrance to true expression.

GARDNER

Certainly it can be taught. But a teacher has to *know* technique to teach it. I've seen a lot of writing teachers because I go around visiting colleges, visiting creative writing classes. A terrible number of awful ones, grotesquely bad. That doesn't mean that one should throw writing out of the curriculum, because when you get a good creative writing class it's magisterial. Most of the writers I know in the world don't know how they do what they do. Most of them feel it out. Bernard Malamud and I had a conversation one time in which he said that he doesn't know how he does those magnificent things he sometimes does. He just keeps writing until it comes out right. If that's the way a writer works, then that's the way he had to work, and that's fine. But I like to be in control as much of the time as possible. One of the first things you have to understand when you are writing fiction—or teaching writing—is that there are different ways of doing things, and each one has a slightly different effect. A misunderstanding of this leads you to the Bill Gass position: that fiction can't tell the truth, because every way you say the thing changes it. I don't think that's to the point. I think that what fiction does is sneak up on the truth by telling it six different ways and finally releasing it. That's what Dante said, that you can't really get at the poetic, inexpressible truths, that the way things are leaps up like steam between them. So you have to determine very accurately the potential of a particular writer's style and help that potential develop at the same time, ignoring what you think of his moral stands.

I hate nihilistic, cynical writing. I hate it. It bothers me and worse yet, bores me. But if I have a student who writes with morbid delight about murder, what I'll have to do—though of course I'll tell him I don't like this kind of writing, that it's immoral, stupid, and bad for civilization—is say what is successful about the work and what is not. I have to swallow every bit of my moral feelings to help the writer write his way, his truth. It may be that the most moral writing of all is writing that shows us how a murderer feels, how it happens. It may be it will protect us from murderers someday.

INTERVIEWER

You've recently had essays appear on the subject of what you call "moral fiction" and "moral criticism." Some readers might have trouble with the word *moral*. Could you explain what you mean by *moral*? The word, as you've acknowledged, has pejorative implications these days.

GARDNER

I know. It shouldn't. I certainly don't mean fiction that preaches. I'm talking mainly—though not exclusively—about works of fiction that are moral in their process. That is to say, the way they *work* is moral. Good works of fiction study values by testing them in imagined/real situations, testing them hard, being absolutely fair to both sides. The real moral writer is the opposite of the minister, the preacher, the rabbi. Insofar as he can, the preacher tries to keep religion as it always was, outlawing contraceptives or whatever; his job is conservative. The writer's job on the other hand, is to be radically open to persuasion. He should, if possible, not be committed to one side more than to the other—which is simply to say that he wants to affirm life, not sneer at it—but he has to be absolutely fair, understand the moral limits of his partisanship. His affirmation has to be earned. If he favors the cop, he must understand the arguments for life on the side of the robber.

INTERVIEWER

What would be "immoral" literature?

GARDNER

Mainly, fiction goes immoral when it stops being fair, when it stops trusting the laboratory experiment. You lie about characters, you make people do what you want them to do. This is characteristic of most hot-shot writers around now. I would agree with people who get nervous around the word *morality*, because usually the people who shout "immoral" are those who want to censor things, or think that all bathroom scenes or bedroom scenes or whatever are wicked. That kind of morality is life-denying, evil. But I *do* think morality is a real thing that's worth talking about. I thought of using some other word so that people wouldn't be mad at me for talking like a minister, but I decided that's the right word. It means what it means, and the fact that it's out of style doesn't matter very much. It's like patriotism, which has got a very bad name because devils keep yelling for it. Ultimately patriotism ought not to mean that you hate all other countries. It ought to mean that you love certain things about your country; you don't want them to change. Unfortunately, when you say "patriotism," everybody goes "aargh." Same thing with morality.

INTERVIEWER

Do you see the risk of dogmatism in your thesis on what fiction and criticism ought to be?

GARDNER

No, only a risk of dogmatism in stubborn or witless misinterpretations of my thesis, of which there have been, alas, many. I'm sure that no matter how carefully I write about true morality, some self-righteous ignoramus will read it too fast and say, Aha, he's on our side. He will use me to support awful ideas, and I'm sorry about that. I don't think real morality can ever be codified. You can't say, Thou shalt not, and you can't say, Thou shalt. What you *can* say is that this is how people feel and why they feel the way they do. My argument in *Moral Fiction* is this: that immoral fiction is indifferent to the real issues. I'm saying that there's good and evil. And in particular situations, maybe the only healthy situation is universal destruction. I would never set up a morality that's goody-goody. Sometimes morality is awful. Fiction can never pronounce ultimate solutions, but it can lead to understanding. It leads, and that's all. It gives visions of what's possible. If I were going to write a book that told people how to live, I would write an incredibly meticulous book about Indian gurus, Jewish heroes, Christian saints. I would present every right argument and show clearly and logically what the wrong sides are. It would be simple, except that logic is never to be trusted. And everybody who read my book would say, if I did my job brilliantly, that's the way to live. The trouble is they wouldn't read the book because it would be boring, and even if they did read and understand, they wouldn't be moved to action. The book wouldn't be interesting because it wouldn't show people we care about growing toward the truth. If you show characters struggling to know what's right, and in the process of the novel you work out their issues more and more clearly, whether the character heroically wins or tragically loses, *then* you move the reader, having first moved yourself. I think morality has to be persuasive. And you can only be persuasive if you start with imperfect human beings. Of course, if you wind up with *perfect* human beings, that's a bore too. I guess the morality of the fiction is the seriousness of the question and the seriousness of the concern with imaginary people's lives and feelings—a reflection of real people's lives and feelings—not the seriousness or logicality of the answer.

Should the writer examine the morality of a piece before, say, the quality of its prose, its interest and salability?

Certainly morality should come first—for writers, critics, and everybody else. People who change tires. People in factories. They should always ask, Is this moral? Not, Will it sell? If you're in construction and building houses out of shingles and you realize that you're wiping out ten thousand acres of Canadian pine every year, you should ask yourself, Can I make it cheaper or as cheaply out of clay? Because clay is inexhaustible. Every place there's dirt. A construction owner should say, I don't have to be committed to this particular product: I can go for the one that will make me money *and* make a better civilization. Occasionally businessmen actually do that. The best will even settle for a profit cut. The same thing is true of writers—ultimately it comes down to, are you making or are you destroying? If you try very hard to create ways of living, create dreams of what is possible, then you win. If you don't, you may make a fortune in ten years, but you're not going to be read in twenty years, and that's that. Why do something cheap? I can't understand people who go for the moment of the book. In the long run, Melville's estate is worth vastly more than the estate of Octave Thanet. Octave Thanet was, I think, the bestselling novelist of the nineteenth century. Melville told the truth, Thanet told high-minded lies. All liars are soon dead, forgotten. Dickens's novels didn't sell half as well as a novel of Octave Thanet's called *A Slave to Duty*. But you haven't heard of her, right? I know of her only because I know obscure facts.

And that is why certain works of fiction have lasted and others have disappeared?

GARDNER

Of course. So I believe. The ones that last are the ones that are true. You look at Faulkner and John O'Hara. John O'Hara outsold Faulkner, he circled Faulkner at the time they were writing. Ten years after his death, O'Hara's books are out of print. We all read Faulkner; nobody reads O'Hara. Dreiser in some ways, some of the time, is one of the worst writers who ever lived. *An American Tragedy*, for instance, is an endless book with terrible sentences like "He found her extremely intellectually interesting." But by the time you finish the book, you've sopped your vest. He's a great writer, though he wrote badly. But what he does morally, that is to say, what he does in terms of analysis of character and honest statement about the way the world is, is very good. Of course, some writers last a long time because of their brilliance, their style. Fitzgerald is a good example—a fine stylist. But he never quite got to the heart of things. *That's* what should concern the critics. If a critic is concerned with only how well the sentences go, or how neat the symbolic structure is, or how new the devices are, he's going to exaggerate the importance of mediocre books. Samuel Beckett—surely one of the great writers of our time, despite my objections—is loved by critics, but except for John Fowles, I hear no one pointing out that the tendency of all he says is wrong. He says it powerfully, with tragicomic brilliance, and he believes it, but what he says is not quite sound. Every night Samuel Beckett goes home to his wife, whom he's lived with all these years, he lies down in bed with her, puts his arms around her, and says, No meaning again today . . . Critics can say, and do say, Well, it doesn't matter what he says, it's how well he says it. But I think in the long run Beckett is in for it. Because great writers tell the truth exactly—and get it right. A man can be a brilliant writer who writes wonderful lines and still say what is just not so, like Sartre, Beckett, and, in his lapses, Faulkner. Faulkner's sentimentality in the bad moments—every reader knows he's missing a little. I like Dilsey. I believe Dilsey really exists, but I just don't believe that Faulkner understands her or really cares. He's more interested in Dilsey as a symbol than as a person. Everything that Faulkner says about Dilsey is no doubt true . . . it's just all those things he didn't say, the things that make her fully human, not just a symbol. Mythologizing her—or accepting the standard mythology of his age—he slightly skews the inevitability of his story. He does the same thing every time he turns on his mannered rhetoric—distorts the inherent emotion of the story and thus gets diverted from the real and inevitable progress of events.

INTERVIEWER

You've said there are exceptions to your thesis on moral fiction. Could you mention a few?

GARDNER

First, there's fiction that's neither moral nor immoral—minor fiction, pure entertainment. I'm accused of not valuing it, but actually all I say is that it's trivial: I'm not at all against it except when some critic takes it seriously. I favor it as on a hot day I favor ice cream. Second, there's fiction I'd call moral only in the earnestness of its concern. This kind of fiction I would *not* call trivial. There's one man whose name is Ernest Finney. He's a wonderful writer. He sent me his fiction, he's been writing for years, unpublished. He writes grim, frightening stories. But I would certainly publish them if I had a magazine. Absolutely no question. One is about a lower-class guy, tough; he's got a good car, a T-Bird, third-hand. He marries this beautiful girl who's kind of a whore. She finally gets his money and disappears. He's making his money stealing. He goes to prison. All the time he's in prison, he plans on killing her. That's all he cares about, that's all he thinks about. His idea is to put a shotgun up her and blow her to smithereens. You understand exactly why he feels the way he does. It's a very powerful, terrifying story. Because you become the character. You would do it too.

INTERVIEWER

How does this fit any standard we've talked about?

GARDNER

Well, I think it's moral fiction, but in a tricky way. Finney does honestly describe a situation. He's not looking for ways that we could live better—the highest way—but he's describing exactly, and with original genius, how it feels to want to kill your wife. Terribly difficult. It's moral fiction of the third degree. Moral fiction can exist in only three forms. The highest form is moral fiction in which you see absolutely accurate description of the best people, fiction that gives you an idea how to live. It's uplifting. You want to be like the hero. You want to be like Jesus, or Buddha, or Moses, whatever. Tolstoy does it. Everybody wants to be like Pierre in *War and Peace*. Everybody wants to be like Levin in *Anna Karenina*. In the next form of moral fiction you see an evil person and you realize you don't want to be like that. Like Macbeth. You see there's an alternative. You don't have to be like Macbeth. It's kind of negative moral fiction, or moral fiction in the tragic mode, where you want to be different than the protagonist—you want to be better. Then there's the third form, wherein alternatives don't exist. Not for fashion's sake or for the cheap love of gruesomeness, but from anger and concern, you stare into the smoking volcano. That's the world of Ernest Finney's fiction, or Constance Urdgang's. You understand exactly why a wife would want to kill her husband, saw up the body, and put it in a suitcase. We've all read the newspaper stories about this kind of thing. It happens. But only a great artist can show it happen so that you feel that you saw it, and saw it from inside the murderer's mind: you understand. That doesn't tell you what you should do. It doesn't tell you, I don't want to be like that. But it makes you understand and, understanding, hunger for a world not like this. It's obviously the least uplifting of the three kinds of moral fiction, but it's morally useful. Mostly what we get, it seems to me, is serious fiction not in any of those three categories. People kill people, we don't understand why they did it, we don't care why they did it, we read it because it's cheaply thrilling, an escape from the common decency we sometimes feel trapped in. Blood drips, people piss on people or live their boring lives of quiet desperation. It's at worst a kind of sick daydream, at best useless actuality, not morally worth reading.

INTERVIEWER

What effect do you think your writing has had?

GARDNER

I think it has given a few readers pleasure. And I suppose it may have depressed a few. I hope it does more good than harm.

Issue 75, 1979

Gabriel García Márquez

The Art of Fiction

Gabriel García Márquez was interviewed in his studio/office located just behind his house in San Angel Inn, an old and lovely section, full of Mexico City's spectacularly colorful flowers. The studio is a short walk from the main house. A low elongated building, it appears to have been originally designed as a guest house. Within, at one end, are a couch, two easy chairs, and a makeshift bar—a small white refrigerator with a supply of acqua minerale on top. The most striking feature of the room is a large blown-up photograph above the sofa of García Márquez alone, wearing a stylish cape and standing on some windswept vista looking somewhat like Anthony Quinn.

García Márquez was sitting at his desk at the far end of the studio. He came to greet me, walking briskly with a light step. He is a solidly built man, only about five feet eight or nine in height, who looks like a good middleweight fighter—broad-chested, but perhaps a bit thin in the legs. He was dressed casually in corduroy slacks with a light turtleneck sweater and black leather boots. His hair is dark and curly brown, and he wears a full mustache.

The interview took place over the course of three late-afternoon meetings of roughly two hours each. Although his English is quite good, García Márquez spoke mostly in Spanish and his two sons shared the translating. When García Márquez speaks, his body often rocks back and forth. His hands too are often in motion, making small but decisive gestures to emphasize a point, or to indicate a shift of direction in his thinking. He alternates between leaning forward toward

El otoño del Patriarca

mustios

pagaron

había hecho

lo sabíamos porque

de los soldados

y sin embargo

civil

era

callejero que por cinco centavos recitaba los versos del
olvidado poeta Rubén Darío y había vuelto feliz con una
morrocota legítima con que le ~~habían premiado~~ un recital que ~~hizo~~ sólo para él, aunque no lo había visto por
supuesto, no porque fuera ciego sino porque ningún mortal lo había visto desde los tiempos del vómito negro,
~~pero~~ sabíamos que él estaba ahí, ~~puesto que~~ el mundo
seguía, la vida seguía, el correo llegaba, la banda muni-
cipal tocaba la retreta de valses bobos bajo las palmeras
polvorientas y los faroles ~~pálidos~~ de la Plaza de Armas,
y otros músicos viejos reemplazaban en la banda a los
músicos muertos. En los últimos años, cuando no se vol-
vieron a oír ruidos humanos ni cantos de pájaros en el
interior y se cerraron para siempre los portones blinda-
dos, sabíamos que había alguien en la casa ~~presidencial~~
porque de noche se veían luces que parecían de navega-
ción a través de las ventanas del lado del mar, y quienes
se atrevieron a acercarse oyeron desastres de pezuñas y
suspiros de animal grande detrás de las paredes fortifi-
cadas, y una tarde de enero habíamos visto una vaca
contemplando el crepúsculo desde el balcón presidencial,
imagínese, una vaca en el balcón de la patria, qué cosa
más inicua, qué país de mierda, pero se hicieron tantas
conjeturas de cómo ~~era~~ posible que una vaca llegara
hasta un balcón si todo el mundo sabía que las vacas
no se trepaban por las escaleras, y menos si eran de
piedra, y mucho menos si estaban alfombradas, que al
final no supimos si en realidad la vimos o si era que
pasamos una tarde por la Plaza de Armas y habíamos
soñado caminando que habíamos visto ~~una vaca en un~~
~~balcón presidencial, y desde entonces nada se volvió a~~
~~ver ni nada se volvió a oír en muchos años, sólo la bon-~~
~~dada densa de gallinazos que vinieron de donde estaban~~

una vaca en un
balcón presiden-
cial donde nada
se había visto ni
había de verse
otra vez en mu-
chos años hasta
el amanecer del
último viernes
cuando empeza-
ron a llegar
los primeros ga-
llinazos que se
alzaron de don-
de estaban

~~cambió~~ también nosotros
nos atrevimos
a entrar

santuario

siempre adormilados en la cornisa del hospital de po-
bres, vinieron más de tierra adentro, vinieron en oleadas
sucesivas desde el horizonte del mar de polvo donde es-
tuvo el mar, volaron todo un día en círculos lentos sobre
la casa del poder hasta que un rey con plumas de novia
y golilla encarnada impartió una orden silenciosa y em-
pezó aquel estropicio de vidrios, aquel viento de muerto
grande, aquel entrar y salir de gallinazos por las ventanas como sólo era concebible en una casa sin autoridad,
de modo que ~~subimos hasta la colina~~ y encontramos en
el ~~interior~~ desierto los escombros de la grandeza, el
cuerpo picoteado, las manos lisas de doncella con el ani-
llo del poder en el hueso anular, y tenía todo el cuerpo
retoñado de líquenes minúsculos y animales parasitarios
de fondo de mar, sobre todo en las axilas y en las ingles,
y tenía el braguero de lona en el testículo herniado que
era lo único que habían eludido los gallinazos a pesar
de ser tan grande como un riñón de buey, pero ni si-
quiera entonces nos atrevimos a creer en su muerte porque era la segunda vez que lo encontraban en aquella
oficina, solo y vestido, y muerto al parecer de muerte
natural durante el sueño, como estaba anunciado desde
hacía muchos años en las aguas premonitorias de los
lebrillos de las pitonisas. La primera vez que lo encon-
traron, en el principio de su otoño, la nación estaba toda-
vía bastante viva como para que él se sintiera amenazado

A manuscript page from The Autumn of the Patriarch
by Gabriel García Márquez.

his listener and sitting far back with his legs crossed when speaking reflectively.

—Peter H. Stone, 1981

INTERVIEWER

How do you feel about using the tape recorder?

GABRIEL GARCÍA MÁRQUEZ

The problem is that the moment you know the interview is being taped, your attitude changes. In my case I immediately take a defensive attitude. As a journalist, I feel that we still haven't learned how to use a tape recorder to do an interview. The best way, I feel, is to have a long conversation without the journalist taking any notes. Then afterward he should reminisce about the conversation and write it down as an impression of what he felt, not necessarily using the exact words expressed. Another useful method is to take notes and then interpret them with a certain loyalty to the person interviewed. What ticks you off about the tape recording everything is that it is not loyal to the person who is being interviewed, because it even records and remembers when you make an ass of yourself. That's why when there is a tape recorder, I am conscious that I'm being interviewed; when there isn't a tape recorder, I talk in an unconscious and completely natural way.

INTERVIEWER

Well, you make me feel a little guilty using it, but I think for this kind of an interview we probably need it.

GARCÍA MÁRQUEZ

Anyway, the whole purpose of what I just said was to put you on the defensive.

INTERVIEWER

So you have never used a tape recorder yourself for an interview?

GARCÍA MÁRQUEZ

As a journalist, I never use it. I have a very good tape recorder, but I just use it to listen to music. But then as a journalist I've never done an interview. I've done reports, but never an interview with questions and answers.

INTERVIEWER

I heard about one famous interview with a sailor who had been shipwrecked.

GARCÍA MÁRQUEZ

It wasn't questions and answers. The sailor would just tell me his adventures and I would rewrite them trying to use his own words and in the first person, as if he were the one who was writing. When the work was published as a serial in a newspaper, one part each day for two weeks, it was signed by the sailor, not by me. It wasn't until twenty years later that it was republished and people found out I had written it. No editor realized that it was good until after I had written *One Hundred Years of Solitude*.

INTERVIEWER

Since we've started talking about journalism, how does it feel being a journalist again, after having written novels for so long? Do you do it with a different feel or a different eye?

GARCÍA MÁRQUEZ

I've always been convinced that my true profession is that of a journalist. What I didn't like about journalism before were the working conditions. Besides, I had to condition my thoughts and ideas to the interests of the newspaper. Now, having worked as a novelist and having achieved financial independence as a novelist, I can really choose the themes that interest me and correspond to my ideas. In any case, I always very much enjoy the chance of doing a great piece of journalism.

INTERVIEWER

What is a great piece of journalism for you?

GARCÍA MÁRQUEZ

Hiroshima by John Hersey was an exceptional piece.

INTERVIEWER

Is there a story today that you would especially like to do?

GARCÍA MÁRQUEZ

There are many, and several I have in fact written. I have written about Portugal, Cuba, Angola, and Vietnam. I would very much like to write on Poland. I think if I could describe exactly what is now going on, it would be a very important story. But it's too cold now in Poland; I'm a journalist who likes his comforts.

INTERVIEWER

Do you think the novel can do certain things that journalism can't?

GARCÍA MÁRQUEZ

Nothing. I don't think there is any difference. The sources are the same, the material is the same, the resources and the language are the same. *A Journal of the Plague Year* by Daniel Defoe is a great novel and *Hiroshima* is a great work of journalism.

INTERVIEWER

Do the journalist and the novelist have different responsibilities in balancing truth versus the imagination?

GARCÍA MÁRQUEZ

In journalism just one fact that is false prejudices the entire work. In contrast, in fiction one single fact that is true gives legitimacy to the entire work. That's the only difference, and it lies in the commitment of the writer. A novelist can do anything he wants so long as he makes people believe in it.

INTERVIEWER

In interviews a few years ago, you seemed to look back on being a journalist with awe at how much faster you were then.

GARCÍA MÁRQUEZ

I do find it harder to write now than before, both novels and journalism. When I worked for newspapers, I wasn't very conscious of every word I wrote, whereas now I am. When I was working for *El Espectador* in Bogotá, I used to do at least three stories a week, two or three editorial notes every day, and I did movie reviews. Then at night, after everyone had gone home, I would stay behind writing my novels. I liked the noise of the Linotype machines, which sounded like rain. If they stopped, and I was left in silence, I wouldn't be able to work. Now, the output is comparatively small. On a good working day, working from nine o'clock in the morning to two or three in the afternoon, the most I can write is a short paragraph of four or five lines, which I usually tear up the next day.

INTERVIEWER

Does this change come from your works being so highly praised or from some kind of political commitment?

GARCÍA MÁRQUEZ

It's from both. I think that the idea that I'm writing for many more people than I ever imagined has created a certain general responsibility that is literary and political. There's even pride involved, in not wanting to fall short of what I did before.

INTERVIEWER

How did you start writing?

GARCÍA MÁRQUEZ

By drawing, by drawing cartoons. Before I could read or write I used to draw comics at school and at home. The funny thing is that I now realize that when I was in high school I had the reputation of being a writer, though I never in fact wrote anything. If there was a pamphlet to be written or a letter of petition, I was the one to do it because I was supposedly the writer. When I entered college I happened to have a very good literary background in general, considerably above the average of my friends. At the university in Bogotá, I started making new friends and acquaintances, who introduced me to contemporary writers. One night a friend lent me a book of short stories by Franz Kafka. I went back to the pension where I was staying and began to read "The Metamorphosis." The first line almost knocked me off the bed. I was so surprised. The first line reads, "When Gregor Samsa woke up one morning from unsettling dreams, he found himself changed in his bed into a monstrous vermin. . . ." When I read the line I thought to myself that I didn't know anyone was allowed to write things like that. If I had known, I would have started writing a long time ago. So I immediately started writing short stories. They are totally intellectual short stories because I was writing them on the basis of my literary experience and had not yet found the link between literature and life. The stories were published in the literary supplement of the newspaper *El Espectador* in Bogotá and they did have a certain success at the time—probably because nobody in Colombia was writing intellectual short stories. What was being written then was mostly about life in the countryside and social life. When I wrote my first short stories I was told they had Joycean influences.

INTERVIEWER

Had you read Joyce at that time?

GARCÍA MÁRQUEZ

I had never read Joyce, so I started reading *Ulysses*. I read it in the only Spanish edition available. Since then, after having read *Ulysses* in English as well as a very good French translation, I can see that the original Spanish translation was very bad. But I did learn something that was to be very useful to me in my future writing—the technique of the interior monologue. I later found this in Virginia Woolf, and I like the way she uses it better than Joyce. Although I later realized that the person who invented this interior monologue was the anonymous writer of the *Lazarillo de Tormes*.

INTERVIEWER

Can you name some of your early influences?

GARCÍA MÁRQUEZ

The people who really helped me to get rid of my intellectual attitude toward the short story were the writers of the American Lost Generation. I realized that their literature had a relationship with life that my short stories didn't. And then an event took place that was very important with respect to this attitude. It was the Bogotazo, on April 9, 1948, when a political leader, Gaitan, was shot and the people of Bogotá went raving mad in the streets. I was in my pension ready to have lunch when I heard the news. I ran toward the place, but Gaitan had just been put into a taxi and was being taken to a hospital. On my way back to the pension, the people had already taken to the streets and they were demonstrating, looting stores, and burning buildings. I joined them. That afternoon and evening, I became aware of the kind of country I was living in, and how little my short stories had to do with any of that. When I was later forced to go back to Barranquilla on the Caribbean, where I had spent my childhood, I realized that that was the type of life I had lived, known, and wanted to write about.

Around 1950 or '51 another event happened that influenced my literary tendencies. My mother asked me to accompany her to Aracataca, where I was born, and to sell the house where I spent my first years. When I got there it was at first quite shocking because I was now twenty-two and hadn't been there since the age of eight. Nothing had really changed, but I felt that I wasn't really looking at the village, but I was *experiencing* it as if I were reading it. It was as if everything I saw had already been written, and all I had to do was to sit down and copy what was already there and what I was just reading. For all practical purposes everything had evolved into literature: the houses, the people, and the memories. I'm not sure whether I had already read Faulkner or not, but I know now that only a technique like Faulkner's could have enabled me to write down what I was seeing. The atmosphere, the decadence, the heat in the village were roughly the same as what I had felt in Faulkner. It was a banana-plantation region inhabited by a lot of Americans from the fruit companies, which gave it the same sort of atmosphere I had found in the writers of the Deep South. Critics have spoken of the literary influence of Faulkner, but I see it as a coincidence: I had simply found material that had to be dealt with in the same way that Faulkner had treated similar material.

From that trip to the village I came back to write *Leaf Storm*, my first novel. What really happened to me in that trip to Aracataca was that I realized that everything that had occurred in my childhood had a literary value that I was only now appreciating. From the moment I wrote *Leaf Storm* I realized I wanted to be a writer and that nobody could stop me and that the only thing left for me to do was to try to be the best writer in the world. That was in 1953, but it wasn't until 1967 that I got my first royalties after having written five of my eight books.

INTERVIEWER

Do you think that it's common for young writers to deny the worth of their own childhoods and experiences and to intellectualize, as you did initially?

GARCÍA MÁRQUEZ

No, the process usually takes place the other way around, but if I had to give a young writer some advice I would say to write about something that has happened to him; it's always easy to tell whether a writer is writing about something that has happened to him or something he has read or been told. Pablo Neruda has a line in a poem that says God help me from inventing when I sing. It always amuses me that the biggest praise for my work comes for the imagination, while the truth is that there's not a single line in all my work that does not have a basis in reality. The problem is that Caribbean reality resembles the wildest imagination.

INTERVIEWER

Whom were you writing for at this point? Who was your audience?

GARCÍA MÁRQUEZ

Leaf Storm was written for my friends who were helping me and lending me their books and were very enthusiastic about my work. In general I think you usually do write for someone. When I'm writing I'm always aware that this friend is going to like this, or that another friend is going to like that paragraph or chapter, always thinking of specific people. In the end all books are written for your friends. The problem after writing *One Hundred Years of Solitude* was that now I no longer know whom of the millions of readers I am writing for; this upsets and inhibits me. It's like a million eyes are looking at you and you don't really know what they think.

INTERVIEWER

What about the influence of journalism on your fiction?

GARCÍA MÁRQUEZ

I think the influence is reciprocal. Fiction has helped my journalism because it has given it literary value. Journalism has helped my fiction because it has kept me in a close relationship with reality.

INTERVIEWER

How would you describe the search for a style that you went through after *Leaf Storm* and before you were able to write *One Hundred Years of Solitude*?

GARCÍA MÁRQUEZ

After having written *Leaf Storm*, I decided that writing about the village and my childhood was really an escape from having to face and write about the political reality of the country. I had the false impression that I was hiding myself behind this kind of nostalgia instead of confronting the political things that were going on. This was the time when the relationship between literature and politics was very much discussed. I kept trying to close the gap between the two. My influence had been Faulkner; now it was Hemingway. I wrote *No One Writes to the Colonel*, *In Evil Hour*, and *Big Mama's Funeral*, which were all written at more or less the same time and have many things in common. These stories take place in a different village from the one in which *Leaf Storm* and *One Hundred Years of Solitude* occur. It is a village in which there is no magic. It is a journalistic literature. But when I finished *In Evil Hour*, I saw that all my views were wrong again. I came to see that in fact my writings about my childhood were *more* political and had more to do with the reality of my country than I had thought. After *The Evil Hour* I did not write anything for five years. I had an idea of what I always wanted to do, but there was something missing and I was not sure what it was until one day I discovered the right tone—the tone that I eventually used in *One Hundred Years of Solitude*. It was based on the way my grandmother used to tell her stories. She told things that sounded supernatural and fantastic, but she told them with complete naturalness. When I finally discovered the tone I had to use, I sat down for eighteen months and worked every day.

INTERVIEWER

How did she express the fantastic so naturally?

GARCÍA MÁRQUEZ

What was most important was the expression she had on her face. She did not change her expression at all when telling her stories, and everyone was surprised. In previous attempts to write *One Hundred Years of Solitude*, I tried to tell the story without believing in it. I discovered that what I had to do was believe in them myself and write them with the same expression with which my grandmother told them: with a brick face.

INTERVIEWER

There also seems to be a journalistic quality to that technique or tone. You describe seemingly fantastic events in such minute detail that it gives them their own reality. Is this something you have picked up from journalism?

GARCÍA MÁRQUEZ

That's a journalistic trick that you can also apply to literature. For example, if you say that there are elephants flying in the sky, people are not going to believe you. But if you say that there are four hundred and twenty-five elephants flying in the sky, people will probably believe you. *One Hundred Years of Solitude* is full of that sort of thing. That's exactly the technique my grandmother used. I remember particularly the story about the character who is surrounded by yellow butterflies. When I was very small there was an electrician who came to the house. I became very curious because he carried a belt with which he used to suspend himself from the electrical posts. My grandmother used to say that every time this man came around, he would leave the house full of butterflies. But when I was writing this, I discovered that if I didn't say the butterflies were yellow, people would not believe it. When I was writing the episode of Remedios the Beauty going to heaven, it took me a long time to make it credible. One day I went out to the garden and saw a woman who used to come to the house to do the wash and she was putting out the sheets to dry and there was a lot of wind. She was arguing with the wind not to blow the sheets away. I discovered that if I used the sheets for Remedios the Beauty, she would ascend. That's how I did it, to make it credible. The problem for every writer is credibility. Anybody can write anything so long as it's believed.

INTERVIEWER

What was the origin of the insomnia plague in *One Hundred Years of Solitude*?

GARCÍA MÁRQUEZ

Beginning with Oedipus, I've always been interested in plagues. I have studied a lot about medieval plagues. One of my favorite books is *A Journal of the Plague Year* by Daniel Defoe, among other reasons because Defoe is a journalist who sounds like what he is saying is pure fantasy. For many years I thought Defoe had written about the London plague as he observed it. But then I discovered it was a novel, because

Defoe was less than seven years old when the plague occurred in London. Plagues have always been one of my recurrent themes—and in different forms. In *The Evil Hour*, the pamphlets are plagues. For many years I thought that the political violence in Colombia had the same metaphysics as the plague. Before *One Hundred Years of Solitude*, I had used a plague to kill all the birds in a story called "One Day After Saturday." In *One Hundred Years of Solitude* I used the insomnia plague as something of a literary trick, since it's the opposite of the sleeping plague. Ultimately, literature is nothing but carpentry.

INTERVIEWER

Can you explain that analogy a little more?

GARCÍA MÁRQUEZ

Both are very hard work. Writing something is almost as hard as making a table. With both you are working with reality, a material just as hard as wood. Both are full of tricks and techniques. Basically very little magic and a lot of hard work are involved. And as Proust, I think, said, it takes ten percent inspiration and ninety percent perspiration. I never have done any carpentry, but it's the job I admire most, especially because you can never find anyone to do it for you.

INTERVIEWER

What about the banana fever in *One Hundred Years of Solitude*? How much of that is based on what the United Fruit Company did?

GARCÍA MÁRQUEZ

The banana fever is modeled closely on reality. Of course, I've used literary tricks on things that have not been proved historically. For example, the massacre in the square is completely true, but while I wrote it on the basis of testimony and documents, it was never known exactly how many people were killed. I used the figure three thousand, which is obviously an exaggeration. But one of my childhood memories was watching a very, very long train leave the plantation supposedly full of bananas. There could have been three thousand dead on it, eventually to be dumped in the sea. What's really surprising is that now they speak very naturally in Congress and the newspapers about the "three thousand dead." I suspect that half of all our history is made in this fashion. In *The Autumn of the Patriarch*, the dictator says it doesn't matter if it's not true now, because sometime in the future it will be true. Sooner or later people believe writers rather than the government.

INTERVIEWER

That makes the writer pretty powerful, doesn't it?

GARCÍA MÁRQUEZ

Yes, and I can feel it too. It gives me a great sense of responsibility. What I would really like to do is a piece of journalism that is completely true and real, but that sounds as fantastic as *One Hundred Years of Solitude*. The more I live and remember things from the past, the more I think that literature and journalism are closely related.

INTERVIEWER

What about a country giving up its sea for its foreign debt, as in *The Autumn of the Patriarch*?

GARCÍA MÁRQUEZ

Yes, but that actually happened. It's happened and will happen many times more. *The Autumn of the Patriarch* is a completely historical book. To find probabilities out of real facts is the work of the journalist and the novelist, and it is also the work of the prophet. The trouble is that many people believe that I'm a writer of fantastic fiction, when actually I'm a very realistic person and write what I believe is the true socialist realism.

INTERVIEWER

Is it utopian?

GARCÍA MÁRQUEZ

I'm not sure if the word *utopian* means the real or the ideal. But I think it's the real.

INTERVIEWER

Are the characters in *The Autumn of the Patriarch*, the dictators, for example, modeled after real people? There seem to be similarities with Franco, Perón, and Trujillo.

GARCÍA MÁRQUEZ

In every novel, the character is a collage: a collage of different characters that you've known, or heard about or read about. I read everything that I could find about Latin American dictators of the last century, and the beginning of this one. I also talked to a lot of people who had lived under dictatorships. I did that for at least ten years. And when I had a clear idea of what the character was going to be like, I made an effort to forget everything I had read and heard, so that I could invent, without using any situation that had occurred in real life. I realized at one point that I myself had not lived for any period of time under a dictatorship, so I thought if I wrote the book in Spain, I could see what the atmosphere was like living in an established dictatorship. But I found that the atmosphere was very different in Spain under Franco from that of a Caribbean dictatorship. So the book was kind of blocked for about a year. There was something missing and I wasn't sure what it was. Then overnight, I decided that the best thing was that we come back to the Caribbean. So we all moved back to Barranquilla in Colombia. I made a statement to the journalists that they thought was a joke. I said that I was coming back because I had forgotten what a guava smelled like. In truth, it was what I really needed to finish my book. I took a trip through the Caribbean. As I went from island to island, I found the elements that were the ones that had been lacking from my novel.

INTERVIEWER

You often use the theme of the solitude of power.

GARCÍA MÁRQUEZ

The more power you have, the harder it is to know who is lying to you and who is not. When you reach absolute power, there is no contact with reality, and that's the worst kind of solitude there can be. A very powerful person, a dictator, is surrounded by interests and people whose final aim is to isolate him from reality; everything is in concert to isolate him.

INTERVIEWER

What about the solitude of the writer? Is this different?

GARCÍA MÁRQUEZ

It has a lot to do with the solitude of power. The writer's very attempt to portray reality often leads him to a distorted view of it. In trying to transpose reality he can end up losing contact with it—in an ivory tower, as they say. Journalism is a very good guard against that. That's why I have always tried to keep on doing journalism, because it keeps me in contact with the real world, particularly political journalism and politics. The solitude that threatened me after *One Hundred Years of Solitude* wasn't the solitude of the writer; it was the solitude of fame, which resembles the solitude of power much more. My friends defended me from that one, my friends who are always there.

INTERVIEWER

How?

GARCÍA MÁRQUEZ

Because I have managed to keep the same friends all my life. I mean I don't break or cut myself off from my old friends, and they're the ones who bring me back to earth; they always keep their feet on the ground, and they're not famous.

INTERVIEWER

How do things start? One of the recurring images in *The Autumn of the Patriarch* is the cows in the palace. Was this one of the original images?

GARCÍA MÁRQUEZ

I've got a photography book that I'm going to show you. I've said on various occasions that in the genesis of all my books there's always an image. The first image I had of *The Autumn of the Patriarch* was a very old man in a very luxurious palace into which cows come and eat the curtains. But that image didn't concretize until I saw the photograph. In Rome I went into a bookshop where I started looking at photography books, which I like to collect. I saw this photograph, and it was just perfect. I just saw that was how it was going to be. Since I'm not a big intellectual, I can find my antecedents in everyday things, in life, and not in the great masterpieces.

INTERVIEWER

Do your novels ever take unexpected twists?

GARCÍA MÁRQUEZ

That used to happen to me in the beginning. In the first stories I wrote I had a general idea of the mood, but I would let myself be taken by chance. The best advice I was given early on was that it was all right to work that way when I was young because I had a torrent of inspiration. But I was told that if I didn't learn technique, I would be in trouble later on when the inspiration had gone and the technique was needed to compensate. If I hadn't learned that in time, I would not now be able to outline a structure in advance. Structure is a purely technical problem, and if you don't learn it early on you'll never learn it.

INTERVIEWER

Discipline then is quite important to you?

GARCÍA MÁRQUEZ

I don't think you can write a book that's worth anything without extraordinary discipline.

INTERVIEWER

What about artificial stimulants?

GARCÍA MÁRQUEZ

One thing that Hemingway wrote that greatly impressed me was that writing for him was like boxing. He took care of his health and his well-being. Faulkner had a reputation of being a drunkard, but in every interview that he gave he said that it was impossible to write one line when drunk. Hemingway said this too. Bad readers have asked me if I was drugged when I wrote some of my works. But that illustrates that they don't know anything about literature or drugs. To be a good writer you have to be absolutely lucid at every moment of writing, and in good health. I'm very much against the romantic concept of writing, which maintains that the act of writing is a sacrifice, and that the worse the economic conditions or the emotional state, the better the writing. I think you have to be in a very good emotional and physical state. Literary creation for me requires good health, and the Lost Generation understood this. They were people who loved life.

INTERVIEWER

Blaise Cendrars said that writing is a privilege compared to most work, and that writers exaggerate their suffering. What do you think?

GARCÍA MÁRQUEZ

I think that writing is very difficult, but so is any job carefully executed. What is a privilege, however, is to do a job to your own satisfaction. I think that I'm excessively demanding of myself and others because I cannot tolerate errors; I think that it is a privilege to do anything to a perfect degree. It is true though that writers are often megalomaniacs and they consider themselves to be the center of the universe and society's conscience. But what I most admire is something well done. I'm always very happy when I'm traveling to know that the pilots are better pilots than I am a writer.

INTERVIEWER

When do you work best now? Do you have a work schedule?

GARCÍA MÁRQUEZ

When I became a professional writer the biggest problem I had was my schedule. Being a journalist meant working at night. When I started writing full-time I was forty years old, my schedule was basically from nine o'clock in the morning until two in the afternoon when my sons came back from school. Since I was so used to hard work, I felt guilty that I was only working in the morning; so I tried to work in the afternoons, but I discovered that what I did in the afternoon had to be done over again the next morning. So I decided that I would just work from nine until two-thirty and not do anything else. In the afternoons I have appointments and interviews and anything else that might come up. I have another problem in that I can only work in surroundings that are familiar and have already been warmed up with my work. I cannot write in hotels or borrowed rooms or on borrowed typewriters. This creates problems because when I travel I can't work. Of course, you're always trying to find a pretext to work less. That's why the conditions you impose on yourself are more difficult all the time. You hope for inspiration whatever the circumstances. That's a word the romantics exploited a lot. My Marxist comrades have a lot of difficulty accepting the word, but whatever you call it, I'm convinced that there is a special state of mind in which you can write with great ease and things just flow. All the pretexts—such as the one where you can only write at home—disappear. That moment and that state of mind seem to come when you have found the right theme and the right ways of treating it. And it has to be something you really like too, because there is no worse job than doing something you don't like.

One of the most difficult things is the first paragraph. I have spent many months on a first paragraph, and once I get it, the rest just comes out very easily. In the first paragraph you solve most of the problems with your book. The theme is defined, the style, the tone. At least, in my case, the first paragraph is a kind of sample of what the rest of the book is going to be. That's why writing a book of short stories is much more difficult than writing a novel. Every time you write a short story, you have to begin all over again.

INTERVIEWER

Are dreams ever important as a source of inspiration?

GARCÍA MÁRQUEZ

In the very beginning I paid a good deal of attention to them. But then I realized that life itself is the greatest source of inspiration, and that dreams are only a very small part of that torrent that is life. What is very true about my writing is that I'm quite interested in different concepts of dreams and interpretations of them. I see dreams as part of life in general, but reality is much richer. But maybe I just have very poor dreams.

INTERVIEWER

Can you distinguish between inspiration and intuition?

GARCÍA MÁRQUEZ

Inspiration is when you find the right theme, one that you really like; that makes the work much easier. Intuition, which is also fundamental to writing fiction, is a special quality that helps you to decipher what is real without needing scientific knowledge or any other special kind of learning. The laws of gravity can be figured out much more easily with intuition than anything else. It's a way of having experience without having to struggle through it. For a novelist, intuition is essential. Basically it's contrary to intellectualism, which is probably the thing that I detest most in the world—in the sense that the real world is turned into a kind of immovable theory. Intuition has the advantage that either it is, or it isn't. You don't struggle to try to put a round peg into a square hole.

INTERVIEWER

Is it the theorists that you dislike?

GARCÍA MÁRQUEZ

Exactly. Chiefly because I cannot really understand them. That's mainly why I have to explain most things through anecdotes, because

I don't have any capacity for abstractions. That's why many critics say that I'm not a cultured person; I don't quote enough.

Do you think that critics type you or categorize you too neatly?

Critics for me are the biggest example of what intellectualism is. First of all, they have a theory of what a writer should be. They try to get the writer to fit their model, and if he doesn't fit, they still try to get him in by force. I'm only answering this because you've asked. I really have no interest in what critics think of me; nor have I read critics in many years. They have claimed for themselves the task of being intermediaries between the author and the reader. I've always tried to be a very clear and precise writer, trying to reach the reader directly without having to go through the critic.

How do you regard translators?

I have great admiration for translators, except for the ones who use footnotes. They are always trying to explain to the reader something that the author probably did not mean; since it's there, the reader has to put up with it. Translating is a very difficult job, not at all rewarding, and very badly paid. A good translation is always a re-creation in another language. That's why I have such great admiration for Gregory Rabassa. My books have been translated into twenty-one languages, and Rabassa is the only translator who has never asked for something to be clarified so he can put a footnote in. I think that my work has been completely re-created in English. There are parts of the book that are very difficult to follow literally. The impression one gets is that the translator read the book and then rewrote it from his recollections. That's why I have such admiration for translators. They are intuitive rather than intellectual. Not only is what publishers pay them completely miserable, but they don't see their work as literary creation. There are some books I would have liked to translate into Spanish, but they would have involved as much work as writing my own books; and I wouldn't have made enough money to eat.

INTERVIEWER

What would you have liked to translate?

GARCÍA MÁRQUEZ

All Malraux. I would have liked to translate Conrad and Saint-Exupéry. When I'm reading I sometimes get the feeling that I would like to translate this book. Excluding the great masterpieces, I prefer reading a mediocre translation of a book than trying to get through it in the original language. I never feel comfortable reading in another language, because the only language I really feel inside is Spanish. However, I speak Italian and French, and I know English well enough to have poisoned myself with *Time* magazine every week for twenty years.

INTERVIEWER

Does Mexico seem like home to you now? Do you feel part of any larger community of writers?

GARCÍA MÁRQUEZ

In general, I'm not a friend of writers or artists just because they are writers or artists. I have many friends of different professions, among them writers and artists. In general terms, I feel that I'm a native of any country in Latin America but not elsewhere. Latin Americans feel that Spain is the only country in which we are treated well, but I personally don't feel as though I'm from there. In Latin America I don't have a sense of frontiers or borders. I'm conscious of the differences that exist from one country to another, but in my mind and heart it is all the same. Where I really feel at home is the Caribbean, whether it is the French, Dutch, or English Caribbean. I was always impressed that when I got on a plane in Barranquilla, a black lady with a blue dress would stamp my passport, and when I got off the plane in Jamaica, a black lady with a blue dress would stamp my passport, but in English. I don't believe that the language makes all that much difference. But anywhere else in the world, I feel like a foreigner, a feeling that robs me of a sense of security. It's a personal feeling, but I always have it when I travel. I have a minority conscience.

INTERVIEWER

Do you think that it's an important thing for Latin American writers to live in Europe for a while?

GARCÍA MÁRQUEZ

Perhaps to have a real perspective from outside. The book of short stories I'm thinking of writing is about Latin Americans going to Europe. I've been thinking about it for twenty years. If you could draw a final conclusion out of these short stories, it would be that Latin Americans hardly ever get to Europe, especially Mexicans, and certainly not to stay. All the Mexicans I've ever met in Europe always leave the following Wednesday.

INTERVIEWER

What effects do you think the Cuban Revolution has had on Latin American literature?

GARCÍA MÁRQUEZ

Up until now it has been negative. Many writers who think of themselves as being politically committed feel obligated to write stories not about what they want, but about what they think they should want. That makes for a certain type of calculated literature that doesn't have anything to do with experience or intuition. The main reason for this is that the cultural influence of Cuba on Latin America has been very much fought against. In Cuba itself, the process hasn't developed to the point where a new type of literature or art has been created. That is something that needs time. The great cultural importance of

Cuba in Latin America has been to serve as a kind of bridge to transmit a type of literature that had existed in Latin America for many years. In a sense, the boom in Latin American literature in the United States has been caused by the Cuban Revolution. Every Latin American writer of that generation had been writing for twenty years, but the European and American publishers had very little interest in them. When the Cuban Revolution started there was suddenly a great interest about Cuba and Latin America. The revolution turned into an article of consumption. Latin America came into fashion. It was discovered that Latin American novels existed that were good enough to be translated and considered with all other world literature. What was really sad is that cultural colonialism is so bad in Latin America that it was impossible to convince the Latin Americans themselves that their own novels were good until people outside *told* them they were.

INTERVIEWER

Are there some lesser-known Latin American writers you especially admire?

GARCÍA MÁRQUEZ

I doubt there are any now. One of the best side effects of the boom in Latin American writing is that publishers are always on the lookout to make sure that they're not going to miss the new Cortázar. Unfortunately, many young writers are more concerned with fame than with their own work. There's a French professor at the University of Toulouse who writes about Latin American literature; many young authors wrote to him telling him not to write so much about me because I didn't need it anymore and other people did. But what they forget is that when I was their age the critics weren't writing about me, but rather about Miguel Angel Asturias. The point I'm trying to make is that these young writers are wasting their time writing to critics rather than working on their own writing. It's much more important to write than to be written about. One thing that I think was very important about my literary career was that until I was forty years old, I never got one cent of author's royalties, though I'd had five books published.

INTERVIEWER

Do you think that fame or success coming too early in a writer's career is bad?

GARCÍA MÁRQUEZ

At any age it's bad. I would have liked for my books to have been recognized posthumously, at least in capitalist countries, where you turn into a kind of merchandise.

INTERVIEWER

Aside from your favorites, what do you read today?

GARCÍA MÁRQUEZ

I read the weirdest things. I was reading Muhammad Ali's memoirs the other day. Bram Stoker's *Dracula* is a great book, and one I probably would not have read many years ago because I would have thought it was a waste of time. But I never really get involved with a book unless it's recommended by somebody I trust. I don't read any more fiction. I read many memoirs and documents, even if they are forged documents. And I reread my favorites. The advantage of rereading is that you can open at any page and read the part that you really like. I've lost this sacred notion of reading only "literature." I will read anything. I try to keep up to date. I read almost all the really important magazines from all over the world every week. I've always been on the lookout for news since the habit of reading the Teletype machines. But after I've read all the serious and important newspapers from all over, my wife always comes around and tells me of news I hadn't heard. When I ask her where she read it, she will say that she read it in a magazine at the beauty parlor. So I read fashion magazines and all kinds of magazines for women and gossip magazines. And I learn many things that I could learn only from reading them. That keeps me very busy.

INTERVIEWER

Why do you think fame is so destructive for a writer?

GARCÍA MÁRQUEZ

Primarily because it invades your private life. It takes away from the time that you spend with friends, and the time that you can work. It tends to isolate you from the real world. A famous writer who wants to continue writing has to be constantly defending himself against fame. I don't really like to say this because it never sounds sincere, but I would really have liked for my books to have been published after my death, so I wouldn't have to go through all this business of fame and being a great writer. In my case, the only advantage in fame is that I have been able to give it a political use. Otherwise, it is quite uncomfortable. The problem is that you're famous for twenty-four hours a day, and you can't say, OK, I won't be famous until tomorrow, or press a button and say, I won't be famous here or now.

INTERVIEWER

Did you anticipate the extraordinary success of *One Hundred Years of Solitude*?

GARCÍA MÁRQUEZ

I knew that it would be a book that would please my friends more than my others had. But when my Spanish publisher told me he was going to print eight thousand copies I was stunned, because my other books had never sold more than seven hundred. I asked him why not start slowly, but he said he was convinced that it was a good book and that all eight thousand copies would be sold between May and December. Actually they were all sold within one week in Buenos Aires.

INTERVIEWER

Why do you think *One Hundred Years of Solitude* clicked so?

GARCÍA MÁRQUEZ

I don't have the faintest idea, because I'm a very bad critic of my own works. One of the most frequent explanations that I've heard is that it is a book about the private lives of the people of Latin America, a book that was written from the inside. That explanation surprises me because in my first attempt to write it the title of the book was going to be *The House*. I wanted the whole development of the novel to take place inside the house, and anything external would be just in terms of its impact on the house. I later abandoned the title *The House*, but once the book goes into the town of Macondo it never goes any further. Another explanation I've heard is that every reader can make of the characters in the book what he wants and make them his own. I don't want it to become a film, since the film viewer sees a face that he may not have imagined.

INTERVIEWER

Was there any interest in making it into a film?

GARCÍA MÁRQUEZ

Yes, my agent put it up for one million dollars to discourage offers and as they approximated that offer she raised it to around three million. But I have no interest in a film, and as long as I can prevent it from happening, it won't. I prefer that it remain a private relationship between the reader and the book.

INTERVIEWER

Do you think any books can be translated into films successfully?

GARCÍA MÁRQUEZ

I can't think of any one film that improved on a good novel, but I can think of many good films that came from very bad novels.

INTERVIEWER

Have you ever thought of making films yourself?

GARCÍA MÁRQUEZ

There was a time when I wanted to be a film director. I studied directing in Rome. I felt that cinema was a medium that had no limitations and in which everything was possible. I came to Mexico because I wanted to work in film, not as a director but as a screenplay writer. But there's a big limitation in cinema in that it's an industrial art, a whole industry. It's very difficult to express in cinema what you really want to say. I still think of it, but it now seems like a luxury that I would like to do with friends but without any hope of really expressing myself. So I've moved further and further away from the cinema. My relation with it is like that of a couple who can't live separated but who can't live together either. Between having a film company or a journal, though, I'd choose a journal.

INTERVIEWER

How would you describe the book on Cuba that you're working on now?

GARCÍA MÁRQUEZ

Actually, the book is like a long newspaper article about what life in Cuban homes is like, how they have managed to survive the shortages. What has struck me during the many trips that I've made to Cuba in the last two years is that the blockade has created in Cuba a kind of "culture of necessity," a social situation in which people have to get along without certain things. The aspect that really interests me is how the blockade has contributed to changing the mentality of the people. We have a clash between an anticonsumer society and the most consumption-oriented society in the world. The book is now at a stage where after thinking that it would be just an easy, fairly short piece of journalism, it is now turning into a very long and complicated book. But that doesn't really matter, because all of my books have been like that. And besides, the book will prove with historical facts that the real world in the Caribbean is just as fantastic as in the stories of *One Hundred Years of Solitude*.

INTERVIEWER

Do you have any long-range ambitions or regrets as a writer?

GARCÍA MÁRQUEZ

I think my answer is the same as the one I gave you about fame. I was asked the other day if I would be interested in the Nobel Prize, but I think that for me it would be an absolute catastrophe. I would certainly be interested in deserving it, but to receive it would be terrible. It would just complicate the problems of fame even more. The only thing I really regret in life is not having a daughter.

INTERVIEWER

Are there any projects now underway you can discuss?

GARCÍA MÁRQUEZ

I'm absolutely convinced that I'm going to write the greatest book of my life, but I don't know which one it will be or when. When I feel something like this—which I have been feeling now for a while—I stay very quiet, so that if it passes by I can capture it.

Issue 82, 1981

Philip Larkin

The Art of Poetry

T emperamentally and geographically remote," *The Times Liter-ary Supplement* wrote of Philip Larkin, "he has refused almost all invitations to judge, recite, review, lecture, pontificate, or to be interviewed."

When the notion of securing a *Paris Review* interview with Larkin arose, the staff was not sanguine. Much to the staff's delight, Larkin consented warily, stating that he wasn't crazy about the idea, but that "the *Paris Review* series is, of course, known to me, and I can see I should be in good company." In the case of this interview, Larkin did not let down his guard sufficiently to be interviewed in person. He stipulated that the interview be conducted entirely by mail: "You will get much better answers that way." He took nearly five months to answer the initial set of questions sent to him at his home in Hull, England, stating, "It has taken rather a long time because, to my surprise, I found writing it suffocatingly boring."

His letterhead—P. A. LARKIN, C.B.E., C.LIT., M.A., D.LIT., D.LITT., F.R.S.L., F.L.A.—is indicative of the measure of worldly recognition his relatively small output has received. Indeed, he has been called the other English poet laureate ("even more loved and needed than the official one, John Betjeman," according to Calvin Bedient in *The New York Times Book Review*). But Larkin transcends his Englishness and is widely read on the Continent and in the United States.

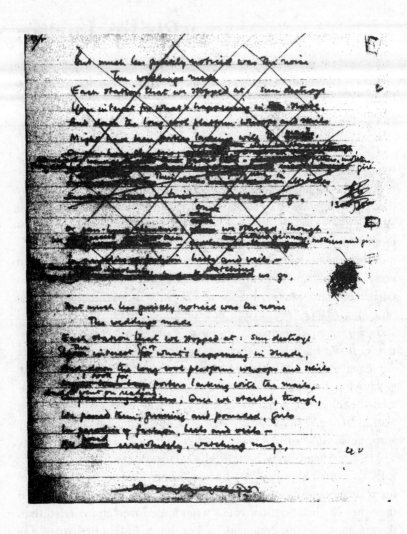

A manuscript page from Philip Larkin's The Whitsun Weddings.

He has said his aim in writing a poem is "to construct a verbal device that would preserve an experience indefinitely by reproducing it in whoever read the poem."

—Robert Phillips, 1982

INTERVIEWER

Can you describe your life at Hull? Do you live in a flat or own a house?

PHILIP LARKIN

I came to Hull in 1955. After eighteen months (during which I wrote "Mr. Bleaney"), I took a university flat and lived there for nearly eighteen years. It was the top flat in a house that was reputedly the American Consulate during the war, and though it might not have suited everybody, it suited me. I wrote most of *The Whitsun Weddings* and all of *High Windows* there. Probably I should never have moved if the university hadn't decided to sell the house, but as it was I had to get out and find somewhere else. It was a dreadful experience, as at that time houses were hard to find. In the end friends reported a small house near the university, and I bought that in 1974. I haven't decided yet whether or not I like it.

INTERVIEWER

How many days a week do you work at the library, and for how many hours a day?

LARKIN

My job as university librarian is a full-time one, five days a week, forty-five weeks a year. When I came to Hull, I had eleven staff; now there are over a hundred of one sort and another. We built one new library in 1960 and another in 1970, so that my first fifteen years were busy. Of course, this was a period of university expansion in England, and Hull grew as much as if not more than the rest. Luckily the vice chancellor during most of this time was keen on the library, which is why it is called after him. Looking back, I think that if the Brynmor Jones Library *is* a good library—and I think it is—the credit should go to him and to the library staff. And to the university as a whole, of course. But you wouldn't be interested in all that.

What is your daily routine?

My life is as simple as I can make it. Work all day, cook, eat, wash up, telephone, hack writing, drink, television in the evenings. I almost never go out. I suppose everyone tries to ignore the passing of time— some people by doing a lot, being in California one year and Japan the next. Or there's my way—making every day and every year exactly the same. Probably neither works.

You didn't mention a schedule for writing . . .

Yes, I was afraid you'd ask about writing. Anything I say about writing poems is bound to be retrospective, because in fact I've written very little since moving into this house, or since *High Windows*, or since 1974, whichever way you like to put it. But when I did write them, well, it was in the evenings, after work, after washing up. (I'm sorry, you would call this "doing the dishes.") It was a routine like any other. And really it worked very well. I don't think you can write a poem for more than two hours. After that you're going round in circles, and it's much better to leave it for twenty-four hours, by which time your subconscious or whatever has solved the block and you're ready to go on.

The best writing conditions I ever had were in Belfast, when I was working at the university there. Another top-floor flat, by the way. I wrote between eight and ten in the evenings, then went to the university bar till eleven, then played cards or talked with friends till one or two. The first part of the evening had the second part to look forward to, and I could enjoy the second part with a clear conscience because I'd done my two hours. I can't seem to organize that now.

INTERVIEWER

Does, or did, writing come easily for you? Does a poem get completed slowly or rapidly?

LARKIN

I've no standards of comparison. I wrote short poems quite quickly. Longer ones would take weeks or even months. I used to find that I was never sure I was going to finish a poem until I had thought of the last line. Of course, the last line was sometimes the first one you thought of! But usually the last line would come when I'd done about two-thirds of the poem, and then it was just a matter of closing the gap.

INTERVIEWER

Why do you write, and for whom?

LARKIN

You've been reading Auden: "To ask the hard question is simple." The short answer is that you write because you have to. If you rationalize it, it seems as if you've seen this sight, felt this feeling, had this vision, and have got to find a combination of words that will preserve it by setting it off in other people. The duty is to the original experience. It doesn't feel like self-expression, though it may look like it. As for *whom* you write for, well, you write for everybody. Or anybody who will listen.

INTERVIEWER

Do you share your manuscripts with anyone before publishing them? Are there any friends whose advice you would follow in revising a poem?

LARKIN

I shouldn't normally show what I'd written to anyone: what would be the point? You remember Tennyson reading an unpublished poem to Jowett; when he had finished, Jowett said, I shouldn't publish that if

I were you, Tennyson. Tennyson replied, If it comes to that, Master, the sherry you gave us at lunch was downright filthy. That's about all that can happen.

But when we were young, Kingsley Amis and I used to exchange unpublished poems, largely because we never thought they could be published, I suppose. He encouraged me, I encouraged him. Encouragement is very necessary to a young writer. But it's hard to find anyone worth encouraging—there aren't many Kingsleys about.

INTERVIEWER

In his *Paris Review* interview, Kingsley Amis states you helped him with the manuscript of *Lucky Jim*. What was the nature of that working relationship? Is part of that novel based upon your own experiences on staff at Leicester University?

LARKIN

Well, it's all so long ago, it's hard to remember. My general conviction was that Kingsley was quite the funniest writer I had ever met—in letters and so on—and I wanted everyone else to think so too. I know he says he got the idea of *Lucky Jim* from visiting me when I was working at University College Leicester. This has always seemed rather tenuous to me: after all, he was working at University College Swansea when he was writing it, and the theme—boy meets apparently nasty girl, but turns her into a nice girl by getting her away from nasty environment—is one I think has always meant a lot to Kingsley. He used it again in *I Want It Now*. When I read the first draft I said, Cut this, cut that, let's have more of the other. I remember I said, Let's have more "faces"—you know, his Edith Sitwell face, and so on. The wonderful thing was that Kingsley could "do" all those faces himself—"Sex Life in Ancient Rome" and so on. Someone once took photographs of them all. I wish I had a set.

INTERVIEWER

How did you come to be a librarian? Had you no interest in teaching? What was your father's profession?

LARKIN

Oh dear, this means a lot of autobiography. My father was a city treasurer, a finance officer. I never had the least desire to "be" anything when I was at school, and by the time I went to Oxford the war was on and there wasn't anything to be except a serviceman or a teacher or a civil servant. In 1943 when I graduated I knew I couldn't be the first, because I'd been graded unfit (I suppose through eyesight), nor the second because I stammered, and then the Civil Service turned me down twice, and I thought, Well, that lets me out, and I sat at home writing *Jill*. But of course in those days the government had powers to send you into the mines or onto the land or into industry, and they wrote quite politely to ask what in fact I was doing. I looked at the daily paper (the *Birmingham Post*—we were living at Warwick then) and saw that a small town in Shropshire was advertising for a librarian, applied for it and got it, and told the government so, which seemed to satisfy them.

Of course, I wasn't a real librarian, more a sort of caretaker—it was a one-man library—and I can't pretend I enjoyed it much. The previous librarian had been there about forty years, and I was afraid I should be there all my life too. This made me start qualifying myself professionally, just in order to get away, which I did in 1946. By then I'd written *Jill*, and *The North Ship*, and *A Girl in Winter*. It was probably the intensest time of my life.

INTERVIEWER

Is Jorge Luis Borges the only other contemporary poet of note who is also a librarian, by the way? Are you aware of any others?

LARKIN

Who is Jorge Luis Borges? The writer-librarian *I* like is Archibald MacLeish. You know, he was made librarian of Congress in 1939, and on his first day they brought him some papers to sign, and he wouldn't sign them until he understood what they were all about. When he did understand, he started making objections and countersuggestions.

The upshot was that he reorganized the whole Library of Congress in five years simply by saying, I don't understand and I don't agree, and in wartime too. Splendid man.

INTERVIEWER

What do you think of the academic world as a milieu for the working creative writer—teaching specifically?

LARKIN

The academic world has worked all right for me, but then, I'm not a teacher. I couldn't be. I should think that chewing over other people's work, writing I mean, must be terribly stultifying. Quite sickens you with the whole business of literature. But then, I haven't got that kind of mind, conceptual or ratiocinative or whatever it is. It would be death to me to have to think about literature as such, to say why one poem was better than another, and so on.

INTERVIEWER

We've heard that you don't give readings from your own work. In America, this has become a business for poets. Do you enjoy attending the readings of others?

LARKIN

I don't give readings, no, although I have recorded three of my collections, just to show how *I* should read them. Hearing a poem, as opposed to reading it on the page, means you miss so much—the shape, the punctuation, the italics, even knowing how far you are from the end. Reading it on the page means you can go your own pace, taking it in properly; hearing it means you're dragged along at the speaker's own rate, missing things, not taking it in, confusing *there* and *their* and things like that. And the speaker may interpose his own personality between you and the poem, for better or worse. For that matter, so may the audience. I don't like hearing things in public, even music. In fact, I think poetry readings grew up on a false analogy with music: the text is the score that doesn't come to life until it's performed. It's false because people can read words, whereas they can't read music. When you write a poem, you put everything into it that's needed: the reader should hear it just as clearly as if you were in the room saying it to him. And of course this fashion for poetry readings has led to a kind of poetry that you *can* understand first go: easy rhythms, easy emotions, easy syntax. I don't think it stands up on the page.

INTERVIEWER

Do you think economic security an advantage to the writer?

LARKIN

The whole of British postwar society is based on the assumption that economic security is an advantage to everyone. Certainly *I* like to be economically secure. But aren't you, really, asking about *work*? This whole question of how a writer actually gets his money—especially a poet—is one to which there are probably as many answers as there are writers, and the next man's answer always seems better than your own.

On the one hand, you can't live today by being a man of letters as easily as a hundred or seventy-five years ago, when there were so many magazines and newspapers all having to be filled. Writers' incomes, as writers, have sunk almost below the subsistence line. On the other hand, you *can* live by being a writer, or being a poet, if you're prepared to join the cultural entertainment industry and take handouts from the Arts Council (not that there are as many of them as there used to be) and be a poet in residence and all that. I suppose I could have said—it's a bit late now—I could have had an agent and said, Look, I will do anything for six months of the year as long as I can be free to write for the other six months. Some people do this, and I suppose it works for them. But I was brought up to think you had to have a job and write in your spare time, like Trollope. Then, when you started earning enough money by writing, you phase the job out. But in fact I was over fifty before I could have lived by my writing—and then only because I had edited a big anthology—and by that time you think, Well, I might as well get my pension, since I've gone so far.

INTERVIEWER

Any regrets?

LARKIN

Sometimes I think, Everything I've written has been done after a day's work, in the evening: what would it have been like if I'd written it in the morning, after a night's sleep? Was I wrong? Some time ago a writer said to me—and he was a full-time writer, and a good one—I wish I had your life. Dealing with people, having colleagues. Being a writer is so lonely.

Everyone envies everyone else. All I can say is, having a job hasn't been a hard price to pay for economic security. Some people, I know, would sooner have the economic insecurity because they have to "feel free" before they can write. But it's worked for me. The only thing that does strike me as odd, looking back, is that what society has been willing to *pay* me for is being a librarian. You get medals and prizes and honorary this and thats—and flattering interviews—but if you turned round and said, Right, if I'm so good, give me an index-linked permanent income equal to what I can get for being an undistinguished university administrator—well, reason would remount its throne pretty quickly.

INTERVIEWER

How did you come to write poems? Was time a factor in choosing poetry over the novel form?

LARKIN

What questions you ask. I wrote prose and poems equally from the age of, say, fifteen. I didn't choose poetry, poetry chose me.

INTERVIEWER

Nicely put. Your last novel, *A Girl in Winter*—which is a small masterpiece—was published twenty-five years ago. Do you think you will ever write another?

LARKIN

I don't know, I shouldn't think so. I tried very hard to write a third novel for about five years. The ability to do so had just vanished. I can't say any more than that . . .

INTERVIEWER

Jill was written when you were about twenty-one, and your second novel only a year or so later. Was it your intention, then, to be a novelist only?

LARKIN

I wanted to be a novelist in a way I never wanted to be a poet, yes. Novels seem to me to be richer, broader, deeper, more enjoyable than poems. When I was young, *Scrutiny* ran a series of articles under the general heading of "The Novel as Dramatic Poem." That was a stimulating, an exciting conception. Something that was both a poem and a novel. Of course, thinking about my own two stories means going back nearly forty years, and at this distance I can't remember what their genesis was.

I seem to recall that *Jill* was based on the idea that running away from life, John's fantasy about an imaginary sister, might lead you straight into it—meeting the real Jill, I mean. With disastrous results.

A Girl in Winter, which I always think of as "The Kingdom of Winter," which was its first title, or "Winterreich," as Bruce Montgomery used to call it—well, that was written when I was feeling pretty low, in this first library job I told you about. It's what Eliot would call an objective correlative. When I look at it today, I do think it's remarkably . . . I suppose the word is *knowing* . . . not really mature, or wise, just incredibly clever. By my standards, I mean. And considering I was only twenty-two. All the same, some people whose opinion I respect prefer *Jill* as being more natural, more sincere, more directly emotional.

INTERVIEWER

In your preface to the reprint of *Jill*, you say it is "in essence an unambitious short story." What is your definition of a novel?

LARKIN

I think a novel should follow the fortunes of more than one character.

INTERVIEWER

At least one critic has cited *Jill* as the forerunner of the new British postwar novel—the literature of the displaced working-class hero that spawned later works by Alan Sillitoe, John Wain, Keith Waterhouse, Amis, and others. Do you feel a part of any of this?

LARKIN

I don't think so, no. Because *Jill* has none of the political overtones of that genre. John's being working class was a kind of equivalent of my stammer, a built-in handicap to put him one down.

I'm glad you mention Keith Waterhouse. I think *Billy Liar* and *Jubb* are remarkably original novels, the first very funny, the second harrowing. Much better than my two.

INTERVIEWER

You're extremely modest. Wouldn't you say that an open assumption of the British sense of class is important to your work—*Jill*, *A Girl in Winter*, a poem like "The Whitsun Weddings"?

LARKIN

Are you suggesting there's no sense of class in America? That's not the impression I get from the works of Mr. John O'Hara.

INTERVIEWER

O'Hara overstated. Did you prefigure a shape to your two novels, or did they evolve? You've stated your mentors in poetry, especially Hardy. But whom in fiction early on did you frequently read and admire?

LARKIN

Hard to say. Of course I had read a great many novels, and knew the mannerisms of most modern writers, but looking back I can't say

I ever imitated anyone. Now don't think I mind imitation in a young writer. It's just a way of learning the job. Really, my novels were more original than my poems at the time. My favorite novelists were Lawrence, Isherwood, Maugham, Waugh—oh, and George Moore. I was on a great Moore kick at that time: probably he was at the bottom of my style then.

INTERVIEWER

A Girl in Winter reminds me stylistically of Elizabeth Bowen's fiction, particularly *The Death of the Heart* and *The House in Paris*. Is Bowen a writer you've also admired?

LARKIN

No, I hadn't read Elizabeth Bowen. In fact, someone lent me *The Death of the Heart* when *A Girl in Winter* came out—two years after it was finished. I quite liked it, but it was never one of my personal favorites.

INTERVIEWER

Let's talk about the structure of *A Girl in Winter* for a moment: did you write it chronologically? That is, did you write Part Two first, then shuffle the pack for effect and counterpoint? Or did you actually conceive the novel as present to past to present?

LARKIN

The second way.

INTERVIEWER

Letters are an important and integral part of both novels, as plot and as texture. Are you a voluminous letter writer?

LARKIN

I suppose I used to write many more letters than I do now, but so did everyone. Nowadays I keep up with one or two people, in the sense of writing when there isn't anything special to say. I love *getting* letters, which means you have to answer them, and there isn't always time. I had a very amusing and undemanding correspondence with the novelist Barbara Pym, who died in 1980, that arose simply out of a fan letter. I wrote her and went on for over ten years before we actually met. I hope she liked getting my letters, I certainly liked hers. I talk about our correspondence in a foreword I provided for the UK edition of her posthumous novel, *An Unsuitable Attachment*.

INTERVIEWER

Can you describe your relationship with the contemporary literary community?

LARKIN

I'm somewhat withdrawn from what you call the "contemporary literary community," for two reasons: in the first place, I don't write for a living and so don't have to keep in touch with literary editors and publishers and television people in order to earn money; and in the second, I don't live in London. Given that, my relations with it are quite amicable.

INTERVIEWER

Is Hull a place where you are likely to stay put? If so, have you as a person changed since the writing of the poem "Places, Loved Ones"—or is the speaker of that poem a persona?

LARKIN

Hull is a place where I *have* stayed. On my twenty-fifth anniversary, I held a little luncheon party for the members of my staff who'd been there as long as I had, or almost as long, and they made me a presentation with a card bearing the very lines you mean. Touché, as the French say.

INTERVIEWER

As a bachelor, have you sometimes felt an outsider? Or, like the speaker of your poems "Reasons for Attendance," "Dockery & Son," and "Self's the Man," have you enjoyed being single and remained so because you liked and preferred living that way?

LARKIN

Hard to say. Yes, I've remained single by choice and shouldn't have liked anything else, but of course most people do get married, and divorced too, and so I suppose I am an outsider in the sense you mean. Of course it worries me from time to time, but it would take too long to explain why. Samuel Butler said life is an affair of being spoilt in one way or another.

INTERVIEWER

Is the character John Kemp in any way based upon your own youth? Were you *that* shy?

LARKIN

I would say, yes, I was and am extremely shy. Anyone who has stammered will know what agony it is, especially at school. It means you never take the lead in anything or do anything but try to efface yourself. I often wonder if I was shy because I stammered, or vice versa.

INTERVIEWER

Was your childhood unhappy?

LARKIN

My childhood was all right, comfortable and stable and loving, but I wasn't a happy child, or so they say. On the other hand, I've never been a recluse, contrary to reports: I've had friends and enjoyed their company. In comparison with some people I know I'm extremely sociable.

INTERVIEWER

Do you feel happiness is unlikely in this world?

LARKIN

Well, I think if you're in good health, and have enough money, and nothing is bothering you in the foreseeable future, that's as much as you can hope for. But "happiness," in the sense of a continuous emotional orgasm, no. If only because you know that you are going to die and the people you love are going to die.

INTERVIEWER

After "Trouble at Willow Gables," did you write any other short stories or tales?

LARKIN

No. I think a short story should be either a poem or a novel. Unless it's just an anecdote.

INTERVIEWER

Have you ever attempted a truly long poem? I've never seen one in print. If not, why?

LARKIN

I've written none. A long poem for me would be a novel. In that sense, *A Girl in Winter* is a poem.

INTERVIEWER

What about a play or a verse play?

LARKIN

I don't like plays. They happen in public, which, as I said, I don't like, and by now I have grown rather deaf, which means I can't hear what's going on. Then again, they are rather like poetry readings—they have to get an instant response, which tends to vulgarize. And of course the intrusion of *personality*—the actor, the producer, or do you call him the director—is distracting.

All the same, I admire *Murder in the Cathedral* as much as anything Eliot ever wrote. I read it from time to time for pleasure, which is the highest compliment I can pay.

INTERVIEWER

Did you ever meet Eliot?

LARKIN

I didn't know him. Once I was in the Faber offices—the old ones, 24 Russell Square, that magic address!—talking to Charles Monteith, and he said, Have you ever met Eliot? I said no, and to my astonishment he stepped out and reappeared with Eliot, who must have been in the next room. We shook hands, and he explained that he was expecting someone to tea and couldn't stay. There was a pause, and he said, I'm glad to see you in this office. The significance of that was that I wasn't a Faber author—it must have been before 1964, when they published *The Whitsun Weddings*—and I took it as a great compliment. But it was a shattering few minutes, I hardly remember what I thought.

INTERVIEWER

What about Auden? Were you acquainted?

LARKIN

I didn't know him either. I met Auden once at Stephen Spender's house, which was very kind of Spender, and in a sense he was more frightening than Eliot. I remember he said, Do you like living in Hull? and I said, I don't suppose I'm unhappier there than I should be anywhere else. To which he replied, Naughty, naughty. I thought that was very funny.

But this business of meeting famous writers is agonizing; I had a dreadful few minutes with Forster. My fault, not his. Dylan Thomas came to Oxford to speak to a club I belonged to, and we had a drink the following morning. *He* wasn't frightening. In fact, and I know it sounds absurd to say so, but I should say I had more in common with Dylan Thomas than with any other "famous writer," in this sort of context.

INTERVIEWER

You mention Auden, Thomas, Yeats, and Hardy as early influences in your introduction to the second edition of *The North Ship*. What in particular did you learn from your study of these four?

LARKIN

Oh for Christ's sake, one doesn't *study* poets! You *read* them and think, That's marvelous, how is it done, could I do it? and that's how you learn. At the end of it you can't say, That's Yeats, that's Auden, because they've gone, they're like scaffolding that's been taken down. Thomas was a dead end. What effects? Yeats and Auden, the management of lines, the formal distancing of emotion. Hardy, well . . . not to be afraid of the obvious. All those wonderful dicta about poetry—"the poet should touch our hearts by showing his own," "the poet takes note of nothing that he cannot feel," "the emotion of all the ages and the thought of his own"—Hardy knew what it was all about.

INTERVIEWER

When your first book, *The North Ship*, appeared, did you feel you were going to be an important poet?

LARKIN

No, certainly not. I've never felt that anyway. You must remember *The North Ship* was published by an obscure press—The Fortune Press—that didn't even send out review copies; it was next door to a vanity press. One had none of the rewards of authorship, neither money (no agreement) nor publicity. You felt you'd cooked your goose.

INTERVIEWER

How can a young poet know if his work is any good?

LARKIN

I think a young poet, or an old poet for that matter, should try to produce something that pleases himself personally, not only when he's written it but a couple of weeks later. Then he should see if it pleases anyone else, by sending it to the kind of magazine he likes reading. But if it doesn't, he shouldn't be discouraged. I mean, in the seventeenth century every educated man could turn a verse and play the lute. Supposing no one played tennis because they wouldn't make

Wimbledon? First and foremost, writing poems should be a pleasure. So should reading them, by God.

How do you account for the great maturity and originality that developed between your first poetry collection and your second, *The Less Deceived*?

You know, I really don't know. After finishing my first books, say by 1945, I thought I had come to an end. I couldn't write another novel; I published nothing. My personal life was rather harassing. Then in 1950 I went to Belfast, and things reawoke somehow. I wrote some poems and thought, These aren't bad, and had that little pamphlet *XX Poems* printed privately. I felt for the first time I was speaking for myself. Thoughts, feelings, language cohered and jumped. They have to do that. Of course they are always lying around in you, but they have to get together.

You once wrote that "the impulse to preserve lies at the bottom of all art." In your case, what is it you are preserving in your poems?

Well, as I said, the experience. The beauty.

Auden admired your forms. But you've stated that form holds little interest for you—content is everything. Could you comment on that?

I'm afraid that was a rather silly remark, especially now when form is so rare. I read poems and I think, Yes, that's quite a nice idea, but why can't he make a *poem* of it? Make it memorable? It's no good just writing it down! At any level that matters, form and content are indivisible. What I meant by content is the experience the poem preserves, what it passes on. I must have been seeing too many poems that were simply agglomerations of words when I said that.

In one early interview you stated that you were not interested in any period but the present, or in any poetry but that written in English. Did you mean that quite literally? Has your view changed?

It has not. I don't see how one can ever know a foreign language well enough to make reading poems in it worthwhile. Foreigners' ideas of good English poems are dreadfully crude: Byron and Poe and so on. The Russians liking Burns. But deep down I think foreign languages irrelevant. If that glass thing over there is a window, then it isn't a *fenster* or a *fenêtre* or whatever. *Hautes fenêtres*, my God! A writer can have only one language, if language is going to mean anything to him.

In D. J. Enright's *Poets of the Nineteen-Fifties*, published in 1955, you made several provocative statements about archetypes and myth that have become well known. Specifically, "As a guiding principle I believe that every poem must be its own sole freshly created universe, and therefore have no belief in 'tradition' or a common myth-kitty. . . . To me the whole of the ancient world, the whole of classical and biblical mythology means very little, and I think that using them today not only fills poems full of dead spots, but dodges the writer's duty to be original." Does this mean you really do not respond to, say, the monstrous manifestation of the Sphinx in Yeats's "The Second Coming"? Or were you merely reacting against bookishness?

My objection to the use in new poems of properties or personae from older poems is not a moral one, but simply because they do not work, either because I have not read the poems in which they appear, or because I have read them and think of them as part of that poem and not a property to be dragged into a new poem as a substitute for securing the effect that is desired. I admit this argument could be pushed to absurd lengths, when a poet could not refer to anything that his readers might not have seen (such as snow, for instance), but in fact poets write for people with the same background and experiences as themselves, which might be taken as a compelling argument in support of provincialism.

INTERVIEWER

The use of archetypes can weaken rather than buttress a poem?

LARKIN

I am not going to fall on my face every time someone uses words such as *Orpheus* or *Faust* or *Judas*. Writers should work for the effects they want to produce, and not wheel out stale old Wardour Street lay figures.

INTERVIEWER

What do you mainly read?

LARKIN

I don't read much. Books I'm sent to review. Otherwise novels I've read before. Detective stories: Gladys Mitchell, Michael Innes, Dick Francis. I'm reading *Framley Parsonage* at the moment. Nothing difficult.

INTERVIEWER

What do you think of the current state of poetry in England today? Are things better or worse in American poetry?

LARKIN

I'm afraid I know very little about American poetry. As regards England, well, before the war, when I was growing up, we had Yeats, Eliot, Graves, Auden, Dylan Thomas, John Betjeman—could you pick a comparable team today?

INTERVIEWER

You haven't been to America, have you?

LARKIN

Oh no, I've never been to America, nor to anywhere else, for that matter. Does that sound very snubbing? It isn't meant to. I suppose I'm pretty unadventurous by nature, partly because that isn't the way I earn my living—reading and lecturing and taking classes and so on. I should hate it.

And of course I'm so deaf now that I shouldn't dare. Someone would say, What about Ashbery? And I'd say, I'd prefer strawberry— that kind of thing. I suppose everyone has his own dream of America. A writer once said to me, If you ever go to America, go either to the East Coast or the West Coast; the rest is a desert full of bigots. That's what I think I'd like: where if you help a girl trim the Christmas tree you're regarded as engaged; and her brothers start oiling their shotguns if you don't call on the minister. A version of pastoral.

INTERVIEWER

How is your writing physically accomplished? At what stage does a poem go through the typewriter?

LARKIN

I write—or used to—in notebooks in pencil, trying to complete each stanza before going on to the next. Then when the poem is finished I type it out and sometimes make small alterations.

INTERVIEWER

You use a lot of idioms and very common phrases—for irony, I'd guess, or to bear more meaning than usual, never for shock value. Do these phrases come late, to add texture or whatever, or are they integral from the beginning?

LARKIN

They occur naturally.

INTERVIEWER

How important is enjambment for you? In certain lines, you seem
to isolate lives by the very line breaks . . .

LARKIN

No device is important in itself. Writing poetry is playing off the
natural rhythms and word order of speech against the artificialities of
rhyme and meter. One has a few private rules—never split an adjec-
tive and its noun, for instance.

INTERVIEWER

How do you decide whether or not to rhyme?

LARKIN

Usually the idea of a poem comes with a line or two of it, and they
determine the rest. Normally one does rhyme. Deciding *not* to is
much harder.

INTERVIEWER

Can you drink and write? Have you tried any consciousness-
expanding drugs?

LARKIN

No, though of course those of my generation are drinkers. Not
druggers.

INTERVIEWER

Can you describe the genesis and working out of a poem based
upon an image that most people would simply pass by? (A clear road
between neighbors, an ambulance in city traffic?)

LARKIN

If I could answer this sort of question, I'd be a professor rather
than a librarian. And in any case, I shouldn't want to. It's a thing you

don't want to think about. It happens, or happened, and if it's something to be grateful for, you're grateful.

I remember saying once, I can't understand these chaps who go round American universities explaining how they write poems; it's like going round explaining how you sleep with your wife. Whoever I was talking to said, They'd do that too, if their agents could fix it.

INTERVIEWER

Do you throw away a lot of poems?

LARKIN

Some poems didn't get finished. Some didn't get published. I never throw anything away.

INTERVIEWER

You included only six of your own poems in *The Oxford Book of Twentieth-Century English Verse* (as opposed, say, to twelve by John Betjeman). Do you consider these to be your half-dozen best, or are they merely "representative"? I was surprised not to find "Church Going," arguably your single most famous poem.

LARKIN

My recollection is that I decided on six as a limit for my generation and anyone younger, to save hurt feelings. Mine were representative, as you say—one pretty one, one funny one, one long one, and so on. As editor, I couldn't give myself much space . . . could I?

INTERVIEWER

In your introduction to that anthology, you make a fine point of saying you didn't include any poems "requiring a glossary for their full understanding." Do you feel your own lucid work has helped close the gap between poetry and the public, a gap that experiment and obscurity have widened?

LARKIN

This was to explain why I hadn't included dialect poems. We have poets who write in pretty dense Lallans. Nothing to do with obscurity in the sense you mean.

INTERVIEWER

OK, but your introduction to *All What Jazz* takes a stance against experiment, citing the trio of Picasso, Pound, and Parker. Why do you distrust the new?

LARKIN

It seems to me undeniable that up to this century literature used language in the way we all use it, painting represented what anyone with normal vision sees, and music was an affair of nice noises rather than nasty ones. The innovation of modernism in the arts consisted of doing the opposite. I don't know why; I'm not a historian. You have to distinguish between things that seemed odd when they were new but are now quite familiar, such as Ibsen and Wagner, and things that seemed crazy when they were new and seem crazy now, like *Finnegans Wake* and Picasso.

INTERVIEWER

What's that got to do with jazz?

LARKIN

Everything. Jazz showed this very clearly because it is such a tele-scoped art, only as old as the century, if that. Charlie Parker wrecked jazz by—or so they tell me—using the chromatic rather than the dia-tonic scale. The diatonic scale is what you use if you want to write a national anthem, or a love song, or a lullaby. The chromatic scale is what you use to give the effect of drinking a quinine martini and hav-ing an enema simultaneously.

If I sound heated on this, it's because I love jazz, the jazz of Arm-strong and Bechet and Ellington and Bessie Smith and Beiderbecke. To have it all destroyed by a paranoiac drug addict made me furious.

Anyway, it's dead now, dead as Elizabethan madrigal singing. We can only treasure the records. And I do.

INTERVIEWER

Let's return to the Oxford anthology for a moment. Some of its critics said your selections not only favored traditional poetic forms, but minor poets as well. How do you respond to that?

LARKIN

Since it was *The Oxford Book of Twentieth-Century English Verse*, I had of course to represent the principal poets of the century by their best or most typical works. I think I did this. The trouble is that if this is all you do, the result will be a worthy but boring book, since there are quite enough books doing this already, and I thought it would be diverting to put in less familiar poems that were good or typical in themselves, but by authors who didn't rank full representation. I saw them as unexpected flowers along an only-too-well-trodden path. I think they upset people in a way I hadn't intended, although it's surprising how they are now being quoted and anthologized themselves.

Most people make anthologies out of other anthologies; I spent five years reading everyone's complete works, ending with six months in the basement of the Bodleian Library handling all the twentieth-century poetry they had received. It was great fun. I don't say I made any major discoveries, but I hope I managed to suggest that there are good poems around that no one knows about. At any rate, I made a readable book. I made twentieth-century poetry sound nice. That's quite an achievement in itself.

INTERVIEWER

Not many have commented upon the humor in your poetry, like the wonderful pun on "the stuff that dreams are made on" in "Toads." Do you consciously use humor to achieve a particular effect, or to avoid an opposite emotion?

LARKIN

One uses humor to make people laugh. In my case, I don't know whether they in fact do. The trouble is, it makes them think you aren't being serious. That's the risk you take.

INTERVIEWER

Your most recent collection, *High Windows*, contains at least three poems I'd call satirical—"Posterity," "Homage to a Government," and "This Be the Verse." Do you consider yourself a satirist?

LARKIN

No, I shouldn't call myself a satirist, or any other sort of *-ist*. The poems you mention were conceived in the same way as the rest. That is to say, as poems. To be a satirist, you have to think you know better than everyone else. I've never done that.

INTERVIEWER

An American poet-critic, Peter Davison, has characterized yours as a "diminutional talent"—meaning you make things clear by making them small—England reduced to "squares of wheat," and so forth. Is this a fair comment? Is it a technique you're aware of?

LARKIN

It's difficult to answer remarks like that. The line "Its postal districts packed like squares of wheat" refers to London, not England. It doesn't seem "diminutional" to me, rather the reverse, if anything. It's meant to make the postal districts seem rich and fruitful.

INTERVIEWER

Davison also sees your favorite subjects as failure and weakness.

LARKIN

I think a poet should be judged by what he does with his subjects, not by what his subjects are. Otherwise you're getting near the totalitarian attitude of wanting poems about steel production figures rather than "Mais où sont les neiges d'antan?" Poetry isn't a kind of paint spray you use to cover selected objects with. A good poem about failure is a success.

INTERVIEWER

Is it intentional that the form of "Toads" is alternating uneven trimeters and dimeters, with alternating off-rhymes, whereas "Toads Revisited" is in trimeters and off-rhymed couplets? What determines the form of a poem for you? Is it the first line, with its attendant rhythms?

LARKIN

Well, yes; I think I've admitted this already. At this distance I can't recall how far the second Toad poem was planned as a companion to the first. It's more likely that I found it turning out to be a poem about work, but different from the first, and so it seemed amusing to link them.

INTERVIEWER

How did you arrive upon the image of a toad for work or labor?

LARKIN

Sheer genius.

INTERVIEWER

As a writer, what are your particular quirks? Do you feel you have any conspicuous or secret flaw as a writer?

LARKIN

I really don't know. I suppose I've used the iambic pentameter a lot; some people find this oppressive and try to get away from it. My secret flaw is just not being very good, like everyone else. I've never been didactic, never tried to make poetry *do* things, never gone out to look for it. I waited for it to come to me, in whatever shape it chose.

INTERVIEWER

Do you feel you belong to any particular tradition in English letters?

LARKIN

I seem to remember George Fraser saying that poetry was either "veeshion"—he was Scotch—or "moaral deescourse," and I was the second, and the first was better. A well-known publisher asked me how one punctuated poetry and looked flabbergasted when I said, The same as prose. By which I mean that I write, or wrote, as everyone did till the mad lads started, using words and syntax in the normal way to describe recognizable experiences as memorably as possible. That doesn't seem to me a tradition. The other stuff, the mad stuff, is more an aberration.

INTERVIEWER

Have you any thoughts on the office of poet laureate? Does it serve a valid function?

LARKIN

Poetry and sovereignty are very primitive things. I like to think of their being united in this way in England. On the other hand, it's not clear what the laureate is, or does. Deliberately so, in a way: it isn't a job, there are no duties, no salary, and yet it isn't quite an honor either or not just an honor. I'm sure the worst thing about it, especially today, is the publicity it brings, the pressure to be involved publicly with poetry, which must be pretty inimical to any real writing.

Of course, the days when Tennyson would publish a sonnet telling Gladstone what to do about foreign policy are over. It's funny that Kipling, who is what most people think of as a poet as national spokesman, never was laureate. He should have had it when Bridges was appointed, but it's typical that he didn't—the post isn't thought of in that way. It really is a genuine attempt to honor someone. But the publicity that anything to do with the Palace gets these days is so fierce, it must be really more of an ordeal than an honor.

INTERVIEWER

Your poetry volumes have appeared at the rate of one per decade. From what you say, though, is it unlikely we'll have another around

1984? Did you really only complete about three poems in any given year?

LARKIN

It's unlikely I shall write any more poems, but when I did, yes, I did write slowly. I was looking at "The Whitsun Weddings" just the other day, and found that I began it sometime in the summer of 1957. After three pages, I dropped it for another poem that in fact was finished but never published. I picked it up again, in March 1958, and worked on it till October, when it was finished. But when I look at the diary I was keeping at the time, I see that the kind of incident it describes happened in July 1955! So in all, it took over three years. Of course, that's an exception. But I did write slowly, partly because you're finding out what to say as well as how to say it, and that takes time.

INTERVIEWER

For someone who dislikes being interviewed, you've responded generously.

LARKIN

I'm afraid I haven't said anything very interesting. You must realize I've never had "ideas" about poetry. To me it's always been a personal, almost physical release or solution to a complex pressure of needs—wanting to create, to justify, to praise, to explain, to externalize, depending on the circumstances. And I've never been much interested in other people's poetry—one reason for writing, of course, is that no one's written what you want to read. Probably my notion of poetry is very simple. Some time ago I agreed to help judge a poetry competition—you know, the kind where they get about thirty-five thousand entries, and you look at the best few thousand. After a bit I said, Where are all the love poems? And nature poems? And they said, Oh, we threw all those away. I expect they were the ones I should have liked.

James Baldwin

The Art of Fiction

This interview was conducted in the two places dearest to James Baldwin's struggle as a writer. We met first in Paris, where he spent the first nine years of a burgeoning career and wrote his first two novels, *Go Tell It on the Mountain* and *Giovanni's Room*, along with his best-known collection of essays, *Notes of a Native Son*. It was in Paris, he says, that he was first able to come to grips with his explosive relationship with himself and America. Our second talks were held at Baldwin's *poutres*-and-stone villa in St. Paul de Vence, where he has made his home for the past ten years. We lunched on an August weekend, together with seasonal guests and his secretary. On Saturday a storm raged amid intolerable heat and humidity, causing Baldwin's minor case of arthritis to pain his writing hand (left) and wrist. Erratic power shortages caused by the storm interrupted the tape machine by our side. During the blackouts we would discuss subjects at random or wait in silence while sipping our drinks.

I returned Sunday at Baldwin's invitation. The sun was shining and we were able to lunch outdoors at a picnic table, shaded by a bower that opened onto property dotted with fruit trees and a spectacular view of the Mediterranean littoral. Baldwin's mood had brightened considerably since the previous day, and we entered the office and study he refers to as his "torture chamber." Baldwin writes in longhand ("you achieve shorter declarative sentences") on the standard legal pad, although a large, old Adler electric sits on one end of his desk—a rectangular oak plank with rattan chairs on either

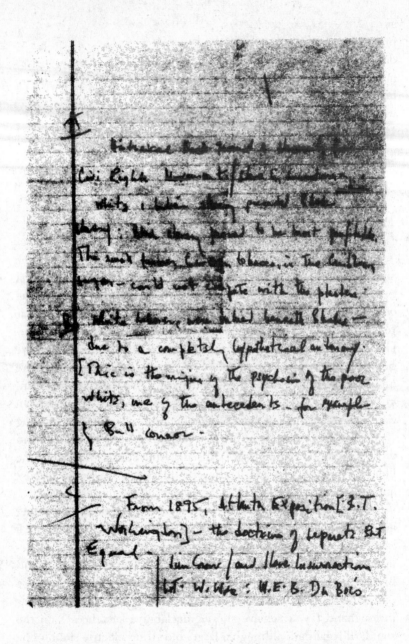

Notes for James Baldwin's lecture "A World I Never Made," delivered in 1984.

side. It is piled with writing utensils and drafts of several works in progress: a novel, a play, a scenario, essays on the Atlanta child murders, these last compiled in *The Evidence of Things Not Seen*. His most recent work includes *The Devil Finds Work*, an attack on racial bias and fear in the film industry, and a novel, *Just Above My Head*, which draws on his experiences as a civil-rights activist in the 1960s.

—*Jordan Elgrably, 1984*

INTERVIEWER

Would you tell us how you came to leave the States?

JAMES BALDWIN

I was broke. I got to Paris with forty dollars in my pocket, but I had to get out of New York. My reflexes were tormented by the plight of other people. Reading had taken me away for long periods at a time, yet I still had to deal with the streets and the authorities and the cold. I knew what it meant to be white and I knew what it meant to be a nigger, and I knew what was going to happen to me. My luck was running out. I was going to go to jail, I was going to kill somebody or be killed. My best friend had committed suicide two years earlier, jumping off the George Washington Bridge.

When I arrived in Paris in 1948 I didn't know a word of French. I didn't know anyone and I didn't want to know anyone. Later, when I'd encountered other Americans, I began to avoid them because they had more money than I did and I didn't want to feel like a freeloader. The forty dollars I came with, I recall, lasted me two or three days. Borrowing money whenever I could—often at the last minute—I moved from one hotel to another, not knowing what was going to happen to me. Then I got sick. To my surprise I wasn't thrown out of the hotel. This Corsican family, for reasons I'll never understand, took care of me. An old, old lady, a great old matriarch, nursed me back to health after three months; she used old folk remedies. And she had to climb five flights of stairs every morning to make sure I was kept alive. I went through this period where I was very much alone, and wanted to be. I wasn't part of any community until I later became the Angry Young Man in New York.

INTERVIEWER

Why did you choose France?

BALDWIN

It wasn't so much a matter of choosing France—it was a matter of getting out of America. I didn't know what was going to happen to me in France but I knew what was going to happen to me in New York. If I had stayed there, I would have gone under, like my friend on the George Washington Bridge.

INTERVIEWER

You say the city beat him to death. You mean that metaphorically.

BALDWIN

Not so metaphorically. Looking for a place to live. Looking for a job. You begin to doubt your judgment, you begin to doubt everything. You become imprecise. And that's when you're beginning to go under. You've been beaten, and it's been deliberate. The whole society has decided to make you *nothing*. And they don't even know they're doing it.

INTERVIEWER

Has writing been a type of salvation?

BALDWIN

I'm not so sure! I'm not sure I've escaped anything. One still lives with it, in many ways. It's happening all around us, every day. It's not happening to me in the same way, because I'm James Baldwin; I'm not riding the subways and I'm not looking for a place to live. But it's still happening. So salvation is a difficult word to use in such a context. I've been compelled in some ways by describing my circumstances to learn to live with them. It's not the same thing as accepting them.

INTERVIEWER

Was there an instant you knew you were going to write, to be a writer rather than anything else?

BALDWIN

Yes. The death of my father. Until my father died I thought I could do something else. I had wanted to be a musician, thought of being a painter, thought of being an actor. This was all before I was nineteen. Given the conditions in this country to be a black writer was impossible. When I was young, people thought you were not so much wicked as sick, they gave up on you. My father didn't think it was possible—he thought I'd get killed, get murdered. He said I was contesting the white man's definitions, which was quite right. But I had also learned from my father what he thought of the white man's definitions. He was a pious, very religious and in some ways a very beautiful man, and in some ways a terrible man. He died when his last child was born and I realized I had to make a jump—a leap. I'd been a preacher for three years, from age fourteen to seventeen. Those were three years that probably turned me to writing.

INTERVIEWER

Were the sermons you delivered from the pulpit very carefully prepared, or were they absolutely off the top of your head?

BALDWIN

I would improvise from the texts, like a jazz musician improvises from a theme. I never wrote a sermon—I studied the texts. I've never written a speech. I can't *read* a speech. It's kind of give-and-take. You have to sense the people you're talking to. You have to respond to what they hear.

INTERVIEWER

Do you have a reader in your mind when you write?

BALDWIN

No, you can't have that.

INTERVIEWER

So it's quite unlike preaching?

BALDWIN

Entirely. The two roles are completely unattached. When you are standing in the pulpit, you must sound as though you know what you're talking about. When you're writing, you're trying to find out something that you don't know. The whole language of writing for me is finding out what you don't want to know, what you don't want to find out. But something forces you to anyway.

INTERVIEWER

Is that one of the reasons you decided to be a writer—to find out about yourself?

BALDWIN

I'm not sure I decided. It was that or nothing, since in my own mind I was the father of my family. That's not quite the way *they* saw it, but still I was the oldest brother, and I took it very seriously, I had to set an example. I couldn't allow anything to happen to me because what then would happen to them? I could have become a junkie. On the roads I traveled and the streets I ran, anything could have happened to a boy like me—in New York. Sleeping on rooftops and in the subways. To this day I'm terrified of public toilets. In any case . . . my father died, and I sat down and figured out what I had to do.

INTERVIEWER

When did you find time to write?

BALDWIN

I was very young then. I could write *and* hold a few jobs. I was for a time a waiter . . . like George Orwell in *Down and Out in Paris and*

London. I couldn't do it now. I worked on the Lower East Side and in what we now call SoHo.

INTERVIEWER

Was there anyone to guide you?

BALDWIN

I remember standing on a street corner with the black painter Beauford Delaney down in the Village, waiting for the light to change, and he pointed down and said, Look. I looked and all I saw was water. And he said, Look again, which I did, and I saw oil on the water and the city reflected in the puddle. It was a great revelation to me. I can't explain it. He taught me how to see, and how to trust what I saw. Painters have often taught writers how to see. And once you've had that experience, you see differently.

INTERVIEWER

Do you think painters would help a fledgling writer more than another writer might? Did you read a great deal?

BALDWIN

I read everything. I read my way out of the two libraries in Harlem by the time I was thirteen. One does learn a great deal about writing this way. First of all, you learn how little you know. It is true that the more one learns the less one knows. I'm still learning how to write. I don't know what technique is. All I know is that you have to make the reader *see it.* This I learned from Dostoyevsky, from Balzac. I'm sure that my life in France would have been very different had I not met Balzac. Even though I hadn't experienced it yet, I understood something about the concierge, all the French institutions and personalities. The way that country and its society works. How to find my way around in it, not get lost in it, and not feel rejected by it. The French gave me what I could not get in America, which was a sense of, If I can do it, I may do it. I won't generalize, but in the years I grew up in the U.S., I could not do that. I'd already been defined.

INTERVIEWER

Did what you wanted to write about come easily to you from the start?

BALDWIN

I had to be released from a terrible shyness—an illusion that I could hide anything from anybody.

INTERVIEWER

I would think that anyone who could address a congregation time after time, and without notes, would never be shy again.

BALDWIN

I was scared then and I'm scared now. Communication is a two-way street, really, it's a matter of listening to one another. During the civil-rights movement I was in the back of a church in Tallahassee and the pastor, who recognized me, called my name and asked me to say a few words. I was thirty-four and had left the pulpit seventeen years before. The moment in which I had to stand up and walk down the aisle and stand in that pulpit was the strangest moment in my life up to that time. I managed to get through it and when I walked down from the pulpit and back up the aisle, a little old black lady in the congregation said to a friend of hers, He's little, but he's loud!

INTERVIEWER

What was the process whereby you were able to write?

BALDWIN

I had to go through a time of isolation in order to come to terms with who and what I was, as distinguished from all the things I'd been told I was. Right around 1950 I remember feeling that I'd come through *something*, shed a dying skin and was naked again. I wasn't, perhaps, but I certainly felt more at ease with myself. And then I was able to write. Throughout 1948 and 1949 I just tore up paper.

Those years were difficult, and yet you received four writing grants
between 1945 and 1956. How much encouragement did they afford
you?

BALDWIN
Well, the first one was the most important in terms of morale—the
Saxton Fellowship in 1945. I was twenty-one. I was launched into the
publishing world, so to speak. And there was the novel, which became *Go Tell It on the Mountain*, several years later.

INTERVIEWER
The Saxton was intended to help you finish the novel you were
working on?

BALDWIN
It helped me finish the novel, it kept me *alive*. The novel didn't
work, but I started doing book reviews for the *New Leader* at ten and
twenty dollars a shot. I had to read everything and had to write all the
time, and that's a great apprenticeship. The people I worked with
were left-of-center Trotskyites, socialist Trotskyites. I was a young
socialist. That was a very nice atmosphere for me; in a sense it saved
me from despair. But most of the books I reviewed were Be Kind to
Niggers, Be Kind to Jews, while America was going through one of its
liberal convulsions. People suddenly discovered they had a Jewish
problem, with books like *Gentleman's Agreement*, *Earth and High
Heaven*, or they discovered they had niggers, with books like *Kings-
blood Royal* and *Quality*.

Thousands of such tracts were published during those years and it
seems to me I had to read every single one of them; the color of my
skin made me an expert. And so, when I got to Paris, I had to dis-
charge all that, which was really the reason for my essay "Everybody's
Protest Novel." I was convinced then—and I still am—that those sort
of books do nothing but bolster up an image. All of this had quite a

bit to do with the direction I took as a writer, because it seemed to me that if I took the role of a victim then I was simply reassuring the defenders of the status quo; as long as I was a victim they could pity me and add a few more pennies to my home-relief check. Nothing would change in that way, I felt, and that essay was a beginning of my finding a new vocabulary and another point of view.

INTERVIEWER

If you felt that it was a white man's world, what made you think that there was any point in writing? And why is writing a white man's world?

BALDWIN

Because they own the business. Well, in retrospect, what it came down to was that I would not allow myself to be defined by other people, white or black. It was beneath me to blame anybody for what happened to me. What happened to me was *my* responsibility. I didn't want any pity. Leave me alone, I'll figure it out. I was very wounded and I was very dangerous because you become what you hate. It's what happened to my father and I didn't want it to happen to me. His hatred was suppressed and turned against himself. He couldn't let it out—he could only let it out in the house with rage, and I found it happening to myself as well. And after my best friend jumped off the bridge, I knew that I was next. So—Paris. With forty dollars and a one-way ticket.

INTERVIEWER

Once in Paris, you spent a lot of time upstairs at the Café de Flore. Is that where *Go Tell It on the Mountain* and *Giovanni's Room* were written?

BALDWIN

A lot of *Go Tell It on the Mountain* had to be written there, between there and the Hotel Verneuil, where I stayed for a lot of the time I was in Paris. After ten years of carrying that book around, I finally finished it in Switzerland in three months. I remember playing

Bessie Smith all the time while I was in the mountains, and playing her till I fell asleep. The book was very hard to write because I was too young when I started, seventeen; it was really about me and my father. There were things I couldn't deal with technically at first. Most of all, I couldn't deal with *me*. This is where reading Henry James helped me, with his whole idea about the center of consciousness and using a single intelligence to tell the story. He gave me the idea to make the novel happen on John's birthday.

INTERVIEWER

Do you agree with Alberto Moravia, who said that one ought only to write in the first person, because the third projects a bourgeois point of view?

BALDWIN

I don't know about that. The first person is the most terrifying view of all. I tend to be in accord with James, who hated the first-person perspective, which the reader has no reason to trust—why should you need this *I*? How is this person real by dint of that bar blaring across the page?

INTERVIEWER

When did you first conceive of leaving black characters out of *Giovanni's Room*?

BALDWIN

I suppose the only honest answer to that is that *Giovanni's Room* came out of something I had to face. I don't quite know when it came, though it broke off from what later turned into *Another Country*. Giovanni was at a party and on his way to the guillotine. He took all the light in the book, and then the book stopped and nobody in the book would speak to me. I thought I would seal Giovanni off into a short story, but it turned into *Giovanni's Room*. I certainly could not possibly have—not at that point in my life—handled the other great weight, the "Negro problem." The sexual-moral light was a hard thing to deal with. I could not handle both propositions in the same book. There was no room for it. I might do it differently today, but then, to have a black presence in the book at that moment, and in Paris, would have been quite beyond my powers.

INTERVIEWER

Was it David who first appeared in *Giovanni's Room*?

BALDWIN

It was, yes, but that novel has a curious history. I wrote four novels before I published one, before I'd even left America. I don't know what happened to them. When I came over they were in a duffel bag, which I lost, and that's that. But the genesis of *Giovanni's Room* is in America. David is the first person I thought of, but that's due to a peculiar case involving a boy named Lucien Carr, who murdered somebody. He was known to some of the people I knew—I didn't know him personally. But I was fascinated by the trial, which also involved a wealthy playboy and his wife in high society. From this fascination came the first version of *Giovanni's Room*, something called *Ignorant Armies*, a novel I never finished. The bones of *Giovanni's Room* and *Another Country* were in that.

INTERVIEWER

Wasn't it after your first two novels, which were in many ways extremely personal, that you introduced more of the political and sociological counterpoint evident in your essays into *Another Country*?

BALDWIN

From my point of view it does not quite work that way, making attempts to be merely personal or to bring in a larger scope. No one knows how he writes his book. *Go Tell It on the Mountain* was about my relationship to my father and to the church, which is the same thing really. It was an attempt to exorcise something, to find out what happened to my father, what happened to all of us, what had happened to me—to John—and how we were to move from one place to another. Of course it seems rather personal, but the book is not *about* John; the book is not *about* me.

INTERVIEWER

"One writes out of one thing only—one's own experience," you've said.

BALDWIN

Yes, and yet one's own experience is not necessarily one's twenty-four-hour reality. Everything happens to you, which is what Whitman means when he says in his poem "Heroes," "I am the man, I suffered, I was there." It depends on what you mean by experience.

INTERVIEWER

Nevertheless, it seems that your struggles with social injustices were kept apart as the material for your essays, while your fiction dealt predominantly with your own past.

BALDWIN

If I wanted to survive as a writer I would eventually have had to write a book like *Another Country*. On the other hand, short stories like "Sonny's Blues" or "Previous Condition," which appeared before *Another Country*, were highly personal and yet went further than the immediate dilemmas of the young writer struggling in the Village or of Sonny in "Sonny's Blues."

INTERVIEWER

Ralph Ellison said in his *Paris Review* interview that he writes "*primarily* not concerned with injustice, but with art," whereas one might almost find you a sort of spokesman for blacks.

BALDWIN

I don't consider myself a spokesman—I have always thought it would be rather presumptuous.

INTERVIEWER

Although you are aware of the fact that many people read and are moved by your essays, as well as your speeches and lectures . . .

BALDWIN

Let's go back now. Those essays really date from the time I was in my early twenties and were written for the *New Leader* and *The Nation* all those years ago. They were an attempt to get me beyond the chaos I mentioned earlier. I lived in Paris long enough to finish my first novel, which was very important for me, or I wouldn't be here at all. What held me in Paris later—from '55 to '57—was the fact that I was going through a kind of breakup in my private life, yet I knew I had to go back to America. And I went. Once I was in the civil-rights milieu, once I'd met Martin Luther King Jr. and Malcolm X and Medgar Evers and all those other people, the role I had to play was confirmed. I didn't think of myself as a public speaker or as a spokesman, but I knew I could get a story past the editor's desk. And once you realize that you can do something, it would be difficult to live with yourself if you didn't do it.

INTERVIEWER

When you were much younger, what distinctions did you make between art and protest?

BALDWIN

I thought of them both as literature and still do. I don't see the contradiction that some people point out as inherent, though I can sense what Ralph, among others, means by that. The only way I could play it, once indeed I found myself on that road, was to assume that if I had the talent, and my talent was important, it would simply have to survive whatever life brought. I couldn't sit somewhere honing my talent to a fine edge after I had been to all those places in the South and seen those boys and girls, men and women, black and white, longing for change. It was impossible for me to drop them a visit and then leave.

INTERVIEWER

You were in utter despair after the death of Martin Luther King Jr. Did you find it difficult to write then, or do you work better out of anguish?

BALDWIN

No one works better out of anguish at all; that's an incredible liter-ary conceit. I didn't think I could write at all. I didn't see any point to it. I was hurt . . . I can't even talk about it. I didn't know how to con-tinue, didn't see my way clear.

INTERVIEWER

How did you eventually find your way out of the pain?

BALDWIN

I think really through my brother, David. I was working on *No Name in the Street* but hadn't touched it after the assassination. He called me and I told him, I just can't finish this book. I don't know what to do with it. And he came across the ocean. I was here in St. Paul, living in Le Hameau across the road. I was sick, went to four or five hospitals. I was very lucky, because I could've gone mad. You see, I had left America after the funeral and gone to Istanbul. Worked—or tried to—there. Got sick in Istanbul, went to London, got sick in Lon-don, and I wanted to die. Collapsed. I was shipped down here, out of the American Hospital in Paris. I'd been in the region in 1949, but I had never dreamt of coming to live in St. Paul. Once I was here, I stayed. I didn't really have anyplace else to go. Well, I could have gone back to America, and I did, to do a *Rap on Race*, which helped me significantly. But principally, David came and he read *No Name in the Street* and sent it on to New York.

INTERVIEWER

In an *Esquire* essay, you once wrote that you've been "schooled in adversity and skilled in compromise." Does that perhaps reflect try-ing to get your work published?

BALDWIN

No, though it has been such a stormy career. It's a terrible way to make a living. I find writing gets harder as time goes on. I'm speaking of the working process, which demands a certain amount of energy and courage (though I dislike using the word), and a certain amount of recklessness. I don't know, I doubt whether anyone—myself at least—knows how to *talk* about writing. Perhaps I'm afraid to.

INTERVIEWER

Do you see it as conception, gestation, accouchement?

BALDWIN

I don't think about it that way, no. The whole process of conception—one talks about it after the fact, if one discusses it at all. But you really don't understand it. After the fact I may discuss a work, yet I'm uncertain that what I do say about it afterward can be taken as gospel.

INTERVIEWER

One critic suggested that James Baldwin's best work was yet to come and would be an autobiographical novel, which *Just Above My Head* was in part.

BALDWIN

He may have a point there. I hope, certainly, that my best work is before me. It depends on what one means by *autobiographical*. I certainly have not told my story yet, I know that, though I've revealed fragments.

INTERVIEWER

Are you, or do you remain, very close to your characters?

BALDWIN

I don't know if I feel close to them, now. After a time you find, however, that your characters are lost to you, making it quite impossible for you to judge them. When you've finished a novel it means, The train stops here, you have to get off here. You never get the book you wanted, you settle for the book you get. I've always felt that when a book ended there was something I didn't see, and usually when I remark the discovery it's too late to do anything about it.

INTERVIEWER

This occurs once it has already been published?

BALDWIN

No, no, it happens when you are right here at the table. The publication date is something else again. It's out of your hands, then. What happens here is that you realize if you try to redo something, you may wreck everything else. But if a book has brought you from one place to another, so that you see something you didn't see before, you've arrived at another point. This then is one's consolation, and you know that you must now proceed elsewhere.

INTERVIEWER

Are there a lot of your characters walking around here?

BALDWIN

No, they begin walking around before you put them on paper. And after you put them on paper you don't see them anymore. They may be wandering around here. *You* might see them.

INTERVIEWER

So once you've captured a character in your work, it is no longer a phantom?

BALDWIN

Actually, what has happened is that the character has tyrannized you for however long it took, and when the novel is over he or she says Ciao, thanks a lot. *Pointe finale*. Before *Another Country*, Ida talked to me for years. We get on very well now.

INTERVIEWER

How soon after you conceived of Rufus, in *Another Country*, did you know he was going to commit suicide, or was he modeled after your adolescent friend who jumped off the George Washington Bridge in New York?

BALDWIN

Oh, he was taken directly from that friend, yet, oddly enough, he was the last person to arrive in the novel. I'd written the book more than once and I'd felt I'd never get it right. Ida was important, but I wasn't sure I could cope with her. Ida and Vivaldo were the first people I was dealing with, but I couldn't find a way to make you understand Ida. Then Rufus came along and the entire action made sense.

INTERVIEWER

And Richard, the rather idealistic writer?

BALDWIN

This is all far beyond my memory. Well, there was Vivaldo, whose name I didn't know for some time. He was called Daniel at first, and at one point was black. Ida, on the other hand, was always Ida. Richard and Cass were part of the decor. From my point of view, there was nothing in the least idealistic about Richard. He was modeled on several liberal American careerists from then and now. In any case, in order to make the reader see Ida, I had to give her a brother, who turned out to be Rufus. It's fascinating from the point of view of styles, and of accomodations to human pain, that it took me so long—from 1946 to 1960—to accept the fact that my friend was dead. From the moment Rufus was gone, I knew that if you knew what had happened to Ida, you'd equally understand Rufus, and you'd see why Ida throughout the book was so difficult with Vivaldo and everybody else—with herself above all, because she wasn't going to be able to live with the pain. The principal action in the book, for me, is the journey of Ida and Vivaldo toward some kind of coherence.

INTERVIEWER

Is there a big shifting of gears between writing fiction and writing nonfiction?

BALDWIN

Shifting gears, you ask. Every form is difficult, no one is easier than another. They all kick your ass. None of it comes easy.

INTERVIEWER

How many pages do you write in a day?

BALDWIN

I write at night. After the day is over, and supper is over, I begin, and work until about three or four A.M.

INTERVIEWER

That's quite rare, isn't it, because most people write when they're fresh, in the morning.

BALDWIN

I start working when everyone has gone to bed. I've had to do that ever since I was young—I had to wait until the kids were asleep. And then I was working at various jobs during the day. I've always had to write at night. But now that I'm established I do it because I'm alone at night.

INTERVIEWER

When do you know something is the way you want it?

BALDWIN

I do a lot of rewriting. It's very painful. You know it's finished when you can't do anything more to it, though it's never exactly the way you want it. In fact, the hardest thing I ever wrote was that suicide scene in *Another Country*. I always knew that Rufus had to commit suicide very early on, because that was the key to the book. But I kept putting it off. It had to do, of course, with reliving the suicide of my friend who jumped off the bridge. Also, it was very dangerous to do from the technical point of view because this central character dies in the first hundred pages, with a couple of hundred pages to go. The point up to the suicide is like a long prologue, and it is the only light on Ida. You never go into her mind, but I had to make you see what is happening to this girl by making you feel the blow of her brother's death—the key to her relationship with everybody. She tries to make everybody pay for it. You cannot do that, life is not like that, you only destroy yourself.

INTERVIEWER

Is that the way a book starts for you, though? Something like that?

BALDWIN

Probably that way for everybody—something that irritates you and won't let you go. That's the anguish of it. Do this book or die. You have to go through that.

INTERVIEWER

Does it purge you in any way?

BALDWIN

I'm not so sure about *that*. For me it's like a journey, and the only thing you know is that if when the book is over you are prepared to continue, you haven't cheated.

INTERVIEWER

What would cheating be?

BALDWIN

Avoiding. Lying.

INTERVIEWER

So there is a compulsion to get it out?

BALDWIN

Oh yes, to get it out and get it right. The word I'm using is *compulsion*. And it is true of the essay as well.

INTERVIEWER

But the essay is a little bit simpler, isn't it, because you're angry about something that you can put your finger on . . .

BALDWIN

An essay is not simpler, though it may seem so. An essay is essentially an argument. The writer's point of view in an essay is always absolutely clear. The writer is trying to make the readers see something, trying to convince them of something. In a novel or a play you're trying to *show* them something. The risks, in any case, are exactly the same.

INTERVIEWER

What are your first drafts like?

BALDWIN

They are overwritten. Most of the rewrite, then, is cleaning. Don't describe it, show it. That's what I try to teach all young writers—take it out! Don't describe a purple sunset, make me see that it is purple.

INTERVIEWER

As your experience about writing accrues, what would you say increases with knowledge?

BALDWIN

You learn how little you know. It becomes much more difficult because the hardest thing in the world is simplicity. And the most fearful thing too. It becomes more difficult because you have to strip yourself of all your disguises, some of which you didn't know you had. You want to write a sentence as clean as a bone. That is the goal.

INTERVIEWER

Do you mind what people say about your writing?

BALDWIN

Ultimately not. I minded it when I was younger. You care about the people you care about, what they say. You care about the reviews so that somebody will read the book. So those things are important, but not of ultimate importance.

INTERVIEWER

The attitudes you found in America that made you go to France—are they still with us, are they exactly the same?

BALDWIN

I always knew I would have to come back. If I were twenty-four now, I don't know if and where I would go. I don't know if I would go to France; I might go to Africa. You must remember when I was twenty-four there was really no Africa to go to, except Liberia. I thought of going to Israel, but I never did, and I was right about that. Now, though, a kid now . . . well, you see, something has happened that no one has really noticed, but it's very important—Europe is no longer a frame of reference, a standard-bearer, the classic model for literature and for civilization. It's not the measuring stick. There are other standards in the world. It's a fascinating time to be living. There's a whole wide world which isn't now as it was when I was younger. When I was a kid the world was white, for all intents and purposes, and now it is struggling to *remain* white—a very different thing.

INTERVIEWER

It's frequently been noted that you are a master of minor characters. How do you respond to that?

BALDWIN

Well, minor characters are the subtext, illustrations of whatever it is you're trying to convey. I was always struck by the minor characters in Dostoyevsky and Dickens. The minor characters have a certain freedom that the major ones don't. They can make comments, they can move, yet they haven't got the same weight or intensity.

INTERVIEWER

You mean to say their actions are less accountable?

BALDWIN

Oh no, if you fuck up a minor character you fuck up a major one. They are more a part of the decor—a kind of Greek chorus. They carry the tension in a much more explicit way than the majors.

INTERVIEWER

Excuse me for asking, but might your mother be standing behind you while you're writing; is she perhaps behind many of your characters?

BALDWIN

I wouldn't think so, but to tell you the truth, I wouldn't know. I've got five sisters. And in a funny way, there have been many women in my life, so it wouldn't be my mother.

INTERVIEWER

Have you been through analysis?

BALDWIN

God no, never got "adjusted."

INTERVIEWER

Both you and William Styron, intentionally or not, write about victims and victimization. Styron has said he has never felt like a victim. Have you?

BALDWIN

Well, I refuse to. Perhaps the turning point in one's life is realizing that to be treated like a victim is not necessarily to become one.

INTERVIEWER

Do you believe in a community of writers? Is that of any interest to you?

BALDWIN

No. I've never *seen* one in any case . . . and I don't think any writer ever has.

INTERVIEWER

But weren't William Styron and Richard Wright, say, important to you in formulating your viewpoints?

BALDWIN

Richard was very important to me. He was much older. He was very nice to me. He helped me with my first novel, really. That was 1944–45. I just knocked on his door out in Brooklyn! I introduced myself, and of course he'd no idea who I was. There were no essays then, no fiction—this was 1944. I adored him. I loved him. We were very unlike each other, as writers, probably as people too. And as I grew older, that became more and more apparent. And after that was Paris.

INTERVIEWER

And Styron?

BALDWIN

Well, as I was saying, Bill is a friend of mine who happens to be a writer.

INTERVIEWER

Did you take a position on his book about Nat Turner?

BALDWIN

I did. My position, though, is that I will not tell another writer what to write. If you don't like their alternative, write yours. I admired him for confronting it, and the result. It brought in the whole enormity of the issue of history versus fiction, fiction versus history, and which is which . . . He writes out of reasons similar to mine—about something that hurt him and frightened him. When I was working on

Another Country and Bill was working on *Nat Turner*, I stayed in his guest house for five months. His hours and mine are very different. I was going to bed at dawn, Bill was just coming up to his study to go to work; his hours going on as mine went off. We saw each other at suppertime.

INTERVIEWER

What kind of conversations would you hold?

BALDWIN

We never spoke about our work, or very rarely. It was a wonderful time in my life, but not at all literary. We sang songs, drank a little too much, and on occasion chatted with the people who were dropping in to see us. We had a certain common inheritance in terms of the music.

INTERVIEWER

What sort of music are you hearing while in the immediate process of writing? Do you experience anything physical or emotional?

BALDWIN

No. I'm very cold—*cold* probably isn't the word I want, *controlled*. Writing for me must be a very controlled exercise, formed by passions and hopes. That is the only reason you get through it, otherwise you may as well do something else. The act of writing itself is cold.

INTERVIEWER

I'm going to presage my own question. Most of the novelists I've spoken to claim they read exceedingly fewer contemporary novels but find themselves drawn to plays, history, memoirs, biographies, and poetry. I believe this is true for you as well.

BALDWIN

In my case it is due to the fact that I'm always doing some kind of research. And yes, I read many plays and a lot of poetry as a kind of apprenticeship. You are fascinated, I am fascinated by a certain *optic*—a process of seeing things. Reading Emily Dickinson, for example, and others who are quite far removed from one's ostensible daily concerns, or obligations. They are freer, for that moment, than you are partly because they are dead. They may also be a source of strength. Contemporary novels are part of a universe in which you have a certain role and a certain responsibility. And, of course, an unavoidable curiosity.

INTERVIEWER

You read contemporary novels out of a sense of responsibility?

BALDWIN

In a way. At any rate, few novelists interest me—which has nothing to do with their values. I find most of them too remote for me. The world of John Updike, for instance, does not impinge on my world. On the other hand, the world of John Cheever *did* engage me. Obviously, I'm not making a very significant judgment about Updike. It's entirely subjective, what I'm saying. In the main, the concerns of most white Americans—to use *that* phrase—are boring, and terribly, terribly self-centered. In the worst sense. Everything is contingent, of course, on what you take yourself to be.

INTERVIEWER

Are you suggesting they are less concerned, somehow, with social injustice?

BALDWIN

No, no, you see, I don't want to make that kind of dichotomy. I'm not asking that anybody get on picket lines or take positions. That is entirely a private matter. What I'm saying has to do with the concept of the self, and the nature of self-indulgence that seems to me to be terribly strangling, and so limited it finally becomes sterile.

INTERVIEWER

And yet in your own writing you deal with personal experiences quite often.

BALDWIN

Yes, but—and here I'm in trouble with the language again—it depends upon how you conceive of yourself. It revolves, surely, around the multiplicity of your connections. Obviously you can only deal with your life and work from the vantage point of your self. There isn't any other vantage point; there is no other point of view. I can't say about any of my characters that they are utter fictions. I do have a sense of what nagged my attention where and when; even in the dimmest sense I know how a character impinged on me in reality, in what we call reality, the daily world. And then, of course, imagination has something to do with it. But it has got to be triggered by something, it cannot be triggered by itself.

INTERVIEWER

What is it about Emily Dickinson that moves you?

BALDWIN

Her use of language, certainly. Her solitude, as well, and the style of that solitude. There is something very moving and in the best sense funny. She isn't solemn. If you really want to know something about solitude, become famous. That is the turn of the screw. That solitude is practically insurmountable. Years ago I thought to be famous would be a kind of ten-day wonder, and then I could go right back to life as usual. But people treat you differently before you realize it. You see it in the wonder and the worry of your intimates. On the other side of that is a great responsibility.

INTERVIEWER

Is one's past cluttered, as a celebrated writer?

BALDWIN

There are many witnesses to my past, people who've disappeared, people who are dead, whom I loved. But I don't feel there are any ghosts, any regrets. I don't feel that kind of melancholy at all. No nostalgia. Everything is always around and before you. Novels that haven't worked, loves, struggles. And yet it all gives you something of immeasurable power.

INTERVIEWER

This brings us to your concern with reality as being history, with seeing the present shaded by everything that occurred in a person's past. James Baldwin has always been bound by his past and his future. At forty, you said you felt much older than that.

BALDWIN

That is one of those things a person says at forty, at forty especially. It was a great shock to me, forty. And I did feel much older than that. Responding to history, I think a person is in sight of his or her death around the age of forty. You see it coming. You are not in sight of your death at thirty, less so at twenty-five. You are struck by the fact of your mortality, that it is unlikely you'll live another forty years. So time alters you, actually becoming either an enemy or a friend.

INTERVIEWER

You seem very troubled—but not by death?

BALDWIN

Yes, true, but not at all by death. I'm troubled over getting my work done and over all the things I've not learned. It's useless to be troubled by death, because then, of course, you can't live at all.

INTERVIEWER

"Essentially, America has not changed that much," you told *The New York Times* when *Just Above My Head* was being published. Have you?

BALDWIN

In some ways I've changed precisely because America has not. I've been forced to change in some ways. I had a certain expectation for my country years ago, which I know I don't have now.

INTERVIEWER

Yes, before 1968, you said, "I love America."

BALDWIN

Long before then. I still do, though that feeling has changed in the face of it. I think that it is a spiritual disaster to pretend that one *doesn't* love one's country. You may disapprove of it, you may be forced to leave it, you may live your whole life as a battle, yet I don't think you can escape it. There isn't any other place to go—you don't pull up your roots and put them down someplace else. At least not in a single life-time, or, if you do, you'll be aware of precisely what it means, knowing that your real roots are always elsewhere. If you try to pretend you don't see the immediate reality that formed you I think you'll go blind.

INTERVIEWER

As a writer, are there any particular battles you feel you've won?

BALDWIN

The battle of becoming a writer at all! I'm going to be a great writer when I grow up, I used to tell my mother when I was a little boy. And I'm still going to be a great writer when I grow up.

INTERVIEWER

What do you tell younger writers who come to you with the usual desperate question: How do I become a writer?

BALDWIN

Write. Find a way to keep alive and write. There is nothing else to say. If you are going to be a writer there is nothing I can say to stop you; if you're not going to be a writer nothing I can say will help you. What you really need at the beginning is somebody to let you know that the effort is real.

INTERVIEWER

Can you discern talent in someone?

BALDWIN

Talent is insignificant. I know a lot of talented ruins. Beyond talent lie all the usual words: discipline, love, luck, but, most of all, endurance.

INTERVIEWER

Would you suggest that a young writer from a minority consecrate himself to that minority, or is his first obligation his own self-realization as a writer?

BALDWIN

Your self and your people are indistinguishable from each other, really, in spite of the quarrels you may have, and your people are all people.

INTERVIEWER

Wasn't *Giovanni's Room* partially an attempt to break down these divisions, pointing out that David could be white, black, or yellow?

BALDWIN

Certainly, for in terms of what happened to him, none of that mattered at all.

INTERVIEWER

Yet, later on, notably in the case of Rufus and *Another Country*, one's race becomes essential to your story.

BALDWIN

Important in that particular novel, yes, but *Another Country* is called that because it is trying to convey the reality of that country. The story would be different if it were in France, or even in England.

INTERVIEWER

What is your present relationship with people like Ralph Ellison, Amiri Baraka, and Eldridge Cleaver?

BALDWIN

I never had a relationship with Cleaver. I was in difficulties because of Cleaver, which I didn't want to talk about then and don't wish to discuss now. My real difficulty with Cleaver, sadly, was visited on me by the kids who were following him, while he was calling me a faggot and the rest of it. I would come to a town to speak, Cleveland, let's say, and he would've been standing on the very same stage a couple of days earlier. I had to try to undo the damage I considered he was doing. I was handicapped with *Soul on Ice*, because what I might have said in those years about Eldridge would have been taken as an answer to his attack on me. So I never answered it, and I'm not answering it now. Cleaver reminded me of an old Baptist minister I used to work with when I was in the pulpit. I never trusted him at all. As for Baraka, he and I have had a stormy time too, but we're very good friends now.

INTERVIEWER

Do you read each other's work?

BALDWIN

Yes—at least I read his. And as for Ralph, I haven't seen him in many years.

INTERVIEWER

You haven't corresponded at all?

BALDWIN

No. I gather Ralph did not like what he considered I was doing to myself on the civil-rights road. And so, we haven't seen each other.

INTERVIEWER

If you were both to meet over lunch tomorrow, what might you talk about?

BALDWIN

I'd love to meet him for lunch tomorrow, and share a bottle of bourbon, and probably talk about the last twenty years we haven't seen each other. I have nothing against him in any case. And I love his great book. We disagreed about tactics, I suppose. But I had to go through the civil-rights movement and I don't regret it at all. And those people trusted me. There was something very beautiful about that period, something life-giving for me to be there, to march, to be a part of a sit-in, to see it through my own eyes.

INTERVIEWER

Do you think that now blacks and whites can write about each other, honestly and convincingly?

BALDWIN

Yes, though I have no overwhelming evidence in hand. But I think of the impact of spokespersons like Toni Morrison and other younger writers. I believe what one has to do as a black American is to take white history, or history as written by whites, and claim it all—including Shakespeare.

INTERVIEWER

"What other people write about me is irrelevant," you once wrote in *Essence*. Was that meant to go unqualified; do you not relate to criticism in any way?

BALDWIN

It is never entirely true that you don't give a shit what others say about you, but you must throw it out of your mind. I went through a very trying period, after all, where on one side of town I was an Uncle Tom and on the other the Angry Young Man. It could make one's head spin, the number of labels that have been attached to me. And it was inevitably painful, and surprising, and indeed, bewildering. I *do* care what certain people think about me.

INTERVIEWER
But not literary critics?

BALDWIN
Literary critics cannot be one's concern. Ideally, however, what a critic can do is indicate where you've been excessive or unclear. As far as any sort of public opinion is a question, I would say that one cannot possibly react to any of it. Things may be said which hurt, and you don't like it, but what are you to do? Write a White Paper, or a Black Paper, defending yourself? You can't do that.

INTERVIEWER
You have often left your home in St. Paul, returning to America and going on the road. Do you feel comfortable as a speaker?

BALDWIN
I have never felt comfortable as a speaker, no.

INTERVIEWER
You feel more at ease behind the typewriter?

BALDWIN
Well, certainly, although I used to be a preacher, which helps on the road.

INTERVIEWER
Can you talk a little more about your relationship to Richard Wright, under whose aegis you received your first writing grant?

BALDWIN
As I said before, I just knocked on his door in New York. I was nineteen. And he was very nice. The only trouble was I didn't drink in those years. He drank bourbon. Now, I'm going to save you the trouble of asking me about writers and alcohol: I don't know any

writers who don't drink. Everybody I've been close to drinks. But you don't drink while you're working. It's funny, because it is all a reflex, like lighting a cigarette. Your drink is made and then you go off to another place. When you finally get back to the drink it's mainly water. And the cigarette has gone out. Talking about Richard and our early hostile period, which I thought was ridiculously blown out of proportion, I should say that when I thought I was dealing with Richard, I was in fact thinking of Harriet Beecher Stowe and *Uncle Tom's Cabin*. Richard's *Native Son* was the only contemporary representation there was of a black person in America. One of the reasons I wrote what I did about the book is a technical objection, which I uphold today. I could not accept the performance of the lawyer at the end of the book. I was very explicit about that. I think it was simply absurd to talk about this monster created by the American public, and then expect the public to save it! Altogether, I found it too simpleminded. Insofar as the American public creates a monster, they are not about to recognize it. You create a monster and destroy it. It is part of the American way of life, if you like. I reserve, in any case, the utmost respect for Richard, especially in light of his posthumous work, which I believe is his greatest novel, *Lawd Today*. Look it up.

INTERVIEWER

Is there any resistance today to black writers in publishing houses?

BALDWIN

There is an enormous resistance, though it differs from Wright's time. When I was young, the joke was, How many niggers you got at your plantation? Or, more snidely, How many niggers you got at your publishing house? And some had one, most had none. That's not true now.

INTERVIEWER

How does it strike you that in many circles James Baldwin is known as a prophetic writer?

BALDWIN

I don't try to be prophetic, as I don't sit down to write literature. It is simply this: a writer has to take all the risks of putting down what he sees. No one can tell him about that. No one can control that reality. It reminds me of something Pablo Picasso was supposed to have said to Gertrude Stein while he was painting her portrait. Gertrude said, I don't look like that. And Picasso replied, You will. And he was right.

Issue 91, 1984

William Gaddis

The Art of Fiction

William Gaddis was interviewed on November 4, 1986, in Budapest, where he had stopped for a day on his way home from a conference in Sofia. The proposal of an interview survived his discouraging reputation for being reclusive and avoiding interviews. A gentle and genial man welcomed me in his Atrium Hyatt suite: gray hair; an absorbed and attentive, hard-featured, longish face with strict yet amiable, contemplative eyes; and a relaxed, unassuming manner. He had a ghastly cold and spoke hoarsely, coughing slightly and sipping meditatively at his whiskey.

He listened to the questions with untiring patience. The remorseless logic as well as the profound care of his answers convinced me that this satiric chronicler of chaotic existence and entropic disintegration is indeed a fearful causal thinker deeply concerned about the human condition.

William Gaddis was born in 1922 in New York, where he lives now. In the mid-fifties he produced *The Recognitions*, an entropic, black humor, postmodern novel. Yet in spite of his books' considerable artistic achievement, Gaddis has still not received the degree of recognition that his talent and work deserve. Animated by a deep-seated humanism, he is a satirist who has no tolerance for stupidity and absurdity. With extraordinary erudition he examines man's relation to the world in witty, sarcastic, often mordant social-epistemological parables. His novels are: *The Recognitions* (1955);

what he was the, he laughed he said next time I go to a dog

fight I'll, I mean that's when everything began to get, when
   began to,
                             did he.
it all when, when he never read to Billy/ He never read to

Billy.

       horm horm mad

   Was it? hand, voice words pacing what had been lost fnd
  lost agn & agn &c; exploring
          idling
-Was it? His hand finding its way under the sheet now, moving

over crest & hummock corrugation of the ribs/ geography
        a   over the rise & fall
over finding its way down its corrugated path from crest to

hummock (paraph his wrds disappntment &c) measuring pacing leading

staying restraining (—wrds, disappntng someone else) exploring
                                   restng
for what been lost & fnd & lost agn & again (into paraph prisoners

of hopes, of othr peoples hopes) & (her) geography, to the hummock

(—wwds as the presumptn effrontry of takng resp for making someone
                   restng
happy) paused/on the hillock now (thrust of his own rise vs

plain flank) to the someone (Irene) who is simply unhappy &c
          dry run
futility of that/effort (agnst her flank)

all of it to provoke her (pulls off the sheet) children choosng prnts

& the heat of her evasion pulled away but her brst pressd at him

—ne, just so they can get born? &c into chance.

Evry? Youll frget me?   (Edie & gypsies)
                  / the abrupt what, reintro of tlescope? rf

prev existnce? into reincarnatn

& does it then turn? his pursuit (limp) into wrds, hers into sx?

   Was it? His hand had idled its way under the sheet now,

returning unseen and as though unattended to pause at her breast,
                                he said
perhaps it had more to do with disappoinment, not of being

disappointed but of being afraid of disappointing someone else,
                    of
hexsmidt his voice unhurried as the movement of his hand, pacing

it, disappointing someone close, of living on the edge of betrayal

that was bound to come along one way or another, sooner or later,

his fingertips failing their search over the soft unbroken rise

under the sheet there and d3scending a corrugated path to (basin &c

A manuscript page from Carpenter's Gothic *by William Gaddis.*

JR, a National Book Award winner (1975); and *Carpenter's Gothic* (1985).

—*Zoltán Abádi-Nagy, 1987*

INTERVIEWER

Since over the years you've acquired a reputation for avoiding interviews, particularly those that address your work, let me ask why you are submitting to this one.

WILLIAM GADDIS

I suppose because I've got some illusion about finally getting the whole thing out of the way once and for all. In the past I've resisted partly because of the tendency I've observed of putting the man in the place of his work, and that goes back more than thirty years; it comes up in a conversation early in *The Recognitions*. That, and the conviction that the work has got to stand on its own—when ambiguities appear they are deliberate and I've no intention of running after them with explanations—and finally, of course, the threat of questions from someone unfamiliar with the work itself: Do you work on a fixed schedule every day? On which side of the paper do you write? That sort of talk-show pap, five-minute celebrity, turning the creative artist into a performing one, which doesn't look to be the case here.

INTERVIEWER

Thank you for the vote of confidence.

GADDIS

And so I've the hope of laying a few things to rest; an interview I can simply refer people to when the threat of another appears, without having to go through it again.

INTERVIEWER

You say a work has got to stand on its own. Isn't it hard for a writer sometimes to adhere to this principle steadfastly? In other words, are you never annoyed by misinterpretations of your works?

GADDIS

What writer is not? And unless you're writing "what they want"—I mean, some formula simply for the money—isn't that our history, from Melville on? It comes with the territory, as the playwright said.

INTERVIEWER

Now that you have decided to step out of your reclusiveness—and before stepping back into it—perhaps you're dissatisfied with the image that is in circulation concerning your life and personality and views that you'd like to correct?

GADDIS

I'd hoped this interview would clear up some of that—what *can* be cleared up, that is to say, because trying to correct one's image is as futile as it is irrelevant. Of course, if your image is really all you've got going—which is hardly uncommon these days; take a Henry Kissinger, for instance—you'll want to deliberately distort the record to make yourself look good. I'd go back to *The Recognitions*, where Wyatt asks what people want from the man they didn't get from his work, because presumably that's where he's tried to distill this "life and personality and views" you speak of. What's any artist but the dregs of his work? I gave that line to Wyatt thirty-odd years ago and as far as I'm concerned it's still valid.

INTERVIEWER

Here is another obligatory question. You have received recognition in the form of various grants and awards, including the substantial MacArthur Prize Fellowship. What is your feeling about that? How have they changed things?

GADDIS

Well, I almost think that if I'd gotten the Nobel Prize when *The Recognitions* was published I wouldn't have been terribly surprised. I mean that's the grand intoxication of youth, or what's a heaven for. And so the book's reception was a sobering experience, quite a humbling

one. When finally help did come along, recognition, as you say, a
Rockefeller Foundation grant, a Guggenheim Fellowship, the National Endowment for the Arts, they came in difficult times and allowed and encouraged me to keep on with the second book and start
the third. Without them, I wonder if I might not just have dropped
the whole damned business, though God knows what else I might
have done, too late even to be any of the things I never wanted to be.
There's always the talk about feeding at the public trough, disdain-
ing grants because you've never been given one. I mean we'd all
wish to come out with the fierce integrity of Samuel Butler, say, who
never wrote simply to publish or published everything he wrote—
The Way of All Flesh was posthumous after all—and that has been
the luxury of the MacArthur. But then I never was a fellow to rush
into print.

INTERVIEWER

Could you say something about the genesis of your own novels?
Can you reconstruct what was involved in your getting started with
The Recognitions?

GADDIS

I think first it was that towering kind of confidence of being quite
young, that one can do anything—"All's brave that youth mounts and
folly guides," as we're told in *As You Like It*. *The Recognitions* started
as a short piece of work, quite undirected, but based on the Faust
story. Then as I got into the idea of forgery, the entire concept of forgery became—I wouldn't say an obsession—but a central part of
everything I thought and saw; so the book expanded from simply the
central character of the forger to forgery, falsification, and cheapen-
ing of values and what have you, everywhere. Looking at it now with
its various faults, I suppose excess would be the main charge. I remember Clive Bell looking back on his small fine book, *Art*, thirty-five
years after it was published in 1913, and listing *its* faults, finding it
too confident and aggressive, even too optimistic—I was never accused of that!—but still feeling, as he said, "a little envious of the adventurous young man who wrote it."

INTERVIEWER

What moved you to write *JR*?

GADDIS

Even though I should have known from *The Recognitions* that the world was not waiting breathlessly for my message, that it already knew and was quite happy to *live* with all these false values, I'd always been intrigued by the charade of the so-called free market, so-called free enterprise system, the stock market conceived of as what was called a "people's capitalism" where you "owned a part of the company," and so forth. All of which is true; you own shares in a company, so you literally do own part of the assets. But if you own a hundred shares out of six or sixty or six hundred million, you're not going to influence things very much. Also, the fact that people buy securities—the very word in this context is comic—not because they are excited by the product—often you don't know what the company makes—but simply for profit: the stock looks good and you buy it. The moment it looks bad you sell it. What had actually happened in the company is not your concern. In many ways I thought . . . the *childishness* of all this. Because JR himself, which is why he is eleven years old, is motivated only by good-natured greed. *JR* was, in other words, to be a commentary on this free enterprise system running out of control. Looking around us now with a two-trillion-dollar federal deficit and billions of private debt and the banks, the farms, basic industry all in serious trouble, it seems to have been rather prophetic.

INTERVIEWER

Carpenter's Gothic?

GADDIS

Well, that was rather different. I cannot really work unless I set a problem for myself to solve. In *Carpenter's Gothic* the problems were largely of style and technique and form. I wanted to write a shorter book, one that observes the unities of time and place to the point that everything, even though it expands into the world, takes place in one house, and a country house at that, with a small number of characters, in a short span of time. It became really largely an exercise in style and technique. And also I wanted to take all these clichés of fiction to bring them to life and make them work. So we have the older man and the younger woman, the marriage breaking up, the obligatory adultery, the locked room, the mysterious stranger, and so forth.

INTERVIEWER

To have a more detailed look at the novels now. *The Recognitions* takes its title from *Recognitions*, a work attributed to St. Clement of Rome. The Wyatt Gwyon of your novel is thus a Clement figure with a dispersed family—there are many more dispersed families in the novel—and with a story that becomes a dialogue between pagan and Christian ideologies, and becomes a search for salvation, to mention the most obvious parallels. What was your main intention in introducing a Clement figure into the twentieth century, in a story that starts a few years after the First World War and takes place mainly at the turn of the decades of the forties and fifties?

GADDIS

We come back to the Faust story and to the original Clementine *Recognitions*, which has been called the first Christian novel (I remember thinking mine was going to be the last one), about his search for salvation, redemption, and so forth. And I had these notions of basing *The Recognitions* on the constant presence of the past and of its imposition of myth in different forms that eventually come down to the same stories in any culture. I think they titled the Italian edition "The Pilgrim" or "The Pilgrimage" or something like that. In a sense it is that: a pilgrimage toward salvation.

INTERVIEWER

Disregarding now the immense symbolic-thematic complexity that the myth itself entails in the novel, I think that the logic of the Faust story lends itself particularly well to the message about the postmodern world, namely, manipulation and forgery. The Faustian pact with the devil is nothing but giving up originality, isn't it? And vice versa, a

painter, Wyatt, manipulated into selling his soul, giving up originality, is bound to be Faustian, besides being emblematic of the artist's
position in a corrupt, manipulative, counterfeit world. Is this a correct
interpretation of Wyatt's central function as a Faust figure?

GADDIS

It is, yes, originality also being Satan's "original sin" if you like. I
think also, further, I tried to make clear that Wyatt was the very height
of a *talent* but not a genius—quite a different thing. Which is why he
shrinks from going ahead in, say, works of originality. He shrinks
from this and takes refuge in what is already there, which he *can* handle, manipulate. He can do quite perfect forgeries, because the pa-
rameters of perfection are already there.

INTERVIEWER

If Joyce's Stephen Dedalus of the *Portrait* was the archetypal
modernist artist, your Wyatt's story seems to be a *postmodern* varia-
tion on the *Künstlerroman*. Wyatt does, in fact, come to be called
Stephen at the end of the novel. He, too, abandons the idea of priest-
hood to become a priest of the imagination. But with a difference. He
will paint *forgeries*; that is, he will become the priest of *other people's*
imaginations. Stephen Dedalus's *non serviam*—an attitude that
echoes down in *Ulysses* too—is no longer possible.

GADDIS

This is quite a complicated question. First, what is interesting is
this business of *Ulysses* . . .

INTERVIEWER

I mean the *Portrait*. I know you had not read *Ulysses* before you
wrote *The Recognitions*.

GADDIS

Right. Many of these similarities that critics and doctoral students
have dug up are absolutely coincidences. Stephen, for instance—the
reason I chose that name is he was the first Christian martyr.

INTERVIEWER

That's why Joyce decided on that name. It was one of his reasons.

GADDIS

News to me. The coincidences turn up down to the smallest details. There is, for instance, a character who has covered the mirrors with handkerchiefs. Apparently this happens somewhere in *Ulysses* too. And they said, Ah! This is where he got that. Where I got it was when I was in a hotel in Panama and I had washed my handkerchiefs and spread them on the windows and the mirrors to dry—they almost look pressed when they're peeled away that way—a Panamanian friend came in and said, All the mirrors are covered. Who's dead? What's happened? I said, No, I'm just drying my handkerchiefs. Then I found the same incident in *McTeague*—in what, 1903 or 1905? whenever *McTeague* was written. This always strikes me as dangerous—finding "sources."

INTERVIEWER

So let's forget about Joyce. Let me repeat the main point of my question to make it clearer, perhaps. It was something like this: Though on the one hand there is this forgery and serving other people's imagination, on the other hand, at a deeper level, isn't there a deeper appreciation of the real, genuine art of the past, an appreciation of tradition as a source of inspiration for the present?

GADDIS

Looking back—of course this is thirty-five years ago—the essential point was that these painters lived in an age of belief, and so they were, from Giotto on, very safely encased in a frame of reference, working in a frame of absolutes for their talents or their genius, in works largely for the Church. And this is exactly what Wyatt does not have around him. So he is really taking refuge in that framework of belief, as Stanley, his counterpoint, is the one who *is* within this framework of belief, the good Catholic boy, who finally pays the price.

INTERVIEWER

The Recognitions is a very serious book. Especially if one considers that it begins and ends with death and that there is much of the apocalyptic in between. If it is read as a piece of satire, it only makes it an even more serious book since it seems to have been written in the best tradition of "noble indignation." On the other hand I wonder if it is not read too earnestly by too many critics. Especially if one considers that it opens on All Saints' Day when somebody—whose body will be canonized as a result of a ridiculous mistake—dies of appendicitis at the hands of a fake doctor, and ends on Easter Sunday when, instead of resurrection, a devout organist—Stanley, the good Catholic boy—is buried in the collapse of a church. This is closer to burlesque.

GADDIS

Well, what I wanted was a large comic novel. I was very frustrated when it came out and so many reviewers saw it as . . . that terrible word *erudition* kept appearing. That it was difficult—

INTERVIEWER

And it *is* difficult.

GADDIS

—that it was among the first books of black humor and so forth, but, of course, we all came out of Mark Twain's vest pocket. No one has ever beaten "The Mysterious Stranger." But that whole world of the amount of information, what they called erudition, frightened off many people. Very very few reviewers said it is often very funny. It was a sometimes heavy-handed satire but I wanted it to be a large comic novel in the great tradition.

INTERVIEWER

In other senses the novel is not read earnestly enough. Most critics point out that the novel is about disintegration, about a world that is in a mess, is entropic. But Steven Moore's arguments about

Wyatt finding human integrity amidst disintegration seem convincing. So the novel itself is negentropic rather than entropic in the last analysis.

GADDIS

Well, we hope. Many reviewers and critics draw attention to all my books as being hopeless, that no good is going to come of anything, that everything is winding down in the entire entropic concept. But Wyatt's line—I think late in the book—says that one must simply live through the corruption, even become part of it. As Esme, the model, is a quite corrupted person but still an innocent in some way. Well, Wyatt has been part of the corruption, but at the end he says we must simply live it through and make a fresh start. I mean you could almost say—though the way the phrase is used now is *not* what I mean—that it is a notion of being born again in *this* life—with no reference to our "born again" Christians—and the next one.

INTERVIEWER

Apropos of Wyatt being born again: can his struggle for originality be regarded as the antihero's struggle to become a hero? He is a student of perspective who reaches "the vanishing point" early in the novel but begins to emerge as a sovereign personality again at the end.

GADDIS

The latter part of what you say is true. The earlier part about antihero and hero is an interesting interpretation. I did want to, in a sense, create a novel without a hero, but while he remains the central figure, facets all about him are carrying out his—the fashionable word today, I guess—persona. Otto is a kind of two-dimensional imitation of Wyatt; he wants to be Wyatt but has none of the equipment. Stanley has the belief and so forth. Anselm has the despair. So they're all reflections of him. They carry the activity—you don't say *action*, you say *activity*—of the novel, while he is not anywhere in sight.

INTERVIEWER

Alchemy has an important role to play in *The Recognitions*. What attracted you to alchemy and what makes it a relevant device in a satiric exploration of early- and mid-twentieth-century reality?

GADDIS

My early impression was that the alchemists were simply trying to turn base metals into gold. Later I came to the more involved reading and better understanding of it all: that it was something between religion and magic and that it did not necessarily mean literally lead and gold. So the gold in many of the symbolic senses in alchemy is the perfection, is the sun, is a kind of redemption. When at some despairing moment Wyatt says—when he realizes that the table of the *Seven Deadly Sins* is the original and not his copy—"Thank God there was the gold to forge," that is very much the key line to the whole book.

INTERVIEWER

The Recognitions—says John Aldridge—was published before the literature to which it was the pioneer came into vogue. Did you discern signs of an influence that your novel exerted on the fabulators and black-humor writers?

GADDIS

No, because I don't read a great deal of current fiction, especially when I'm working on my own. I don't look for these influences. Even if I did, I would prefer not to say, Yes, I think he learnt from me, or what have you. Let the critics do that.

INTERVIEWER

While *The Recognitions* prefigured the style of the Pynchon generation, I wonder if there was any Pynchonian influence that went into your second novel, *JR*, which opens with a *direct* discussion of the questions of energy, disorder, chaos, entropy—the second law of thermodynamics?

GADDIS

Well, going back a bit further, Nathanael West had sketched entropy nicely in *Miss Lonelyhearts* in the early thirties. Norbert Wiener extrapolated the concept to communications around 1950, and, of course, entropy was mentioned in connection with *The Recognitions*. So I think both Pynchon and I—and I don't know him—are simply involved with different aspects of the same problems. I would doubt that my work has influenced him; his has certainly not influenced mine in any way at all.

INTERVIEWER

Although there is a time-honored tradition of the satirical treatment of human stupidity from Aristophanes through Erasmus, Swift, Twain, to Vonnegut—it is Vonnegut's Jonah, the narrator of *Cat's Cradle*, with his interest in "the history of human stupidity," that I am especially reminded of by your theoretician of stupidity, McCandless, in *Carpenter's Gothic*.

GADDIS

Again, I think writers work from their own energies, their own concepts. I don't think there is any influence among us. After all, stupidity—and I don't mean ignorance—is a central issue of our time. In my own case, going back to entropy, I'm most intrigued by its correlation as the loss of available energy in a closed system with stupidity as the corresponding loss of available intelligence in our own political establishment, especially as regards foreign policy and the economy—its collapse, that is to say—where Wiener sees physics' view of the world as it actually exists replaced by one as we observe it, a kind of one-way communication.

INTERVIEWER

The story of the dwarfish sixth grader, who begins with mail-order enterprise and becomes the head of a huge business conglomerate, is also about the American family—a bitter indictment of the corroding effect that profit-oriented corporate operations exert not only on education and art in particular, but also on social values and human relationships in general.

GADDIS

It is insofar as it is very much about the absence of the family. We know nothing about his father. All that we know about his mother is that she's a nurse who keeps odd hours because of her work. He has no past, in other words, and so he's obliged to invent himself, not in the terms of a father, a mother, and a family, but in terms of what he sees around him. And all he sees around him—in all discussions in the principal's office at the school—there is never any mention of actual educational content. They talk about nothing but paving the parking lot, about buying new teaching machines and teaching equipment and storing what they already have because no one knows how to use it, and so forth.

INTERVIEWER

And there is that other family, the musician's. I forget the name . . .

GADDIS

Yes, Bast, who is, of course, a captive remnant of the past, of the "old family," Turgenev's romantic Arkady meeting up with the hard-nosed pragmatist Bazarov, as it were. Speaking of influences, I think mine are more likely to be found going from Eliot *back* rather than forward to my contemporaries.

INTERVIEWER

Is JR's story something you extrapolated from life only, or did you rely on sociologies devoted to how the corporate world works upon social values, human qualities, and relationships in American culture?

GADDIS

The boy himself is a total invention, completely sui generis. The reason he is eleven is because he is in this prepubescent age where he is amoral, with a clear conscience, dealing with people who are immoral, unscrupulous; they realize what scruples are but push them aside, whereas his good cheer and greed he considers perfectly normal. He thinks this is what you're supposed to do; he is not going to

wait around; he is in a hurry, as you should be in America—get on
with it, get going. He is very scrupulous about obeying the *letter* of
the law and then (never making the distinction) evading the *spirit* of
the law at every possible turn. He is in these ways an innocent and is
well-meaning, a sincere hypocrite. With Bast, he does think he's helping him out. As for the corporate world, I do read the newspapers,
clip things, ideas, articles, and just use them as fodder. But all that
hardly requires a text in sociology. And this may be the place to make
a further point. I'm frequently seen in the conservative press as being
out there on the barricades shouting: Down with capitalism! I do see
it in the end as really the most workable system we've produced. So
what we're talking about is not the system itself, but its abuses. I don't
mean criminal but the abundant abuses just *within* the letter of the
law. The essential question is whether it can survive these abuses
given free rein and whether these abuses are inherent in the system itself. I should think it is perfectly clear in my work—calling attention,
satirizing these abuses—that our best hope lies in bringing things under better and more equitable control, cutting back the temptations to
unmitigated greed and bemused dishonesty . . . in other words, that
these abuses the system has fostered are not essential, but running out
of moral or ethical control can certainly threaten its survival.

INTERVIEWER

What *JR* is about is a radically new situation from the point of
view of the American dream too, and radically new as a literary treatment of that theme: the novel seems to be about how the American
dream claims you before you are socially mature enough to dream it.

GADDIS

Fine, yes, well put. Very much the heart of it in fact.

INTERVIEWER

But the *writer* of *JR* must have commanded an immense inward
knowledge of the mentality and the clichés of the jungle of speculation and manipulation to enable him to write the book. Is this formidable "documentation" mainly veristic or intuitive?

GADDIS

I think both, in the sense that the earlier book was too. It is getting a central idea—in one case the forgery, in the other case the American dream turned inside out—and *then* seeking the documentation, in areas that essentially don't greatly interest me, that simply provide vehicles. But I wanted them right, thinking *if* someone who is well versed and familiar with the world of finance, with what goes on in the market and so forth, read *JR* . . . that even though it's a quite improbable story, it is still possible. So that JR backs into the situation; he isn't sure really what is happening. But in the beginning, what is very important, he is not viewed as one of these computer-wizard brilliant kids. He buys defaulted bond issues simply because they're cheap—it says a thousand dollars up in the corner, but selling at seven cents on the dollar, he's getting them for seventy dollars apiece. So it's simple, cheerful greed. Then, when finally the corporation is thrown into bankruptcy and they wipe out all of the stock, all the equities, he becomes the largest holder of preferred stock and takes control pretty much by default. This is not through his brilliance. But, of course, when he does end up with this textile mill, Eagle Mills, and reads in the paper about this brilliant financial person in New York who has taken over, he believes the myth that has been created around him. And finally, by the end of the book, he is a prisoner of his own myth: he thinks that he *is* a brilliant financial operator. When it all collapses, he says, "Well, why do they blame me?"

INTERVIEWER

Earlier you mentioned the irrelevant activities of educators in JR's world. Your satire concerning education is quite passionate. You must have had bad experiences.

GADDIS

No, really the opposite, in fact. I went to boarding school in New England when I was very young, and to college at Harvard, and had a good education. And so it was: looking around me as I became thirty and forty and fifty at what goes on, thinking this is not what serious education is all about.

The humanities can do anything but humanize these schoolchildren in *JR*. And your view of art has not changed since *The Recognitions*, as evidenced by figures like Bast, the composer; Eigen, the novelist; and Gibbs, the encyclopedist. What makes you place art at the center of fraud and counterfeit in the modern world?

Let me start off with this observation, touching perhaps on my earlier ones on the crushing abuses of capitalism. Frequently enough, careless or predisposed readers, John Gardner for instance, see these books as chronicles of the dedicated artist crushed by commerce, which is, of course, to miss, or misread, or simply disregard all the evidence of *their own* appetite for destruction, their frequently eager embrace of the forces to be blamed for their failure to pursue the difficult task for which their talents have equipped them, failure to pursue their destiny, if you like, taking art at the center, as you say, as redemption in and of and from a world of material values, overwhelmed by the material demands it imposes. The embittered character in *JR*, for instance, who is Eigen, is obviously based in part on my own experience with *The Recognitions*, that it was not a success when it was published and I was obliged to go and work in a pharmaceutical company, which I did not like, but I had a family and had to make a living. Next, Gibbs, who is very much a persona; obviously his name is from Willard Gibbs of the second law of thermodynamics and the concept of entropy. Gibbs is the man who has all of the feelings and the competency but is overcome, overwhelmed by a sense of the futility of doing anything and the consequent question of what is worth doing, which he cannot respond to. And so even though he *could've* done this, he *could've* done this, he *could've* done this, he doesn't *finish* anything because he just thinks it's not worth it, whatever it is. So that finally, when he has been quite a negative figure all the way through, and he meets a woman who has great confidence and faith and love for him and wants him to complete his own work, he tries to go back, but it's too late. Bast starts with great confidence, the sort I mentioned earlier, that confidence of youth. He's going to write grand opera. And gradually, if you noticed—because of pressures of reality on him and money and so forth—his ambitions shrink. The grand opera becomes a cantata where we have the orchestra and the voices. Then it becomes a piece for orchestra, then a piece for small orchestra, and finally at the end he's writing a piece for unaccompanied cello, his own that is to say, one small voice trying to rescue it all and say, Yes, there *is* hope. Again, like Wyatt, living it through, and in his adventure with JR, having lived through all the nonsense, he will rescue this one small, hard, gemlike flame, if you like. Because it is that *real* note of hope in *JR* that is very important. It's the kind of thing that someone like John Gardner totally missed. Finally, it's the artist as "inner-directed" confronting a materialistic world—brokers, bankers, salesmen, factory workers, most politicians, the lot—that JR himself represents, and which is "outer-directed," if you want it in sociological terms.

INTERVIEWER

What do the letters *J* and *R* stand for?

GADDIS

A sort of abbreviation for Junior.

INTERVIEWER

And also his class at school perhaps. He is going to 6J. If that has got anything to do with it at all.

GADDIS

No, no, no, that *J* is Mrs. Joubert, the teacher. This is what I mean about being wary of tracing down sources, inferences; Gardner, I think, traced the name Bast down to some Greek reference, which was, of course, nonsense.

INTERVIEWER

Africa seems to be very much on your mind both in *JR* and in *Carpenter's Gothic*. Why does Africa figure so conspicuously in your imagination?

GADDIS

In this last book, in *Carpenter's Gothic*, it is very important because of what the scheme of the book becomes, which is the book of Genesis emerging from the fiery holocaust that created the Great Rift Valley from Lebanon down through Israel, down through the Red Sea and all the way down East Africa, as where man was born, where he emerged, as in fact much of modern paleontology confirms. In Genesis we have prehistory told in the Lord raining down fire and brimstone, and by the time we get to the last book of the New Testament in Revelation, this whole apocalyptic notion, which many people, especially in the fundamentalist Christian movement in America, read literally, and feel that all this talk about the bomb is a kind of logical apocalypse and Marxism the great beast, and they put that together with what they read in Revelation. And so, as McCandless says in the book, many of these people who feel that apocalypse is coming must make peace, not with God, but with Jesus, as the go-between, take Jesus as one's savior so that when he does appear and calls up the faithful, they all rise to heaven and are saved in this self-fulfilling prophecy. If a war did start in Africa or any place else with the nuclear bombs and so forth, they would feel, Ah! now the wrongdoers, the ones who did not accept Jesus, are going to get it, that we are going to be—of course they're also going to be—incinerated.

INTERVIEWER

The title of *Carpenter's Gothic* is explained in the novel by the owner of the Victorian house built in that style as the Hudson Valley country architects' derivative style, "to be seen from the outside," "a patchwork of conceits, borrowings, deceptions." More than one critic suggested that the other meaning of *gothic* functions in the novel too, the novel being "a spoof of gothic romances," as Peter S. Prescott puts it. Let me wonder about the first half of the title, *carpenter*, though. Has it got anything to do with the town carpenter of *The Recognitions*—Wyatt's maternal grandfather, who is a storehouse of adventurous stories just as McCandless in *Carpenter's Gothic* is the mysterious adventurer whose adventures turn out to exist in a madman's imagination in the end, mere stories?

GADDIS

It never occurred to me—we're back with this second-guessing of sources, connections—but ideas do come forth and then submerge and come out in another form, which in a way both books are all about. One critical discussion I read discussed Wyatt's first job with a bridge-building concern, which I'd conceived simply to get across his fascination with the idea of tensions, the delicacy of bridges and the tensions that are involved, the idea of strength in delicacy, in tension, but this dissertation ingeniously related his career as bridge builder to his father as pontifex, a priest, the bridge between God and man, and I thought this was marvelous. When I read things like that, I just keep quiet. I think, Well, if they want to think I'm that clever—fine.

INTERVIEWER

McCandless is a good "carpenter," anyway, since he exposes what is behind the fanciful religious and political facade of those other "carpenters": Reverend Ude, the fake evangelist, and Senator Teakell, the corrupt politician. So contrary to what his name suggests—"candleless," namely, absence of light (perhaps a reference to his madness)—this "mad" carpenter is a molder of *correct* theories about how things fall into a pattern in the world, theories that *do* shed light on what is going on. But why must a seer be a lunatic?

GADDIS

A seer being an illuminated person and an illuminator—is this what you . . .

INTERVIEWER

I meant the wife's revelation about him at the end, with the implication that he has spent time in a mental institution.

GADDIS

But that's simply an implication, isn't it? I mean, these are areas in my work that I don't care to comment on. I think it says somewhere in *The Recognitions* that you cannot run along after your work saying what I really meant was this or this or this. Generally of all these questions: when I've worked on a book, I've put just as much into it as I wanted to, and if there are ambiguities, well, life is filled with them.

INTERVIEWER

I'm not asking if he was or was not really mad. What I mean is that the hint that he was, or even the ambiguity created about his sanity, makes one wonder why it is that an illuminator should be at least potentially mad?

GADDIS

Well, you may make that inference—or comment. I have no objection.

INTERVIEWER

McCandless is ironically undercut as a messiah at the end—this much is perhaps safe to say. Where does it leave us with the novel? Is the ironic undercutting "a straw of hope" as Cynthia Ozick hopes it is: that the world is not so dark after all, that it was only a madman's vision?

GADDIS

Again, there's an informed and positive interpretation; after all, if our situation—or what I see as our situation—were utterly hopeless, why would I have written the book at all? But I will say that this novel probably contains the least hope of the three. Because McCandless, who had got it all figured out, comes out at the end—when we realize that he is just leaving the scene and wants Liz to go with him—as hardly the great hero. It is sort of *sauve-qui-peut* and she refuses him. Incidentally, *carpenter* without the apostrophe, *carpenter gothic*, is the correct phrase for this style of architecture, as Lester mentions in the book. So the apostrophe, yes, is a play on the architectural style, and on McCandless, and on the Lord's Father's ramshackle house wherein "are many mansions," and on the author too as "the carpenter."

INTERVIEWER

What Paul helps the fundamentalist Ude and other antievolutionist carpenters to cut, frame, join, and hammer into shape is something political that may turn out to be an Armageddon for America, according to the novel. Amidst all this Liz is "the only straight number." If this is a bit exaggerated, the second half of what her brother, Billy— yet another carpenter of yet another counterfeit front (counterculture)—says is true: Liz is "the only thing that holds things together." It occurs to me to ask if she is not an embodiment of the female universe that Wyatt's quest is for in *The Recognitions?* The female universe is not absent from the world of *Carpenter's Gothic*, as it was not from the world of *The Recognitions*; rather, the world stifles it, kills it—Liz is asthmatic and is dead in the end.

GADDIS

I think that is valid. Just as in *JR* where Madame Joubert *is* this force of love, trust, hope, what have you. The *Ewigweibliche* and so forth, but the thwarted, betrayed-by-lack-of-love *Ewigweibliche*, the defeated *Frau, nach der man sich sehnt* (as is Esme in *The Recognitions*). They are all the realm of intuitive wisdom in a world of masculine materialism and so, as you may have noticed, at the end of *JR* it is the two unloved women who are going to be locked in a legal battle, reduced to being men, you might say, after the men have messed everything up. In that book they're the despairing survivors.

INTERVIEWER

Although *Carpenter's Gothic* seems to be a little like the schoolbooks that are criticized in the novel—questions are asked to which

no firm answers are offered—it *is* a book of beliefs and not, as Gardner would have said, "dramatization without belief." This is satire
and the beliefs are present indirectly: the satirist believes in those
things whose absence is resented when what is negative is destroyed.

GADDIS

Deeply resented, yes, because we're really back to the heart of it
here, aren't we? What we're really talking about—what the book is so
largely talking about, leaving behind alchemy and Wyatt's "thank
God there was the gold to forge"—is precisely this courage to live without absolutes, which is, really, nothing more than growing up, the
courage to accept a relative universe and even one verging upon chance,
certainly at least in its human component, since these absolutes are essentially childish, born out of fear of a purposeless existence, and, finally, out of the desperate denial of the one unacceptable inevitable
outrage, the prospect of one's own death itself. Of course all this
leads us into the sketchy refuge of situation ethics, old foes with new
faces, because looked at another way, this collapse of absolutes going
on around us may be simply another form of entropy, a spiritual entropy winding down eventually to total equilibrium, the ultimate
chaos where everything equals everything else: the ultimate senseless
universe. But then that, fighting that off, or succumbing to it, isn't
that what Dostoyevsky, what the great fictions have always been
about?

INTERVIEWER

The man who wrote these three books seems to be just about fed
up with two thousand years of wars and especially with the modern
world, which is all fraud and forgery. Is it that bad?

GADDIS

I think it *is* but we must simply live with it.

INTERVIEWER

The Gaddis novels are also difficult books; this has become a critical commonplace.

GADDIS

I'm afraid.

INTERVIEWER

So let me ask some obligatory questions about your art in general. First, why the proliferation of characters in the first two books?

GADDIS

In the first two books. Well, as I say, the first one I wanted to be a large comic novel . . . with characters reflecting facets of the central figure who, for all practical purposes, disappears; they carry on. This was part of the reason for *that* proliferation. In *JR* it was much more in the realm of these theories of entropy in communication and the breakdown of communication. So that especially in the school, where most of the time no one is listening to anyone else—they're all talking—there's some attempt in their patterns of speech to differentiate. Some readers have said: I don't know who's talking about what, and I give up. But that's the chance, the risk that I took.

INTERVIEWER

Are you guided by theoretical preconceptions concerning the human personality and character when you sit down to write your—as they have also been called—postpsychological novels?

GADDIS

Insofar as these are a culmination of one's experiences and ideas and impressions, one's prejudices and inner doubts—of course. But the task is to make the characters alive and come off the page as real. In *JR* it's much more a number of voices creating the story, the world they live in. In *Carpenter's Gothic* it's much more the point of very few characters, each of whom is forcefully and severely self-delineated.

INTERVIEWER

Do you deploy preconceived aesthetic philosophies concerning language and communication when you sit down to work?

GADDIS

As I say, it is all simply *in* sitting down to work and the working, not with any theoretical notions. I did make *the* basic decision in *JR* largely, as I've said, in terms of setting a problem to solve. Often it's very frustrating, but otherwise I would die of boredom at the typewriter. So I have to—in order to avoid boredom, to have the energy—set a problem. In *JR* it was writing a long book almost entirely in dialogue with no chapter breaks and so forth, which led me into the problem of real time because I could not say "Chapter Four" or "two weeks later." I had somehow to make that time pass in dialogue.

INTERVIEWER

So there must have been aesthetic decisions . . .

GADDIS

But they're not out of a theory.

INTERVIEWER

I call your book-length dialogues floated dialogue because while you present everything through dialogues—background information, letters, newspaper articles, radio texts, TV texts—too many outlines become blurred, persons and objects are externally undifferentiated, everything is allowed to be viewed through what is spoken only. The omniscient narrator gives insignificant, descriptive details of the physical situation in which the dialogue is carried on, but he is of no help with what the reader would be really interested in.

GADDIS

I will tell you something in that area, if you like a theory, which I may have come up with after I wrote the book—I'm not sure. It is the notion that the reader is brought in almost as a collaborator in creating the picture that emerges of the characters, of the situation, of what they look like—everything. So this authorial absence, which everyone from Flaubert to Barthes talks about, is the sense that the book is a collaboration between the reader and what is on the pages.

INTERVIEWER

But the floated dialogue makes the reader's part very difficult. The omniscient narrator expresses no view of his own. The reader is left to imagine the psychological motivation behind what is said. What the reader is left with—in the absence of reliable authorial/narratorial information and of the psychologically more reliable direct interior monologue form—is what could be called vocal behaviorism.

GADDIS

Well, this interior monologue you speak of *is* just too easy, obvious, boring, lazy, and I would agree right up to the last; I always cringe at the word *behaviorism*. But again it is very much this notion of what the reader is obliged to supply. We go back to McLuhan and his talk about hot and cool media. Television is the hot medium, to which one contributes nothing except a blank state, and the next day you say, What was that show we saw last night on television? It disappears because you put nothing into it. So nothing remains, as Gibbs remarks in *JR*. In this case it was my hope—for many readers it worked, for others it did not—that having made some effort they would not read too agonizedly slowly and carefully, trying to figure out who is talking and so forth. It was the *flow* that I wanted, for the readers to read and be swept along—to participate. And enjoy it. And occasionally chuckle, laugh along the way.

INTERVIEWER

But if they read along like that, they may miss a lot.

GADDIS

This is a risk I take, but isn't that what life is, after all? Missing something that's right there before you?

INTERVIEWER

The flood of dialogues may intensify the sense of claustrophobia some readers experience. Several critics believe that you lose control over your talent in your first two novels, and this is why they are so long, 956 pages and 726 pages. Are you concerned with structure when you write?

GADDIS

Of course, acutely so, with outline after outline even to paragraphs. And this sounds very odd for me to say—not of *The Recognitions* perhaps, but of *JR* and *Carpenter's Gothic* both—*JR* especially is a very economical novel. That is one thing I hope I learned from Evelyn Waugh, economy. No one would believe this. *I* think a great deal of information is there of every sort, very economically got together. But critics will say whatever . . .

INTERVIEWER

Do you write the way you do because this is the easiest way for you to write, or are such "difficult" works difficult to write too? What is it that causes particular difficulty in creating this type of a novel?

GADDIS

Well, as I've tried to make clear, if the work weren't difficult I'd die of boredom. After *The Recognitions*, where there is a great deal of authorial intrusion and little essays along the way—on alchemy or what have you—I found it was too easy and I didn't want to do it again. I wanted to write something different. I wanted to do something that was challenging, to create other problems, to force this discipline on myself, particularly with the last book. It's all discipline. But I certainly can't agree with that notion of whatever talent I may have going out of control. I think whatever talent there may be has been very painfully controlled, perhaps too much so.

INTERVIEWER

Do you regard yourself an experimental writer?

GADDIS

No. I think of "experimental" as something that may not work. When I sit down with a concept and what I've said about discipline and so on—what I'm going to do—I don't think it's experimental.

INTERVIEWER

It's probably the dialogue form primarily that makes people label you as experimental. The novel is turned into a drama, as if it were staged almost—"theatricalized." The narrator is just a kind of stage director who does not interfere with the play.

GADDIS

But that's exactly the point, isn't it—not to interfere. The attempt in the last two books was to make the characters create themselves, which is true of movies or the stage, and essentially of life itself. Of course, on the stage you can *see* the people. You see that he's tall or short or fat or what have you. Here the only devices are: Where did you get that terrible suit? Or one person may say to the other something that *is* descriptive of that person. But only if it's essential because this, to me, is again for the reader to supply, and, I think, to feel rewarded in doing so.

INTERVIEWER

Creative reading. Critics have also created various labels that they affixed to your work: the encyclopedic novel, the novel of excess, and so on. If you were to stamp a label that would describe your works best the way *you* see them, what would that label be?

GADDIS

Maybe in ten years, when I am finished, I will give you an answer to that.

INTERVIEWER

What do you think of labels like *postmodern*, *black humor*, *metafiction*?

GADDIS

I don't read a great deal of this kind of criticism. When it's applied to me . . . When I'm put in one of these areas, I think, Well, then *that* is what "postmodernism" is. But I don't either court it or pursue it or protest. I mean there are fashions—the most extreme, I gather now, being structuralism, deconstruction, what have you, much of which I just read askance. I'm not sure what is going on, but it's surely not on my mind when I write.

INTERVIEWER

Isn't one of the commonly accepted features of the postmodern that there is a suspension of causation? Is this illustrated in your work?

GADDIS

No, no, there is always a thread of causation—threads, many of them—and on a different level I would say that form and content must coalesce; they must reflect each other. So particularly with *JR*, being very largely about a shattered world, about a fragmented world, the style there is fragmentation. So that was a basic early decision: to try to reflect the fragmentation, but to create the fabric threaded with causation of however attenuated or even illogical a sort.

INTERVIEWER

Do you want readers to like what you do?

GADDIS

Heavens, yes.

INTERVIEWER

What kind of audience do you think of when you write?

GADDIS

When I write I *don't* think of the audience. After the fact I think, Well there. I hope they like it.

INTERVIEWER

Somehow it is always emphasized in connection with *The Recognitions* that it is an underground classic, that it is for a very small audience. Did you want to break out of this when you wrote more accessible novels? If not, what is it that made your second novel more accessible than the first, and the third more accessible than the second?

GADDIS

That's interesting. *I* think of the first one, *The Recognitions*, as being the most accessible. Much the most. If we get into this terrible word, *accessible*, which has been used in many reviews usually with the prefix *in-*, I should think that because of the demand on the reader to put in a little work, *JR* is the least accessible of the three. The last one, I think, is quite accessible. Although because of the background that the first two created, they're inclined to pursue it in the same way. The daily reviewer for *The New York Times* was relieved because it was short, so I believe he actually read it. Though he reviewed *JR* ten years before, in reviewing *Carpenter's Gothic* he said he had *not* read *JR*—couldn't follow it, too long and complicated. That kind of irresponsibility doesn't cheer a writer up, but, of course, these things are not on my mind when I'm working.

INTERVIEWER

The self-reflexive element is gone from your work at this point.

GADDIS

I want to get rid of it, yes. None of the books has got any interior monologue, easy effects, any of "he wished he could see her that afternoon." I mean he's got to show it, to *tell* someone, "I wish I could see her this afternoon." Authorial absence so that the characters create the situation. I find this much more provocative to me both as a writer, when I'm working on it, and as a reader. Interestingly, *The Recognitions*, which came out thirty-five years ago, was regarded as quite inaccessible at the time. *Now* I think it is read without much difficulty.

INTERVIEWER

Which is the novel *you* care most for?

GADDIS

I think that I care most for *JR* because I'm awfully fond of the boy himself.

INTERVIEWER

What are your feelings about the American novel today?

GADDIS

I wouldn't make a great statement on that, but I do think there is a good number of excellent novelists, and then there is the usual . . . the others. But I think—since they say American novel in contradistinction to the French, the British, or what have you—we are turning out proportionately much more good fiction of all kinds in America.

INTERVIEWER

What is happening in the novel is happening mostly in America. What, in your view, can the goal of literary workmanship be in the last quarter of the twentieth century?

GADDIS

In Bulgaria, when we were talking at a conference dedicated to peace, the hope of the planet, there were some two hundred writers there from fifty-two countries, discussing what the writer can do for peace. Obviously peace is the issue driving everyone mad, so that most of that conference was sheer and desperate propaganda. I suppose in all three books I constantly try to call attention to what my mother had told me once at some paranoid moment of mine: You must always remember that there is much more stupidity than there is malice in the world. This is what I talked about in Sofia. This is what we must—if we can't teach it, which we can't—at least call attention to.

INTERVIEWER

Plans?

GADDIS

I have got another novel nicely under way.

INTERVIEWER

This conversation is being conducted in Budapest. Being a Hungarian, I am particularly interested in why Hungary, and Hungarian literature and language, have a relatively large role to play in *The Recognitions*.

GADDIS

I think because I pictured them—Hungary and Budapest—as mysterious, exciting, highly civilized, sophisticated. But *mysterious*, mainly.

INTERVIEWER

One of the central characters, Valentine, is Hungarian. Why?

GADDIS

I suppose for these reasons; and that he is completely cynical, in that traditional American mistrust of European guile going back, again, to Mark Twain.

INTERVIEWER

Is he purely fictional or is he somebody you knew? I am asking this because he is the one in *The Recognitions* who informs Willie— obviously the author, William Gaddis—about Clement's *Recognitions*.

GADDIS

No. He is a totally fictional character.

INTERVIEWER

And the references to Sámuel Brassai, Pázmány, Mikszáth, Bródy, Gárdonyi, Móricz, Molnár? Is there more behind it than the *Encyclopaedia Britannica*? Even if there is not, why Hungarian literature? Because Valentine and Inononu are Hungarian characters in the novel?

GADDIS

I was trying to make them legitimately characters of this very sophisticated, very cynical, very mysterious world as I viewed it thirty-five years ago.

INTERVIEWER

Where did you pick up the Hungarian phrases?

GADDIS

Well, I had written those scenes in English. I try to get things right, so if they are in Hungary, if they're in a Hungarian hospital, obviously they are speaking Hungarian. So I took these passages to a bar in the Upper East Side of New York, where there is a large Hungarian community, had a drink, and approached the bartender. I told him I had a problem, that I wanted these passages in Hungarian. He called someone over. Finally there must have been ten people around me arguing about exactly the correct accent, the nuance of the phrase. When I had written it all down, he said, Now, the man who was the leading figure in this conversation, whom everyone else bowed to, as it were, is a great Hungarian actor. If he said you got it right, you know you have it right. And, of course, as it all turned out, when I'd gone up there ready to buy a drink for anyone who would help me, it was they who bought mine.

INTERVIEWER

If there are Hungarian phrases and literary references, why couldn't the two Hungarian characters have Hungarian names?

GADDIS

Valentine, of course, is named after the alchemist, Basil Valentine, who . . .

INTERVIEWER

So there were more important thematic concerns.

GADDIS

Yes—who knows, maybe he changed his name. I don't know.

INTERVIEWER

Did you visit Hungary in the years when you were writing *The Recognitions*?

GADDIS

I've never been to Hungary until today.

INTERVIEWER

And since you flew in yesterday, it's too early to ask you about the impressions.

GADDIS

What I see of Budapest is splendid. It is everything one has been led to imagine.

Issue 105, 1987

Harold Bloom

The Art of Criticism

Recently, Harold Bloom has been under attack not just in scholarly journals and colloquia, but also in newspapers, on the op-ed page, on television and radio. The barrage is due to the bestseller *The Book of J*, in which Bloom argues that the J-Writer, the putative first author of the Hebrew Bible, not only existed (a matter under debate among Bible historians for the last century) but, quite specifically, was a woman who belonged to the Solomonic elite and wrote during the reign of Rehoboam of Judah in competition with the Court Historian. The attacks have come from Bible scholars, rabbis, and journalists, as well as from the usual academic sources, and Bloom has never been more isolated in his views or more secure in them. He has become, by his own description, "a tired, sad, humane old creature," who greets his many friends and detractors with an endearing, melancholy exuberance.

He is happy to talk about most anything—politics, romance, sports—although he admits he is "too used to" some topics to get into them. One sets out to disagree with him, and the response is, "Oh, no, no, my dear . . ." In a class on Shakespeare, a mod-dressed graduate student suggests that Iago may be sexually jealous of Othello; Bloom tilts his furry eyebrows, his stockinged feet crossed underneath him, his hand tucked in his shirt, and cries out, "That will not do, my dear. I must protest!" Not surprisingly, it is by now a commonplace of former students' articles and lectures to start off with a quarrel with Bloom, and in his view, this is only as it should be. He

Introduction

It is reasonable to assert
that Jay Gatsby is the major literary
character of the United States in the
Twentieth Century. No single figure
created by Faulkner or Hemingway,
or by our principal major dramatists, has is
become as central a presence in
our national mythology as Gatsby has.
There are few living Americans, of
whatever gender, race, ethnic origin,
or social class, who do not have at
least a little touch of Gatsby in
them. Whatever the American Dream has
become, its truest contemporary
representative remains Jay Gatsby, at
once a gangster and a Romantic
idealist, and above all a victim of
his own High Romantic, Keatsian dream
of love. Like his creator, Scott Fitzgerald,
Gatsby is the American hero of
romance, a vulnerable quester whose
fate has the aesthetic dignity of
the romance mode at its strongest.
Gatsby is neither pathetic nor tragic,
because as a quester he meets his
appropriate fate, which is to die still
lacking in the knowledge that would
destroy the spell of his enchantment.
His death preserves his greatness, and
justifies the title of his story, a title
that is anything but ironic.
Gatsby, doom-eager yet desiring
a perfect love, or perhaps doom-eager but

A manuscript page from the introduction to Major Literary Characters: Gatsby, *edited and with an introduction by Harold Bloom.*

likes to quote the Emersonian adage: "That which I can gain from another is never tuition but only provocation."

The interview was conducted at the homes he shares with his
wife, Jeanne, in New Haven and New York—the one filled with four
decades' accrual of furniture and books, the other nearly bare, although stacks of works in progress and students' papers are strewn
about in both. If the conversation is not too heavy, Bloom likes to
have music on, sometimes Baroque, sometimes jazz. (His New York
apartment, which is in Greenwich Village, allows him to take in
more live jazz.) The phone rings nonstop. Friends, former students,
colleagues drop by. Talk is punctuated by strange exclamatories:
Zoombah, for one—Swahili for "libido"—is an all-purpose flavoring
particle, with the accompanying, adjectival *zoombinatious* and the
verb *to zoombinate*. Bloom speaks as if the sentences came to him
off a printed page, grammatically complex, at times tangled. But
they are delivered with great animation, whether ponderous or
joyful—if also with finality. Because he learned English by reading
it, his accent is very much his own, with some New York inflec-
tions: "*You* try and learn English in an all-Yiddish household in the
East Bronx by sounding out the words of Blake's *Prophecies*," he
explains. Often, he will start a conversation with a direct, at times
personal question, or a sigh: "Oh, how the Bloomian feet ache today!"

—*Antonio Weiss, 1991*

INTERVIEWER

What are your memories of growing up?

HAROLD BLOOM

That was such a long time ago. I'm sixty years old. I can't remember much of my childhood that well. I was raised in an Orthodox East
European Jewish household where Yiddish was the everyday language. My mother was very pious, my father less so. I still read Yiddish poetry. I have a great interest and pleasure in it.

What are your recollections of the neighborhood in which you grew up?

Almost none. One of my principal memories is that I and my friends, just to survive, had constantly to fight street battles with neighborhood Irish toughs, some of whom were very much under the influence of a sort of Irish-American Nazi organization called the Silver Shirts. This was back in the 1930s. We were on the verge of an Irish neighborhood over there in the East Bronx. We lived in a Jewish neighborhood. On our border, somewhere around Southern Boulevard, an Irish neighborhood began, and they would raid us, and we would fight back. They were terrible street fights, involving broken bottles and baseball bats. They were very nasty times. I say this even though I've now grown up and find that many of my best friends are Irish.

Do you think your background helped in any way to shape your career?

Obviously it predisposed me toward a great deal of systematic reading. It exposed me to the Bible as a sort of definitive text early on. And obviously too, I became obsessed with interpretation as such. Judaic tradition necessarily acquaints one with interpretation as a mode. Exegesis becomes wholly natural. But I did not have very Orthodox religious beliefs. Even when I was quite a young child I was very skeptical indeed about Orthodox notions of spirituality. Of course, I now regard normative Judaism as being, as I've often said, a very strong misreading of the Hebrew Bible undertaken in the second century in order to meet the needs of the Jewish people in a Palestine under Roman occupation. And that is not very relevant to matters eighteen centuries later. But otherwise, I think the crucial experiences for me as a reader, as a child, did not come reading the Hebrew Bible. It came in reading poetry written in English, which can still work on me with the force of a Bible conversion. It was the aesthetic experience of first reading Hart Crane and William Blake—those two poets in particular.

INTERVIEWER

How old were you at this point?

BLOOM

I was preadolescent, ten or eleven years old. I still remember the extraordinary delight, the extraordinary force that Crane and Blake brought to me—in particular Blake's rhetoric in the longer poems—though I had no notion what they were about. I picked up a copy of the *Collected Poems* of Hart Crane in the Bronx Library. I still remember when I lit upon the page with the extraordinary trope, "O Thou steeled Cognizance whose leap commits / The agile precincts of the lark's return." I was just swept away by it, by the Marlovian rhetoric. I still have the flavor of that book in me. Indeed it's the first book I ever owned. I begged my oldest sister to give it to me, and I still have the old black and gold edition she gave me for my birthday back in 1942. It's up on the third floor. Why is it you can have that extraordinary experience (preadolescent in my case, as in so many other cases) of falling violently in love with great poetry . . . where you are moved by its power before you comprehend it? In some, a version of the poetical character is incarnated and in some like myself the answering voice is from the beginning that of the critic. I suppose the only poet of the twentieth century that I could secretly set above Yeats and Stevens would be Hart Crane. Crane was dead at the age of thirty-two, so one doesn't really know what he would have been able to do. An immense loss. As large a loss as the death of Shelley at twenty-nine or Keats at twenty-five. Crane had to do it all in only seven or eight years.

INTERVIEWER

Did you read children's stories, fairy tales?

I don't think so. I read the Bible, which is, after all, a long fairy tale. I didn't read children's literature until I was an undergraduate.

Did you write verse as a child?

In spite of my interest, that never occurred to me. It must have had something to do with the enormous reverence and rapture I felt about poetry, the incantatory strength that Crane and Blake had for me from the beginning. To be a poet did not occur to me. It was indeed a threshold guarded by demons. To try to write in verse would have been a kind of trespass. That's something that I still feel very strongly.

How was your chosen career viewed by your family?

I don't think they had any idea what I would be. I think they were disappointed. They were Jewish immigrants from Eastern Europe with necessarily narrow views. They had hoped that I would be a doctor or a lawyer or a dentist. They did not know what a professor of poetry was. They would have understood, I suppose, had I chosen to be a rabbi or a Talmudic scholar. But finally, I don't think they cared one way or the other.

When I was a small boy already addicted to doing nothing but reading poems in English, I was asked by an uncle who kept a candy store in Brooklyn what I intended to do to earn a living when I grew up. I said, I want to read poetry. He told me that there were professors of poetry at Harvard and Yale. That's the first time I'd ever heard of those places or that there was such a thing as a professor of poetry. In my five- or six-year-old way I replied, I'm going to be a professor of poetry at Harvard or Yale. Of course, the joke is that three years ago I was simultaneously Charles Eliot Norton Professor of Poetry at

Harvard and Sterling Professor of the Humanities at Yale! So in that sense I was prematurely overdetermined in my profession. Sometimes I think that is the principal difference between my own work and the work of many other critics. I came to it very early, and I've been utterly unswerving.

INTERVIEWER

You are known as someone who has had a prodigious memory since childhood. Do you find that your power of recall was triggered by the words themselves, or were there other factors?

BLOOM

Oh no, it was immediate and it was always triggered by text, and indeed always had an aesthetic element. I learned early that a test for a poem for me was whether it seemed so inevitable that I could remember it perfectly from the start. I think the only change in me in that regard has come mainly under the influence of Nietzsche. It is the single way he has influenced me aesthetically. I've come to understand that the quality of memorability and inevitability that I assumed came from intense pleasure may actually have come from a kind of pain. That is to say that one learns from Nietzsche that there is something painful about meaning. Sometimes it is the pain of difficulty, sometimes the pain of being set a standard that one cannot attain.

INTERVIEWER

Did you ever feel that reading so much was an avoidance of experience?

BLOOM

No. It was for me a terrible rage or passion that was a drive. It was fiery. It was an absolute obsession. I do not think that speculation on my own part would ever convince me that it was an attempt to substitute a more ideal existence for the life that I had to live. It was love. I fell desperately in love with reading poems. I don't think that one should idealize such a passion. I certainly no longer do. I mean, I still love reading a poem when I can find a really good one to read. Just recently, I was sitting down, alas for the first time in several years, reading through Shakespeare's *Troilus and Cressida* at one sitting. I found it to be an astonishing experience, powerful and superb. That hasn't dimmed or diminished. But surely it is a value in itself, a reality in its own right; surely it cannot be reduced or subsumed under some other name. Freud, doubtless, would wish to reduce it to the sexual thought, or rather the sexual past. But increasingly it seems to me that literature, and particularly Shakespeare, who *is* literature, is a much more comprehensive mode of cognition than psychoanalysis can be.

INTERVIEWER

Who are the teachers who were important to you? Did you study with the New Critics at Yale?

BLOOM

I did not study with any of the New Critics, with the single exception being William K. Wimsatt. Bill was a formalist and a very shrewd one, and from the moment I landed in the first course that I took with him, which was in theories of poetry, he sized me up. His comment on my first essay for him was, This is Longinian criticism. You're an instance of exactly what I don't like or want. He was quite right. He was an Aristotelian; as far as I was concerned, Aristotle had ruined Western literary criticism almost from the beginning. What I thought of as literary criticism really *did* begin with the pseudo-Longinus. So we had very strong disagreements about that kind of stuff. But he was a remarkable teacher. We became very close friends later on. I miss him very much. He was a splendid, huge, fascinating man, almost seven feet tall, a fierce, dogmatic Roman Catholic, very intense. But very fair-minded. We shared a passion for Dr. Samuel Johnson. I reacted so violently against him that antithetically he was a great influence on me. I think that's what I meant by dedicating *The Anxiety of Influence* to Bill. I still treasure the note he wrote me after I gave him one of the early copies of the book. I find the dedication extremely surprising, he said, and then added mournfully, I suppose it entitles you to be Plotinus to Emerson's Plato in regard to American neoromanticism, a doctrine that I despise. Oh, yes, we had serious differences in our feelings about poetry.

What were your earliest essays like?

I don't think I wrote any essays until I was an undergraduate at Cornell. But then a few years ago Bob Elias, one of my teachers there, sent me an essay I had written on Hart Crane (which I had completely forgotten about) when I was a Cornell freshman of sixteen or seventeen. I couldn't get myself to read it. I even destroyed it. I shouldn't have. I should have waited until I could bear to look at it. I'm very curious as to what kind of thing it was.

Are there other literary figures who were important to you early on?

A real favorite among modern critics, and the one I think influenced me considerably, though no one ever wants to talk about him, was George Wilson Knight. He was an old friend. Utterly mad. He made Kenneth Burke and Harold Bloom look placid and mild. George died quite old. He was very interested in spiritualism and in survival after death. He told me a couple of times that he believed it quite literally. There is a moment in *The Christian Renaissance* that I think is the finest moment in modern criticism, because it is the craziest. He is citing a spiritualist, F. W. H. Myers, and he quotes something that Myers wrote and published, and then he quotes something from a séance at which Myers "came back" and said something through a medium, this astonishing sentence, which I give to you verbatim: "These quotations from F. W. H. Myers, so similar in style, composed before and after his own earthly 'death,' contain together a wisdom which our era may find it hard to assimilate." I mean, perfectly straight about it! But the early books of Wilson

Knight are very fine indeed—certainly one of the most considerable figures of twentieth-century criticism, though he's mostly forgotten now.

[*At this point we wander into the kitchen, where Mrs. Bloom is watching the evening news.*]

BLOOM

Now let's wait for the news about this comeback for the wretched Yankees. I've been denouncing them. They haven't won since 1979. That's ten years and they're not going to win this year. They're terrible . . . What's this?

[*TV: The Yankees with their most dramatic win of the year this afternoon . . . And the Tigers lost again.*]

BLOOM

Oh my God! That means we're just four games out. How very up-cheering.

MRS. BLOOM

Jessica Hahn.

BLOOM

Jessica Hahn is back!

[*TV: . . . hired on as an on-air personality at a Top 40 radio station in Phoenix.*]

BLOOM

How marvelous!

[*TV:* Playboy *magazine had counted on Hahn to come through. She appeared nude in a recent issue.*]

BLOOM

Splendid . . . Let us start again, Antonio. What were we talking about?

[*We return to the living room.*]

INTERVIEWER

We were talking about your teachers and I was going to ask about the poets you've known over the years.

BLOOM

Auden I knew pretty well, mostly through John Hollander. Eliot I never met. Stevens I met just once. I was still a Cornell undergraduate. I came up to Yale to hear him read the shorter version of "Ordinary Evening in New Haven." It was the first time I was ever in New Haven, or at Yale for that matter. I got to talk to him afterward. It was a formidable experience meeting him. We talked about Shelley, and he quoted a stanza of the "Witch of Atlas" to me, which impressed me. "Men scarcely know how beautiful fire is," it starts. It's a chilly, rather beautiful poem. Robert Penn Warren and I were close friends. Miss Bishop was of that younger generation also. Archie Ammons and I are very close. There are quite a few others. Sometimes I used to correspond with James Merrill when he was writing *The Changing Light at Sandover.* He kept sending parts to me as it went along, and I kept writing him letters saying: can't we have more J.M. and less of this stuff in capital letters? He said this was the way it had to be, this was the way it was actually coming to him. I realized I was going against my cardinal rule, which is don't argue with it, just appreciate it.

INTERVIEWER

Are there any authors you'd like to have known but haven't?

BLOOM

No. I should like to have known fewer authors than I have known, which is to say nothing against all my good friends.

INTERVIEWER

Because it interferes with an honest assessment?

No. It's just that as one gets older, one is doomed, in this profession, to know personally more and more authors. Most of them are in fact quite nice ladies and gentlemen, but they have trouble—even one's very close friends—talking to the tired, sad, humane old creature that one is. They seem to be more conscious of one's profession as literary critic than one is necessarily conscious of their profession as novelist or poet.

INTERVIEWER

Are there characters you would like to have known?

BLOOM

No, no. The only person I would like to have known, whom I have never known, but it's just as well, is Sophia Loren. I have been in love with Sophia Loren for at least a third of a century. But undoubtedly it would be better never to meet her. I'm not sure I ever shall, though my late friend Bart Giamatti had breakfast with her. Judging by photographs and recent film appearances, she has held up quite well, though a little too slender now—no longer the same gorgeous Neapolitan beauty, now a much more sleek beauty.

INTERVIEWER

Could you give us your opinion of some novelists? We could start with Norman Mailer.

BLOOM

Oh, I have written on Norman a lot. I reviewed *Ancient Evenings* at some length in *The New York Review of Books* and I came forth with a sentence that did not please Norman, which I'm still proud of. It was, "Subscribers to the Literary Guild will find in it more than enough humbuggery and bumbuggery to give them their money's worth." I had counted up the number of homosexual and heterosexual bumbuggeries; I was rather impressed by the total, including, unless I misremember, at one point the protagonist or perhaps it was the godking successfully bumbuggering the lion. But then Norman is immensely inventive in this regard. He told me the last time I saw him that he is completing a manuscript of several thousand pages on the CIA. That should be an amazing nightmare of a book since Norman's natural grand paranoid vision is one of *everything* being a conspiracy. So I should think that might be very interesting indeed. What can one say? Mailer is an immense imaginative energy. One is not persuaded that in the sheer mode of the fantastic, he has found his proper mètier. Beyond a doubt his most impressive single book is *The Executioner's Song*, and that is, of course, very close indeed to a transcript of what we want to call reality. So it's rather ironic that Norman should be more effective in the mode of Theodore Dreiser, giving us a kind of contemporary *American Tragedy* or *Sister Carrie* in *The Executioner's Song* than in the modes he himself has wanted to excel in. I would think that he is likely to impress future literary historians as having been a knowing continuator of Dreiser, which is not an inconsiderable achievement.

INTERVIEWER

And William Gaddis?

BLOOM

Like everyone else, I've never gotten over *The Recognitions*, but I differ from those who have found the other two books worthy of him. I have had great difficulty working my way through them. I assume that there is more to be heard from him, but I am afraid that he is an instance of someone who in that vast initial anatomy of a book, to use Mister Frye's phrase for that kind of fictional writing, seems to have surpassed himself at the start . . . which is, of course, in the famous American tradition.

INTERVIEWER

And Saul Bellow?

BLOOM

He's an enormous pleasure but he does not make things difficult enough for himself or for us. Like many others, I would commend him for the almost Dickensian exuberance of his minor male characters who have carried every one of his books. The central protagonist, always being some version of himself, even in *Henderson*, is invariably an absurd failure, and the women, as we all know, are absurdities; they are third-rate pipe dreams. The narrative line is of no particular interest. His secular opinions are worthy of Allan Bloom, who seems to derive from them. And I'm not an admirer of the "other Bloom," as is well known. In general, Bellow seems to me an immensely wasted talent though he certainly would not appreciate my saying so. I would oppose to him a most extraordinary talent—Philip Roth. It does seem to me that Philip Roth goes from strength to strength and is at the moment startlingly unappreciated. It seems strange to say Philip is unappreciated when he has so wide a readership and so great a notoriety, but *Deception* was not much remarked upon and it's an extraordinary tour de force.

INTERVIEWER

It was seen as an experiment or a sort of a leftover from—

BLOOM

—from *The Counterlife*. Well, *The Counterlife*, of course, deserved the praise that it received. It's an astonishing book, though I would put it a touch below the *Zuckerman Bound* trilogy with its marvelous *Prague Orgy* postlude or coda. I still think *My Life as a Man* as well as, of course, *Portnoy's Complaint* are remarkable books. There's the great episode of Kafka's whore in *The Professor of Desire*. I've written a fair amount about Philip. After a rather unfortunate personal book called *The Facts*, which I had trouble getting through, he has written a book about his late father called *Patrimony*, which is both beautiful and immensely moving, a real achievement. The man is a prose artist of great accomplishment. He has immense narrative exuberance, and also—I would insist upon this—since it's an extremely difficult thing, as we all know, to write successful humorous fiction and, though the laughter Philip evokes is very painful indeed, he is an authentic comic novelist. I'm not sure at the moment that we have any other authentic comic novelist of the first order.

INTERVIEWER

You have written that poetry is in an especially strong stage now. Is the same true of fiction?

BLOOM

Although I've been reading extensively and writing about it over the last few years, it is very difficult for me to get a steady fix on the current kaleidoscope of American fiction. Our most distinguished living writer of narrative fiction—I don't think you would quite call him a novelist—is Thomas Pynchon, and yet that recent book *Vineland* was a total disaster. In fact, I cannot think of a comparable disaster in modern American fiction. To have written the great story of Byron the lightbulb in *Gravity's Rainbow*, to have written *The Crying of Lot 49* and then to give us this piece of sheer ineptitude, this hopelessly hollow book that I read through in amazement and disbelief, and which has not got in it a redeeming sentence, hardly a redeeming phrase, is immensely disheartening.

INTERVIEWER

Do you have any response to the essay Tom Wolfe wrote urging the big, Victor Hugo–like novel?

BLOOM

He is, of course, praising his own *Bonfire of the Vanities*, which is a wholly legitimate thing for an essayist-turned-novelist to do. But with all honor to Tom Wolfe, a most amiable fellow and a former classmate of mine at Yale, and as someone who enjoyed reading *The Bonfire of the Vanities*, I found very little difference between it and his book of essays. He has merely taken his verve and gift for writing the journalistic essay and moved it a little further over the edge; but the characters are names on the page—he does not try to make them more than that. The social pressure is extraordinarily and vividly conveyed. But he's always been remarkable for that. He's still part of that broad movement which has lifted a particular kind of high-pitched journalism into a realm that may very nearly be aesthetic. On the other hand, I must say I would rather reread

The Bonfire of the Vanities than reread another Rabbit volume by Mr. Updike. But then Mr. Updike and I, we are not a mutual admiration society.

INTERVIEWER

Have you had run-ins with friends or writers whose books you've reviewed?

BLOOM

I wouldn't say run-ins exactly. Mr. Styron, who has, of course, his difficulties and I sympathize with them, once at Robert Penn Warren's dinner table, when I dared to disagree with him on a question of literary judgment, spoke up and said, Your opinion doesn't matter; you are only a schoolteacher—which still strikes me as perhaps the most memorable single thing that has been said to me by any contemporary novelist.* I felt that Warren's poetry was greatly preferable to his recent novels and was trying to persuade Red to stop writing novels. *A Place to Come To*, which Red to his dying day thought was a novel of the eminence of *World Enough and Time*, *At Heaven's Gate*, *All the King's Men*, and *Night Rider*, is a stillborn book and a terrible bore, though I say that with great sadness. Whereas Red Warren's poetry from the *Incarnations* in 1966 down to the end (he stopped writing poetry in the last few years because he was too ill) was consistently the work of a great poet.

INTERVIEWER

Are there younger writers you enjoy reading?

BLOOM

I like this fellow Ted Mooney. I think something is going on there. *Traffic and Laughter*, which I've just read through, certainly has éclat—it certainly has a lot of intensity. I don't know; there are so many that it is difficult to choose among them. It's easier on the whole these days to think of poets than novelists. It's very difficult for a novelist to

---

*Mr. Styron wishes to point out that his annoyance was not with H.B.'s critical views—with which he agrees—but that they were offered in Warren's presence. [—Ed.]

break through. The form is not showing a great deal of fecundity, except perhaps in Don DeLillo, who is a superb inventor.

INTERVIEWER

What direction do you see the form taking?

BLOOM

I would suppose that in America we are leaning more and more towards terrible millennial visions. I would even expect a religious dimension, a satiric dimension, an even more apocalyptic dimension than we have been accustomed to. I would expect the mode of fantasy to develop new permutations.

INTERVIEWER

Do you think that fiction—or poetry for that matter—could ever die out?

BLOOM

I'm reminded of that great trope of Stevens's in "The Auroras of Autumn," when he speaks of a "great shadow's last embellishment." There's always a further embellishment. It looks like a last embellishment and then it turns out not to be—yet once more, and yet once more. One is always saying farewell to it, it is always saying farewell to itself, and then it perpetuates itself. One is always astonished and delighted. When I introduced John Ashbery at one of the poetry readings in the old days at Yale, I heard for the first time "Wet Casements." How it ravished my heart away the moment I heard it! Certainly when I recite that poem myself and remember the original experience of hearing him deliver it, it's hard to see how any poem could be more adequate. Clearly it is not a diminished or finished art form as long as a poem like "Wet Casements" is still possible.

INTERVIEWER

I wanted to ask you about a period of time in the mid-sixties, which you have described as a period of great upheaval and transition for you. You were immersed in the essays of Emerson.

BLOOM

Yes, I started reading him all day long, every day, and pretty much simultaneously reading Freud. People would look at me with amazement and say, Well, what about Thoreau? He at least counts for something. And I would look back at them in amazement and tell them what indeed was and is true, that Thoreau is deeply derivative of Emerson and very minor compared to him. Emerson is God.

INTERVIEWER

You were in analysis during this period. How did that go?

BLOOM

As my distinguished analyst said to me at the end, there had never been a proper transference.

INTERVIEWER

You were unable to accept his authority?

BLOOM

I thought and still think that he is a very nice man, but as he wryly remarked, I was paying him to give him lectures several times a week on the proper way to read Freud. He thought this was quite self-defeating for both of us.

INTERVIEWER

Can a successful therapy ever be so closely allied to a reading of Freud?

BLOOM

I take it that a successful therapy is an oxymoron.

INTERVIEWER

It's always interminable?

BLOOM

I do not know anyone who has ever benefited from Freudian or any other mode of analysis, except by being, to use the popular trope for it, so badly shrunk that they become quite dried out. That is to say, all passion spent. Perhaps they become better people, but they also become stale and uninteresting people with very few exceptions. Like dried-out cheese, or wilted flowers.

INTERVIEWER

Were you worried about losing your creativity?

BLOOM

No, no. That was not the issue at all.

INTERVIEWER

You were having trouble writing at the time.

BLOOM

Oh yes. I was having all kinds of crises. I was, in every sense, "in the middle of a journey." On the other hand, this has been recurrent. Here I am sixty years old and as much as ever I'm in the middle of the journey. That is something that goes with the territory. One just keeps going.

INTERVIEWER

Do you see yourself as a difficult critic, in the sense that you qualify certain poets and prose fiction writers as "difficult"?

BLOOM

I would think, my dear, that most people these days might be kind enough to call me difficult. The younger members of my profession and the members of what I have called the school of resentment describe me, I gather, as someone who partakes of a cult of personality or self-obsession rather than their wonderful, free, and generous social vision. One of them, I understand, refers to me customarily as

Napoleon Bonaparte. There is no way of dealing with these people. They have not been moved by literature. Many of them are my former students and I know them all too well. They are now gender and power freaks.

But, no. *The Anxiety of Influence* is a difficult book. So is *Kabbalah and Criticism*. They're books in which one is trying to discover something. But *Ruin the Sacred Truths* is a very different book from these earlier ones, a very simple book, to me quite transparent. Besides the aging process and, I hope, the maturing process, the major reason is that I am writing more for that Johnsonian ideal—which, of course, does not exist anymore—the common reader. I wouldn't dream of using a too-technical word or term now if I could possibly help it, and I don't think there are any in *Ruin the Sacred Truths* except for *facticity*. I use that term and then dismiss it. I don't think that any of my own special vocabulary, for which I have been condemned in the past (and which was meant to expose how arbitrary all critical and rhetorical terminology always is and has to be) is in that book. Nor do I think it's necessary to have read *Kabbalah and Criticism* or *A Map of Misreading* or any other to understand the book. It is general literary criticism.

INTERVIEWER

How do you account historically for the school of resentment?

BLOOM

In the universities, the most surprising and reprehensible development came some twenty years ago, around 1968, and has had a very long-range effect, one that is still percolating. Suddenly all sorts of people, faculty members at the universities, graduate and undergraduate students, began to blame the universities not just for their own palpable ills and malfeasances but for all the ills of history and society. They were blamed, and to some extent still are, by the budding school of resentment and its precursors, as though they were not only representative of these ills but, weirdly enough, as though they had somehow helped *cause* these ills and, even more weirdly, quite surrealistically, as though they were somehow capable of ameliorating these ills. It's still going on—this attempt to ascribe both culpability and apocalyptic potential to the universities. It's really asking the universities to take the place that was once occupied by religion, philosophy, and science. These are our conceptual modes. They have all failed us. The entire history of Western culture, from Alexandrian days until now, shows that when a society's conceptual modes fail it, then willy-nilly it becomes a literary culture. This is probably neither good nor bad, but just the way things become. And we can't really ask literature or the representatives of a literary culture, in or out of the university, to save society. Literature is not an instrument of social change or an instrument of social reform. It is more a mode of human sensations and impressions, which do not reduce very well to societal rules or forms.

INTERVIEWER

How does one react to the school of resentment? By declaring oneself an aesthete?

BLOOM

Well, I do that now, of course, in furious reaction to their school and to so much other pernicious nonsense that goes on. I would certainly see myself as an aesthete in the sense advocated by Ruskin, indeed to a considerable degree by Emerson, and certainly by the divine Walter and the sublime Oscar. It is a very engaged kind of mode. Literary criticism in the United States increasingly is split between very-low-level literary journalism and what I increasingly regard as a disaster, which is literary criticism in the academies, particularly in the younger generations. Increasingly scores and scores of graduate students have read the absurd Lacan but have never read Edmund Spenser, or have read a great deal of Foucault or Derrida but scarcely read Shakespeare or Milton. That's obviously an absurd defeat for literary study. When I was a young man back in the fifties starting out on what was to be my career, I used to proclaim that my chosen profession seemed to consist of secular clergy or clerisy. I was thinking, of course, of the highly Anglo-Catholic New Criticism under the sponsorship or demigodness of T. S. Eliot. But I realized in latish middle age that, no better or worse, I was surrounded by a pride of displaced social workers, a rabblement of lemmings, all rushing down to the sea carrying their subject down to destruction with them. The school of resentment is an extraordinary sort of mélange of latest-model feminists, Lacanians, that whole semiotic cackle, latest-model pseudo-Marxists, so-called New Historicists, who are neither new nor historicist, and third-generation deconstructors, who I believe have no relationship whatever to literary values. It's really a very paltry kind of a phenomenon. But it is pervasive, and it seems to be waxing rather than waning. It is a very rare thing indeed to encounter one critic, academic or otherwise, not just in the English-speaking world, but also in France or Italy, who has an authentic commitment to aesthetic values, who reads for the pleasure of reading, and who values poetry or story as such, above all else. Reading has become a very curious kind of activity. It has become tendentious in the extreme. A sheer deliquescence has taken place because of this obsession with the methods or supposed method. Criticism starts—it *has* to start—with a real passion for reading. It can come in adolescence, even in your twenties, but you must fall in love with poems. You must fall in love with what we used to call "imaginative literature." And when you are in love that way, with or without provocation from good teachers, you will pass on to encounter what used to be called the sublime. And as soon as you do this, you pass into the agonistic mode, even if your own nature is anything but agonistic. In the end, the spirit that makes one a fan of a particular athlete or a particular team is different only in degree, not in kind, from the spirit that teaches one to prefer one poet to another, or one novelist to another. That is to say there is some element of competition at every point in one's experience as a reader. How could there not be? Perhaps you learn this more fully as you get older, but in the end you choose between books, or you choose between poems, the way you choose between people. You can't become friends with every acquaintance you make, and I would not think that it is any different with what you read.

INTERVIEWER

Do you foresee any change, or improvement, in the critical fashions?

BLOOM

I don't believe in myths of decline or myths of progress, even as regards to the literary scene. The world does not get to be a better or a worse place; it just gets more senescent. The world gets older, without getting either better or worse and so does literature. But I do think that the drab current phenomenon that passes for literary studies in the university will finally provide its own corrective. That is to say, sooner or later, students and teachers are going to get terribly bored with all the technocratic social work going on now. There will be a return to aesthetic values and desires, or these people will simply do something else with their time. But I find a great deal of hypocrisy in what they're doing now. It is tiresome to be encountering myths called "the Social Responsibility of the Critic" or "the Political Responsibility of the Critic." I would rather walk into a bookstore and find a book called "the Aesthetic Responsibilities of the Statesman," or "the Literary Responsibilities of the Engineer." Criticism is not a program for social betterment, not an engine for social change. I don't see how it possibly could be. If you look for the best instance of a socially radical critic, you find a very good one indeed in William Hazlitt. But you will not find that his social activism on the left in any way conditions his aesthetic judgments, or that he tries to make imaginative literature a machine for revolution. You would not find much difference in aesthetic response between Hazlitt and Dr. Samuel Johnson on Milton, though Dr. Johnson is very much on the right politically and Hazlitt, of course, very much an enthusiast for the French Revolution and for English radicalism. But I can't find much in the way of a Hazlittian or Johnsonian temperament in life and literature anywhere on the current scene. There are so many tiresomenesses going on. Everyone is so desperately afraid of being called a racist or a sexist that they connive—whether actively or passively—the almost total breakdown of standards that has taken place both in and out of the universities, where writings by blacks or Hispanics or in many cases simply women are concerned.

This movement has helped focus attention on some great novels, though. You're an admirer, for example, of Ralph Ellison's *Invisible Man*.

BLOOM

Oh, but that is a very, very rare exception. What else is there like *Invisible Man*? Zora Neale Hurston's *Their Eyes Were Watching God* has a kind of superior intensity and firm control. It's a very fine book indeed. It surprised and delighted me when I first read it and it has sustained several rereadings since. But that and *Invisible Man* are the only full-scale works of fiction I have read by American blacks in this century that have survival possibilities at all. Alice Walker is an extremely inadequate writer, and I think that is giving her the best of it. A book like *The Color Purple* is of no aesthetic interest or value whatsoever, yet it is exalted and taught in the academies. It clearly is a time in which social and cultural guilt has taken over.

INTERVIEWER

I know you find this to be true of feminist criticism.

BLOOM

I'm very fond of feminist critics, some of whom are my close friends, but it is widely known I'm not terribly fond of feminist criticism. The true test is to find work, whether in the past or present, by women writers that we had undervalued, and thus bring it to our attention and teach us to study it more closely or more usefully. By that test they have failed, because they have added not one to the canon. The women writers who mattered—Jane Austen, George Eliot, Emily Dickinson, Edith Wharton, Willa Cather, and others who have always mattered on aesthetic grounds—still matter. I do not appreciate Elizabeth Bishop or May Swenson any more or less than I would have appreciated them if we had no feminist literary criticism at all. And I stare at what is presented to me as feminist literary criticism and I shake my head. I regard it at best as being well-intentioned. I do not regard it as being literary criticism.

INTERVIEWER

Can it be valued as a form of social or political literary criticism?

BLOOM

I'm not concerned with political or social criticism. If people wish to practice it, that is entirely their business. It is not mine, heavens! If it does not help me to read a work of aesthetic value then I'm not going to be interested in it at all. I do not for a moment yield to the notion that any social, racial, ethnic, or "male" interest could determine my aesthetic choices. I have a lifetime of experience, learning, and insight that tells me this.

INTERVIEWER

What do you make of all this recent talk of the "canonical problem"?

BLOOM

It is no more than a reflection of current academic and social politics in the United States. The old test for what makes a work canonical is if it has engendered strong readings that come after it, whether as overt interpretations or implicitly interpretive forms. There's no way the gender and power boys and girls, or the New Historicists, or any of the current set are going to give us new canonical works, any more than all the agitation of feminist writing or nowadays what seems to be called African American writing is going to give us canonical works. Alice Walker is not going to be a canonical poet no matter how many lemmings stand forth and proclaim her sublimity. It really does seem to me a kind of bogus issue. I am more and more certain that a great deal of what now passes for literary study of the so-called politically correct variety will wash aside. It is a ripple. I give it five years. I have seen many fashions come and go since I first took up literary study. After forty years one begins to be able to distinguish an ephemeral surface ripple from a deeper current or an authentic change.

INTERVIEWER

You teach Freud and Shakespeare.

BLOOM

Oh yes, increasingly. I keep telling my students that I'm not interested in a Freudian reading of Shakespeare but a kind of Shakespearean reading of Freud. In some sense Freud has to be a prose
version of Shakespeare, the Freudian map of the mind being in fact
Shakespearean. There's a lot of resentment on Freud's part because I
think he recognizes this. What we think of as Freudian psychology is
really a Shakespearean invention and, for the most part, Freud is
merely codifying it. This shouldn't be too surprising. Freud himself
says "the poets were there before me," and the poet in particular is
necessarily Shakespeare. But you know, I think it runs deeper than
that. Western psychology is much more a Shakespearean invention
than a Biblical invention, let alone, obviously, a Homeric, or Sopho-
clean, or even Platonic, never mind a Cartesian or Jungian invention.
It's not just that Shakespeare gives us most of our representations of
cognition as such; I'm not so sure he doesn't largely invent what we
think of as cognition. I remember saying something like this to a seminar consisting of professional teachers of Shakespeare and one of
them got very indignant and said, You are confusing Shakespeare with
God. I don't see why one shouldn't, as it were. Most of what we know
about how to represent cognition and personality in language was per-
manently altered by Shakespeare. The principal insight that I've had
in teaching and writing about Shakespeare is that there isn't anyone
before Shakespeare who actually gives you a representation of characters or human figures speaking out loud, whether to themselves or to
others or both, and then brooding out loud, whether to themselves or
to others or both, on what they themselves have said. And then, in the
course of pondering, undergoing a serious or vital change, they become a different kind of character or personality and even a different
kind of mind. We take that utterly for granted in representation. But it
doesn't exist before Shakespeare. It doesn't happen in the Bible. It
doesn't happen in Homer or in Dante. It doesn't even happen in Euripides. It's pretty clear that Shakespeare's true precursor—where he
took the hint from—is Chaucer, which is why I think the Wife of Bath
gets into Falstaff, and the Pardoner gets into figures like Edmund and

Iago. As to where Chaucer gets that from, that's a very pretty question. It is a standing challenge I have put to my students. That's part of Chaucer's shocking originality as a writer. But Chaucer does it only in fits and starts, and in small degree. Shakespeare does it all the time. It's his common stock. The ability to do that and to persuade one that this is a natural mode of representation is purely Shakespearean and we are now so contained by it that we can't see its originality anymore. The originality of it is bewildering.

By the way, I was thinking recently about this whole question as it relates to the French tradition. I gave what I thought was a remarkable seminar on *Hamlet* to my undergraduate Shakespeare seminar at Yale. About an hour before class, I had what I thought was a very considerable insight, though I gather my students were baffled by it. I think that I was trying to say too much at once. It had suddenly occurred to me that the one canon of French neoclassical thought that was absolutely, indeed religiously, followed by French dramatists—and this means everyone, even Molière and Racine—was that there were to be no soliloquies and no asides. No matter what dexterity or agility had to be displayed, a confidante had to be dragged onto the stage so that the protagonist could have someone to whom to address cogitations, reflections. This accounts not only for why Shakespeare has never been properly absorbed by the French, as compared to his effect on every other European culture, language, literature, dramatic tradition, but also for the enormous differences between French and Anglo-American modes of literary thought. It also helps account for why the French modes, which are having so absurd an effect upon us at this time, are so clearly irrelevant to our literature and our way of talking about literature. I can give you a further illustration. I gave a faculty seminar a while ago, in which I talked for about two hours about my notions of Shakespeare and originality. At the end of it, a woman who was present, a faculty member at Yale, who had listened with a sort of amazement and a clear lack of comprehension, said with considerable exasperation, Well, you know, Professor Bloom, I don't really understand why you're talking about originality. It is as outmoded as, say, private enterprise in the economic sphere. An absurdity to have put myself in a situation where I had to address a member of the school of resentment! I was too courteous, especially since my colleague Shoshana Felman jumped in to try to explain to the lady what I was up to. But I realized it was hopeless. Here was a lady who came not out of Racine and Molière but in fact out of Lacan, Derrida, and Foucault. Even if she *had* come out of Racine and Molière, she could never have hoped to understand. I remember what instantly flashed through my head was that I had been talking about the extraordinary originality of the way Shakespeare's protagonists ponder to themselves and, on the basis of that pondering, change. She could not understand this because it never actually happens in the French drama; the French critical mind has never been able to believe that it is appropriate for this to happen. Surely this is related to a mode of apprehension, a mode of criticism in which authorial presence was never very strong anyway, and so indeed it could die.

INTERVIEWER

Can you explain how you came to notice this about Shakespeare's protagonists?

BLOOM

Yes, I can even remember the particular moment. I was teaching *King Lear*, and I'd reached a moment in the play that has always fascinated me. I suddenly saw what was going on. Edmund is the most remarkable villain in all Shakespeare, a manipulator so strong that he makes Iago seem minor in comparison. Edmund is a sophisticated and sardonic consciousness who can run rings around anyone else on the stage in *King Lear*. He is so foul that it takes Goneril and Regan, really, to match up to him . . . He's received his death wound from his brother; he's lying there on the battlefield. They bring in word that Goneril and Regan are dead—one slew the other and then committed suicide for his sake. Edmund broods out loud and says, quite extraordinarily (it's all in four words), "Yet Edmund was belov'd." One looks at those four words totally startled. As soon as he says it, he starts to ponder out loud. What are the implications that, though two monsters of the deep, the two loved me so much that one of them killed the other and then murdered herself. He reasons it out. He says, "The one the other poison'd for my sake / And after slew herself."

And then he suddenly says, "I pant for life," and then amazingly he says, "Some good I mean to do / despite of mine own nature," and he suddenly gasps out, having given the order for Lear and Cordelia to be killed, "Send in time," to stop it. They don't get there in time. Cordelia's been murdered. And then Edmund dies. But that's an astonishing change. It comes about as he hears himself say in real astonishment, "Yet Edmund was belov'd," and on that basis, he starts to ponder. Had he not said that, he would not have changed. There's nothing like that in literature before Shakespeare. It makes Freud unnecessary. The representation of inwardness is so absolute and large that we have no parallel to it before then.

INTERVIEWER

So that the Freudian commentary on *Hamlet* by Ernest Jones is unnecessary.

BLOOM

It's much better to work out what Hamlet's commentary on the Oedipal complex might be. There's that lovely remark of A. C. Bradley's that Shakespeare's major tragic heroes can only work in the play that they're in—that if Iago had to come onto the same stage with Hamlet, it would take Hamlet about five seconds to catch on to what Iago was doing and so viciously parody Iago that he would drive him to madness and suicide. The same way, if the ghost of Othello's dead father appeared to Othello and said that someone had murdered him, Othello would grab his sword and go and hack the other fellow down. In each case there would be no play. Just as the plays would make mincemeat of one another if you tried to work one into the other, so Shakespeare chops up any writer you apply him to. And a Shakespearean reading of Freud would leave certain things but not leave others. It would make one very impatient, I think, with Freud's representation of the Oedipal complex. And it's a disaster to try to apply the Freudian reading of that to Hamlet.

INTERVIEWER

Have you ever acted Shakespeare?

BLOOM

Only just once, at Cornell. I was pressed into service because I knew Father Falstaff by heart. But it was a disaster. I acted as though there were no one else on stage, something that delights my younger son when I repeat it. As a result, I never heard cues, I created a kind of gridlock on stage. I had a good time, but no one else did. Not long ago President Reagan, who should be remembered only for his jokes because his jokes I think are really very good, was asked how it was he could have managed eight years as president and still look so wonderful. Did you see this?

INTERVIEWER

No.

BLOOM

It was in the *Times.* He said, "Let me tell you the story about the old psychiatrist being admired by a young psychiatrist who asks, 'How come you still look so fresh, so free of anxiety, so little worn by care, when you've spent your entire life sitting as I do every day, getting worn out listening to the miseries of your patients?' To which the older psychiatrist replies, 'It's very simple, young man. I never listen.'" Such sublime, wonderful, and sincere self-revelation on the part of Reagan! In spite of all one's horror at what he has done or failed to do as president, it takes one's breath away with admiration. That's the way I played the part of Falstaff. I'm occasionally asked by old friends, who don't yet know me well enough, if I had ever considered becoming a psychoanalyst. I look at them in shock and say, Psychoanalyst! My great struggle as a teacher is to stop answering my own questions! I still think, though no one in the world except me thinks so and no one's ever going to give me an award as a great teacher, I'm a pretty good teacher, but only in terms of the great Emersonian maxim "that which I can receive from another is never tuition but only provocation." I think that if the young woman or man listens to what I am saying, she or he will get very provoked indeed.

INTERVIEWER

Do you ever teach from notes? Or do you prefer to improvise?

BLOOM

I have never made a note in my life. How could I? I have internalized the text. I externalized it in different ways at different times. We cannot step even once in the same river. We cannot step even once in the same text.

INTERVIEWER

What do you think of creative-writing workshops?

BLOOM

I suppose that they do more good than harm, and yet it baffles me. Writing seems to me so much an art of solitude. Criticism is a teachable art, but like every art it too finally depends upon an inherent or implicit gift. I remember remarking somewhere in something I wrote that I gave up going to the Modern Language Association some years ago because the idea of a convention of twenty-five or thirty thousand critics is every bit as hilarious as the idea of going to a convention of twenty-five thousand poets or novelists. There *aren't* twenty-five thousand critics. I frequently wonder if there are *five* critics alive at any one time. The extent to which the art of fiction or the art of poetry is teachable is a more complex problem. Historically, we know how poets become poets and fiction writers become fiction writers—they read. They read their predecessors and they learn what is to be learned. The idea of Herman Melville in a writing class is always distressing to me.

INTERVIEWER

Do you think that the word processor has had or is having any effect on the study of literature?

BLOOM

There cannot be a human being who has fewer thoughts on the whole question of word processing than I do. I've never even seen a word processor. I am hopelessly archaic.

INTERVIEWER

Perhaps you see an effect on students' papers then?

BLOOM

But for me the typewriter hasn't even been invented yet, so how can I speak to this matter? I protest! A man who has never learned to type is not going to be able to add anything to this debate. As far as I'm concerned, computers have as much to do with literature as space travel, perhaps much less. I can only write with a ballpoint pen, with a Rolling Writer, they're called, a black Rolling Writer on a lined yellow legal pad on a certain kind of clipboard. And then someone else types it.

INTERVIEWER

And someone else edits?

BLOOM

No one edits. I edit. I refuse to be edited.

INTERVIEWER

Do you revise much?

BLOOM

Sometimes, but not often.

INTERVIEWER

Is there a particular time of day when you like to write?

BLOOM

There isn't one for me. I write in desperation. I write because the pressures are so great, and I am simply so far past a deadline that I must turn out something.

INTERVIEWER

So you don't espouse a particular work ethic on a daily basis?

BLOOM

No, no. I lead a disordered and hurried life.

INTERVIEWER

Are there days when you do not work at all?

BLOOM

Yes, alas, alas, alas. But one always thinks about literature. I don't recognize a distinction between literature and life. I am, as I keep moaning, an experimental critic. I've spent my life proclaiming that what is called "critical objectivity" is a farce. It is deep subjectivity which has to be achieved, which is difficult, whereas objectivity is cheap.

INTERVIEWER

What is it that you think keeps you from writing when you're unable to write?

BLOOM

Despair, exhaustion. There are long periods when I cannot write at all. Long, long periods, sometimes lasting many years. Sometimes one just has to lie fallow. And also, you know, interests change. One goes into such different modes. What was incredibly difficult was the commentary on the J-Writer, which underwent real change for me as I became more and more convinced that she was a woman, which made some considerable difference. I mean, obviously it's just a question of imagining it one way or another. No one will ever demonstrate it, that he was a man or she was a woman. But I find that if I imagine it that J was a woman, it produces, to me, more imaginatively accurate results than the other way around.

INTERVIEWER

But do you think that the importance of the J-Writer's being a woman has been exaggerated?

BLOOM

Oh, immensely exaggerated. In an interview that was published in *The New York Times*, the extremely acute Richard Bernstein allowed me to remark at some length on my strong feeling, more intense than before, that on the internal, that is to say psychological and literary, evidence, it is much more likely to have been a woman than a man. I also said—I believe this quite passionately—that if I had it to do over again, I wouldn't have mentioned the putative gender of the author. It has served as a monstrous red herring that has diverted attention away from what is really controversial and should be the outrage and scandal of the book, which is the fact that the god—the literary character named Yahweh or God—has absolutely nothing in common with the God of the revisionists in the completed Torah and therefore of the normative Jewish tradition and of Christianity and Islam and all their branches.

INTERVIEWER

Certainly that aspect of the book has caught the notice of the normative Jewish reviewers.

BLOOM

The normative Jewish reviewers have reacted very badly, in particular Mr. Robert Alter. And the other Norman Podhorrors-type review was by his henchman, Neil Kozody, a subscriber to the Hotel Hilton Kramer criteria. (The marvelous controversialist Gore Vidal invariably refers to that dubiety as the Hotel Hilton Kramer.) Mr. Kozody, in playing Tonto to the Lone Ranger, went considerably further than Mr. Alter in denouncing me for what he thought was my vicious attack on normative Judaism. And indeed, I've now heard this from many quarters, including from an absurd rabbinical gentleman who reviewed it in *Newsday* and proclaimed, "What makes Professor Bloom think there was such a thing as irony three thousand years ago?"—which may be the funniest single remark that anyone could make about this or any other book.

But I'm afraid it isn't over. It's just beginning. There was a program at Symphony Space, where Claire Bloom and Fritz Weaver read aloud from the Bible, and I spoke for ten minutes at the beginning and end. I got rather carried away. In the final ten minutes I allowed myself not only to answer my normative Jewish critics, but to start talking about what I feel are the plain spiritual inadequacies for a contemporary intellectual Jewry. It has been subsequently broadcast, and all hell may break loose. Many a rabbi and Jewish bureaucrat has been after my scalp.

INTERVIEWER

What did you say?

BLOOM

Well, I allowed myself to tell the truth, which is always a great mistake. I said that I could not be the only contemporary Jewish intellectual who was very unhappy indeed that the Holocaust had been made part of our religion. I did not like this vision of six million versions of what the Christians call Jesus, and I did not believe that if this was going to be offered to me as Judaism it would be acceptable. I also allowed myself to say that the god of the J-Writer seems to me a god in whom I scarcely could fail to believe, since that god was all of our breath and vitality. Whereas what the Redactor, being more a censor than an author of the Hebrew Bible, and the priestly authors and those that came after in Jewish, Christian, and Islamic tradition, gave us are simply not acceptable to a person with literary sensibility or any high spirituality at this time.

INTERVIEWER

How have you found being in the public eye? *The Book of J* is your first book on the bestseller list.

BLOOM

Though it's the first time, I'm informed, that a work of literary criticism or commentary has been on the bestseller list, it has not been a pleasant experience.

INTERVIEWER

How so?

BLOOM

I did not, on the whole, relish the television and radio appearances, which I undertook because of the plain inadequacies of the publisher. The people who work for that publisher did the best they could, but they were understaffed, undermanned, never printed enough books, and have most inadequate advertising. I know that all authors complain about that, but this is manifest.

INTERVIEWER

You were on *Good Morning America* of all things.

BLOOM

I was on *Good Morning America*, I was on *Larry King*, and many others. I must say that I came away with two radically opposed insights. One is the remarkably high degree of civility and personal civilization of both my radio and TV interlocutors. In fact, they're far more civilized and gentlemanly or gentlewomanly than journalistic interviewers usually are, and certainly more so than the so-called scholarly and academic reviewers, who are merely assassins and thugs. But also, after a lifetime spent teaching, it was very difficult to accept emotionally that huge blank eye of the TV camera, or the strange bareness of the radio studio. There is a terrible unreality about it that I have not enjoyed at all.

INTERVIEWER

You have mentioned you might write on the aesthetics of outrage as a topic.

BLOOM

Yes, the aesthetics of *being* outraged. But I don't mean being outraged in that other sense, you know, that sort of postsixties phenomenon. I mean in the sense in which Macbeth is increasingly outraged. What fascinates me is that we so intensely sympathize with a successful or strong representation of someone in the process of being outraged, and I want to know why. I suppose it's ultimately that we're outraged at mortality, and it is impossible not to sympathize with that.

This is a topic that would somehow include W. C. Fields.

BLOOM

Oh yes, certainly, since I think his great power is that he perpetu-
ally demonstrates the enormous comedy of being outraged. I have
never recovered from the first time I saw the W. C. Fields short, *The
Fatal Glass of Beer*. It represents for me still the high point of cinema,
surpassing even Groucho's *Duck Soup*. Have you seen *The Fatal
Glass of Beer*? I don't think I have the critical powers to describe it.
Throughout much of it, W. C. Fields is strumming a zither and
singing a song about the demise of his unfortunate son, who expires
because of a fatal glass of beer that college boys persuade the abstain-
ing youth to drink. He then insults a Salvation Army lassie, herself a
reformed high-kicker in the chorus line, and she stuns him with a single high kick. But to describe it in this way is to say that *Macbeth* is
about an ambitious man who murders the King.

INTERVIEWER

So in addition to being an outrageous critic, are you an outraged
critic, in that sense?

BLOOM

No, no. I hope that I am not an outrageous critic, but I suppose I
am. But that's only because most of the others are so dreadfully tame
and senescent, or indeed are now politically correct or content to be
social reformers who try to tell us there is some connection between
literature and social change. Outraged? No, I am not outraged. I am
not outraged as a person. I am beyond it now. I'm sixty years and seven
months old. It's too late for me to be outraged. It would really shorten
my life if I let myself be outraged. I don't have the emotional strength
anymore. It would be an expense of spirit that I cannot afford. Besides, by now nothing surprises me. You know, the literary situation is
one of a surpassing absurdity. Criticism in the universities, I'll have to
admit, has entered a phase where I am totally out of sympathy with

95 percent of what goes on. It's Stalinism without Stalin. All the traits of the Stalinist in the 1930s and 1940s are being repeated in this whole resentment in the universities in the 1990s. The intolerance, the self-congratulation, smugness, sanctimoniousness, the retreat from imaginative values, the flight from the aesthetic. It's not worth being truly outraged about. Eventually these people will provide their own antidote, because they will perish of boredom. I will win in the end. I must be the only literary critic of any eminence who is writing today (I cannot think of another, I'm sad to say, however arrogant or difficult this sounds) who always asks about what he reads and likes, whether it is ancient, modern, or brand new, or has always been laying around, who always asks: How good is it? What is it better than? What is it less good than? What does it mean? and Is there some relation between what it means and how good or bad it is, and not only how is it good or bad, but why it is good or bad? Mr. Frye, who was very much my precursor, tried to banish all of that from criticism, just as I tried to reintroduce a kind of dark sense of temporality, or the sorrows of temporality, into literary criticism as a correction to Frye's Platonic idealism. I have also raised more explicitly than anyone else nowadays, or indeed anyone since Johnson or Hazlitt, the question of why does it matter. There has to be some relation between the way in which we matter and the way in which we read. A way of speaking and writing about literature that addresses itself to these matters must seem impossibly naïve or old-fashioned or not literary criticism at all to the partisans of the school of resentment. But I believe that these have been the modes of Western literary criticism ever since Aristophanes invented the art of criticism by juxtaposing Euripides with Aeschylus (to the profound disadvantage of Euripides), or indeed ever since Longinus started to work off his own anxieties about Plato by dealing with Plato's anxieties about Homer. This is the stuff literary criticism has always done and, if it is finally to be of any use to us, this is what I think it must get back to. It really must answer the questions of good and bad and how and why. It must answer the question of what the relevance of literature is to our lives, and why it means one thing to us when we are one way and another thing to us when we are another. It astonishes me that I cannot find any other contemporary critic who

still discusses the pathos of great literature or is willing to talk about why a particular work does or does not evoke great anguish in us. This is of course dismissed as the merest subjectivity.

INTERVIEWER

Can essays like Hazlitt's or Ruskin's or Pater's still be written today?

BLOOM

Most people would say no. I can only say I do my best. That's as audacious a thing as I can say. I keep saying, though nobody will listen, or only a few will listen, that criticism is either a genre of literature or it is nothing. It has no hope for survival unless it is a genre of literature. It can be regarded, if you wish, as a minor genre, but I don't know why people say that. The idea that poetry or, rather, verse writing, is to take priority over criticism is on the face of it absolute nonsense. That would be to say that the verse writer Felicia Hemans is a considerably larger figure than her contemporary William Hazlitt. Or that our era's Felicia Hemans, Sylvia Plath, is a considerably larger literary figure than, say, the late Wilson Knight. This is clearly not the case. Miss Plath is a bad verse writer. I read Knight with pleasure and profit, if at times wonder and shock. These are obvious points but obviously one will have to go on making them. Almost everything now written and published and praised in the United States as verse isn't even verse, let alone poetry. It's just typing, or word processing. As a matter of fact, it's usually just glib rhetoric or social resentment. Just as almost everything that we now call criticism is in fact just journalism.

INTERVIEWER

Or an involvement with what you refer to as the "easier pleasures." What are these easier pleasures?

BLOOM

Well, I take the notion from my friend and contemporary Angus Fletcher, who takes it from Shelley and Longinus. It's perfectly clear some very good writers offer only easier pleasures. Compare two writers exactly contemporary with one another—Harold Brodkey and John Updike. Updike, as I once wrote, is a minor novelist with a major style. A quite beautiful and very considerable stylist. I've read many novels by Updike, but the one I like best is *The Witches of Eastwick*. But for the most part it seems to me that he specializes in the easier pleasures. They are genuine pleasures, but they do not challenge the intellect. Brodkey, somewhat imperfectly perhaps, does so to a much more considerable degree. Thomas Pynchon provides very difficult pleasures, it seems to me, though not of late. I am not convinced, in fact, that it was he who wrote *Vineland*. Look at the strongest American novelist since Melville, Hawthorne, and James. That would certainly have to be Faulkner. Look at the difference between Faulkner at his very best in *As I Lay Dying* and at his very worst in *A Fable*. *A Fable* is nothing but easier pleasures, but they're not even pleasures. It is *so* easy it becomes, indeed, vulgar, disgusting, and does not afford pleasure. *As I Lay Dying* is a very difficult piece of work. To try to apprehend Darl Bundren takes a very considerable effort of the imagination. Faulkner really surpasses himself there. It seems to me an authentic instance of the literary sublime in our time. Or, if you look at modern American poetry, in some sense the entire development of Wallace Stevens is from affording us easier pleasures, as in "The Idea of Order at Key West," and before that "Sunday Morning," to the very difficult pleasures of "Notes Toward a Supreme Fiction" and then the immensely difficult pleasures of a poem like "The Owl in the Sarcophagus." You have to labor with immense intensity in order to keep up. It is certainly related to the notion propounded by both Burckhardt and Nietzsche, which I've taken over from them, of the agonistic. There is a kind of standard of measurement starting with Plato on through Western thought where one asks a literary work, implicitly, to answer the question "More, equal to, or less than?" In the end, the answer to that question is the persuasive force enabling a reader to say, I will sacrifice an easier pleasure for something that takes me beyond myself. Surely that must be the difference between Marlowe's *The Jew of Malta* and Shakespeare's *The Merchant of Venice*, an enigmatic and to me in many ways unequal play. I get a lot more pleasure out of Barabas than I do out of the equivocal Shylock, but I'm well aware that my pleasure in Barabas is an easier pleasure, and that my trouble in achieving any pleasure in reading or viewing Shylock is because other factors are getting in the way of apprehending the Shakespearean sublime. The whole question of the fifth act of *The Merchant of Venice* is for me one of the astonishing tests of what I would call the sublime in poetry. One has the trouble of having to accommodate oneself to it.

INTERVIEWER

You recently completed a stint as general editor for the Chelsea House series, a sort of encyclopedia of literary criticism, consisting of some five hundred volumes.

BLOOM

I haven't completed it, but it has slowed down. It has been a very strange kind of a process. It swept me away in a kind of fantastic rush. I couldn't do it again like that and I wouldn't want to do it again, but it was very intense while it lasted. When it reached its height I was writing fifteen of those introductions a month, so that every two days I had to write another. I had to reread everything and crystallize my views very quickly. But I like that kind of writing. I learned a great deal doing it, because you couldn't waste any time. You had to get to the kernel of it immediately, and in seven to twelve pages say what you really thought about it without wasting time on scholarly outreaches or byways.

INTERVIEWER

How do you manage to write so quickly? Is it insomnia?

BLOOM

Partly insomnia. I think I usually write therapeutically. That is what Hart Crane really taught one. I was talking to William Empson about this once. He never wrote any criticism of Crane, and he didn't know whether he liked his poetry or not, but he said that the desperation of Crane's poetry appealed to him. Using his funny kind of parlance, he said that Hart Crane's poetry showed that poetry is now a mug's game, that Crane always wrote every poem as though it were going to be his last. That catches something in Crane which is very true, that he writes each lyric in such a way that you literally feel he's going to die if he can't bring it off, that his survival not just as a poet but as a person depends upon somehow articulating that poem. I don't have the audacity to compare myself to Crane, yet I think I write criticism in the spirit in which he wrote poems. One writes to keep going, to keep oneself from going mad. One writes to be able to write the next piece of criticism or to live through the next day or two. Maybe it's an apotropaic gesture, maybe one writes to ward off death. I'm not sure. But I think in some sense that's what poets do. They write their poems to ward off dying.

INTERVIEWER

You were for some time writing a major work on Freud to be called "Transference and Authority." What's become of that?

BLOOM

Well, it's a huge, yellowing manuscript. I don't know whether I would have finished it, but for the five years before the Chelsea House New Haven factory closed down I increasingly had to give my work to writing those introductions. I don't regret it, since it allowed me for the first time to become a really general literary critic. But I had to set the Freud aside. Perhaps in four or five years I'll get back to it. I would still like to write a book on Freud, but I don't think it will be the "Transference and Authority" book. I've got a huge manuscript that tries to comment on every important essay or monograph of Freud's, but I don't think I would want to publish it. I would not want to write on Freud as though he were a kind of scripture. I would have to re-think the whole thing. The title was a giveaway, I now realize. I could never work out my own transference relationship with regard to the text of Freud, and I could never decide how much authority it did or didn't have for me. I suppose I foundered upon that, so it's a kind of tattered white elephant. It's up in the attic—seven or eight hundred pages of typescript. But I think I have abandoned in manuscript more books and essays than I've ever printed. The attic is full of them. Eventually I may make a bonfire of the whole thing.

INTERVIEWER

You've also referred to a sequel to *The Flight to Lucifer*, your one novel.

BLOOM

I wrote about half the sequel to it, called "The Lost Travelers' Dream," about a changeling child, a kind of gnostic concept, though it was much less doctrinal than *The Flight to Lucifer*. I thought it was a much better piece of writing, and a couple of people whom I showed it to thought it had real promise. But I brooded on it one night, about 1981 or 1982, and I shut my notebook, took the manuscript, and put it up in the attic. It's still up there, and if I ever live long enough and there are no changes in my life I might take it down. *Flight to Lucifer* is certainly the only book that I wish I hadn't published. It was all right to have composed it, but I wish I hadn't published it. I sat down one night, six months after it came out, and read through it. I thought it was—particularly in the last third or so—quite well written, but I also felt it was an atrociously bad book. It failed as narrative, as negative characterization. Its overt attempt to be a sort of secret sequel to that sublime and crazy book *A Voyage to Arcturus* failed completely. It had no redeeming virtues. It was a kind of tractate in the understanding of gnosticism. It clearly had many obsessive critical ideas in it. *The Flight to Lucifer* now reads to me as though Walter Pater were trying to write *Star Wars*. That's giving it the best of it.

INTERVIEWER

Do you find you have "slowed down" at all since your incredibly prolific period in the seventies?

BLOOM

I don't know that I'm a burned-out husk but one becomes so dialectically aware of the history of literature that one requires some multiple consciousness of oneself in regard to the total work of others. One gets more and more addicted to considering the relationship between literature and life in teaching and writing. In fact, there are certain things that had been possible at an early age that are not possible anymore. I find that anything of any length I'm now trying to write is what once would have been called religious. I'm writing this book called "The American Religion: A Prophecy," whose title, of course, echoes Blake's *America: A Prophecy*. It is meant to be a somewhat outrageous but I hope a true and useful book. It begins with our last election and leads into the whole question of the American spirit and American literature and above all the American religion—which existed before Emerson but to which Emerson gave the decisive terms. The religion of the United States is not Christianity; perhaps it never was Christianity, but is a curious form of American gnosis. It is a mighty queer religion, exhilarating in some ways but marked by destructiveness. It seems to me increasingly that George Bush won hands down and had to win because of the two candidates he more nearly incarnated the ideals and visions of the American religion. Our foreign policy basically amounts to making the world safe for gnosticism.

INTERVIEWER

You've written that the Christian Bible is, on the whole, a disappointment.

BLOOM

The aesthetic achievement is so much less than that of the Old—or original—Testament. The New Testament is a very curious work from a literary point of view. So much of it is written by writers who are thinking in Aramaic and writing in demotic Greek. And that curious blend of Aramatic syntax with a Greek vocabulary is a very dubious medium. It's particularly egregious in the Revelation of St. John the Divine, the Apocalypse, which is a very bad and hysterical and nasty piece of writing. Even the most powerful parts of the New Testament from a literary point of view—certain epistles of Paul and the Gospel of John—are not works that can sustain a close aesthetic comparison with the stronger parts of the Hebrew Bible. It is striking how the Apocalypse of John has had an influence out of all proportion to its aesthetic, or for that matter, I would think, its spiritual value. It is not only an hysterical piece of work, but a work lacking love or compassion. In fact, it is the archetypal text of resentment, and it is the proper foundation for every school of resentment ever since.

INTERVIEWER

Is belief anything more than a trope for you now?

BLOOM

Belief is not available to me. It is a stuffed bird, up on the shelf. So is philosophy, let me point out, and so, for that matter, is psychoanalysis—an institutional church founded upon Freud's writings, praxis, and example. These are not live birds that one can hold in one's hand. We live in a literary culture, as I keep saying. This is not necessarily good—it might even be bad—but it is where we are. Our cognitive modes have failed us.

INTERVIEWER

Can belief be as individual and idiosyncratic as fiction?

BLOOM

The religious genius is a dead mode. Belief should be as passionate and individual a fiction as any strong, idiosyncratic literary work, but it isn't. It almost never is. Religion has been too contaminated by society, by human hatreds. The history of religion as an institutional or social mode is a continuous horror. At this very moment we see this with the wretched Mr. Rushdie, who, by the way, alas, is not much of a writer. I tried to read *Midnight's Children* and found myself quite bored; I have tried to read *The Satanic Verses*, which seems to me very wordy, very neo-Joycean, very much an inadequate artifice. It is not much better than an upper-middlebrow attempt at serious fiction. Poor wretched fellow, who can blame him? There's no way for him to apologize because the world is not prepared to protect him from the consequences of having offended a religion. All religions have always been pernicious as social, political, and economic entities. And they always will be.

INTERVIEWER

Are you still watching the TV evangelists?

BLOOM

Oh yes, I love the TV evangelists, especially Jimmy Swaggart. I loved above all his grand confession starting "I have sinned . . . ," which he delivered to all of America with his family in the front row of the auditorium. One of the most marvelous moments in modern American culture! I enjoyed it immensely. It was his finest performance. And then the revelation by the lady, when she published her article, that he never touched her! And he was paying her these rather inconsiderable sums for her to *zoombinate* herself while he watched. Oh dear. It's so sad. It's so terribly sad.

INTERVIEWER

I've heard that you occasionally listen to rock music.

BLOOM

Oh sure. My favorite viewing, and this is the first time I have ever admitted it to anyone, but what I love to do, when I don't watch evangelicals, when I can't read or write and can't go out walking, and don't want to just tear my hair and destroy myself, I put on, here in New Haven, cable channel thirteen and I watch rock television endlessly. As a sheer revelation of the American religion it's overwhelming. Yes, I like to watch the dancing girls too. The sex part of it is fine. Occasionally it's musically interesting, but you know, ninety-nine out of a hundred groups are just bilge. And there hasn't been any good American rock since, alas, The Band disbanded. I watch MTV endlessly, my dear, because what is going on there, not just in the lyrics but in its whole ambience, is the real vision of what the country needs and desires. It's the image of reality that it sees, and it's quite weird and wonderful. It confirms exactly these two points: first, that no matter how many are on the screen at once, not one of them feels free except in total self-exaltation. And second, it comes through again and again in the lyrics and the way one dances, the way one moves, that what is best and purest in one is just no part of the creation—that myth of an essential purity before and beyond experience never goes away. It's quite fascinating. And notice how pervasive it is! I spent a month in Rome lecturing and I was so exhausted at the end of each day that my son David and I cheerfully watched the Italian MTV. I stared and I just couldn't believe it. Italian MTV is a sheer parody of its American counterpart, with some amazing consequences—the American religion has made its way even into Rome! It is nothing but a religious phenomenon. Very weird to see it take place.

INTERVIEWER

Has the decision to be a critic . . . or it's not really a decision, I suppose . . .

BLOOM

It's not a decision, it's an infliction.

INTERVIEWER

Has the vocation of criticism been a happy one?

BLOOM

I don't think of it in those terms.

INTERVIEWER

Satisfying?

BLOOM

I don't think of it in those terms.

INTERVIEWER

Inevitable only?

BLOOM

People who don't like me would say so. Denis Donoghue, in his review of *Rain the Sacred Truths*, described me as the Satan of literary criticism. That I take as an involuntary compliment. Perhaps indeed it was a voluntary compliment. In any case, I'm delighted to accept that. I'm delighted to believe that I am by merit raised to that bad eminence.

INTERVIEWER

Are there personal costs to being the Satan of literary criticism?

BLOOM

I can't imagine what they would be. All of us are, as Mr. Stevens said, "condemned to be that inescapable animal, ourselves." Or as an even greater figure, Sir John Falstaff, said, " 'Tis no sin for a man to labor in his vocation." I would much rather be regarded, of course, as the Falstaff of literary criticism than as the Satan of literary criticism. Much as I love my Uncle Satan, I love my Uncle Falstaff even more. He's much wittier than Satan. He's wiser than Satan. But then, Shakespeare's an even better poet than Milton.

INTERVIEWER

Is there anything you feel especially required to complete right now, as a teacher or as a critic? Something just beyond view?

BLOOM

Well, I intend to teach Shakespeare for the rest of my life. I would like to write a general, comprehensive study on Shakespeare, not necessarily commenting on every play or every scene, but trying to arrive at a total view of Shakespeare. One always wants to write about Shakespeare. But by then I may be too old I think.

INTERVIEWER

Are you being fruitfully misread, as you would say, by anyone?

BLOOM

I hope that somewhere in the world there is a young critic or two who will strongly misread me to their advantage. Lord knows, one is not Samuel Johnson or William Hazlitt or John Ruskin, or even Walter Pater or Oscar Wilde as critic. But, yes, I hope so.

You know, I've learned something over the years, picking up copies of my books in secondhand bookstores and in libraries, off people's shelves. I've written so much and have now looked at so many of these books that I've learned a great deal. You also learn this from reviews and from things that are cited in other people's books and so on, or from what people say to you—what you pride yourself on, the things that you think are your insight and contribution . . . no one ever even *notices* them. It's as though they're just for you. What you say in passing or what you expound because you know it too well, because it really bores you, but you feel you have to get through this in order to make your grand point, *that's* what people pick up on. *That's* what they underline. *That's* what they quote. *That's* what they attack or cite favorably. *That's* what they can use. What you really think you're doing may or may not be what you're doing, but it certainly isn't communicated to others. I've talked about this to other critics, to other writers; they haven't had quite my extensive sense of this, but it strikes an answering chord in them. One's grand ideas are indeed one's grand ideas, but there are none that seem to be useful or even recognizable to anyone else. It's a very strange phenomenon. It must have something to do with our capacity for not knowing ourselves.

Issue 118, 1991

Toni Morrison

The Art of Fiction

Toni Morrison detests being called a "poetic writer." She seems
to think that the attention that has been paid to the lyricism of
her work marginalizes her talent and denies her stories their power
and resonance. As one of the few novelists whose work is both popular and critically acclaimed, she can afford the luxury of choosing
what praise to accept. But she does not reject all classifications, and,
in fact, embraces the title "black woman writer." Her ability to transform individuals into forces and idiosyncrasies into inevitabilities has
led some critics to call her the "D. H. Lawrence of the black psyche."
She is also a master of the public novel, examining the relationships
between the races and sexes and the struggle between civilization and
nature, while at the same time combining myth and the fantastic with
a deep political sensitivity.

We talked with Morrison one summer Sunday afternoon on the
lush campus of Princeton University. The interview took place in her
office, which is decorated with a large Helen Frankenthaler print,
pen-and-ink drawings an architect did of all the houses that appear in
her work, photographs, a few framed book-jacket covers, and an apology note to her from Hemingway—a forgery meant as a joke. On her
desk is a blue glass teacup emblazoned with the likeness of Shirley
Temple filled with the No. 2 pencils that she uses to write her first
drafts. Jade plants sit in a window and a few more potted plants hang
above. A coffeemaker and cups are at the ready. Despite the high ceil-
ings, the big desk, and the high-backed black rocking chairs, the

American; it could be Catholic, it could be Midwestern. I'm those things too, and they are all important.

INTERVIEWER

Why do you think people ask, "Why don't you write something that we can understand?" Do you threaten them by not writing in the typical western, linear, chronological way?

MORRISON

I don't think that they mean that. ~~When they say,~~ "Are you ever going to write a book about white people?" ~~they think that~~ that's a kind of a compliment. They're saying, "You write well enough, I would even let you write about me." couldn't say that to anybody else. I mean, could I ~~go~~ up to Andre Gide and say, "Yes, but when are you going to get serious and start writing about black people?" I don't think he would know how to answer that question. Just as I don't. He would say, "What?" "I will if I want" or "Who are you?" What is behind that question is, there's the center, which is ~~you~~, and then there are these regional blacks or Asians, sort of marginal people. That question can only be asked from the center. Bill Moyers asked me that when-are-you-going-to-write-about question on television. I just said, "Well, maybe one day ..." but I couldn't say to him, you know, you can only ask that question from the center. The center of the world! I mean he's a white male. He's asking a marginal person, "When are you going to get to the center? When are you going to write about white people?" ~~But I can't say, "Leo Tolstoy, when are you gonna write about black people?"~~ I can't say, "Bill, why are you asking me that question?" The point is that he's ~~complimenting~~; he's saying, "You write room had the warm feeling of a kitchen, maybe because talking to Morrison about writing is the intimate kind of conversation that often seems to happen in kitchens; or perhaps it was the fact that as our energy started flagging she magically produced mugs of cranberry juice. We felt that she had allowed us to enter into a sanctuary, and that, however subtly, she was completely in control of the situation.

Outside, high canopies of oak leaves filtered the sunlight, dappling her white office with pools of yellowy light. Morrison sat behind her big desk, which despite her apologies for the "disorder" appeared well organized. Stacks of books and piles of paper resided on a painted bench set against the wall. She is smaller than one might imagine, and her hair, gray and silver, is woven into thin steel-colored braids that hang just at shoulder length. Occasionally during the interview Morrison let her sonorous, deep voice break into rumbling laughter and punctuated certain statements with a flat smack of her hand on the desktop. At a moment's notice she can switch from raging about violence in the United States to gleefully skewering the hosts of the trash TV talk shows through which she confesses to channel surfing sometimes late in the afternoon if her work is done.

—*Elissa Schappell, Claudia Brodsky Lacour, 1993*

INTERVIEWER

You have said that you begin to write before dawn. Did this habit begin for practical reasons, or was the early morning an especially fruitful time for you?

TONI MORRISON

Writing before dawn began as a necessity—I had small children when I first began to write and I needed to use the time before they said, Mama—and that was always around five in the morning. Many years later, after I stopped working at Random House, I just stayed at home for a couple of years. I discovered things about myself I had never thought about before. At first I didn't know when I wanted to eat, because I had always eaten when it was lunchtime or dinnertime or breakfast time. Work and the children had driven all of my habits . . . I didn't know the weekday sounds of my own house; it all made me feel a little giddy.

I was involved in writing *Beloved* at that time—this was in 1983—and eventually I realized that I was clearer-headed, more confident, and generally more intelligent in the morning. The habit of getting up early, which I had formed when the children were young, now became my choice. I am not very bright or very witty or very inventive after the sun goes down.

Recently I was talking to a writer who described something she did whenever she moved to her writing table. I don't remember exactly what the gesture was—there is something on her desk that she touches before she hits the computer keyboard—but we began to talk about little rituals that one goes through before beginning to write. I, at first, thought I didn't have a ritual, but then I remembered that I always get up and make a cup of coffee while it is still dark—it must be dark—and then I drink the coffee and watch the light come. And she said, Well, that's a ritual. And I realized that for me this ritual comprises my preparation to enter a space that I can only call nonsecular . . . Writers all devise ways to approach that place where they expect to make the contact, where they become the conduit, or where they engage in this mysterious process. For me, light is the signal in the transition. It's not being *in* the light, it's being there *before it arrives*. It enables me, in some sense.

I tell my students one of the most important things they need to know is when they are their best creatively. They need to ask themselves, What does the ideal room look like? Is there music? Is there silence? Is there chaos outside or is there serenity outside? What do I need in order to release my imagination?

INTERVIEWER

What about your writing routine?

MORRISON

I have an ideal writing routine that I've never experienced, which is to have, say, nine uninterrupted days when I wouldn't have to leave the house or take phone calls. And to have the space—a space where I have huge tables. I end up with this much space [*she indicates a small square spot on her desk*] everywhere I am, and I can't beat my way out of it. I am reminded of that tiny desk that Emily Dickinson wrote on and I chuckle when I think, Sweet thing, there she was. But that is all any of us have: just this small space and no matter what the filing system or how often you clear it out—life, documents, letters, requests, invitations, invoices just keep going back in. I am not able to write regularly. I have never been able to do that—mostly because I have always had a nine-to-five job. I had to write either in between those hours, hurriedly, or spend a lot of weekend and predawn time.

INTERVIEWER

Could you write after work?

MORRISON

That was difficult. I've tried to overcome not having orderly spaces by substituting compulsion for discipline, so that when something is urgently there, urgently seen or understood, or the metaphor was powerful enough, then I would move everything aside and write for sustained periods of time. I'm talking to you about getting the first draft.

INTERVIEWER

You have to do it straight through?

MORRISON

I do. I don't think it's a law.

INTERVIEWER

Could you write on the bottom of a shoe while riding on a train like Robert Frost? Could you write on an airplane?

MORRISON

Sometimes something that I was having some trouble with falls into place, a word sequence, say, so I've written on scraps of paper, in hotels on hotel stationery, in automobiles. *If* it arrives you *know.* If you know it *really* has come, then you *have* to put it down.

INTERVIEWER

What is the physical act of writing like for you?

MORRISON

I write with a pencil.

INTERVIEWER

Would you ever work on a word processor?

MORRISON

Oh, I do that also, but that is much later when everything is put together. I type that into a computer and then I begin to revise. But everything I write for the first time is written with a pencil, maybe a ballpoint if I don't have a pencil. I'm not picky, but my preference is for yellow legal pads and a nice No. 2 pencil.

INTERVIEWER

Dixon Ticonderoga No. 2 soft?

MORRISON

Exactly. I remember once trying to use a tape recorder, but it doesn't work.

INTERVIEWER

Did you actually dictate a story into the machine?

MORRISON

Not the whole thing, but just a bit. For instance, when two or three sentences seemed to fall into place, I thought I would carry a tape recorder in the car, particularly when I was working at Random House going back and forth every day. It occurred to me that I could just record it. It was a disaster. I don't trust my writing that is not written, although I work very hard in subsequent revisions to remove the writerly-ness from it, to give it a combination of lyrical, standard, and colloquial language. To pull all these things together into something that I think is much more alive and representative. But I don't trust something that occurs to me and then is spoken and transferred immediately to the page.

INTERVIEWER

Do you ever read your work out loud while you are working on it?

MORRISON

Not until it's published. I don't trust a performance. I could get a response that might make me think it was successful when it wasn't at all. The difficulty for me in writing—*among* the difficulties—is to write language that can work quietly on a page for a reader who doesn't hear anything. Now for that, one has to work very carefully with what is *in between* the words. What is not said. Which is measure, which is rhythm, and so on. So, it is what you don't write that frequently gives what you do write its power.

INTERVIEWER

How many times would you say you have to write a paragraph over to reach this standard?

MORRISON

Well, those that need reworking I do as long as I can. I mean, I've revised six times, seven times, thirteen times. But there's a line between revision and fretting, just working it to death. It is important to know when you are fretting it; when you are fretting it because it is not working, it needs to be scrapped.

INTERVIEWER

Do you ever go back over what has been published and wish you had fretted more over something?

MORRISON

A lot. Everything.

INTERVIEWER

Do you ever rework passages that have already been published before reading them to an audience?

MORRISON

I don't change it for the audience, but I know what it ought to be and isn't. After twenty-some years you can figure it out; I know more about it now than I did then. It is not so much that it would have been different or even better; it is just that, taken into context with what I was trying to effect, or what consequence I wanted it to have on the reader, years later the picture is clearer to me.

INTERVIEWER

How do you think being an editor for twenty years affected you as a writer?

MORRISON

I am not sure. It lessened my awe of the publishing industry. I understood the adversarial relationship that sometimes exists between writers and publishers, but I learned how important, how critical an editor was, which I don't think I would have known before.

INTERVIEWER

Are there editors who are helpful critically?

MORRISON

Oh yes. The good ones make all the difference. It is like a priest or a psychiatrist; if you get the wrong one, then you are better off alone. But there are editors so rare and so important that they are worth searching for, and you always know when you have one.

INTERVIEWER

Who was the most instrumental editor you've ever worked with?

MORRISON

I had a very good editor, superlative for me—Bob Gottlieb. What made him good for me was a number of things—knowing what not to touch; asking all the questions you probably would have asked yourself had there been the time. Good editors are really the third eye. Cool. Dispassionate. They don't love you or your work; for me that is what is valuable—not compliments. Sometimes it's uncanny; the editor puts his or her finger on exactly the place the writer knows is weak but just couldn't do any better at the time. Or perhaps the writer thought it might fly but wasn't sure. Good editors identify that place and sometimes make suggestions. Some suggestions are not useful because you can't explain everything to an editor about what you are trying to do. I couldn't possibly explain all of those things to an editor, because what I do has to work on so many levels. But within the relationship if there is some trust, some willingness to listen, remarkable things can happen. I read books all the time that I know would have profited from not a copy editor but somebody just talking through it. And it is important to get a great editor at a certain time, because if you don't have one in the beginning, you almost can't have one later. If you work well without an editor, and your books are well received for five or ten years, and then you write another one—which is successful but not very good—why should you then listen to an editor?

INTERVIEWER

You have told students that they should think of the process of revision as one of the major satisfactions of writing. Do you get more pleasure out of writing the first draft or in the actual revision of the work?

MORRISON

They are different. I am profoundly excited by thinking up or having the idea in the first place . . . before I begin to write.

INTERVIEWER

Does it come in a flash?

MORRISON

No, it's a sustained thing I have to play with. I always start out with an idea, even a boring idea, that becomes a question I don't have any answers to. Specifically, since I began the *Beloved* trilogy, the last part of which I'm working on now, I have been wondering why women who are twenty, thirty years younger than I am are no happier than women who are my age and older. What on earth is that about, when there are so many more things that they can do, so many more choices? *All right*, so this is an embarrassment of riches, but so what. Why is everybody so miserable?

INTERVIEWER

Do you write to figure out exactly how you feel about a subject?

MORRISON

No, I know how I *feel*. My feelings are the result of prejudices and convictions like everybody else's. But I am interested in the complexity, the vulnerability of an idea. It is not "This is what I believe," because that would not be a book, just a tract. A book is "This may be what I believe, but suppose I am wrong . . . what could it be?" Or, "I don't know what it is, but I am interested in finding out what it might mean to me, as well as to other people."

INTERVIEWER

Did you know as a child that you wanted to be a writer?

MORRISON

No. I wanted to be a reader. I thought everything that needed to be written had already been written or would be. I only wrote the first book because I thought it wasn't there, and I wanted to read it when I got through. I am a pretty good reader. I love it. It is what I do, really. So, if I can read it, that is the highest compliment I can think of. People say, I write for myself, and it sounds so awful and so narcissistic, but in a sense if you know how to read your own work—that is, with the necessary critical distance—it makes you a better writer and editor. When I teach creative writing, I always speak about how you have to learn how to read your work; I don't mean enjoy it because you wrote it. I mean, go away from it, and read it as though it is the first time you've ever seen it. Critique it that way. Don't get all involved in your thrilling sentences and all that . . .

INTERVIEWER

Do you have your audience in mind when you sit down to write?

MORRISON

Only me. If I come to a place where I am unsure, I have the characters to go to for reassurance. By that time they are friendly enough to tell me if the rendition of their lives is authentic or not. But there are so many things only I can tell. After all, this is my work. I have to take full responsibility for doing it right as well as doing it wrong. Doing it wrong isn't bad, but doing it wrong and thinking you've done it right is. I remember spending a whole summer writing something I was very impressed with, but couldn't get back to until winter. I went back confident that those fifty pages were really first-rate, but when I read them each page of the fifty was terrible. It was really ill-conceived. I knew that I could do it over, but I just couldn't get over the fact that I thought it was so good at the time. And that is scary because then you think it means you don't know.

INTERVIEWER

What about it was so bad?

MORRISON

It was pompous. Pompous and unappetizing.

INTERVIEWER

I read that you started writing after your divorce as a way of beating back the loneliness. Was that true, and do you write for different reasons now?

MORRISON

Sort of. Sounds simpler than it was. I don't know if I was writing for that reason or some other reason—or one that I don't even suspect. I do know that I don't like it here if I don't have something to write.

INTERVIEWER

Here, meaning where?

MORRISON

Meaning out in the world. It is not possible for me to be unaware of the incredible violence, the willful ignorance, the hunger for other people's pain. I'm always conscious of that though I am less aware of it under certain circumstances—good friends at dinner, other books. Teaching makes a big difference, but that is not enough. Teaching could make me into someone who is complacent, unaware, rather than part of the solution. So what makes me feel as though I belong here out in this world is not the teacher, not the mother, not the lover, but what goes on in my mind when I am writing. Then I belong here and then all of the things that are disparate and irreconcilable can be useful. I can do the traditional things that writers always say they do, which is to make order out of chaos. Even if you are reproducing the disorder, you are sovereign at that point. Struggling through the work is extremely important—more important to me than publishing it.

INTERVIEWER

If you didn't do this, then the chaos would—

MORRISON

Then I would be part of the chaos.

INTERVIEWER

Wouldn't the answer to that be either to lecture about the chaos or to be in politics?

MORRISON

If I had a gift for it. All I can do is read books and write books and edit books and critique books. I don't think that I could show up on a regular basis as a politician. I would lose interest. I don't have the resources for it, the gift. There are people who can organize other people and I cannot. I'd just get bored.

INTERVIEWER

When did it become clear to you that your gift was to be a writer?

MORRISON

It was very late. I always thought I was probably adept, because people used to say so, but their criteria might not have been mine. So I wasn't interested in what they said. It meant nothing. It was by the time I was writing *Song of Solomon*, the third book, that I began to think that this was the central part of my life. Not to say that other women haven't said it all along, but for a woman to say, I am a writer, is difficult.

INTERVIEWER

Why?

MORRISON

Well, it isn't so difficult *anymore*, but it certainly was for me and for women of my generation or my class or my race. I don't know that all those things are folded into it, but the point is you're moving yourself out of the gender role. You are not saying, I am a mother, I am a wife. Or if you're in the labor market, I am a teacher, I am an editor. But when you move to *writer*, what is that supposed to mean? Is that a job? Is this the way you make your living? It's an intervention into terrain that you are not familiar with—where you have no provenance. At the time I certainly didn't personally know any other women writers who were successful; it looked very much like a male preserve. So you sort of hope you're going to be a little minor person around the edges. It's almost as if you needed permission to write. When I read women's biographies and autobiographies, even accounts of how they got started writing, almost every one of them had a little anecdote that told about the moment someone gave them permission to do it. A mother, a husband, a teacher—somebody—said, OK, go ahead— you can do it. Which is not to say that men have never needed that; frequently when they are very young, a mentor says, You're good, and they take off. The entitlement was something they could take for granted. I couldn't. It was all very strange. So, even though I knew that writing was central to my life, that it was where my mind was, where I was most delighted and most challenged, I couldn't say it. If someone asked me, What do you do? I wouldn't say, Oh I'm a writer. I'd say, I'm an editor, or, I'm a teacher. Because when you meet people and go to lunch, if they say, What do you do? and you say, I'm a writer, they have to think about that, and then they ask, What have you written? Then they have to either like it or not like it. People feel obliged to like or not like and say so. It is perfectly all right to hate my work. It really is. I have close friends whose work I loathe.

INTERVIEWER

Did you feel you had to write in private?

MORRISON

Oh yes, I wanted to make it a private thing. I wanted to own it myself. Because once you say it, then other people become involved. As a matter of fact, while I was at Random House I never said I was a writer.

INTERVIEWER

Why not?

MORRISON

Oh, it would have been awful. First of all they didn't hire me to do that. They didn't hire me to be one of *them*. Secondly, I think they would have fired me.

INTERVIEWER

Really?

MORRISON

Sure. There were no in-house editors who wrote fiction. Ed Doctorow quit. There was nobody else—no real buying, negotiating editor in trade who was also publishing her own novels.

INTERVIEWER

Did the fact that you were a woman have anything to do with it?

MORRISON

That I didn't think about too much. I was so busy. I only know that I will never again trust my life, my future, to the whims of men, in companies or out. Never again will their judgment have anything to do with what I think I can do. That was the wonderful liberation of being divorced and having children. I did not mind failure, ever, but I minded thinking that someone male knew better. Before that, all the men I knew *did* know better, they really did. My father and teachers were smart people who knew better. Then I came across a smart person who was very important to me who *didn't* know better.

INTERVIEWER

Was this your husband?

MORRISON

Yes. He knew better about his life, but not about mine. I had to stop and say, Let me start again and see what it is like to be a grown-up. I decided to leave home, to take my children with me, to go into publishing and see what I could do. I was prepared for that not to work either, but I wanted to see what it was like to be a grown-up.

INTERVIEWER

Can you talk about that moment at Random House when they suddenly realized that they had a writer in their midst?

MORRISON

I published a book called *The Bluest Eye*. I didn't tell them about it. They didn't know until they read the review in *The New York Times*. It was published by Holt. Somebody had told this young guy there that I was writing something and he had said in a very offhand way, If you ever complete something send it to me. So I did. A lot of black men were writing in 1968, 1969, and he bought it, thinking that there was a growing interest in what black people were writing and that this book of mine would also sell. He was wrong. What was selling was: Let me tell you how powerful I am and how horrible you are, or some version of that. For whatever reasons, he took a small risk. He didn't pay me much, so it didn't matter if the book sold or not. It got a really horrible review in *The New York Times Book Review* on Sunday and then got a very good daily review.

INTERVIEWER

You mentioned getting permission to write. Who gave it to you?

MORRISON

No one. What I needed permission to do was to succeed at it. I never signed a contract until the book was finished because I didn't want it to be homework. A contract meant somebody was waiting for it, that I *had* to do it, and they could ask me about it. They could get up in my face and I don't like that. By not signing a contract, I do it, and if I want you to see it, I'll let you see it. It has to do with self-esteem. I am sure for years you have heard writers constructing illusions of freedom, anything in order to have the illusion that it is all mine and only I can do it. I remember introducing Eudora Welty and saying that nobody could have written those stories but her, meaning that I have a feeling about most books that at some point somebody would have written them *anyway*. But then there are some writers without whom certain stories would never have been written. I don't mean the subject matter or the narrative but just the way in which they did it—their slant on it is truly unique.

INTERVIEWER

Who are some of them?

MORRISON

Hemingway is in that category, Flannery O'Connor. Faulkner, Fitzgerald . . .

INTERVIEWER

Haven't you been critical of the way these authors depicted blacks?

MORRISON

No! Me, critical? I have been revealing how white writers imagine black people, and some of them are brilliant at it. Faulkner was brilliant at it. Hemingway did it poorly in places and brilliantly elsewhere.

INTERVIEWER

How so?

MORRISON

In not using black characters, but using the aesthetic of blacks as anarchy, as sexual license, as deviance. In his last book, *The Garden of Eden*, Hemingway's heroine is getting blacker and blacker. The woman who is going mad tells her husband, I want to be your little African queen. The novel gets its charge that way: Her white white hair and her black, black skin . . . almost like a Man Ray photograph. Mark Twain talked about racial ideology in the most powerful, eloquent, and instructive way I have ever read. Edgar Allan Poe did not. He loved white supremacy and the planter class, and he wanted to be a gentleman, and he endorsed all of that. He didn't contest it or critique it. What is exciting about American literature is that business of how writers say things under, beneath, and around their stories. Think of *Pudd'nhead Wilson* and all these inversions of what race is, how sometimes nobody can tell, or the thrill of discovery? Faulkner in *Absalom, Absalom!* spends the entire book tracing race and you can't find it. No one can see it, even the character who *is* black can't see it. I did this lecture for my students that took me forever, which was tracking all the moments of withheld, partial, or disinformation, when a racial fact or clue *sort* of comes out but doesn't quite arrive. I just wanted to chart it. I listed its appearance, disguise, and disappearance on every page—I mean every phrase! Everything, and I delivered this thing to my class. They all fell asleep! But I was so fascinated, technically. Do you know how hard it is to withhold that kind of information but hinting, pointing all of the time? And then to reveal it in order to say that it is *not* the point anyway? It is technically just astonishing. As a reader you have been forced to hunt for a drop of black blood that means everything and nothing. The insanity of racism. So the structure is the argument. Not what this one says or that one says . . . it is the *structure* of the book, and you are there hunting this black thing that is nowhere to be found and yet makes all the difference. No one has done anything quite like that ever. So, when I critique, what I am saying is, I don't care if Faulkner is a racist or not; I don't personally care but I am fascinated by what it means to write like this.

INTERVIEWER

What about black writers . . . how do they write in a world dominated by and informed by their relationship to a white culture?

MORRISON

By trying to alter language, simply to free it up, not to repress it or confine it, but to open it up. Tease it. Blast its racist straitjacket. I wrote a story entitled "Recitatif," in which there are two little girls in an orphanage, one white and one black. But the reader doesn't know which is white and which is black. I use class codes, but no racial codes.

INTERVIEWER

Is this meant to confuse the reader?

MORRISON

Well, yes. But to provoke and enlighten. I did that as a lark. What was exciting was to be forced as a writer not to be lazy and rely on obvious codes. Soon as I say, Black woman . . . I can rest on or provoke predictable responses, but if I leave it out then I have to talk about her in a complicated way—as a person.

INTERVIEWER

Why wouldn't you want to say, The black woman came out of the store?

MORRISON

Well, you can, but it has to be important that she is black.

INTERVIEWER

What about *The Confessions of Nat Turner*?

MORRISON

Well, here we have a very self-conscious character who says things like, I looked at my black hand. Or, I woke up and I felt black. It is very much on Bill Styron's mind. He feels charged in Nat Turner's skin . . . in this place that feels exotic to him. So it reads exotically to us, that's all.

INTERVIEWER

There was a tremendous outcry at that time from people who felt that Styron didn't have a right to write about Nat Turner.

MORRISON

He has a right to write about whatever he wants. To suggest otherwise is outrageous. What they should have criticized, and some of them did, was Styron's suggestion that Nat Turner hated black people. In the book Turner expresses his revulsion over and over again . . . he's so distant from blacks, so superior. So the fundamental question is why would anybody follow him? What kind of leader is this who has a fundamentally racist contempt that seems unreal to any black person reading it? Any white leader would have some interest and identification with the people he was asking to die. That was what these critics meant when they said Nat Turner speaks like a white man. That racial distance is strong and clear in that book.

INTERVIEWER

You must have read a lot of slave narratives for *Beloved*.

MORRISON

I wouldn't read them for information because I knew that they had to be authenticated by white patrons, that they couldn't say everything they wanted to say because they couldn't alienate their audience; they had to be quiet about certain things. They were going to be as good as they could be under the circumstances and as revelatory, but they never say how terrible it was. They would just say, Well, you know, it was really awful, but let's abolish slavery so life can go on. Their narratives had to be very understated. So while I looked at the documents and felt *familiar* with slavery and overwhelmed by it, I wanted it to be truly *felt*. I wanted to translate the historical into the personal. I spent a long time trying to figure out what it was about slavery that made it so repugnant, so personal, so indifferent, so intimate, and yet so public.

In reading some of the documents I noticed frequent references to something that was never properly described—*the bit*. This thing was put into the mouth of slaves to punish them and shut them up without preventing them from working. I spent a long time trying to find out what it looked like. I kept reading statements like, I put the bit on Jenny, or, as Equiano says, "I went into a kitchen" and I saw a woman standing at the stove, and she had a brake (*b-r-a-k-e*, he spells it) "in her mouth," and I said, What is that? and somebody told me what it was, and then I said, I never saw anything so awful in all my life. But I really couldn't image the thing—did it look like a horse's bit or what?

Eventually I did find some sketches in one book in this country, which was the record of a man's torture of his wife. In South America, Brazil, places like that, they kept such mementos. But while I was searching, something else occurred to me—namely, that this bit, this item, this personalized type of torture, was a direct descendant of the Inquisition. And I realized that of course you can't buy this stuff. You can't send away for a mail-order bit for your slave. Sears doesn't carry them. So you have to make it. You have to go out in the backyard and put some stuff together and construct it and then affix it to a person. So the whole process had a very personal quality for the person who made it, as well as for the person who wore it. Then I realized that describing it would never be helpful; that the reader didn't need to *see* it so much as *feel* what it was like. I realized that it was important to imagine the bit as an active instrument, rather than simply as a curio or an historical fact. And in the same way I wanted to show the reader what slavery *felt* like, rather than how it looked.

There's a passage in which Paul D. says to Sethe, "I've never told anybody about it, I've sung about it sometimes." He tries to tell her what wearing the bit was like, but he ends up talking about a rooster that he swears smiled at him when he wore it—he felt cheapened and lessened and that he would never be worth as much as a rooster sitting on a tub in the sunlight. I make other references to the desire to spit, to sucking iron, and so on; but it seemed to me that describing what it *looked* like would distract the reader from what I wanted him or her to experience, which was what it *felt* like. The kind of information you can find between the lines of history. It sort of falls off the page, or it's a glance and a reference. It's right there in the intersection where an institution becomes personal, where the historical becomes people with names.

INTERVIEWER

When you create a character is it completely created out of your own imagination?

MORRISON

I never use anyone I know. In *The Bluest Eye* I think I used some gestures and dialogue of my mother in certain places, and a little geography. I've never done that since. I really am very conscientious about that. It's never based on anyone. I don't do what many writers do.

INTERVIEWER

Why is that?

MORRISON

There is this feeling that artists have—photographers, more than other people, and writers—that they are acting like a succubus . . . this process of taking from something that's alive and using it for one's own purposes. You can do it with trees, butterflies, or human beings. Making a little life for oneself by scavenging other people's lives is a big question, and it does have moral and ethical implications.

In fiction, I feel the most intelligent, and the most free, and the most excited, when my characters are fully invented people. That's part of the excitement. If they're based on somebody else, in a funny way it's an infringement of a copyright. That person *owns* his life, has a patent on it. It shouldn't be available for fiction.

INTERVIEWER

Do you ever feel like your characters are getting away from you, out of your control?

MORRISON

I take control of them. They are very carefully imagined. I feel as though I know all there is to know about them, even things I don't write—like how they part their hair. They are like ghosts. They have nothing on their minds but themselves and aren't interested in anything but themselves. So you can't let them write your book for you. I have read books in which I know that has happened—when a novelist has been totally taken over by a character. I want to say, You can't do that. If those people could write books they would, but they can't. *You* can. So, you have to say, Shut up. Leave me alone. I am doing this.

INTERVIEWER

Have you ever had to tell any of your characters to shut up?

MORRISON

Pilate, I did. Therefore she doesn't speak very much. She has this long conversation with the two boys and every now and then she'll say something, but she doesn't have the dialogue the other people have.

I had to do that, otherwise she was going to overwhelm everybody. She got terribly interesting; characters can do that for a little bit. I had to take it back. It's *my* book; it's not called "Pilate."

INTERVIEWER

Pilate is such a strong character. It seems to me that the women in your books are almost always stronger and braver than the men. Why is that?

MORRISON

That isn't true, but I hear that a lot. I think that our expectations of women are very low. If women just stand up straight for thirty days, everybody goes, Oh! How brave! As a matter of fact, somebody wrote about Sethe, and said she was this powerful, statuesque woman who wasn't even human. But at the end of the book, she can barely turn her head. She has been zonked; she can't even feed herself. Is that tough?

INTERVIEWER

Maybe people read it that way because they thought Sethe made such a hard choice slashing Beloved's throat. Maybe they think that's being strong. Some would say that's just bad manners.

MORRISON

Well, Beloved surely didn't think it was all that tough. She thought it was lunacy. Or, more importantly, How do you know death is better for me? You've never died. How could you know? But I think Paul D., Son, Stamp Paid, even Guitar, make equally difficult choices; they are principled. I do think we are too accustomed to women who don't talk back or who use the weapons of the weak.

INTERVIEWER

What are the weapons of the weak?

MORRISON

Nagging. Poison. Gossip. Sneaking around instead of confrontation.

INTERVIEWER

There have been so few novels about women who have intense friendships with other women. Why do you think that is?

MORRISON

It has been a discredited relationship. When I was writing *Sula*, I was under the impression that for a large part of the female population a woman friend was considered a secondary relationship. A man and a woman's relationship was primary. Women, your own friends, were always secondary relationships when the man was not there. Because of this, there's that whole cadre of women who don't like women and prefer men. We had to be taught to like one another. *Ms.* magazine was founded on the premise that we really have to stop complaining about one another, hating, fighting one another, and joining men in their condemnation of ourselves—a typical example of what dominated people do. That is a big education. When much of the literature was like that—when you read about women together (not lesbians or those who have formed long relationships that are covertly lesbian, like in Virginia Woolf's work), it is an overtly male view of females together. They are usually male-dominated—like some of Henry James's characters—or the women are talking about men, like Jane Austen's girlfriends . . . talking about who got married, and how to get married, and are you going to lose him, and I think she wants him and so on. To have heterosexual women who are friends, who are talking only about themselves to each other, seemed to me a very radical thing when *Sula* was published in 1971 . . . but it is hardly radical now.

INTERVIEWER

It is becoming acceptable.

MORRISON

Yes, and it's going to get boring. It will be overdone and as usual it will all run amok.

INTERVIEWER

Why do writers have such a hard time writing about sex?

MORRISON

Sex is difficult to write about because it's just not sexy enough. The only way to write about it is not to write much. Let the reader bring his own sexuality into the text. A writer I usually admire has written about sex in the most off-putting way. There is just too much information. If you start saying "the curve of . . ." you soon sound like a gynecologist. Only Joyce could get away with that. He said all those forbidden words. He said *cunt*, and that was shocking. The forbidden word can be provocative. But after a while it becomes monotonous rather than arousing. Less is always better. Some writers think that if they use dirty words they've done it. It can work for a short period and for a very young imagination, but after a while it doesn't deliver. When Sethe and Paul D. first see each other, in about half a page they get the sex out of the way, which isn't any good anyway— it's fast and they're embarrassed about it—and then they're lying there trying to pretend they're not in that bed, that they haven't met, and then they begin to think different thoughts, which begin to merge so you can't tell who's thinking what. That merging to me is more tactically sensual than if I had tried to describe body parts.

INTERVIEWER

What about plot? Do you always know where you're going? Would you write the end before you got there?

MORRISON

When I really know what it is about, then I can write that end scene. I wrote the end of *Beloved* about a quarter of the way in. I wrote the end of *Jazz* very early and the end of *Song of Solomon* very early on. What I really want is for the plot to be *how* it happened. It is like a detective story in a sense. You know who is dead and you want to find out who did it. So, you put the salient elements up front and the reader is hooked into wanting to know how did that happen. Who did that and why? You are forced into having a certain kind of language that will keep the reader asking those questions. In *Jazz*, just as I did before with *The Bluest Eye*, I put the whole plot on the first page. In fact, in the first edition the plot was on the cover, so that a person in a bookstore could read the cover and know right away what the book was about, and could, if they wished, dismiss it and buy another book. This seemed a suitable technique for *Jazz* because I thought of the plot in that novel, the threesome, as the melody of the piece, and it is fine to follow a melody—to feel the satisfaction of recognizing a melody whenever the narrator returns to it. That was the real art of the enterprise for me—bumping up against that melody time and again, seeing it from another point of view, seeing it afresh each time, playing it back and forth.

When Keith Jarrett plays "Ol' Man River," the delight and satisfaction is not so much in the melody itself but in recognizing it when it surfaces and when it is hidden, and when it goes away completely, what is put in its place. Not so much in the original line as in all the echoes and shades and turns and pivots Jarrett plays around it. I was trying to do something similar with the plot in *Jazz*. I wanted the story to be the vehicle that moved us from page one to the end, but I wanted the delight to be found in moving away from the story and coming back to it, looking around it, and through it, as though it was a prism, constantly turning.

This playful aspect of *Jazz* may well cause a great deal of dissatisfaction in readers who just want the melody, who want to know what happened, who did it and why. But the jazzlike structure wasn't a secondary thing for me—it was the raison d'être of the book. The process of trial and error by which the narrator revealed the plot was as important and exciting to me as telling the story.

INTERVIEWER

You also divulge the plot early on in *Beloved*.

MORRISON

It seemed important to me that the action in *Beloved*—the fact of infanticide—be immediately known but deferred, unseen. I wanted to give the reader all the information and the consequences surrounding the act, while avoiding engorging myself or the reader with the violence itself. I remember writing the sentence where Sethe cuts the throat of the child very, very late in the process of writing the book. I remember getting up from the table and walking outside for a long time—walking around the yard and coming back and revising it a little bit and going back out and in and rewriting the sentence over and over again . . . Each time I fixed that sentence so that it was exactly right, or so I thought, but then I would be unable to sit there and would have to go away and come back. I thought that the act itself had to be not only buried but also understated, because if the language was going to compete with the violence itself it would be obscene or pornographic.

INTERVIEWER

Style is obviously very important to you. Can you talk about this in relation to *Jazz*?

MORRISON

With *Jazz*, I wanted to convey the sense that a musician conveys—that he has more but he's not gonna give it to you. It's an exercise in restraint, a holding back—not because it's not there, or because one had exhausted it, but because of the riches, and because it can be done again. That sense of knowing when to stop is a learned thing and I didn't always have it. It was probably not until after I wrote *Song of Solomon* that I got to feeling secure enough to experience what it meant to be thrifty with images and language and so on. I was very conscious in writing *Jazz* of trying to blend that which is contrived and artificial with improvisation. I thought of myself as like the jazz musician—someone who practices and practices and practices in order to be able to invent and to make his art look effortless and graceful. I was always conscious of the constructed aspect of the writing process, and that art appears natural and elegant only as a result of constant practice and awareness of its formal structures. You must practice thrift in order to achieve that luxurious quality of wastefulness—that sense that you have enough to waste, that you are holding back—without actually wasting anything. You shouldn't overgratify, you should never satiate. I've always felt that that peculiar sense of hunger at the end of a piece of art—a yearning for more—is really very, very powerful. But there is at the same time a kind of contentment, knowing that at some other time there will indeed be more because the artist is endlessly inventive.

INTERVIEWER

Were there other ingredients, structural entities?

MORRISON

Well, it seems to me that migration was a major event in the cultural history of this country. Now, I'm being very speculative about all of this—I guess that's why I write novels—but it seems to me something modern and new happened after the Civil War. Of course, a number of things changed, but the era was most clearly marked by the disowning and dispossession of ex-slaves. These ex-slaves were sometimes taken into their local labor markets, but they often tried to escape their problems by migrating to the city. I was fascinated by the thought of what the city must have meant to them, these second- and third-generation ex-slaves, to rural people living there in their own number. The city must have seemed so exciting and wonderful, so much the place to be.

I was interested in how the city worked. How classes and groups and nationalities had the security of numbers within their own turfs and territories, but also felt the thrill of knowing that there were other turfs and other territories, and felt the real glamour and excitement of being in this throng. I was interested in how music changed in this country. Spirituals and gospel and blues represented one kind of response to slavery—they gave voice to the yearning for escape, in code, literally on the Underground Railroad.

I was also concerned with personal life. How did people love one another? What did they think was free? At that time, when the ex-slaves were moving into the city, running away from something that was constricting and killing them and dispossessing them over and over and over again, they were in a very limiting environment. But when you listen to their music—the beginnings of jazz—you realized that they are talking about something else. They are talking about love, about loss. But there is such grandeur, such satisfaction in those lyrics . . . they're never happy—somebody's always leaving—but they're not whining. It's as though the whole tragedy of choosing somebody, risking love, risking emotion, risking sensuality, and then losing it all didn't matter, since it was their choice. Exercising choice in who you love was a major, major thing. And the music reinforced the idea of love as a space where one could negotiate freedom.

Obviously, jazz was considered—as all new music is—to be devil music; too sensual and provocative, and so on. But for some black people jazz meant claiming their own bodies. You can imagine what that must have meant for people whose bodies had been owned, who had been slaves as children, or who remembered their parents' being slaves. Blues and jazz represented ownership of one's own emotions. So of course it is excessive and overdone: tragedy in jazz is relished, almost as though a happy ending would take away some of its glamour, its flair. Now advertisers use jazz on television to communicate authenticity and modernity; to say "trust me," and to say "hip."

These days the city still retains the quality of excitement it had in the jazz age—only now we associate that excitement with a different kind of danger. We chant and scream and act alarmed about the homeless; we say we want our streets back, but it is from our awareness of homelessness and our employment of strategies to deal with it that we get our sense of the urban. Feeling as though we have the armor, the shields, the moxie, the strength, the toughness, and the smarts to be engaged and survive encounters with the unpredictable, the alien, the strange, and the violent is an intrinsic part of what it means to live in the city. When people "complain" about homelessness they are actually bragging about it: New York has more homeless than San Francisco. No, no, no, San Francisco has more homeless. No, you haven't been to Detroit. We are almost competitive about our endurance, which I think is one of the reasons why we accept homelessness so easily.

INTERVIEWER

So the city freed the ex-slaves from their history?

MORRISON

In part, yes. The city was seductive to them because it promised forgetfulness. It offered the possibility of freedom—freedom, as you put it, from history. But although history should not become a straitjacket, which overwhelms and binds, neither should it be forgotten. One must critique it, test it, confront it, and understand it in order to achieve a freedom that is more than license, to achieve true, adult agency. If you penetrate the seduction of the city, then it becomes possible to confront your own history—to forget what ought to be forgotten and use what is useful—such true agency is made possible.

INTERVIEWER

How do visual images influence your work?

MORRISON

I was having some difficulty describing a scene in *Song of Solomon* . . . of a man running away from some obligations and himself. I used an Edvard Munch painting almost literally. He is walking and there is nobody on his side of the street. Everybody is on the other side.

INTERVIEWER

Song of Solomon is such a painted book in comparison with some of your others, like *Beloved*, which is sepia toned.

MORRISON

Part of that has to do with the visual images that I got being aware that in historical terms women, black people in general, were very attracted to very bright-colored clothing. Most people are frightened by color anyway.

INTERVIEWER

Why?

MORRISON

They just are. In this culture quiet colors are considered elegant.
Civilized Western people wouldn't buy bloodred sheets or dishes.
There may be something more to it than what I am suggesting. But
the slave population had no access even to what color there was, because they wore slave clothes, hand-me-downs, work clothes made
out of burlap and sacking. For them a colored dress would be luxurious; it wouldn't matter whether it was rich or poor cloth . . . just to
have a red or a yellow dress. I stripped *Beloved* of color so that there
are only the small moments when Sethe runs amok buying ribbons
and bows, enjoying herself the way children enjoy that kind of color.
The whole business of color was why slavery was able to last such a
long time. It wasn't as though you had a class of convicts who could
dress themselves up and pass themselves off. No, these were people
marked because of their skin color, as well as other features. So color
is a signifying mark. Baby Suggs dreams of color and says, "Bring me
a little lavender." It is a kind of luxury. We are so inundated with
color and visuals. I just wanted to pull it back so that one could feel
that hunger and that delight. I couldn't do that if I had made it the
painterly book *Song of Solomon* was.

INTERVIEWER

Is that what you are referring to when you speak about needing to
find a controlling image?

MORRISON

Sometimes, yes. There are three or four in *Song of Solomon*. I
knew that I wanted it to be painterly, and I wanted the opening to be
red, white, and blue. I also knew that in some sense he would have to
"fly." In *Song of Solomon* it was the first time that I had written about
a man who was the central, the driving engine of the narrative; I was a
little unsure about my ability to feel comfortable inside him. I could
always look at him and write from the outside, but those would have
been just perceptions. I had to be able not only to look at him but to
feel how it really must have felt. So in trying to think about this, the

image in my mind was a train. All the previous books have been women centered, and they have been pretty much in the neighborhood and in the yard; this was going to move out. So, I had this feeling about a train . . . sort of revving up, then moving out as he does, and then it sort of highballs at the end; it speeds up, but it doesn't brake, it just highballs and leaves you sort of suspended. So that image controlled the structure for me, although that is not something I articulate or even make reference to; it only matters that it works for me. Other books look like spirals, like *Sula*.

INTERVIEWER

How would you describe the controlling image of *Jazz*?

MORRISON

Jazz was very complicated because I wanted to re-represent two contradictory things—artifice and improvisation—where you have an artwork, planned, thought through, but at the same time appears invented, like jazz. I thought of the image being a book. Physically a book, but at the same time it is writing itself. Imagining itself. Talking. Aware of what it is doing. It watches itself think and imagine. That seemed to me to be a combination of artifice and improvisation— where you practice and plan in order to invent. Also the willingness to fail, to be wrong, because jazz is performance. In a performance you make mistakes, and you don't have the luxury of revision that a writer has; you have to make something out of a mistake, and if you do it well enough it will take you to another place where you never would have gone had you not made that error. So, you have to be able to risk making that error in performance. Dancers do it all the time, as well as jazz musicians. *Jazz* predicts its own story. Sometimes it is wrong because of faulty vision. It simply did not imagine those characters well enough, admits it was wrong, and the characters talk back the way jazz musicians do. It has to listen to the characters it has invented and then learn something from them. It was the most intricate thing I had done, though I wanted to tell a very simple story about people who do not know that they are living in the jazz age and to never use the word.

INTERVIEWER
One way to achieve this structurally is to have several voices speaking throughout each book. Why do you do this?

MORRISON
It's important not to have a totalizing view. In American literature we have been so totalized—as though there is only one version. We are not one indistinguishable block of people who always behave the same way.

INTERVIEWER
Is that what you mean by *totalized*?

MORRISON
Yes. A definitive or an authoritarian view from somebody else or someone speaking for us. No singularity and no diversity. I try to give some credibility to all sorts of voices, each of which is profoundly different. Because what strikes me about African-American culture *is* its variety. In so much of contemporary music everybody sounds alike. But when you think about black music, you think about the difference between Duke Ellington and Sidney Bechet or Satchmo or Miles Davis. They don't sound anything alike, but you know that they are all black performers, because of whatever that quality is that makes you realize, Oh yes, this is part of something called the African-American music tradition. There is no black woman popular singer, jazz singer, blues singer who sounds like any other. Billie Holiday does not sound like Aretha, doesn't sound like Nina, doesn't sound like Sarah, doesn't sound like any of them. They are really powerfully different. And they will tell you that they couldn't possibly have made it as singers if they sounded like somebody else. If someone comes along sounding like Ella Fitzgerald, they will say, Oh we have one of those . . . It's interesting to me how those women have this very distinct, unmistakable image. I would like to write like that. I would like to write novels that were unmistakably mine, but nevertheless fit first into African-American traditions and second of all, this whole thing called literature.

INTERVIEWER

First African-American?

MORRISON

Yes.

INTERVIEWER

. . . rather than the whole of literature?

MORRISON

Oh yes.

INTERVIEWER

Why?

MORRISON

It's richer. It has more complex sources. It pulls from something that's closer to the edge; it's much more modern. It has a human future.

INTERVIEWER

Wouldn't you rather be known as a great exponent of literature than as an African-American writer?

MORRISON

It's very important to me that my work be African-American; if it assimilates into a different or larger pool, so much the better. But I shouldn't be *asked* to do that. Joyce is not asked to do that. Tolstoy is not. I mean, they can all be Russian, French, Irish, or Catholic, they write out of where they come from, and I do too. It just so happens that that space for me is African-American; it could be Catholic, it could be Midwestern. I'm those things too, and they are all important.

Why do you think people ask, Why don't you write something that we can understand? Do you threaten them by not writing in the typical Western, linear, chronological way?

MORRISON
I don't think that they mean that. I think they mean, Are you ever going to write a book about white people? For them perhaps that's a kind of a compliment. They're saying, You write well enough, I would even let you write about me. They couldn't say that to anybody else. I mean, could I have gone up to André Gide and said, Yes, but when are you going to get serious and start writing about black people? I don't think he would know how to answer that question. Just as I don't. He would say, What? I will if I want to, or, Who are you? What is behind that question is, there's the center, which is white, and then there are these regional blacks or Asians, or any sort of marginal people. That question can only be asked from the center. Bill Moyers asked me that when-are-you-going-to-write-about question on television. I just said, Well, maybe one day . . . but I couldn't say to him, you know, you can only ask that question from the center. The center of the world! I mean he's a white male. He's asking a marginal person when are you going to get to the center, when are you going to write about white people. I can't say, Bill, why are you asking me that question? Or, As long as that question seems reasonable is as long as I won't, can't. The point is that he's patronizing; he's saying, You write well enough; you could come on into the center if you wanted to. You don't have to stay out there on the margins. And I'm saying, Yeah, well, I'm gonna stay out here on the margin, and let the center look for me.

Maybe it's a false claim, but not fully. I'm sure it was true for the ones we think of as giants now. Joyce is a good example. He moved here and there, but he wrote about Ireland wherever he was, didn't care where he was. I am sure people said to him, Why . . . ? Maybe the French asked, When you gonna write about Paris?

INTERVIEWER

What do you appreciate most in Joyce?

MORRISON

It is amazing how certain kinds of irony and humor travel. Some-times Joyce is hilarious. I read *Finnegans Wake* after graduate school and I had the great good fortune of reading it without any help. I don't know if I read it right, but it was hilarious! I laughed constantly! I didn't know what was going on for whole blocks but it didn't matter because I wasn't going to be graded on it. I think the reason everyone still has so much fun with Shakespeare is because he didn't have any literary critic. He was just doing it, and there were no reviews except for people throwing stuff on stage. He could just do it.

INTERVIEWER

Do you think if he had been reviewed he would have worked less?

MORRISON

Oh, if he'd cared about it, he'd have been very self-conscious. That's a hard attitude to maintain, to pretend you don't care, pretend you don't read.

INTERVIEWER

Do you read your reviews?

MORRISON

I read everything.

INTERVIEWER

Really? You look deadly serious.

MORRISON

I read everything written about me that I see.

INTERVIEWER

Why is that?

MORRISON

I have to know what's going on!

INTERVIEWER

You want to see how you're coming across?

MORRISON

No, no. It's not about me or my work, it's about what is going on. I have to get a sense, particularly of what's going on with women's work or African-American work, contemporary work. I teach a literature course. So I read any information that's going to help me teach.

INTERVIEWER

Are you ever really surprised when they compare you to the magic realists, such as Gabriel García Márquez?

MORRISON

Yes, I used to be. It doesn't mean anything to me. Schools are only important to me when I'm teaching literature. It doesn't mean anything to me when I'm sitting here with a big pile of blank yellow paper . . . What do I say? I'm a magic realist? Each subject matter demands its own form, you know.

INTERVIEWER

Why do you teach undergraduates?

MORRISON

Here at Princeton they really do value undergraduates, which is nice because a lot of universities value only the graduate school or the professional research schools. I like Princeton's notion. I would have loved that for my own children. I don't like freshmen and sophomores being treated as the staging ground or the playground or the canvas on which graduate students learn how to teach. They need the best instruction. I've always thought the public schools needed to study the best literature. I always taught *Oedipus Rex* to all kinds of what they used to call remedial or development classes. The reason those kids are in those classes is that they're bored to death, so you can't give them boring things. You have to give them the best there is to engage them.

INTERVIEWER

One of your sons is a musician. Were you ever musical; did you ever play the piano?

MORRISON

No, but I come from a family of highly skilled musicians. "Highly skilled" meaning most of them couldn't read music but they could play everything that they heard . . . instantly. They sent us, my sister and me, to music lessons. They were sending me off to learn how to do something that they could do naturally. I thought I was deficient, retarded. They didn't explain that perhaps it's more important that you learn how to *read* music . . . that it's a good thing, not a bad thing. I thought we were sort of lame people going off to learn how to walk, while, you know, they all just stood up and did it naturally.

INTERVIEWER

Do you think there is an education for becoming a writer? Reading perhaps?

MORRISON

That has only limited value.

INTERVIEWER

Travel the world? Take courses in sociology, history?

MORRISON

Or stay home . . . I don't think they have to go anywhere.

Some people say, Oh, I can't write a book until I've lived my life, until I've had experiences.

MORRISON

That may be—maybe they can't. But look at the people who never went anywhere and just thought it up. Thomas Mann. I guess he took a few little trips . . . I think you either have or you acquire this sort of imagination. Sometimes you do need a stimulus. But I myself don't ever go anywhere for stimulation. I don't want to go anywhere. If I could just sit in one spot I would be happy. I don't trust the ones who say I have to go do something before I can write. You see, I don't write autobiographically. First of all, I'm not interested in real-life people as subjects for fiction—including myself. If I write about somebody who's a historical figure like Margaret Garner, I really don't know anything about her. What I knew came from reading two interviews with her. They said, Isn't this extraordinary. Here's a woman who escaped into Cincinnati from the horrors of slavery and was not crazy. Though she'd killed her child, she was not foaming at the mouth. She was very calm; she said, I'd do it again. That was more than enough to fire my imagination.

INTERVIEWER

She was sort of a cause célèbre?

MORRISON

She was. Her real life was much more awful than it's rendered in the novel, but if I had known all there was to know about her I never would have written it. It would have been finished; there would have been no place in there for me. It would be like a recipe already cooked. There you are. You're already this person. Why should I get to steal from you? I don't like that. What I really love is the process of invention. To have characters move from the curl all the way to a full-fledged person, that's interesting.

INTERVIEWER

Do you ever write out of anger or any other emotion?

MORRISON

No. Anger is a very intense but tiny emotion, you know. It doesn't last. It doesn't produce anything. It's not creative . . . at least not for me. I mean these books take at least three years!

INTERVIEWER

That is a long time to be angry.

MORRISON

Yes. I don't trust that stuff anyway. I don't like those little quick emotions, like, I'm lonely, *ohhh*, God . . . I don't like those emotions as fuel. I mean, I have them, but—

INTERVIEWER

—they're not a good muse?

MORRISON

No, and if it's not your brain thinking cold, cold thoughts, which you can dress in any kind of mood, then it's nothing. It has to be a cold, cold thought. I mean cold, or cool at least. Your brain. That's all there is.

Issue 128, 1993

Alice Munro

The Art of Fiction

There is no direct flight from New York City to Clinton, Ontario, the Canadian town of three thousand where Alice Munro lives most of the year. We left LaGuardia early on a June morning, rented a car in Toronto, and drove for three hours on roads that grew smaller and more rural. Around dusk, we pulled up to the house where Munro lives with her second husband, Gerry Fremlin. It has a deep backyard and an eccentric flower garden and is, as she explained, the house where Fremlin was born. In the kitchen, Munro was preparing a simple meal with fragrant local herbs. The dining room is lined floor to ceiling with books; on one side a small table holds a manual typewriter. It is here that Munro works.

After a while, Munro took us to Goderich, a bigger town, the county seat, where she installed us in the Bedford Hotel on the square across from the courthouse. The hotel is a nineteenth-century building with comfortable rooms (twin beds and no air-conditioning) that would seem to lodge a librarian or a frontier schoolteacher in one of Munro's stories. Over the next three days, we talked in her home, but never with the tape recorder on. We conducted the interview in our small room at the hotel, as Munro wanted to keep "the business out of the house." Both Munro and her husband grew up within twenty miles of where they now live; they knew the history of almost every building we passed, admired, or ate inside. We asked what sort of literary community was available in the immediate area. Although there is a library in Goderich, we were told the nearest good bookstore was

and suchlike dreary stuff. And thank the Lord, one of them was a divinity
student. A different kind of young man went into the church in those days
if you remember.Good-looking and ambitious, rather the type who might go
into politics now. This one was set to be a success. He wasn't so far out
of the family influence as to speak up first,at his father's table, but
once I spoke to him, he started to talk. He could even step in and answer
for the others when they could not. For at least a couple of them absolutely
could not. She's helping at home, he'd say. or, He's in the second form.x

    We had a chat about Toronto,where he was going to Know College.
The number of motor-cars there, a trip to ~~Toronto Island,the mummy~~ in the
Hanlen's Point, the giraffe
in the Riverdale Zoo
~~Museum~~.He seemed to want to let me know that the divinity regulations were
Tobogganing in High Park.
not too stringent. He went ~~skating in the winter~~. He had been to see a
play. We could have talked on, but were defeated by the silence around
us, or rather the speechlessness, for there was clinking and chewing and
swallowing. Conversation could seem affected here, pure clatter and self-
display. It seemed as if all the social rules I had been brought up with
were turned on their heads.I even began to wonder if they suffered as I
had thought, if they didn't have an altogether different idea than I had,
of what this dinner should be. A ceremony. Where everything was done
right. Where everything had taken a lot of work and was done right. I could
see that conversation might seem bewildering, unnecessary. Even ~~disrespectful~~
disrespectful. I could see myself as a giddy sort of foreigner,embarrassing
them, and I could see that the divinity student was embarrassing them,in a
way, by being willing to keep me company. So I dried up, and he did ~~Everybody~~
Everybody managed to eat a lot. Especially the two ~~sisters~~, I thought.
They munched along in a kind of eating trance.

    I went out to the kitchen afterwards offering to help with the
dishes,thinking that was what you did on the farm, but of course they were
not having any of me. They wouldn't let your uncle's wife do anything
~~but she must have~~

A manuscript page from Alice Munro's story "Wilderness Station."

in Stratford, some thirty miles away. When we asked whether there were any other local writers, she drove us past a ramshackle house where a man sat bare chested on the back stoop, crouched over a typewriter, surrounded by cats. "He's out there every day," she said. "Rain or shine. I don't know him, but I'm dying of curiosity to find out what he's up to."

Our last morning in Canada, supplied with directions, we sought out the house in which Alice Munro had grown up. Her father had built the house and raised mink there. After several dead ends, we found it, a pretty brick house at the very end of a country road, facing an open field where an airplane rested, alighted temporarily it seemed. It was, from our spot, easy to imagine the glamour of the air, the pilot taking a country wife away, as in "White Dump," or the young aviation stuntsman who lands in a field like this in "How I Met My Husband."

Like the house, like the landscape of Ontario, which resembles the American Midwest, Munro is not imposing. She is gracious, with a quiet humor. She is the author of seven books of short stories, including the forthcoming *Open Secrets*, and one novel, *Lives of Girls and Women*; she has received the Governor-General's Award (Canada's most prestigious literary prize), and is regularly featured in Best American Short Stories (Richard Ford recently included two Alice Munro stories in the volume he edited), and Prize Stories: The O. Henry Awards; she also is a regular contributor to *The New Yorker*. Despite these considerable accomplishments, Munro still speaks of writing with some of the reverence and insecurity one hears in the voices of beginners. She has none of the bravura or bluster of a famous writer, and it is easy to forget that she is one. Speaking of her own work, she makes what she does sound not exactly easy but possible, as if anyone could do it if they only worked hard enough. As we left, we felt that contagious sense of possibility. It seems simple—but her writing has a perfect simplicity that takes years and many drafts to master. As Cynthia Ozick has said, "She is our Chekhov and is going to outlast most of her contemporaries."

—*Jeanne McCulloch, Mona Simpson, 1994*

INTERVIEWER

We went back to the house where you grew up this morning: did you live there your entire childhood?

ALICE MUNRO

Yes. When my father died, he was still living in that house on the farm, which was a fox and mink farm. It's changed a lot though. Now it's a beauty parlor called Total Indulgence. I think they have the beauty parlor in the back wing, and they've knocked down the kitchen entirely.

INTERVIEWER

Have you been inside it since then?

MUNRO

No I haven't, but I thought if I did I'd ask to see the living room. There's the fireplace my father built and I'd like to see that. I've sometimes thought I should go in and ask for a manicure.

INTERVIEWER

We noticed a plane on the field across the road and thought of your stories "White Dump" and "How I Met My Husband."

MUNRO

Yes, that was an airport for a while. The man who owned that farm had a hobby of flying planes, and he had a little plane of his own. He never liked farming so he got out of it and became a flight instructor. He's still alive. In perfect health and one of the handsomest men I've ever known. He retired from flight instruction when he was seventy-five. Within maybe three months of retirement he went on a trip and got some odd disease you get from bats in caves.

INTERVIEWER

The stories in your first collection, *Dance of the Happy Shades*, are very resonant of that area, the world of your childhood. At what point in your life were those stories written?

MUNRO

The writing of those stories stretched over fifteen years. "The Day of the Butterfly" was the earliest one. That was probably written when I was about twenty-one. And I can remember very well writing "Thanks for the Ride" because my first baby was lying in the crib beside me. So I was twenty-two. The really late stories were written in my thirties. "Dance of the Happy Shades" is one; "The Peace of Utrecht" is another. "Images" is the very latest. "Walker Brothers Cowboy" was also written after I was thirty. So there's a really great range.

INTERVIEWER

How do they seem to hold up now? Do you reread them?

MUNRO

There's an early one in that collection called "The Shining Houses," which I had to read at Harborfront in Toronto two or three years ago for a special event celebrating the history of *Tamarack Review*. Since it was originally published in one of the early issues of that magazine, I had to get up and read it, and it was very hard. I think I wrote that story when I was twenty-two. I kept editing as I read, catching all the tricks I used at that time which now seemed very dated. I was trying to fix it up fast, with my eyes darting ahead to the next paragraph as I read, because I hadn't read it ahead of time. I never do read things ahead of time. When I read an early story I can see things I wouldn't do now, things people were doing in the fifties.

INTERVIEWER

Do you ever revise a story after it's been published? Apparently, before he died, Proust rewrote the first volumes of *Remembrance of Things Past*.

MUNRO

Yes, and Henry James rewrote simple, understandable stuff so it was obscure and difficult. Actually I've done it recently. The story

"Carried Away" was included in *Best American Short Stories 1991*. I read it again in the anthology, because I wanted to see what it was like and I found a paragraph that I thought was really soggy. It was a very important little paragraph, maybe two sentences. I just took a pen and rewrote it up in the margin of the anthology so that I'd have it there to refer to when I published the story in book form. I've often made revisions at that stage that turned out to be mistakes because I wasn't really in the rhythm of the story anymore. I see a little bit of writing that doesn't seem to be doing as much work as it should be doing, and right at the end I will sort of rev it up. But when I finally read the story again it seems a bit obtrusive. So I'm not too sure about this sort of thing. The answer may be that one should stop this behavior. There should be a point where you say, the way you would with a child, this isn't mine anymore.

INTERVIEWER

You've mentioned that you don't show your works in progress to friends.

MUNRO

No, I don't show anything in progress to anybody.

INTERVIEWER

How much do you rely on your editors?

MUNRO

The New Yorker was really my first experience with serious editing. Previously I'd more or less just had copyediting with a few suggestions—not much. There has to be an agreement between the editor and me about the kind of thing that can happen. An editor who thought nothing happened in William Maxwell's stories, for example, would be of no use to me. There also has to be a very sharp eye for the ways that I could be deceiving myself. Chip McGrath at *The New Yorker* was my first editor, and he was so good. I was amazed that anybody could see that deeply into what I wanted to do. Sometimes we didn't do much, but occasionally he gave me a lot of direction. I rewrote one story called "The Turkey Season," which he had already bought. I thought he would simply accept the new version but he didn't. He said, Well, there are things about the new version I like better, and there are things about the old version I like better. Why don't we see? He never says anything like, We will. So we put it together and got a better story that way, I think.

INTERVIEWER

How was this accomplished? By phone or by mail? Do you ever go into *The New Yorker* and hammer it out?

MUNRO

By mail. We have a very fruitful phone relationship, but we've only seen each other a few times.

INTERVIEWER

When did you first publish in *The New Yorker*?

MUNRO

"Royal Beatings" was my first story, and it was published in 1977. But I sent all my early stories to *The New Yorker* in the 1950s, and then I stopped sending for a long time and sent only to magazines in Canada. *The New Yorker* sent me nice notes though—penciled, informal messages. They never signed them. They weren't terribly encouraging. I still remember one of them: The writing is very nice, but the theme is a bit overly familiar. It was, too. It was a romance between two aging people—an aging spinster who knows this is it for her when she's proposed to by an aging farmer. I had a lot of aging spinsters in my stories. It was called "The Day the Asters Bloomed." It was really awful. And I didn't write this when I was seventeen; I was twenty-five. I wonder why I wrote about aging spinsters. I didn't know any.

INTERVIEWER

And you married young. It's not as though you were anticipating a life as an aging spinster.

MUNRO

I think I knew that at heart I was an aging spinster.

INTERVIEWER

Were you always writing?

MUNRO

Since about grade seven or eight.

INTERVIEWER

Were you a serious writer by the time you went to college?

MUNRO

Yes. I had no chance to be anything else because I had no money. I knew I would only be at university two years because the scholarships available at that time lasted only two years. It was this little vacation in my life, a wonderful time. I had been in charge of the house at home when I was in my teens, so university was about the only time in my life that I haven't had to do housework.

INTERVIEWER

Did you get married right after your two years?

MUNRO

I got married right after the second year. I was twenty. We went to Vancouver. That was the big thing about getting married—this huge adventure, moving. As far away as we could get and stay in the country. We were only twenty and twenty-two. We immediately set up a very proper kind of middle-class existence. We were thinking of getting a house and having a baby, and we promptly did these things. I had my first baby at twenty-one.

INTERVIEWER

And you were writing all through that?

MUNRO

I was writing desperately all the time I was pregnant because I thought I would never be able to write afterward. Each pregnancy spurred me to get something big done before the baby was born. Actually I didn't get anything big done.

INTERVIEWER

In "Thanks for the Ride," you write from the point of view of a rather callous city boy who picks up a poor town girl for the night and sleeps with her and is alternately attracted to and revolted by the poverty of her life. It seems striking that this story came from a time when your life was so settled and proper.

MUNRO

A friend of my husband's came to visit us the summer when I was pregnant with my eldest daughter. He stayed for a month or so. He worked for the National Film Board, and he was doing a film up there. He told us a lot of stuff—we just talked the way you do, anecdotally about our lives. He told the story about being in a small town on Georgian Bay and going out with a local girl. It was the encounter of a middle-class boy with something that was quite familiar to me but not familiar to him. So I immediately identified strongly with the girl and her family and her situation, and I guess I wrote the story fairly soon afterward because my baby was looking at me from the crib.

INTERVIEWER

How old were you when that first book came out?

MUNRO

I was about thirty-six. I'd been writing these stories over the years and finally an editor at Ryerson Press, a Canadian publisher that has since been taken over by McGraw-Hill, wrote and asked me if I had enough stories for a book. Originally he was going to put me in a book with two or three other writers. That fell through, but he still had a bunch of my stories. Then he quit but passed me on to another editor, who said, If you could write three more stories, we'd have a book. And so I wrote "Images," "Walker Brothers Cowboy," and "Postcard" during the last year before the book was published.

INTERVIEWER

Did you publish those stories in magazines?

MUNRO

Most of them got into *Tamarack Review*. It was a nice little magazine, a very brave magazine. The editor said he was the only editor in Canada who knew all his readers by their first names.

INTERVIEWER

Have you ever had a specific time to write?

MUNRO

When the kids were little, my time was as soon as they left for school. So I worked very hard in those years. My husband and I owned a bookstore, and even when I was working there I stayed at home until noon. I was supposed to be doing housework, and I would also do my writing then. Later on, when I wasn't working every day in the store, I would write until everybody came home for lunch and then after they went back, probably till about two-thirty, and then I would have a quick cup of coffee and start doing the housework, trying to get it all done before late afternoon.

INTERVIEWER

What about before the girls were old enough to go to school?

MUNRO

Their naps.

INTERVIEWER

You wrote when they had naps?

MUNRO

Yes. From one to three in the afternoon. I wrote a lot of stuff that wasn't any good, but I was fairly productive. The year I wrote my second book, *Lives of Girls and Women*, I was enormously productive. I had four kids because one of the girls' friends was living with us, and I worked in the store two days a week. I used to work until maybe one o'clock in the morning and then get up at six. And I remember thinking, You know, maybe I'll *die*, this is terrible, I'll have a heart attack. I was only about thirty-nine or so, but I was thinking this. Then I thought, Well even if I do, I've got that many pages written now. They can see how it's going to come out. It was a kind of desperate, desperate race. I don't have that kind of energy now.

INTERVIEWER

What was the process involved in writing *Lives*?

MUNRO

I remember the day I started to write that. It was in January, a Sunday. I went down to the bookstore, which wasn't open Sundays, and locked myself in. My husband had said he would get dinner, so I had the afternoon. I remember looking around at all the great literature that was around me and thinking, You fool! What are you doing here? But then I went up to the office and started to write the section called "Princess Ida," which is about my mother. The material about my mother is my central material in life, and it always comes the most readily to me. If I just relax, that's what will come up. So, once I started to write that, I was off. Then I made a big mistake. I tried to make it a regular novel, an ordinary sort of childhood adolescence novel. About March I saw it wasn't working. It didn't feel right to me, and I thought I would have to abandon it. I was very depressed. Then it came to me that what I had to do was pull it apart and put it in the story form. Then I could handle it. That's when I learned that I was never going to write a real novel because I could not think that way.

INTERVIEWER

The Beggar Maid, too, is a sort of a novel because it's interconnected stories.

MUNRO

I don't want to second-guess things too much, but I've often wanted to do another series of stories. In my new book, *Open Secrets*, there are characters who reappear. Bea Doud in "Vandals" is mentioned as the little girl in "Carried Away," which is the first story I wrote for the collection. Billy Doud is the son of the librarian. They're all mentioned in "Spaceships Have Landed." But I mustn't let this sort of plan overtake the stories themselves. If I start shaping one story so it will fit with another, I am probably doing something wrong, using force on it that I oughtn't. So I don't know that I'll ever do that kind of series again, though I love the idea of it. Katherine Mansfield said something in one of her letters like, Oh, I hope I write a novel, I hope I don't die just leaving these bits and pieces. It's very hard to wean yourself away from this bits-and-pieces feeling if all you're leaving behind is scattered stories. I'm sure you could think of Chekhov and everything, but still.

INTERVIEWER

And Chekhov always wanted to write a novel. He was going to call it "Stories from the Lives of My Friends."

MUNRO

I know. And I know that feeling that you could have this achievement of having put everything into one package.

INTERVIEWER

When you start writing a story do you already know what the story will be? Is it already plotted out?

MUNRO

Not altogether. Any story that's going to be any good is usually going to change. Right now I'm starting a story cold. I've been working on it every morning, and it's pretty slick. I don't really like it, but I think maybe at some point I'll be into it. Usually, I have a lot of acquaintance with the story before I start writing it. When I didn't have regular time to give to writing, stories would just be working in my head for so long that when I started to write I was deep into them. Now I do that work by filling notebooks.

INTERVIEWER

You use notebooks?

MUNRO

I have stacks of notebooks that contain this terribly clumsy writing, which is just getting anything down. I often wonder, when I look at these first drafts, if there was any point in doing this at all. I'm the opposite of a writer with a quick gift, you know, someone who gets it piped in. I don't grasp it very readily at all, the "it" being whatever I'm trying to do. I often get on the wrong track and have to haul myself back.

INTERVIEWER

How do you realize you're on the wrong track?

MUNRO

I could be writing away one day and think I've done very well; I've done more pages than I usually do. Then I get up the next morning and realize I don't want to work on it anymore. When I have a terrible reluctance to go near it, when I would have to push myself to continue, I generally know that something is badly wrong. Often, in about three quarters of what I do, I reach a point somewhere, fairly early on, when I think I'm going to abandon this story. I get myself through a day or two of bad depression, grouching around. And I think of something else I can write. It's sort of like a love affair: you're getting out of all the disappointment and misery by going out with some new man you don't really like at all, but you haven't noticed that yet. Then, I will suddenly come up with something about the story that I abandoned; I will see how to do it. But that only seems to happen after I've said, No, this isn't going to work, forget it.

INTERVIEWER

Can you always do that?

MUNRO

Sometimes I can't, and I spend the whole day in a very bad mood. That's the only time I'm really irritable. If Gerry talks to me or keeps going in and out of the room or bangs around a lot, I am on edge and enraged. And if he sings or something like that, it's terrible. I'm trying to think something through, and I'm just running into brick walls; I'm not getting through it. Generally I'll do that for a while before I'll give it up. This whole process might take up to a week, the time of trying to think it through, trying to retrieve it, then giving it up and thinking about something else, and then getting it back, usually quite unexpectedly, when I'm in the grocery store or out for a drive. I'll think, Oh well, I have to do it from the point of view of so-and-so, and I have to cut this character out, and of course these people are not married, or whatever. The big change, which is usually the radical change.

INTERVIEWER

That makes the story work?

MUNRO

I don't even know if it makes the story better. What it does is make it possible for me to continue to write. That's what I mean by saying I don't think I have this overwhelming thing that comes in and dictates to me. I only seem to get a grasp on what I want to write about with the greatest difficulty. And barely.

INTERVIEWER

Do you often change perspective or tone?

MUNRO

Oh yes, sometimes I'm uncertain, and I will do first person to third over and over again. This is one of my major problems. I often do first person to get myself into a story and then feel that for some reason it isn't working. I'm quite vulnerable to what people tell me to do at that point. My agent didn't like the first person in "The Albanian Virgin," which I think, since I wasn't perfectly sure anyway, made me change it. But then I changed it back to first again.

INTERVIEWER

How consciously, on a thematic level, do you understand what you're doing?

MUNRO

Well, it's not very conscious. I can see the ways a story could go wrong. I see the negative things more easily than the positive things. Some stories don't work as well as others, and some stories are lighter in conception than others.

INTERVIEWER

Lighter?

MUNRO

They *feel* lighter to me. I don't feel a big commitment to them. I've been reading Muriel Spark's autobiography. She thinks, because she is a Christian, a Catholic, that God is the real author. And it behooves us not to try to take over that authority, not to try to write fiction that is about the meaning of life, that tries to grasp what only God can grasp. So one writes entertainments. I think this is what she says. I think I write stories sometimes that I intend as entertainments.

INTERVIEWER

Can you give an example?

MUNRO

Well I think that "Jack Randa Hotel," which I quite like, works as an entertainment. I want it to, anyway. Although a story like "Friend of my Youth" does not work as an entertainment. It works in some other way. It works at my deepest level.

INTERVIEWER

Do you agonize just as much over those pieces you consider entertainments as over your central material?

MUNRO

Yes, that's true.

INTERVIEWER

Are there stories that haven't been any trouble at all to write?

MUNRO

I actually wrote "Friend of My Youth" very quickly. From an anecdote. There is a young man I know who works in the library in Goderich and researches things for me. He was at our house one night and he began to talk about neighbors of his family, neighbors who lived on the next farm. They belonged to a religion that forbade them to play card games, and so they played Crokinole, which is a board game. He just told me about that, and then I asked him about the family, their religion, what they were like. He described these people and then told me about the marriage scandal: the young man who comes along who is a member of their church and gets engaged to the older daughter. Then, low and behold, the *younger* sister was pregnant so the marriage has to be switched. And they go on all living together in the same house. The stuff about fixing the house, painting it over is all true too. The couple painted their half, and the older sister didn't—half the house got painted.

INTERVIEWER

Was there really a nurse?

MUNRO

No, the nurse I invented, but I was given the name. We had a fundraising event at the Blyth Theater, about ten miles away from here. Everybody contributed something to be auctioned off to raise money, and somebody came up with the idea that I could auction off the right to have the successful bidder's name used for a character in my next story. A woman from Toronto paid four hundred dollars to be a character. Her name was Audrey Atkinson. I suddenly thought, That's the nurse! I never heard from her. I hope she didn't mind.

INTERVIEWER

What was the inception of that story?

MUNRO

When I started to write the story we were on one of our trips from Ontario to British Columbia; we drive out every year in fall and drive back in spring. So I wasn't writing, but I was thinking about this family in the motels at night. Then the whole story of my mother closed around it, and then me telling the story closed around my mother, and I saw what it was about. I would say that story came easily. I didn't have any difficulty. I've done the character of my mother so often, and my feelings toward her, I didn't have to look for those.

INTERVIEWER

You have several mothers in your work. That particular mother appears in other stories, and she seems very real. But so does Flo, Rose's stepmother in "The Beggar Maid."

MUNRO

But Flo wasn't a real person. She was someone very like people I've known, but she was one of these composite characters that writers talk about. I think Flo was a force because I wrote that story when I had just come back to live here after being away for twenty-three years. The whole culture here hit me with a tremendous bang. I felt that the world I had been using, the world of my childhood, was a glazed-over world of memory once I came back and confronted the real thing. Flo was an embodiment of the real thing, so much harsher than I had remembered.

INTERVIEWER

You obviously travel a great deal, but your work seems fundamentally informed by a rural sensibility. Do you find that stories you hear around here are more resonant for you, or did you use just as much material from your life when you lived in cities?

MUNRO

When you live in a small town you hear more things, about all sorts of people. In a city you mainly hear stories about your own sort of people. If you're a woman there's always a lot from your friends. I got "Differently" from my life in Victoria, and a lot of "White Dump." I got the story "Fits" from a real and terrible incident that happened here—the murder-suicide of a couple in their sixties. In a city, I would only have read about it in the paper; I wouldn't have picked up all the threads.

INTERVIEWER

Is it easier for you to invent things or to do composites?

MUNRO

I'm doing less personal writing now than I used to for a very simple obvious reason. You use up your childhood, unless you're able, like William Maxwell, to keep going back and finding wonderful new levels in it. The deep, personal material of the latter half of your life is your children. You can write about your parents when they're gone, but your children are still going to be here, and you're going to want them to come and visit you in the nursing home. Maybe it's advisable to move on to writing those stories that are more observation.

INTERVIEWER

Unlike your family stories, a number of your stories could be called historical. Do you ever go looking for this kind of material, or do you just wait for it to turn up?

MUNRO

I never have a problem with finding material. I wait for it to turn up, and it always turns up. It's dealing with the material I'm inundated with that poses the problem. For the historical pieces I have had to search out a lot of facts. I knew for years that I wanted to write a story about one of the Victorian lady writers, one of the authoresses of this area. Only I couldn't find quite the verse I wanted; all of it was so bad that it was ludicrous. I wanted to have it a little better than that. So *I* wrote it. When I was writing that story I looked in a lot of old newspapers, the kind of stuff my husband has around—he does historical research about Huron County, our part of Ontario. He's a retired geographer. I got very strong images of the town, which I call Walley. I got very strong images from newspaper clippings. Then, when I needed specific stuff, I'd sometimes get the man at the library to do it for me. To find out things about old cars or something like that, or the Presbyterian church in the 1850s. He's wonderful. He loves doing it.

INTERVIEWER

What about those aunts, the wonderful aunts who appear?

MUNRO

My great-aunt and my grandmother were very important in our lives. After all, my family lived on this collapsing enterprise of a fox and mink farm, just beyond the most disreputable part of town, and *they* lived in real town, in a nice house, and they kept up civilization. So there was always tension between their house and ours, but it was very important that I had that. I loved it when I was a little girl. Then, when I was an adolescent, I felt rather burdened by it. My mother was not in the role of the lead female in my life by that time, though she was an enormously important person; she wasn't there as the person who set the standards anymore. So these older women moved into that role, and though they didn't set any standards that I was at all interested in, there was a constant tension there that was important to me.

INTERVIEWER

Then you didn't actually move into town as the mother and daughter do in "Lives of Girls and Women"?

MUNRO

We did for one winter. My mother decided she wanted to rent a house in town for one winter, and she did. And she gave the ladies' luncheon party, she tried to break into society, which was totally impenetrable to her. She couldn't do it. There was just no understanding there. I do remember coming back to the farmhouse that had been occupied by men, my father and my brother, and you couldn't see the pattern on the linoleum anymore. It seemed as if mud had flowed into the house.

INTERVIEWER

Is there a story you like that others don't? Are there any stories your husband doesn't like, for instance?

MUNRO

I liked "The Moon in the Orange Street Skating Rink" a lot, but Gerry didn't like that story. It was from anecdotes he'd told me about his childhood, so I think he expected them to come out quite differently. Because I thought he would like it, I didn't have qualms. And then he said, Well, not one of your best. That's the only time we ever had trouble about anything I wrote. Since then he's been really careful about not reading something until I'm away, and then if he likes it he will mention it, but maybe he won't mention it at all. I think that's the way you have to manage in a marriage.

INTERVIEWER

Gerry's from here, less than twenty miles from where you grew up. Are his anecdotes and his memories more useful to you than those of Jim, your first husband?

MUNRO

No, Jim was from near Toronto. But he was from a very different background. He lived in a sort of upper-middle-class commuter town where most of the men worked in Toronto and were professional. Cheever wrote about towns like that around New York. I'd never known people of this class before, so the way they thought about things was interesting as hell, but it wasn't anecdotal. I guess I was too hostile for a long time to appreciate it; I was more left-wing then. Whereas the things that Gerry tells me are further extensions of all the stuff I remember from growing up—though there's an entire difference between a boy's life in town and a girl's life on the farm. The greatest part of Gerry's life was probably between the ages of seven and fourteen, when the boys roamed the town in gangs. They weren't delinquents or anything, but they did more or less as they pleased, like a subculture within the town. Girls were not part of that, I don't think ever. We were always in little knots of girlfriends, we just didn't have the freedom. So it was interesting to learn all this.

INTERVIEWER

How long did you live outside of this region?

MUNRO

I got married the end of 1951, went to live in Vancouver, and stayed there until 1963, and then we moved to Victoria where we started our bookstore, Munro's. And I came back, I think it would be, in the summer of 1973. So I had only been ten years in Victoria. I was married for twenty years.

INTERVIEWER

Did you move back east because you met Gerry, or for work?

MUNRO

For work. And also because I had been living with my first husband in Victoria for ten years. The marriage was unraveling for a year or two. It's a small city. You have a circle of friends who all know each other, and it seems to me that if a marriage is breaking up, it's very hard to stay in the same environment. I thought it would be better for us, and he couldn't leave because he had the bookstore. I got an offer of a job teaching creative writing at York University outside of Toronto. But I didn't last at that job at all. I hated it, and even though I had no money, I quit.

INTERVIEWER

Because you didn't like teaching fiction?

MUNRO

No! It was terrible. This was 1973. York was one of the more radical Canadian universities, yet my class was all male except for one girl who hardly got to speak. They were doing what was fashionable at the time, which had to do with being both incomprehensible and trite; they seemed intolerant of anything else. It was good for me to learn to shout back and express some ideas about writing that I hadn't sharpened up before, but I didn't know how to reach them, how not to be an adversary. Maybe I'd know now. But it didn't seem to have anything to do with writing—more like good training for going into television or something, getting really comfortable with clichés. I should have been able to change that, but I couldn't. I had one student who wasn't in the class who brought me a story. I remember tears came into my eyes because it was so good, because I hadn't seen a good piece of student writing in so long. She asked, How can I get into your class? And I said, Don't! Don't come near my class, just keep bringing me your work. And she has become a writer. The only one who did.

INTERVIEWER

Has there been a proliferation of creative-writing schools in Canada as in the United States?

MUNRO

Maybe not quite as much. We don't have anything up here like Iowa. But careers are made by teaching in writing departments. For a while I felt sorry for these people because they weren't getting published. The fact that they were making three times as much money as I would ever see didn't quite get through to me.

INTERVIEWER

It seems the vast majority of your stories are based in Ontario. Would you choose to live here now, or was it circumstance?

MUNRO

Now that I've been here I would choose to. It was Gerry's mother's house, and he was living there to take care of her. And my father and my stepmother lived in the region too; we felt that there was a limited period of time when we would be at the service of these old people, and then we would move on. Then, of course, for various reasons, that didn't happen; they've been gone a long time, and we're still here. One of the reasons to stay now is that the landscape is so important to both of us. It's a great thing that we have in common. And thanks to Gerry, I appreciate it in such a different way. I couldn't possess any other landscape or country or lake or town in this way. And I realize that now, so I'll never leave.

INTERVIEWER

How did you meet Gerry?

MUNRO

I had known Gerry when we were in university together. He was a senior, and I was a freshman. He was a returned World War II veteran, which meant that there were seven years between us. I had a terrific crush on him when I was eighteen, but he did not notice me at all. He was noticing other people. It was a small university so you sort of knew everybody and who they were. And he was one of that small group of people who seemed—I think we called them bohemian, when they still said *bohemian*. They wrote poetry for the literary magazine, and they were dangerous, got drunk, and so on. I thought he was connected with the magazine, and when I wrote my first story, part of my plan was that I would take this manuscript to him. Then we would fall into conversation, and he would fall in love with me, and everything would go on from there. I took the story to him, and he said, John Cairns is the editor, he's down the hall. That was our only exchange.

INTERVIEWER

That was your only exchange all through your years in college?

MUNRO

Yes. But then, after I had published the story, he had left university. I was working as a waitress between my first and second years, I got a letter from Gerry. It was really a wonderful letter all about the story. It was my first fan letter. But it wasn't about me at all, and it didn't mention my beauty, or that it would be nice for us to get together or any of that. It was simply a literary appreciation. So that I appreciated it less than I might have if it had been from anybody else because I was hoping that it would be more. But it was a nice letter. Then, after I moved back to London and had the job at Western, he somehow heard me on the radio. I did an interview. I must have said where I was living and given the impression that I was not married anymore, because he then came to see me.

INTERVIEWER

And this was twenty-some-odd years later?

MUNRO

Easily. More than twenty years later, and we hadn't seen each other in the meantime. He didn't look at all as I'd expected. He just called me up and said, This is Gerry Fremlin. I'm in Clinton, and I was wondering if we could have lunch together sometime. I knew his home was in Clinton and I thought he had probably come home to see his parents. I think by this time I knew that he was working in Ottawa; I'd heard that from somebody. And I thought the wife and children were back in Ottawa, and he's home to visit his parents and he thought he'd like to have lunch with an old acquaintance. So this is what I expected until he turned up and I learned that he was living in Clinton and there was no wife and no children. We went to the faculty club and had three martinis each, at lunch. I think we were nervous. But we rapidly became very well acquainted. I think we were talking about living together by the end of the afternoon. It was very quick. I guess I finished out that term teaching at Western and then came up to Clinton, and we started living together there in the home where he had moved back to look after his mother.

INTERVIEWER

You hadn't made the decision to come back here for writing.

MUNRO

I never made a decision with any thought of my writing. And yet I never thought that I would abandon it. I guess because I didn't understand that you could have conditions for writing that would be any better than any other conditions. The only things that ever stopped me writing were the jobs—when I was defined publicly as a writer and given an office to work in.

INTERVIEWER

That seems reminiscent of your early story "The Office": the woman who rents an office in order to write and is so distracted by her landlord she eventually has to move out.

MUNRO

That was written because of a real experience. I did get an office, and I wasn't able to write anything there at all—except that story. The landlord did bug me all the time, but even when he stopped I couldn't work. This has happened anytime I've had a setup for writing, an office. When I worked as writer-in-residence at the University of Queensland in Australia, I had an office there, in the English Department, a really posh, nice office. Nobody had heard of me, so nobody came to see me. Nobody was trying to be a writer there anyway. It was like Florida; they went around in bikinis all the time. So I had all this time, and I was in this office, and I would just sit there thinking. I couldn't reach anything. I meant to, but it was paralyzing.

INTERVIEWER

Was Vancouver less useful for material?

MUNRO

I lived in the suburbs, first in North Vancouver, then in West Vancouver. In North Vancouver, the men all went away in the morning and came back at night; all day it was housewives and children. There was a lot of informal togetherness, and it was hard to be alone. There was a lot of competitive talk about vacuuming and washing the woolies, and I got quite frantic. When I had only one child, I'd put her in the stroller and walk for miles to avoid the coffee parties. This was much more narrow and crushing than the culture I grew up in. So many things were forbidden—like taking anything seriously. Life was very tightly managed as a series of permitted recreations, permitted opinions, and permitted ways of being a woman. The only outlet, I thought, was flirting with other people's husbands at parties; that was really the only time anything came up that you could feel was real, because the only contact you could have with men, that had any reality to it, seemed to me to be sexual. Otherwise, men usually didn't talk to you, or if they did they talked very much from high to low. I'd meet a university professor or someone, and if I knew something about what he knew, that would not be considered acceptable conversation. The men didn't like you to talk, and the women didn't like it either. So the world you had was female talk about the best kind of diet, or the best care of woolies. I was with the wives of the climbing men. I hated it so much I've never been able to write about it. Then in West Vancouver, it was more of a mixed suburb, not all young couples, and I made great friends there. We talked about books and scandal and laughed at everything like high-school girls. That's something I'd like to write about and haven't, that subversive society of young women, all keeping each other alive. But going to Victoria and opening a bookstore was the most wonderful thing that ever happened. It was great because all the crazy people in town came into the bookstore and talked to us.

INTERVIEWER

How did you get the idea to start the bookstore?

MUNRO

Jim wanted to leave Eatons, the big department store in town. We were talking about how he wanted to go into business of some kind, and I said, Look, if we had a bookstore I could help. Everybody thought that we would go broke, and, of course, we almost did. We were very poor, but at that time my two older girls were both in school, so I could work all the time in the store, and I did. That was the happiest period in my first marriage.

INTERVIEWER

Did you always have the sense that the marriage wouldn't last?

MUNRO

I was like a Victorian daughter—the pressure to marry was so great, one felt it was something to get out of the way: Well, I'll get that done, and they can't bug me about it, and then I'll be a real person and my life will begin. I think I married to be able to write, to settle down and give my attention back to the important thing. Sometimes now when I look back at those early years I think, This was a hard-hearted young woman. I'm a far more conventional woman now than I was then.

INTERVIEWER

Doesn't any young artist, on some level, have to be hard-hearted?

MUNRO

It's worse if you're a woman. I want to keep ringing up my children and saying, Are you sure you're all right? I didn't mean to be such a . . . Which of course would make them furious because it implies that they're some kind of damaged goods. Some part of me was absent for those children, and children detect things like that. Not that I neglected them, but I wasn't wholly absorbed. When my oldest daughter was about two, she'd come to where I was sitting at the type-writer, and I would bat her away with one hand and type with the other. I've told her that. This was bad because it made her the adversary to what was most important to me. I feel I've done everything backward: this totally driven writer at the time when the kids were little and desperately needed me. And now, when they don't need me at all, I love them so much. I moon around the house and think, There used to be a lot more family dinners.

INTERVIEWER

You won the Governor-General's Award for your first book, which is roughly equivalent to the Pulitzer Prize in our country. It happens only very rarely in the States that a first book wins such a big prize. When it does, the writer's career often seems to suffer afterward.

MUNRO

Well, I wasn't young, for one thing. But it was difficult. I had about a year when I couldn't write anything because I was so busy thinking I had to get to work on a novel. I didn't have the burden of having produced a huge bestseller that everyone was talking about, as Amy Tan did with her first book, for instance. The book sold very badly, and nobody—even though it had won the Governor-General's Award—nobody had heard of it. You would go into bookstores and ask for it, and they didn't have it.

INTERVIEWER

Do reviews matter much to you? Do you feel you've ever learned from them? Have you ever been hurt by them?

MUNRO

Yes and no, because really you can't learn much from reviews, but you can nevertheless be very hurt. There's a feeling of public humiliation about a bad review. Even though it doesn't really matter to you, you would rather be clapped than booed off stage.

INTERVIEWER

Were you a big reader growing up? What work if any had an influence?

MUNRO

Reading was my life really until I was thirty. I was living in books. The writers of the American South were the first writers who really moved me because they showed me that you could write about small towns, rural people, and that kind of life I knew very well. But the thing about the Southern writers that interested me, without my being really aware of it, was that all the Southern writers whom I really loved were women. I didn't really like Faulkner that much. I loved Eudora Welty, Flannery O'Connor, Katherine Anne Porter, Carson McCullers. There was a feeling that women could write about the freakish, the marginal.

INTERVIEWER

Which you've always done as well.

MUNRO

Yes. I came to feel that was our territory, whereas the mainstream big novel about real life was men's territory. I don't know how I got that feeling of being on the margins; it wasn't that I was *pushed* there. Maybe it was because I grew up on a margin. I knew there was something about the great writers I felt shut out from, but I didn't know quite what it was. I was terribly disturbed when I first read D. H. Lawrence. I was often disturbed by writers' views of female sexuality.

INTERVIEWER

Can you put your finger on what it was that disturbed you?

MUNRO

It was: how I can be a writer when I'm the object of other writers?

INTERVIEWER

What is your reaction to magic realism?

MUNRO

I did love *One Hundred Years of Solitude*. I loved it, but it can't be imitated. It looks easy but it's not. It's wonderful when the ants carry off the baby, when the virgin rises into the sky, when the patriarch dies, and it rains flowers. But just as hard to pull off and just as wonderful is William Maxwell's *So Long, See You Tomorrow*, where the dog is the character. He's dealing with a subject that potentially is so banal and makes it brilliant.

INTERVIEWER

Some of your newer stories seem to mark a change in direction.

MUNRO

About five years ago, when I was still working on the stories that were in *Friend of My Youth*, I wanted to do a story with alternate realities. I resisted this because I worried it would end up a *Twilight Zone* kind of stuff. You know, really junky stuff. I was scared of it. But I wrote "Carried Away," and I just kept fooling around with it and wrote that weird ending. Maybe it's something to do with age. Changing your perceptions of what is possible, of what has happened—not just what *can* happen but what really *has* happened. I have all these disconnected realities in my own life, and I see them in other people's lives. That was one of the problems—why I couldn't write novels, I never saw things hanging together any too well.

INTERVIEWER

What about your confidence? Has that changed over the years?

MUNRO

In writing, I've always had a lot of confidence, mixed with a dread that this confidence is entirely misplaced. I think in a way that my confidence came just from being dumb. Because I lived so out of any mainstream, I didn't realize that women didn't·become writers as readily as men, and that neither did people from a lower class. If you know you can write fairly well in a town where you've hardly met any-one else who reads, you obviously think this is a rare gift indeed.

INTERVIEWER

You've been a master at steering clear of the literary world. Has this been conscious or largely circumstantial?

MUNRO

It certainly was circumstantial for a long time, but then became a matter of choice. I think I'm a friendly person who is not very sociable. Mainly because of being a woman, a housewife, and a mother, I want to keep a lot of time. It translates as being scared of it. I would have lost my confidence. I would have heard too much talk I didn't under-stand.

INTERVIEWER

So you were glad to be out of the mainstream?

MUNRO

This is maybe what I'm trying to say. I probably wouldn't have survived very well otherwise. It may have been that I would lose my confidence when I was with people who understood a lot more than I did about what they were doing. And talked a lot about it. And were confident in a way that would be acknowledged to have a more solid basis than mine. But then, it's very hard to tell about writers—who *is* confident?

INTERVIEWER

Was the community you grew up in pleased about your career?

MUNRO

It was known there had been stories published here and there, but my writing wasn't fancy. It didn't go over well in my hometown. The sex, the bad language, the incomprehensibility . . . The local newspa-per printed an editorial about me: A soured introspective view of life . . . And, A warped personality projected on . . . My dad was already dead when they did that. They wouldn't do it while Dad was alive, because everyone really liked him. He was so liked and respected that everybody muted it a bit. But after he died, it was different.

INTERVIEWER

But he liked your work?

MUNRO

But he liked my work, yes, and he was very proud of it. He read a lot, but he always felt a bit embarrassed about reading. And then he wrote a book just before he died that was published posthumously. It was a novel about pioneer families in the southwest interior, set in a period just before his life, ending when he was a child. He had real gifts as a writer.

INTERVIEWER

Can you quote us a passage?

MUNRO

In one chapter he describes what the school was like for a boy who lived a little earlier than he did: "On other walls were some faded brown maps. Interesting places like Mongolia were shown, where scattered residents rode in sheepskin coats on small ponies. The center of Africa was a blank space marked only by crocodiles with mouths agape and lions who held dark people down with huge paws. In the very center Mr. Stanley was greeting Mr. Livingston, both wearing old hats."

INTERVIEWER

Did you recognize anything of your own life in his novel?

MUNRO

Not of my life, but I recognized a great deal of my style. The angle of vision, which didn't surprise me because I knew we had that in common.

INTERVIEWER

Had your mother read any of your work before she died?

MUNRO

My mother would not have liked it. I don't think so—the sex and the bad words. If she had been well, I would have had to have a big fight and break with the family in order to publish anything.

INTERVIEWER

Do you think you would have done it?

MUNRO

I think so, yes, because as I said I was more hard-hearted then. The tenderness I feel now for my mother, I didn't feel for a long time. I don't know how I would feel if one of my daughters wrote about me. They're about at the age now where they should be coming out with a first novel that is all about childhood. It must be a dreadful experience to go through, becoming a character in your kid's novel. People write carelessly wounding things in reviews like, oh, that my father was a seedy fox farmer, and things like this, reflecting on the poverty. A feminist writer interpreted "My Father," in *Lives of Girls and Women*, as straight autobiographical representation. She made me into someone who came out of this miserable background, because I had a "feckless father." This was an academic at a Canadian university, and I was so mad, I tried to find out how to sue her. I was furious. I didn't know what to do because I thought, It doesn't matter for me, I've had all this success, but all my father had was that he was my father. He's dead now. Is he going to be known as a feckless father because of what I did to him? Then I realized she represented a younger generation of people who had grown up on a totally different economic planet. They live in a welfare state to a certain extent—Medicare. They're not aware of the devastation something like illness could cause to a family. They've never gone through any kind of real financial trouble. They look at a family that's poor and they think this is some kind of choice. Not wanting to better yourself is fecklessness, it's stupidity or something. I grew up in a house that had no indoor toilet, and this to this generation is so appalling, truly squalid. Actually it wasn't squalid. It was fascinating.

INTERVIEWER

We didn't ask you questions about your writing day. How many days a week do you actually write?

MUNRO

I write every morning, seven days a week. I write starting about eight o'clock and finish up around eleven. Then I do other things the rest of the day, unless I do my final draft or something that I want to keep working on—then I'll work all day with little breaks.

INTERVIEWER

Are you rigid about that schedule, even if there's a wedding or some other required event?

MUNRO

I am so compulsive that I have a quota of pages. If I know that I am going somewhere on a certain day, I will try to get those extra pages done ahead of time. That's so compulsive, it's awful. But I don't get too far behind; it's as if I could lose it somehow. This is something about aging. People get compulsive about things like this. I'm also compulsive now about how much I walk every day.

INTERVIEWER

How much do you walk?

MUNRO

Three miles every day, so if I know I'm going to miss a day, I have to make it up. I watched my father go through this same thing. You protect yourself by thinking if you have all these rituals and routines then nothing can get you.

INTERVIEWER

After you've spent five months or so completing a story, do you take time off?

MUNRO

I go pretty much right into the next one. I didn't use to when I had the children and more responsibilities, but these days I'm a little panicked at the idea of stopping—as if, if I stopped, I could be stopped for good. I have a backlog of ideas. But it isn't just ideas you need and it isn't just technique or skill. There's a kind of excitement and faith that I can't work without. There was a time when I never lost that, when it was just inexhaustible. Now I have a little shift sometimes when I feel what it would be like to lose it, and I can't even describe what *it* is. I think it's being totally alive to what this story is. It doesn't even have an awful lot to do with whether the story will work or not. What happens in old age can be just a draining away of interest in some way that you don't foresee, because this happens with people who may have had a lot of interest and commitment to life. It's something about the living for the next meal. When you travel you see a lot of this in the faces of middle-aged people in restaurants, people my age—at the end of middle age and the beginning of old age. You see this, or you feel it like a snail, this sort of chuckling along looking at the sights. It's a feeling that the capacity for responding to things is being shut off in some way. I feel now that this is a possibility. I feel it like the possibility that you might get arthritis, so you exercise so you won't. Now I am more conscious of the possibility that everything could be lost, that you could lose what had filled your life before. Maybe keeping on, going through the motions, is actually what you have to do to keep this from happening. There are parts of a story where the story fails. That's not what I'm talking about. The story fails but your faith in the importance of doing the story doesn't fail. That it might is the danger. This may be the beast that's lurking in the closet in old age—the loss of the feeling that things are worth doing.

INTERVIEWER

One wonders though, because artists do seem to work to the very end.

MUNRO

I think it's possible that you do. You may have to be a little more vigilant. It's something I never would have been able to think of losing twenty years ago—the faith, the desire. I suppose it's like when you don't fall in love anymore. But you can put up with that because falling in love has not really been as necessary as something like this. I guess that's why I keep doing it. Yes, I don't stop for a day. It's like my walk every day. My body loses tone now in a week if I don't exercise. The vigilance has to be there all the time. Of course it wouldn't matter if you did give up writing. It's not the giving up of the writing that I fear. It's the giving up of this excitement or whatever it is that you feel that makes you write. This is what I wonder: what do most people do once the necessity of working all the time is removed? Even the retired people who take courses and have hobbies are looking for something to fill this void, and I feel such horror of being like that and having that kind of life. The only thing that I've ever had to fill my life has been writing. So I haven't learned how to live a life with a lot of diversity. The only other life I can imagine is a scholarly life, which I probably idealize.

INTERVIEWER

They are very different lives too, the life of a single pursuit as opposed to the serial.

MUNRO

You go and play golf and you enjoy that, and then you garden, and then you have people in to dinner. But I sometimes think what if writing stops? What if it just peters out? Well, then I would have to start learning about something. You can't go from writing fiction to writing nonfiction, I don't think. Writing nonfiction is so hard on its own that it would be learning a whole new thing to do, but maybe I would try to do that. I've made a couple of attempts to plan a book, the sort of book everybody's writing about their family. But I haven't got any framework for it, any center.

INTERVIEWER

What about the essay "Working for a Living" that appears in *The Grand Street Reader*? That reads like a memoir.

MUNRO

Yes. I'd like to do a book of essays and include it.

INTERVIEWER

Well, William Maxwell wrote about his family in that way in *Ancestors*.

MUNRO

I love that book, yes. I asked him about it. He had a lot of material to draw on. He did the thing you have to do, which is to latch the family history onto something larger that was happening at the time—in his case, the whole religious revival of the early eighteen hundreds, which I didn't know anything about. I didn't know that America had been practically a godless country, and that suddenly all over the country people had started falling down in fits. That was wonderful. If you get something like that, then you've got the book. It would take a while. I keep thinking I'm going to do something like this, and then I get the idea for one more story, and that one more story always seems so infinitely more important, even though it's only a story, than the other work. I read that interview in *The New Yorker* with William Trevor, when he said something like, And then another little story comes along and that solves how life has got to be.

Peter Carey

The Art of Fiction

When I arrived at Peter Carey's apartment on a chilly March morning for the first of the two conversations that make up this interview, Carey took my coat and hung it up. When we met again ten days later, he gestured toward the closet and said, "You know where the hangers are." He is a casual man, usually found in jeans and sneakers, and given to genial profanity. For much of our four hours of conversation he reclined in his chair, his feet up on the kitchen table. But if his posture was laid-back, his expression was lively, and he laughed frequently. When talk turned to his childhood in Australia, he hopped up to show me family photographs—of his grandfather, Robert Graham Carey, an aviator, posing in a monoplane in Adelaide in 1917; and of Carey Motors, the car dealership Carey's parents ran in Ballarat, near the small town of Bacchus Marsh, where he was born in 1943. From a kitchen drawer Carey produced a fistful of comment slips from his boarding-school days, which he displayed with self-deprecatory glee. "Very hard-working," wrote his housemaster at Geelong Grammar School, in 1960. "Very intense and serious-minded. He needs to have his leg pulled and learn to laugh at himself. It may be better to concentrate on the Pure Maths next term."

Carey has instead concentrated on fiction, with prodigious results. Since 1974 he has published two collections of stories, nine novels, a children's book, and several short works of nonfiction, and he is one of only two novelists to have been awarded the Booker Prize twice:

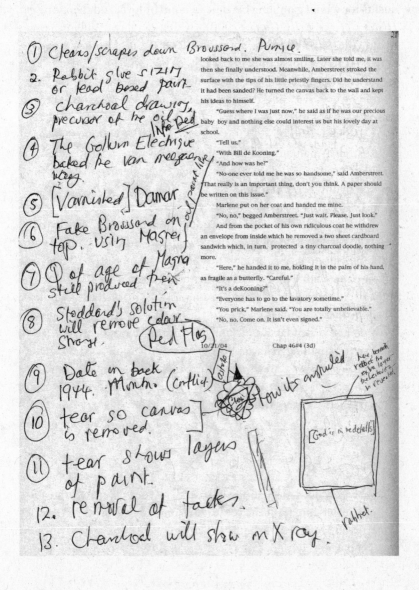

① Cleans/scrapes down Broussard. Pumice.

2. Rabbit glue sizing or lead based paint

③ charcoal drawing, precursor of the oil bed. Into bed

④ The Gollum Electrique baked he van meegeren way.

⑤ [Varnished] Damar. oil paint line

⑥ Fake Broussard on top. Using Masrei

⑦ ① of age of Magna still produced then

⑧ Stoddard's solution will remove colour shows. Red Flos

⑨ Date on back 1944. Month (conflict) Carbole

⑩ tear so canvas is removed.

⑪ tear shows layers of paint.

12. removal of tacks.

13. Charcoal will show in X ray.

How its annulled here beneath rabbet no extra layer believing n revealed.

[God is in the details]

Rabbet.

---

looked back to me she was almost smiling. Later she told me, it was then she finally understood. Meanwhile, Amberstreet stroked the surface with the tips of his little priestly fingers. Did he understand it had been sanded? He turned the canvas back to the wall and kept his ideas to himself.

"Guess where I was just now," he said as if he was our precious baby boy and nothing else could interest us but his lovely day at school.

"Tell us."

"With Bill de Kooning."

"And how was he?"

"No-one ever told me he was so handsome," said Amberstreet. That really is an important thing, don't you think. A paper should be written on this issue."

Marlene put on her coat and handed me mine.

"No, no," begged Amberstreet. "Just wait. Please. Just look."

And from the pocket of his own ridiculous coat he withdrew an envelope from inside which he removed a two sheet cardboard sandwich which, in turn, protected a tiny charcoal doodle, nothing more.

"Here," he handed it to me, holding it in the palm of his hand, as fragile as a butterfly. "Careful."

"It's a deKooning?"

"Everyone has to go to the lavatory sometime."

"You prick," Marlene said. "You are totally unbelievable."

"No, no. Come on. It isn't even signed."

10/21/04   Chap 46#4 (3d)

A manuscript page from a bound draft of Theft: A Love Story *by Peter Carey.*

first for *Oscar and Lucinda* (1988), the story of two Victorian-era misfits for whom gambling becomes a bond of love; and then for *True History of the Kelly Gang* (2000)—which sold two million copies worldwide—a novel in the form of a letter from Australia's outlaw-hero Ned Kelly, horse thief and bank robber, who was hanged at the age of twenty-six. In his recent novels Carey has explored the intersection of creativity and deception. *My Life as a Fake* (2003) was inspired by a notorious Australian poetry hoax. And in *Theft: A Love Story*, which was published this May, Carey intertwines the voices of an Australian painter, Michael "Butcher" Boone, and his mentally disabled brother, Hugh, as they navigate an international art world marked by forgery and fraud.

In 1990 Carey moved to New York, where he has lived since. For his last few novels, he has had drafts bound into what he calls "working notebooks." The first one, made for *The Kelly Gang*, was "huge, heavy, and annoying to carry through the bush"; the more recent ones use lighter paper with wide margins for notes. The pages are rough ("I type so badly, it's appalling," he said), with passages highlighted to indicate where further research is necessary; the margins hold chapter plans and plot points, calendars and timelines, and occasionally pasted-in postcards—anything relevant to the story in progress. Though the notebooks speak to Carey's talent for weaving history and legend into his own richly invented worlds, they also illustrate his editorial rigor. "For a writer," he says, "the greatest thing is to be able to pare away."

—*Radhika Jones, 2006*

INTERVIEWER

You were raised in small-town Australia—your parents ran an automobile dealership and sent you to Geelong Grammar, the country's most prestigious prep school. What did they think when you told them you were a writer?

PETER CAREY

I didn't tell them. I got a job in advertising. So even though I was writing, I was always supporting myself. That's the thing that would matter for my father, who was absolutely a creature of the Great Depression. He would worry every time I got a raise. He'd think, Well, Peter can't be worth all that money; he'll be the first to be fired. When I finally began to publish, my father never read my work. He'd say, Oh, that's your mother's sort of thing. But my mother found the books rather upsetting. I figure she read just enough to know that she didn't want to go there. I don't think my brother read my books, but he may have started recently. My sister was the only one who read me.

None of it had to do with disapproval. My mother and father were very proud of my success. Mind you, by the time I won the Booker Prize my mother's mind had started to wander a little. I'd gone to London, and I called her and said, Mum, you remember that prize? Oh yes, dear, she said. I said, I've won it! Oh, that's good, dear. There were some people here from your work. I said, What work? I don't know, she said—they had cameras.

A tabloid television crew had arrived at her doorstep. It was some crappy TV show. They said to her, Mrs. Carey, you must be really pleased! Oh yes, she said, Peter always was special. They said, Did he ring you? And my mother said, Ring me? Why would he ring me? He never rings me.

INTERVIEWER

They sound like regular parents. How did they come to send you to this fancy boarding school?

CAREY

My father left school at the age of fourteen, so this was a man with no deep experience of formal education. My mother was the daughter of a poor schoolteacher—well, that's a tautology—a country schoolteacher. I think she might have gone one year to a sort of posh school, but she would have been noticeably not well off. So you have to imagine these two people, my parents, in this little town, working obsessively hard in this small-time car business. The local high school was not particularly distinguished—I think it stopped at a certain level—and my mother was a working mother. Geelong Grammar? Because it was the best. It cost six hundred pounds a year in 1954, which was an unbelievable amount of money—and they really weren't that well off—and they did it. So I think she thought they were doing the very best thing they could do. I suppose it did solve a few child-care problems. I never felt I was being exiled or sent away, but I was only eleven years old. No one could have guessed that the experience would finally produce an endless string of orphan characters in my books.

INTERVIEWER

Is that where they come from—your boarding-school experience?

CAREY

Well, it took me ages to figure that out. I thought the orphans were there because it's just easier—you don't have to invent a complicated family history. But I think in retrospect that it's not a failure of imagination. I'm writing a book now about an orphan. But it's also the story of Australia, which is a country of orphans. I have the good fortune that my own personal trauma matches my country's great historical trauma. Our first fleet was cast out from "home." Nobody really wanted to be there. Convicts, soldiers were all going to starve or survive together. Later, the state created orphans among the aboriginal population through racial policies, stealing indigenous kids from their communities and trying to breed out their blackness. Then there were all these kids sent from England to Dr. Barnardo's Homes, which were institutions for homeless and destitute children, some of them run in the most abusive, horrible circumstances. There was one near us in Bacchus Marsh called Northcote Farm. This continued until almost 1970.

INTERVIEWER

Was that experience—of being sent off to school, of being orphaned in that way—what made you think of becoming a writer?

CAREY

Good God, no. I thought I would be an organic chemist. I went off to university, and when I couldn't understand the chemistry lectures

I decided that I would be a zoologist, because zoologists seemed like life-loving people. They looked at art, they read poetry. But I was faking my physics experiments, which is very exhausting. You'd think it's easy enough to start with the answer and work backwards, but my experimental method was terrible. Then I fell in love and everything went to hell. Then I had a very bad car accident, which I thought was a gift from God—because it was just before final exams. I remember waking up in the wreck, my scalp peeled back, blood pouring down my face, and thinking, Fantastic, I've got an excuse to fail.

INTERVIEWER

What happened?

CAREY

The bastards gave me supplementary examinations. So there was no escape. But I failed all of those as well, and then I had to get a job. I finally found a job at an advertising agency. It was a strange agency, as it turns out—full of writers and artists and run by a former member of the Communist Party. It sounds ridiculous, but I worked at three different agencies all run by former Communists. If you think about it, it's not so strange. It was Australia, not the U.S. It was after the war, and they were young intellectuals of the left. In my first job I worked alongside a man named Barry Oakley, an English teacher in his thirties who had come into advertising to support his wife and six children. He was certainly startled to find himself where he was. But he was writing every day, and he ended up being the literary editor of an Australian newspaper and also a distinguished playwright and novelist. There were also some good painters. None of us were real copywriters. I don't think I got a single piece of copy accepted all the time I worked there. We used to write copy all day, but then our boss would come down from meetings and put on his cardigan, which was a sign that he was going to be creative, and he would rewrite everything we'd done. So Barry and I were a little hysterical because we couldn't imagine why we were not being fired.

INTERVIEWER

What did you get out of the experience?

CAREY

I was put into an environment where people were writing and talking about books. Geelong Grammar was known as a "good school," but this reputation turned out to be more about class than anything else. My education really began at this little advertising agency. I started to read. I read all sorts of things in a great huge rush. James Joyce and Graham Greene and Jack Kerouac and William Faulkner, week after week. No nineteenth-century authors at all. No Australian authors, because I thought they were worthless, of course—that's good colonial self-hatred. I read haphazardly but with great passion. I would sit there earnestly annotating Pound's *Cantos*, for instance, almost building a wall between myself and the possibility of reading them.

INTERVIEWER

How did you make the shift from reading voraciously to thinking that you could do this yourself?

CAREY

If you don't know anything, you don't know how difficult it is. I looked at Barry and the others tapping away and thought, If they can do it, I can do it. Also, all of my friends were still at university. They weren't exactly Marxists, but they did have a good old-style repugnance for trade, advertising in particular. So my choice of employment was subjected to some intensely moral weather. I would go to parties and people would ask what I was doing and I would say, I work in advertising, but I am also writing a novel. There was a redemptive aspect to it. I went to work in 1962, and by '64 I was writing all the time, every night and every weekend. It didn't occur to me that, having read nothing and knowing nothing, I was in no position to write a book. I wish I could say I was the last person to suffer from this misunderstanding.

Were you starting to publish your work?

Not right away. I wrote a novel between '64 and '65. The next year I wrote another novel. Then I wrote a story that got published around that time. I was married for the first time, very young, at twenty-one. We traveled to a few places and then went to London and stayed there and worked, and I wrote another novel in London. I had small successes with all of those books. A portion of my first novel was published in an anthology. The second novel was accepted by Geoffrey Dutton, who had a publishing house, Sun Books, in Australia. He wrote me a letter saying, This is fantastic, we love the character, we'd love to publish it. Imagine, I was twenty-four years old. I was about to leave Australia for the first time, so on my passport application, in the space where they ask your profession, I wrote *author*. Then I went to a meeting in Melbourne with Dutton and his partner. The partner spent all of the meeting looking for a spelling mistake he'd discovered on page three or four. And I slowly realized that they weren't going to publish it. They told me that the English publisher André Deutsch was in Australia looking for Australian novels, and that they'd given my novel to him.

I went to Europe, traveled for three months, arrived in London, found out where André Deutsch's offices were, presented myself at reception. Can I see Mr. Deutsch, please—he brought my manuscript back from Australia, I believe. The receptionist said, Wait a second. She came back in fifteen minutes and gave me my manuscript and said, Thank you very much.

That was the end of that novel?

Yes, but I was already writing something else. When I reread the novel André Deutsch didn't like, I didn't like it either. I went on to finish the new novel in London, a wildly difficult, odd book about a bureaucratic investigation into a man's life. It was rather loveless—like dragging your tongue over a gray blanket—with reproductions of sixty-five newspaper photographs of car accidents, people in hoods, notes on cornflakes packets, mad graffiti beside Melbourne railway lines. I was a little crazy. I was about twenty-five. I saw Fellini's *8½* and was convinced that I was the only person in the whole cinema who understood it and that my book was sort of like that. No one would ever publish it because it was so good.

I finally decided that the only person who would really understand it was Kenneth Tynan. I don't know why I thought this. Tynan was staging *Oh! Calcutta!* in London, and he would understand my book. So I sent it to him and went back to Australia. Of course I didn't know Tynan and I now think him a very peculiar choice but the *idea* of him kept me going for a while. By the time I realized he was never going to write to me, I no longer needed him. But I was so exhausted—I had been writing all of these novels with such high hopes. Each one, by the time I had finished it, I knew what was wrong with it. I knew there was something mistaken, misshapen, wrong in their DNA.

INTERVIEWER

Did you think about giving up?

CAREY

No, I got a job with another Melbourne Communist's ad agency and started to write short stories. I wrote one story one week, and the next week I wrote another one, and then two weeks later I wrote one more. I didn't really understand that something had changed, but something had. I was finally a writer.

INTERVIEWER

What was it that was clicking?

CAREY

Age, experience, a simpler form, practice, reading, influence, getting beyond influence. Somewhere along the way I read Borges, who taught me, at the very least, that it might be possible to reinvent the world in just a few pages. Until then I'd imagined that the only really serious form was the novel, but when I returned to Australia I began to write a whole lot of what-if stories.

INTERVIEWER

What was appealing about that for you?

CAREY

I had been trying to build grand palaces, and now I was building little sheds and huts. If they fell down and rotted it didn't matter. In the end I had a collection of them published in Australia. It was praised, so then immediately—a totally Pavlovian response—I wrote another book of short stories. Later, the best of them went into one book in Britain and the U.S. That felt a lot better than being rejected. At the start my agent told me that it would be easier to sell the stories if I said I was writing a novel. So I said, Sure. But of course I just wanted to sell the stories. I had no intention of writing a novel.

INTERVIEWER

It wasn't at all tempting to say, Yes, I have three novels?

CAREY

They were no good to start with, and they hadn't gotten any better. But the point is, my lie came true. When I said I'd write a novel, I had no intention of doing so. Then I started to worry about it, and I thought about this failed short story about this complacent bourgeois who thinks he's died and gone to hell and hasn't. I started to write it as a novel, *Bliss*, and that was published and was, in its own small way, successful.

INTERVIEWER

Have you written any short stories since?

CAREY

No. Bill Buford came to New York in 1995 to be fiction editor of *The New Yorker*. He had published me before, and he felt that something new had to happen with the short stories in *The New Yorker*. So we had lunch at Da Silvano and he offered me a shitpile of money to write a short story for *The New Yorker*, a commission. I couldn't do it. I did a little memoir piece instead. It was at that lunch, with all that money on the table, that I realized I had no interest in doing short fiction anymore. I had become addicted to the dangers and pleasures of the novel. A novel is a lot more fun. It's so much more interesting. You go so far beyond what you know and what you think.

INTERVIEWER

Now that you've published nine novels, do you have a routine? How do you start writing every day?

CAREY

It's like standing on the edge of a cliff. This is especially true of the first draft. Every day you're making up the earth you're going to stand on. Normally I know what I want to achieve in a chapter, and I have an idea about where events should take place and I'll have some rough idea of the characters involved. But I might not have fully invented the place. And I certainly won't fully know the characters. So in the first draft, I'm inventing people and place with a broad schematic idea of what's going to happen. In the process, of course, I discover all sorts of bigger and more substantial things. Within those successive drafts, my characters keep on doing the same things over and over; it's like some hellish repetition of events. But the reasons they do them gradually become more complex and layered and deeply rooted in the characters. Every day's a miracle: Wow, I did that, I didn't know any of that yesterday.

INTERVIEWER

So you're discovering your characters as you go?

CAREY

Always. The big question for me is, What sort of person would do that thing—not just because it suits a story or suits something symbolically, but who would really, *really* do that? When I continue to ask myself that question and I don't take the easy answer, compli-cated characters are born. There's a scene near the beginning of *The Unusual Life of Tristan Smith* where I wanted one of the characters, Wally, to jump off a very high platform onto the stage, right in the middle of a performance. I couldn't even rationally explain to myself why I wanted him to do it, but I did. So I wrote it and wrote it and wrote it until it worked. There's some stubbornness and some belief in the action, and that's what the characters are born from.

INTERVIEWER

Do you revise as you go?

CAREY

I can't leave a chapter alone until I think it's as good as I can make it at that time. Often I will reach a stage, say, a third of the way into the book, where I realize there's something very wrong. Everything starts to feel shallow and false and unsatisfactory. At that stage I'll go back to the beginning. I might have written only fifty pages, but it's like a cantilever and the whole thing is getting very shaky because I haven't thought things through properly. So I'll start again and I'll write all the way through and then just keep going until it starts to get shaky again, and then I'll go back because I'll know that there's some-thing really considerable, something deeply necessary waiting to be discovered or made. Often these are unbelievably big things. Some-times they are things that readers will ultimately think the book is about.

For example, in *Illywhacker* I wanted to tell the story of a family over three generations, its descent from naïve nationalism—Australian nationalism, which is so much more fragile than, say, German nationalism—to a sort of mercantile opportunism. The first genera-tion was this character Herbert Badgery, and in the original plan he was going to die off or recede from the story. But I loved him so much that after I had written the first section I didn't want to let go of him. I remember I had bronchitis at the time, I was sitting in a doctor's office in Sydney with a notebook, and I said, Oh I know what I'm going to do, he's going to be there all the time and he's going to be a liar. And

I wrote in the doctor's office, "My name is Herbert Badgery. I am a hundred and thirty-nine years old and something of a celebrity" . . . dah dah dah dah dah. I realized, This is my book. But I had been working for a year before I got to that point.

A lying first-person narrator allowed me to use the immediacy of first person, but also the third person, because he's a liar—he will tell you everything. He didn't have to be there. There's a great thing to be had from the energy of first person. There's also something precious about third person, that godlike view and the wisdom that comes from it. With Badgery, I could have them both.

INTERVIEWER

Do you prepare for a book before you begin writing it—or do you just plunge in?

CAREY

I recently found a photograph that was taken in the seventies when I was working on some failed movie script that gives an idea of what I do. In the picture I'm using index cards and dividing up chapters and asking myself, What will happen in that chapter? I'll often look at those chapters as little boxes or rooms, and I'll start to ask myself what happens within each room. But I'll also be faking it by making notes and just wandering off into sentences to see where I end up.

INTERVIEWER

Is that how it tends to go for you with a novel? You don't know where you're going to end up?

CAREY

It wasn't always like that. I used to begin with an image—a strong, symbolic picture—and then ask myself, What do you have to do to arrive at this point? It's like one of those houses of cards where everything underneath has to hold up the top two cards. In the case of *Illywhacker*, I knew that the family was going to end up as pets in their own pet shop. The pet shop seemed to me pretty much what Australia had become, for all its blustering. With *Oscar and Lucinda* it started with the image of the glass church floating down the river, which is the end. And I knew from the very beginning that Oscar was going to drown. Readers used to say to me, How could you do that to him? They'd say, I threw the book across the room! Well, if I'd known who Oscar was I couldn't have done it to him. But at the beginning, when I was deciding his fate, I didn't know who he was. At that stage I'm like a bomber pilot, causing pain a long way beneath me because I'm dealing with something abstract.

INTERVIEWER

If there's no strong visual image, where do you begin?

CAREY

Recently I've been inhabiting voices. When I got to *True History of the Kelly Gang*, I let myself do something that goes back to the beginning of my reading. I was nineteen and just discovering literature. I was reading Joyce, and at the same time I read the Jerilderie Letter, a letter written by Ned Kelly in a town where he was robbing a bank. It's a very Irish voice. I know it's not Joyce, but it does suggest even to a nineteen-year-old the possibility of creating a poetic voice that grows out of Australian soil, that is true to its place and hasn't existed before. I had that in my mind from very, very early. It was astonishing to me that I could finally do it. In the next book, *My Life as a Fake*, I found myself doing something similar. At the time it never occurred to me that there was any similarity, but it was a continuation of the same practice, a book about voices telling stories.

In *Theft*, Butcher's voice is a very Australian voice—full of high and low, very profane but also grappling with quite substantial intellectual and artistic issues. What you have with Butcher is a lot of resentment, a lot of rage, a quality that the English would call *chippy*. I liked that. Here is an artist talking like a plumber, but he's discussing Clement Greenberg, or even his own art. That results in a particular language mix that gives you the ability to produce interesting sentences. I thought, This really is how we talk. This is so common. And yet I'd never read sentences like these in Australian literature. But I also realized that Butcher is quite well armored. He's not going to tell you a whole lot of things. So I wanted another view, another angle. That's where Hugh, his brother, comes from. As it developed I saw that Hugh's voice was going to be one of the really strong cables that runs through the book.

The book I'm writing now also has a particular voice. It's the voice of an American man recalling himself as a runaway child in Australia in the early seventies. He's put in situations and in a landscape that he doesn't understand at all. That produces very particular sorts of sentences. The actual narrator is thirty or forty and knows Australia very well, but he's imagining himself as an eight-year-old American. The reader won't have to think about that at all, but I do, and it guides me and gives me the limitations to create—I hope—a pleasurable and interesting verbal texture. I think *True History of the Kelly Gang* liberated that sense of possibility, that ability to disrupt and tear sentences. It's very pleasant.

INTERVIEWER

Do you do that kind of work with editors too—disrupting and tearing sentences?

CAREY

For many books my primary editor was Robert McCrum at Faber and Faber. Robert was not at all interested in sentences, and he was very good with the big issues. When I was writing *Illywhacker* and I had written two of the sections and was halfway through the third, and I was in a panic because I thought no one would publish such a long book, he asked me three questions. I can't even remember what they were—only that the answers allowed me to go back to work and finish the book. That's the sort of editor he was, gutsy and courageous. And he was very reckless as a publisher. So I felt comfortable with him. But Robert had a stroke and after that we really didn't work together.

Then Sonny Mehta became my editor, and Gary Fisketjon. Sonny and Gary have taken turns with the recent books. With Sonny, you sit down and talk at lunch, and you make notes. He is not particularly interested in the sentences either. Sonny is a fabulously good reader and I love sitting down with him. It all happens very quietly and sub-tly. He is a great publisher in the grand tradition. There are not so many left.

Gary rolls up his shirtsleeves and gets right in there. When I was do-ing *The Kelly Gang*, he was the person I wanted to work with. Being a writer is like being an individual proprietor or a taxi driver: You don't like the way I do things, get out of my shop. But Gary interrogates every sentence. Every page comes back covered with green ink. As a younger man I could not have borne it, but I'm older and finally understand that it's there to help me. I'd sit there and the pages would come in and I would respond to them—Yes, No, Yes, No, No, Yes. If anything was worth stealing I would steal it. If there was something I didn't like I wouldn't do it. Gary was passionately detailed. He was always worry-ing about what was the rule for this and when did you do that. I re-member being on holiday in Provence and he was on the phone in the middle of the night talking for four hours about fucking ampersands. He was obsessed about the jacket design, he was obsessed with the sell-ing and is very close to many booksellers. I was blessed.

INTERVIEWER

These days you run a graduate writing program at Hunter College. But the way you became a writer was completely informal, right? You had no training.

CAREY

In one way that's true, but it would be too smug to go along with it uncritically. Yes, we tend to be self-taught, and there's a part of me that thinks that's the way it should be—you do it alone, you learn to endure loneliness. I never said, I think I'll just workshop this with twelve other people. But I did have help. I mentioned Barry Oakley, who'd been a schoolteacher. He encouraged me, he gave me books. He read my writing and infuriated me by telling me it didn't work. I somehow managed to cast him in the role of an old conservative fa-ther to my young radical. But when I wrote my first successful stories, he was the one who said, They're good. By then I couldn't bear to be rejected by anyone. Barry gave stories to this person and that person, and with his help they found their way into magazines. It wasn't an MFA program, but it was hugely helpful. If that had not happened I wouldn't have been a writer.

INTERVIEWER

When do you write?

CAREY

Mostly in the mornings. Nonfiction writers tend not to understand this; they can write for eighteen hours straight, it seems. At the very end of a book I can manage to work for longer stretches, but mostly, making stuff up for three hours, that's enough. I can't do any more. At the end of the day I might tinker with my morning's work and maybe write some again. But I think three hours is fine. There are writers who go to the gym when they finish working, and there are writers who go to lunch. I'm enthusiastic about lunch. Three hours, then lunch. Now I have the Hunter program to keep me out of pool halls in the afternoon.

No one is particularly interested that I teach, but advertising was a different matter. You win the Booker Prize, the papers say "Ad-man Wins Booker Prize." It used to drive me nuts. But the wonderful thing about advertising—which I became quite good at and ended up doing for about twenty years—was that it provided this situation where I could be employed two afternoons a week or one week a month, so it was like having a fantastic patron or a great scholarship. From 1976 onward I never worked full-time. That meant that every day I could write.

INTERVIEWER

You mentioned that you never read any Victorian novels, but your 1997 novel, *Jack Maggs*, takes *Great Expectations* and turns it on its head. How did that come about?

CAREY

When my country began the European phase of its history there had already been some fifty thousand years of aboriginal settlement.

Then this penal colony arrives and marks the beginning of what is called Australia. This was the traumatic moment of the nation's birth, and the moment of its birth affects it forever. We grew up denying it, of course. Certainly it never occurred to us that the land was stolen, or that we had anything to do with the agony of the transported convicts. When we imagined who we were, we somehow imagined ourselves on the soldier's end of the whip. I wanted to write about this false consciousness for a long, long time, but I was not at all engaged with the idea of writing about a penal colony. Still, it was in my head.

INTERVIEWER

What released it?

CAREY

I recall very well. I was writing *The Unusual Life of Tristan Smith*. I had two kids and was at one of those resorts in Jamaica where theoretically the children go off and play happily and the parents read. Most of them seem to read John Grisham novels. I took *Culture and Imperialism* by Edward Said. I removed its dust jacket, because it seemed tasteless. You've got all of these not particularly wealthy Jamaicans around—and Jamaicans are continually suffering from imperialism and colonialism and are actively aware of it—so you do feel like a terrible hypocrite sitting there reading *Culture and Imperialism* by the swimming pool.

When people in America write about colonialism, it often becomes about color. It may not be immediately apparent that Australia was blighted in a similar way. But Said got it very well. Said was writing about Magwitch, the convict from *Great Expectations*, who is a classic Australian figure. There he is, transported to Australia, a free man after serving his seven-year sentence. He is an Englishman, but only as long as he doesn't go to England. But he is so fucked by it all that he'd rather risk his life to go back to England and sit at the feet of his invented gentleman child and have cakes and ale. I thought, Oh, that's so good.

Up until that stage of my life I hadn't read much Dickens. I'd always had trouble with the saccharine little girls—in *Bleak House*, for instance. Much easier to watch on television for me. But after reading

Said I thought, I better read Dickens. I was astonished that I enjoyed *The Pickwick Papers*. I found in *Great Expectations* a perfect book, and not a lot of saccharine little girls either. Then I started to read about Dickens. That's how I got to *Jack Maggs*.

People talk about historical fiction, but for me, in Australia, *Jack Maggs* addresses contemporary life. It was published at a time when Australians were still squabbling among themselves about whether Australia was going to be a republic. The issues of *Jack Maggs* are being played out in this argument about the republic and whether they are going to go and sit by the fire with the Queen of England having cakes and ale or whether they are going to understand their situation. To label it historical fiction is to risk misunderstanding its context.

INTERVIEWER

How did you manage the historical setting?

CAREY

Well, I'm a bloody colonial, aren't I? London is not my place and Britain is not my country. How was I going to have the authority to invent London in 1837? First I had to know something that's different from what anybody ever thought about the period. I couldn't steal from literature even if I wanted to—for the most part metropolitan literature takes the place for granted. So I spent a lot of time reading about people visiting London from abroad. They're going to see things that would not occur to the Englishman. There was a German visitor to London, for instance, who spends all this time describing this weird English breakfast that turns out to be toast. That was terrific—the familiar defamiliarized. I was trying to imagine—what was it *really* like? We generally think of London in that period as gloomy and sooty and filthy, but in the New York Public Library I found an account by an American visitor who described London as ablaze with light. That's not how anyone thinks of that period, but if you came from Australia or America at that time it was bright. I thought, that's it—this story will start at night, and it will be blazing bright. That's the first way in which I can colonize London for myself, take imaginative possession of the territory.

INTERVIEWER

So the research gives you a way in?

CAREY

Permission. And a sense of authority. It's important. I am writing that book for Australians, but I'm going to have well-educated British readers as well. Not long after *Jack Maggs* was published I met Anthony Minghella, the director, and he said, I saw it just like you wrote it. Of course he saw so much more than I imagined, but I had provided him with a sort of a matrix where he could plug in all of his knowledge and experience and it would illuminate the book for him.

INTERVIEWER

You said you were writing for Australian readers. Are they the first readers who come to mind when you are working?

CAREY

Yes. They have to be. Though in the case of *Jack Maggs* I was thinking about English readers as well, of course, and I liked the idea that I was messing with Dickens. In the case of *The Kelly Gang*, I was absolutely writing a story for Australians. But living in New York reminded me that people didn't know the story, so I couldn't assume anything, and that made the story better.

INTERVIEWER

Do you feel pressure to go back to Australia?

CAREY

From myself, but it's a confused sort of pressure. Australia is a nation of castoffs—we were sent to the place of punishment, like people sent to Mars. There is a great self-hatred and doubt that runs through Australian culture. If I had this conversation tomorrow with an Australian journalist, the journalist would say, Do you think we really are still like that? And I would say, We want that self-doubting colonial period to be over, but things don't go away that quickly. So when one leaves, the unsaid accusation is that you're going somewhere else because Australia is not good enough for you. But that has nothing to do with why I came to live in the States. It was strictly to do with a personal relationship. My friends made excuses for me, saying, Well, Pete, I suppose it will help you see us better if you are away.

INTERVIEWER

But isn't that true?

CAREY

Sure, but I thought that was a cop-out. I said, I'm just going, it is not *for* anything. Of course, there is a specially reserved position in Australian culture for the expatriate. The prime expatriates—people like Clive James, Germaine Greer, Robert Hughes—belong to an earlier generation than mine. When these people return to Australia, they are asked, What do you think of us? How are we doing? The expatriate is occasionally lauded and occasionally fiercely criticized for daring to come back and judge. I try to stay away from that as much as humanly possible. I don't feel at all like an expatriate. I can read the *Sydney Morning Herald* in a second, and I often did, before it developed its current tabloid sensibility. I have e-mail, I talk to my friends, everybody travels. It's not like we're weeping as the ship leaves the wharf and we're never going to see our home again. Though when my first wife and I left in '68, it was a little like that. But we were the first generation to take the plane.

INTERVIEWER

Critics have sometimes described your characters as failures, but they strike me as risk takers and mavericks.

CAREY

The people we call battlers, Americans call losers. It's an honorable position, to be a battler. Who are you thinking of? Butcher? What a loser, right?

INTERVIEWER

Also Herbert Badgery in *Illywhacker*. And Lucinda. She runs a glassworks in Victorian Sydney—that goes against the grain.

CAREY

They're both mavericks, I guess.

INTERVIEWER

Ned Kelly.

CAREY

He's our great hero, of course. But it's worth considering the nature of our heroes. You have Ned Kelly, who was hanged for shooting and killing policemen. Burke and Wills, the explorers who got lost and died. Phar Lap, who was really a New Zealand horse but we think of him as Australian, came to this country and was nobbled and died. Gallipoli, our great national story, is completely about loss—a military adventure devised by Winston Churchill that was totally misconceived and tragic, and is still celebrated today. These are all about loss. Landscape forms character, of course, and ours is a killer. In America the narrative is, Go west. You might eat a few people on the way, but basically it will be wealth and success. We just get lost and we die.

INTERVIEWER

You go into the bush and then—

CAREY

You're fucked. It's a hostile place, with droughts and fires. There's no frontier that triumphs over space in Australia. Also we have a big Irish component, a folkloric culture, about being robbed, tortured, and oppressed. And then we have the convict narrative, which is certainly about loss. And under all of this lies the knowledge that the land we love is also stolen. The horror of the destruction of aboriginal society is there every day. In Australian stories we trust loss and we are very suspicious of success. We have an affection for outcasts and oddballs. My stories and novels tend to fit into that tradition. We don't have many love stories either. There's a film called *Angel Baby* made by Michael Rymer, a love story between a boy who is schizophrenic and a girl who is not yet diagnosed—that's a love found only in Australia.

INTERVIEWER

"A Love Story" is *Theft*'s subtitle.

CAREY

Well, I'm always trying to do something new.

INTERVIEWER

The brothers, Butcher and Hugh, are from your home town of Bacchus Marsh.

CAREY

Yes. And then they go to Bellingen in northern New South Wales, where I also lived. But I'd warn against reading it in any autobiographical way. Think of it like Robert Rauschenberg picking up a sock from the floor and using it in a painting. It's still a sock, but it's no longer a sock. When I write I look at what's lying on the floor of my life. So I can pick up that river and that land and rip them up and glue them down to serve a whole new purpose. None of my other books was driven by such a personal and powerful memory of place. I left Bacchus Marsh when I was eleven, and it's been twenty years since I lived in Bellingen—I was astonished by how clearly I could see lost places.

INTERVIEWER

You spent some time living in an alternative community in Australia in the late seventies. Would you tell me about that?

CAREY

Like many things in my life, I didn't really mean to do it. I was living with a woman who inherited a little money, and she saw a photograph of this picturesque hut in a health-food shop window in Sydney, and I went up with her to look at it. She decided she wanted to go there, and I went with her. It was really wonderful. I suddenly found myself in a different physical environment, learning how to do all sorts of things. It was very tropical. We didn't have a telephone; at first we didn't even have any water. I spent a while trying to be a carpenter, fixing the leak on the roof and collecting water from it. People came up to see us and went back disgusted because there were flies crawling over every surface. One moment I was in Sydney, working in an advertising agency trying to write mornings and nights, using credit cards and drinking nice wine, and the next I am living in this very shaky hippie hut with policemen coming around threatening to plant dope on me if I didn't tell them my name and date of birth. Hanging out with people who saw wood nymphs wearing hats and neat little boots. Arguing about, when you did a collective *om*, which way the energy flowed from person to person around the circle. Though that makes them sound silly, which they weren't. They were all sorts of interesting people and we were living in paradise. Most of my friends lived on unemployment benefits. But once a month I would sneak out of the valley and fly down to Sydney and work in the advertising agency for five days.

INTERVIEWER

Were you able to write while you were there?

CAREY

Yes. I wrote a book of short stories there, and I wrote *Bliss* there.

INTERVIEWER

You adapted *Bliss* for film, and you wrote a screenplay with Wim Wenders, *Until the End of the World*. How did that experience impact your fiction?

CAREY

My fiction is now far more informed by an understanding of dramatic art. When I adapted *Bliss* I was ridiculously complacent and stupid, but the film looks great and the actors were really extraordinary. After that, Wim Wenders approached me about working on *Until the End of the World*. We had lunch and he told me this long complicated story of what he wanted the film to be. I thought, This is great, it'll be like there's this weird beast and I'm going to invent its lungs and kidneys and skeletal structure and where it eats and lives, and I'll discover character. For various reasons it did not work out like that at all. Soon afterward, when I was writing *Tristan Smith*, which is set in the theater, I began to think more about how you make a scene work through action. You start to conceive of dialogue as the disturbance on the surface that occurs as the result of tectonic shifts beneath.

INTERVIEWER

You've been publishing regularly for more than thirty years. Do you read reviews of your work?

CAREY

Yes and no. There is no good reason to read a review except vanity and insecurity. I never learned anything from a review. But one wants to be liked, of course. In an ideal world I have someone else read them first. When people say, You are better off not to read this, it is easy for me not to read it.

INTERVIEWER

Is it strange to hear your work described as falling into a particular framework, like postcolonial or postmodern, or is that irrelevant?

CAREY

There are writers whom I think I belong with, if one is talking about postcolonialism. I think of Salman Rushdie and Derek Walcott and most writers from the former British empire. I'm at home with them. We have huge amounts in common; we are dealing with astonishingly similar sorts of shit in different ways. On the other hand, I also think of English writers as my peers and friends. Julian Barnes, Ian McEwan, Martin Amis—I'd say that we are all engaged in the same sort of business, though I'm not an English writer. I'm in a relatively peripheral spot. We Australian writers occupy some weird little place.

INTERVIEWER

When Patrick White won the Nobel Prize in 1973, did that have an effect on you at all?

CAREY

I think I had a much bigger response to Thomas Keneally's winning the Booker Prize for *Schindler's Ark* in 1982. I remember that very clearly, and I remember being terrifically happy. It never occurred to me that I might be in that position at all, although that must have been when I was writing *Illywhacker*, which did get short-listed. I took it for granted that Patrick White was known internationally to be a great writer. I never would have imagined that in 2006 I could walk around bookstores in New York and be unable to find a copy of his work.

INTERVIEWER

What is your reception like in Australia? Is it different than elsewhere?

CAREY

I think there are things about the new book that Australians will get a greater degree of pleasure from than people in other countries—recognition of certain places and characters. Language too. On the other hand, Australians are more likely to get angry or agitated in a way that puzzles readers in other countries. People there got upset about *The Tax Inspector*. They thought I didn't like my country, because I said some things about Sydney being continually corrupt from its beginnings. It's an edgy, unsettling sort of book.

INTERVIEWER

Yes, you don't have to be Australian to be unsettled by it, with its graphic descriptions of violence and incestuous abuse. Did you feel a moral imperative in taking on that kind of material?

CAREY

Well, yes. There had been a sadistic rape and murder in Sydney—really, really horrible. At the same time, my first son was born. I had the idea of putting these two things in magical opposition—the birth of a child, which is this powerful thing, and this rape. I wanted in my simplistic, sentimental heart for birth to triumph. The end of the book is the birth of the child, and there's Benny Catchprice, the fucked-up little boy, who is intent on some weird rape. All of the time that I was writing the book—you asked about the moral imperative—I thought, it's easy, he's been abused. I didn't really think about what a morass I was creating. If he had been abused, how had he been abused? Do you really want to think about that? Do you really want to see the mother finding the father sucking the little boy's penis? Oh no. I really didn't want to think about that, and it took me forever to write it. It was the most difficult thing I've ever written. All the time I was thinking, Does the world need this book? What purpose does it serve? I was half sick with worrying. At that time I saw the movie *The Silence of the Lambs*. I was so disgusted. Did we really need to imagine this? For what reason? And I was writing *The Tax Inspector*, which is dark and disturbing. So the answer is yes. Yes. If you are going to break a taboo or imagine evil and put it on the earth you better have a good moral reason. You better hope that it is doing something that justifies its existence.

INTERVIEWER

You talked earlier about meeting with Bill Buford in the nineties and writing a memoir piece for *The New Yorker*. It's a painful piece, about your first wife's abortion, and lost children. What makes you turn occasionally to nonfiction?

CAREY

I'd had that story in my head for twenty-five years. In retrospect I think I shouldn't have written it. The thing I didn't think about was that it would also be published in Australia, and my first wife had a life there and I couldn't protect her privacy. She was terrifically generous about it, but I think I had presumed a right that I didn't really have. That's a sort of arrogance and self-involvement of writers that's not very attractive.

INTERVIEWER

What was the reaction to it here?

CAREY

When it appeared, I couldn't walk five yards in my neighborhood without someone coming up to me and saying, God that must have been so painful to write. Well, the curious thing about it was that it was easy to write. It was easy to write because I didn't need to make it up—it had been in my head all that time. I can think of things that were way more painful to write that I've made up.

One of the things that happens to me—particularly when I do interviews in Australia—is that journalists find it hard to believe in fiction. They want to know what really happened. They'll be looking at Ned Kelly—what's the real story? *My Life as a Fake*—they want the historical story, the poetry hoax. They'll want to look at what's personal. In a funny way I am always pleased to have that memoir piece so that I can say, Look, I am not frightened—I should have been more frightened—but I am not frightened to write about myself. I do not need the cloak of fiction to write about myself. I am involved in something completely different.

In fact, the two little books of mine that are considered memoir are not memoir at all. *30 Days in Sydney* is called "a wildly distorted account." The book about when I went with my son to Tokyo, *Wrong About Japan*, has an invented character in it. In the rest of the world this is clearly acknowledged on the cover, but in the U.S.—for reasons that still escape me—this important piece of information was not revealed. So I had to go around telling everybody about the made-up character. I was very anxious that my readers understood the contract I was making with them.

INTERVIEWER

Is there something that ties all your novels together in your mind?

CAREY

There was a stage where I might have said, "the invention of my country," but I think that as time goes on it's a much looser bundle. Those things are for other people to see, not for me. It's a little bit like being asked, Why do you walk the way you do? How do you walk? You don't really know.

INTERVIEWER

For all your talk about stories of loss, I sense a great level of optimism in your works.

CAREY

Historically, I'm pessimistic. Is the world going to be better in five years? I don't think so. Is it going to be better in twenty years? I don't think so. So I am a pessimist. But my pessimism has an indecent amount of energy and humor in it. And my working life, which is a huge part of my life, has given me every reason to be ridiculously optimistic. I can believe that anything is possible and be proved right. One of the great privileges of being an artist in Australia is that you can do any damn thing you like. Of course, the period that I grew up in was really culturally impoverished, very insular, threatened. But you didn't have the deadweight of history pushing your nose down into the soil. All of English literature was at once yours and not yours. You could do things for the first time, you could name things that hadn't been named, at least in English.

INTERVIEWER

You mentioned being addicted to the "dangers and pleasures" of writing a novel. What are they, exactly?

CAREY

The dangers are the risks you take in doing something that you don't know how to do. It is very dangerous to presume to write a novel like *My Life as a Fake*, set predominantly in Malaysia—a place you've visited four or five times. How are you going to do that without

being a colonial pig? How are you going to write a novel about a painter when you don't know shit about painting? How are you going to
write about the Kelly Gang—a group of horse thieves—when you are
basically frightened of horses? And write it so that people who really
know and love horses feel it? Even the novel I am writing now—and I
am well into it—I still can't be sure it's going to work, and I certainly
don't know how it's all going to come together and I don't even know
quite yet what it means, and that makes it dangerous to plow ahead
every day. I like the sense of risk that ends up with me sitting in a cab
coming in from Heathrow for the launch of *Jack Maggs*, thinking,
What have I done? What sort of idiot is going to take on Dickens?
Or taking the Ned Kelly story, which is my country's big story, and
messing with that and writing it in long breathless sentences with no
punctuation other than an occasional period. All of those things are
dangerous and thrilling, and I like that.

The huge pleasures are discovering things that you didn't know
and creating characters who are not based on anybody you've ever
seen. When I first set out to be a writer I had no real interest in character and certainly no aptitude or ability to create character. The
pleasures of having created those characters are enormous. It's a very
privileged way to spend your mornings. When you realize that you've
made some nice sentences—how thrilling is that? And then you get to
go to lunch.

Issue 177, 2006

Stephen King

The Art of Fiction

S tephen King began this interview in the summer of 2001, two
years after he was struck by a minivan while walking near his
home in Center Lovell, Maine. He was lucky to have survived the accident, in which he suffered scalp lacerations, a collapsed right lung,
and multiple fractures of his right hip and leg. Six pounds of metal
that had been implanted in King's body during the initial surgery
were removed shortly before the author spoke to *The Paris Review*,
and he was still in constant pain. "The orthopedist found all this in-
fected tissue and outraged flesh," said King. "The bursas were stick-
ing right out, like little eyes." The interview was held in Boston,
where King, an avid Red Sox fan, had taken up temporary residence
to watch his team make its pennant run. Although he was still frail, he
was back to writing every day, and by night he would take his manuscript to Fenway Park so that he could edit between innings and during pitching changes.

A second interview session with King was conducted early this
year at his winter home in Florida, which happens to be within easy
driving distance of the Red Sox's spring training compound in Fort
Myers. The house lies at the end of a sandy key, and looks—by virtue
of a high vaulted ceiling—something like an overturned sailboat. It
was a hot, sunny morning and King sat on his front steps in blue
jeans, white sneakers, and a Tabasco hot sauce T-shirt, reading the
local newspaper. The day before, the same paper had printed his
home address in its business section, and fans had been driving by all

moment there, grappling with that screaming, twenty kid, trying to get the muzzle of his .45 ~~into~~ socket into the cup of the kid's ear, it had almost felt like the old days, when the thing had been more than just an empty ritual, when it had been—

"Ron?" It was Johnny Speck again. He was looking at Darling anxiously.

"What?" he asked, annoyed. It was hard enough to think about these things at all without being jerked rudely out of your own head every ten seconds.

"It's Harry," Johnny said. "Something's wrong with Harry Drake."

* * *

Marsha:
(New doc. starts here)

Chapter 3

Last night I dreamt I went to Manderley again. If there ~~[crossed out]~~ is any more beautiful and haunting first line in English fiction, then I have never read it. And it was a line I had come to think of a lot during the winter of 1997 and the spring of 1998. I didn't dream of Manderley, of course, but of Sarah Laughs, a lodge so far up in the western Maine woods that it's not really even in a town ~~[crossed out]~~ at all, but in an unincorporated area designated as TR-90 on the maps.

The last of these dreams was a nightmare, but until that one, they had a kind of surreal simplicity. You know how the air feels before a thunderstorm, how everything gets still and colors seem to stand out with the brilliance of things seen during a high fever? My winter dreams of Sarah Laughs were like that, and I would awake from them with a feeling that was not quite fear. I *have dreamed* again of Manderley, I would think sometimes, and sometimes I would awake thinking that Rebecca deWinter hadn't drowned in the ocean but in the lake — Dark Score Lake. That she had gone down while the loons cried out in the twilight. Sometimes after these dreams I would get up and drink a glass of water. Sometimes I just rolled

A manuscript page from Bag of Bones *by Stephen King.*

morning to get a peek at the world-famous author. "People forget," he said, "I'm a real person."

King was born on September 21, 1947, in Portland, Maine. His father abandoned his family when King was very young, and his mother moved around the country before settling back in Maine—this time in the small inland town of Durham. King's first published story, "I Was a Teenage Grave Robber," appeared in 1965 in a fan magazine called *Comics Review*. Around that time he received a scholarship to attend the University of Maine in Orono, where he met his wife, Tabitha, a novelist with whom he has three children and to whom he is still married. For several years he struggled to support his young family by washing motel linens at a laundry, teaching high-school English, and occasionally selling short stories to men's magazines. Then, in 1973, he sold his novel *Carrie*, which quickly became a bestseller. Since then, King has sold over three hundred million books.

In addition to forty-three novels, King has written eight collections of short stories, eleven screenplays, and two books on the craft of writing, and he is a coauthor with Stewart O'Nan of *Faithful*, a day-by-day account of the Red Sox's 2004 championship season. Virtually all of his novels and most of his short stories have been adapted for film or television. Although he was dismissed by critics for much of his career—one *New York Times* review called King "a writer of fairly engaging and preposterous claptrap"—his writing has received greater recognition in recent years, and in 2003 he won the Medal for Distinguished Contribution to American Letters from the National Book Foundation. King has also been honored for his devoted efforts to support and promote the work of other authors. In 1997 he received the Writers for Writers Award from *Poets & Writers* magazine, and he was recently selected to edit the 2007 edition of Best American Short Stories.

In person, King has a gracious, funny, sincere manner and speaks with great enthusiasm and candor. He is also a generous host. Halfway through the interview he served lunch: a roasted chicken—which he proceeded to hack at with a frighteningly sharp knife—potato salad, coleslaw, macaroni salad, and, for dessert, key lime pie. When asked what he was currently working on, he stood up and led the way to the beach that runs along his property. He explained that two other houses once stood at the end of the key. One of them collapsed during a storm five years earlier, and bits of wall, furniture, and personal effects still wash ashore at high tide. King is setting his next novel in the other house. It is still standing, though it is abandoned and, undoubtedly, haunted.

—*Christopher Lehmann-Haupt, Nathaniel Rich, 2006*

INTERVIEWER

How old were you when you started writing?

STEPHEN KING

Believe it or not, I was about six or seven, just copying panels out of comic books and then making up my own stories. I can remember being home from school with tonsillitis and writing stories in bed to pass the time. Film was also a major influence. I loved the movies from the start. I can remember my mother taking me to Radio City Music Hall to see *Bambi*. Whoa, the size of the place, and the forest fire in the movie—it made a big impression. So when I started to write, I had a tendency to write in images because that was all I knew at the time.

INTERVIEWER

When did you begin reading adult fiction?

KING

In 1959 probably, after we had moved back to Maine. I would have been twelve, and I was going to this little one-room schoolhouse just up the street from my house. All the grades were in one room, and there was a shithouse out back, which stank. There was no library in town, but every week the state sent a big green van called the bookmobile. You could get three books from the bookmobile and they didn't care which ones—you didn't have to take out kid books. Up until then what I had been reading was Nancy Drew, the Hardy Boys, and things like that. The first books I picked out were these Ed

McBain 87th Precinct novels. In the one I read first, the cops go up to question a woman in this tenement apartment and she is standing there in her slip. The cops tell her to put some clothes on, and she grabs her breast through her slip and squeezes it at them and says, "In your eye, cop!" And I went, Shit! Immediately something clicked in my head. I thought, That's real, that could really happen. That was the end of the Hardy Boys. That was the end of all juvenile fiction for me. It was like, See ya!

INTERVIEWER

But you didn't read popular fiction exclusively.

KING

I didn't know what popular fiction was, and nobody told me at the time. I read a wide range of books. I read *The Call of the Wild* and *The Sea-Wolf* one week, and then *Peyton Place* the next week, and then a week later *The Man in the Gray Flannel Suit*. Whatever came to mind, whatever came to hand, I would read. When I read *The Sea-Wolf*, I didn't understand that it was Jack London's critique of Nietzsche, and when I read *McTeague*, I didn't know that was naturalism, that it was Frank Norris saying, You can never win, the system always beats you. But I did understand them on another level. When I read *Tess of the d'Urbervilles*, I said to myself two things. Number one, if she didn't wake up when that guy fucked her, she must have really been asleep. And number two, a woman couldn't catch a break at that time. That was my introduction to women's lit. I loved that book, so I read a whole bunch of Hardy. But when I read *Jude the Obscure*, that was the end of my Hardy phase. I thought, This is fucking ridiculous. Nobody's life is this bad. Give me a break, you know?

INTERVIEWER

In *On Writing*, you mention how the idea for your first novel, *Carrie*, came to you when you connected two unrelated subjects: adolescent cruelty and telekinesis. Are such unlikely connections often a starting point for you?

KING

Yes, that's happened a lot. When I wrote *Cujo*—about a rabid dog—I was having trouble with my motorcycle, and I heard about a place I could get it fixed. We were living in Bridgton, Maine, which is a resort-type town—a lake community in the western part of the state—but over in the northern part of Bridgton, it's really rough country. There are a lot of farmers just making their own way in the old style. The mechanic had a farmhouse and an auto shop across the road. So I took my motorcycle up there, and when I got it into the yard, it quit entirely. And the biggest Saint Bernard I ever saw in my life came out of that garage, and it came toward me.

Those dogs look horrible anyway, particularly in summer. They've got the dewlaps, and they've got the runny eyes. They don't look like they're well. He started growling at me, way down in his throat: *arrrrrrrrrrrggggggghhhhhh*. At that time I weighed about two hundred and twenty pounds, so I outweighed the dog by maybe ten pounds. The mechanic came out of the garage and said to me, Oh, that's Bowser, or whatever the dog's name was. It wasn't Cujo. He said, Don't worry about him. He does that to everybody. So I put my hand out to the dog, and the dog went for my hand. The guy had one of those socket wrenches in his hand, and he brought it down on the dog's hindquarters. A steel wrench. It sounded like a rug beater hitting a rug. The dog just yelped once and sat down. And the guy said something to me like, Bowser usually doesn't do this, he must not have liked your face. Right away it's my fault.

I remember how scared I was because there was no place to hide. I was on my bike but it was dead, and I couldn't outrun him. If the man wasn't there with the wrench and the dog decided to attack . . . But that was not a story, it was just a piece of something. A couple of weeks later I was thinking about this Ford Pinto that my wife and I had. It was the first new car we ever owned. We bought it with the Doubleday advance for *Carrie*, twenty-five hundred dollars. We had problems with it right away because there was something wrong with the needle valve in the carburetor. It would stick, the carburetor would flood, and the car wouldn't start. I was worried about my wife getting stuck in that Pinto, and I thought, What if she took that car to get fixed like I did my motorcycle and the needle valve stuck and she couldn't get it going—but instead of the dog just being a mean dog, what if the dog was really crazy?

Then I thought, Maybe it's rabid. That's when something really fired over in my mind. Once you've got that much, you start to see all the ramifications of the story. You say to yourself, Well, why didn't somebody come and rescue her? People live there. It's a farmhouse. Where are they? Well, you say, I don't know, that's the story. Where is her husband? Why didn't her husband come rescue her? I don't know, that's part of the story. What happens if she gets bitten by this dog? And that was going to be part of the story. What if she starts to get rabid? After I got about seventy or eighty pages into the book I found out the incubation period for rabies was too long, so her becoming rabid ceased to be a factor. That's one of the places where the real world intruded on the story. But it's always that way. You see something, then it clicks with something else, and it will make a story. But you never know when it's going to happen.

INTERVIEWER

Are there other sources for your material besides experience?

KING

Sometimes it's other stories. A few years ago I was listening to a book on tape by John Toland called *The Dillinger Days*. One of the stories is about John Dillinger and his friends Homer Van Meter and Jack Hamilton fleeing Little Bohemia, and Jack Hamilton being shot in the back by a cop after crossing the Mississippi River. Then all this other stuff happens to him that Toland doesn't really go into. And I thought, I don't need Toland to tell me what happens, and I don't need to be tied to the truth. These people have legitimately entered the area of American mythology. I'll make up my own shit. So I wrote a story called "The Death of Jack Hamilton."

Or sometimes I'll use film. In *Wolves of the Calla*, one of the seven books in the Dark Tower series, I decided to see if I couldn't retell *Seven Samurai*, that Kurosawa film, and *The Magnificent Seven*. The story is the same, of course, in both cases. It's about these farmers who hire gunslingers to defend their town against bandits who keep coming to steal their crops. But I wanted to up the ante a little bit. So in my version, instead of crops, the bandits steal children.

INTERVIEWER

What happens when the real world intrudes, as with the incubation period of rabies in *Cujo*? Do you go back?

KING

You can never bend reality to serve the fiction. You have to bend the fiction to serve reality when you find those things out.

INTERVIEWER

Cujo is unusual in that the entire novel is a single chapter. Did you plan that from the start?

KING

No, *Cujo* was a standard novel in chapters when it was created. But I can remember thinking that I wanted the book to feel like a brick that was heaved through your window at you. I've always thought that the sort of book that I do—and I've got enough ego to think that every novelist should do this—should be a kind of personal assault. It ought to be somebody lunging right across the table and grabbing you and messing you up. It should get in your face. It should upset you, disturb you. And not just because you get grossed out. I mean, if I get a letter from somebody saying, I couldn't eat my dinner, my attitude is, Terrific!

INTERVIEWER

What do you think it is that we're afraid of?

KING

I don't think there's anything that I'm not afraid of, on some level. But if you mean, What are *we* afraid of, as humans? Chaos. The outsider. We're afraid of change. We're afraid of disruption, and that is what I'm interested in. I mean, there are a lot of people whose writing I really love—one of them is the American poet Philip Booth—who write about ordinary life straight up, but I just can't do that.

I once wrote a short novel called "The Mist." It's about this mist that rolls in and covers a town, and the story follows a number of people who are trapped in a supermarket. There's a woman in the checkout line who's got this box of mushrooms. When she walks to the window to see the mist coming in, the manager takes them from her. And she tells him, "Give me back my mushies."

We're terrified of disruption. We're afraid that somebody's going to steal our mushrooms in the checkout line.

INTERVIEWER

Would you say then that this fear is the main subject of your fiction?

KING

I'd say that what I do is like a crack in the mirror. If you go back over the books from *Carrie* on up, what you see is an observation of ordinary middle-class American life as it's lived at the time that particular book was written. In every life you get to a point where you have to deal with something that's inexplicable to you, whether it's the doctor saying you have cancer or a prank phone call. So whether you talk about ghosts or vampires or Nazi war criminals living down the block, we're still talking about the same thing, which is an intrusion of the extraordinary into ordinary life and how we deal with it. What that shows about our character and our interactions with others and the society we live in interests me a lot more than monsters and vampires and ghouls and ghosts.

INTERVIEWER

In *On Writing*, that's how you define popular fiction: fiction in which readers recognize aspects of their own experience—behavior, place, relationships, and speech. In your work, do you consciously set out to capture a specific moment in time?

KING

No, but I don't try to avoid it. Take *Cell*. The idea came about this way: I came out of a hotel in New York and I saw this woman talking on her cell phone. And I thought to myself, What if she got a message over the cell phone that she couldn't resist, and she had to kill people until somebody killed her? All the possible ramifications started bouncing around in my head like pinballs. If everybody got the same message, then everybody who had a cell phone would go crazy. Normal people would see this, and the first thing they would do would be to call their friends and families on their cell phones. So the epidemic would spread like poison ivy. Then, later, I was walking down the street and I see some guy who is apparently a crazy person yelling to himself. And I want to cross the street to get away from him. Except he's not a bum; he's dressed in a suit. Then I see he's got one of these plugs in his ear and he's talking into his cell phone. And I thought to myself, I really want to write this story.

It was an instant concept. Then I read a lot about the cell-phone business and started to look at the cell-phone towers. So it's a very current book, but it came out of a concern about the way we talk to each other today.

INTERVIEWER

Do you think *Cell*, because of its timeliness, might look dated in ten years?

KING

It might. I'm sure other books, like *Firestarter* for instance, look antique now. But that doesn't bother me. One hopes that the stories and the characters stand out. And even the antique things have a certain value.

INTERVIEWER

Do you think about which of your books will last?

KING

It's a crapshoot. You never know who's going to be popular in fifty years. Who is going to be in, in a literary sense, and who's not. If I had to predict which of my books people will pick up a hundred years from now, if they pick up any, I'd begin with *The Stand* and *The Shining*. And *'Salem's Lot*—because people like vampire stories, and its premise is the classic vampire story. It doesn't have any particular bells or whistles. It's not fancy; it's just scary. So I think people will pick that up for a while.

INTERVIEWER

When you look back on your novels, do you group them in any way?

KING

I do two different kinds of books. I think of books like *The Stand*, *Desperation*, and the Dark Tower series as books that go out. Then there are books like *Pet Sematary*, *Misery*, *The Shining*, and *Dolores Claiborne* that go in. Fans usually will either like the outies or they'll like the innies. But they won't like both.

INTERVIEWER

But even in the more supernatural books the horror is psychological, right? It's not just the bogeyman jumping out from behind a corner. So couldn't they all be characterized as innies?

KING

Well, my categorization is also about character, and the number of characters. Innies tend to be about one person and go deeper and deeper into a single character. *Lisey's Story*, my new novel, is an innie, for instance, because it's a long book and there are only a few characters, but a book like *Cell* is an outie because there are a lot of people and it's about friendship and it's kind of a road story. *Gerald's Game* is the innie-est of all the innie books. It's about only one person, Jessie, who's been handcuffed naked to her bed. The little things all get so big—the glass of water, and her trying to get the shelf above the bed to tip up so she can escape. Going into that book, I remember thinking that Jessie would have been some sort of gymnast at school, and at the end of it she would simply put her feet back over her head, over the bedstead, and wind up standing up. About forty pages into writing it, I said to myself, I'd better see if this works. So I got my son—I think it was Joe because he's the more limber of the two boys—and I took him into our bedroom. I tied him with scarves to the bedposts. My wife came in and said, What are you doing? And I said, I'm doing an experiment, never mind.

Joe tried to do it, but he couldn't. He said, My joints don't work that way. And again, it's what I was talking about with the rabies in *Cujo*. I'm saying, Jesus Christ! This isn't going to work! And the only thing you can do at that point is say, Well, I could make her double-jointed. Then you go, Yeah, right, that's not fair.

Misery was just two characters in a bedroom, but *Gerald's Game* goes that one better—one character in a bedroom. I was thinking that eventually there's going to be another book that will just be called "Bedroom." There won't be any characters at all.

INTERVIEWER

Mark Singer wrote in *The New Yorker* that you lost part of your audience with *Cujo* and *Pet Sematary* and *Gerald's Game* because those novels were too painful for readers to bear. Do you think that's actually the case?

KING

I think that I lost some readers at various points. It was just a natural process of attrition, that's all. People go on, they find other things. Though I also think that I have changed as a writer over the years, in the sense that I'm not providing exactly the same level of escape that *'Salem's Lot*, *The Shining*, or even *The Stand* does. There are people out there who would have been perfectly happy had I died in 1978, the people who come to me and say, Oh, you never wrote a book as good as *The Stand*. I usually tell them how depressing it is to hear them say that something you wrote twenty-eight years ago was your best book. Dylan probably hears the same thing about *Blonde on Blonde*. But you try to grow as a writer and not just do the same thing over and over again, because there's absolutely no point to that.

And I can afford to lose fans. That sounds totally conceited, but I don't mean it that way: I can lose half of my fan base and still have enough to live on very comfortably. I've had the freedom to follow my own course, which is great. I might have lost some fans, but I might've gained some too.

INTERVIEWER

You have written a lot about children. Why is that?

KING

I wrote a lot about children for a couple of reasons. I was fortunate to sell my writing fairly young, and I married young and had children young. Naomi was born in 1971, Joe was born in 1972, and Owen was born in 1977—a six-year spread between three kids. So I had a chance to observe them at a time when a lot of my contemporaries were out dancing to KC and the Sunshine Band. I feel that I got the better part of that deal. Raising the kids was a lot more rewarding than pop culture in the seventies.

So I didn't know KC and the Sunshine Band, but I did know my kids inside out. I was in touch with the anger and exhaustion that you can feel. And those things went into the books because they were what I knew at that time. What has found its way into a lot of the recent books is pain, and people who have injuries, because that's what I know right now. Ten years from now maybe it will be something else, if I'm still around.

INTERVIEWER

Bad things happen to children in *Pet Sematary*. Where did that come from?

KING

That book was pretty personal. Everything in it—up to the point where the little boy is killed in the road—everything is true. We moved into that house by the road. It was Orrington instead of Ludlow, but the big trucks did go by, and the old guy across the street did say, You just want to watch 'em around the road. We did go out in the field. We flew kites. We did go up and look at the pet cemetery. I did find my daughter's cat, Smucky, dead in the road, run over. We buried him up in the pet cemetery, and I did hear Naomi out in the garage the night after we buried him. I heard all these popping noises—she was jumping up and down on packing material. She was crying and saying, Give me my cat back! Let God have his own cat! I just dumped that right into the book. And Owen really did go charging for the road. He was this little guy, probably two years old. I'm yelling, Don't do that! And of course he runs faster and laughs, because that's what they do at that age. I ran after him and gave him a flying tackle and pulled him down on the shoulder of the road, and a truck just thundered by him. So all of that went into the book.

And then you say to yourself, You have to go a little bit further. If you're going to take on this grieving process—what happens when you lose a kid—you ought to go all the way through it. And I did. I'm proud of that because I followed it all the way through, but it was so gruesome by the end of it, and so awful. I mean, there's no hope for anybody at the end of that book. Usually I give my drafts to my wife Tabby to read, but I didn't give it to her. When I finished I put it in the desk and just left it there. I worked on *Christine*, which I liked a lot better, and which was published before *Pet Sematary*.

INTERVIEWER

Was *The Shining* also based on personal experience? Did you ever stay in that hotel?

KING

Yes, the Stanley Hotel in Estes Park, Colorado. My wife and I went up there in October. It was their last weekend of the season, so the hotel was almost completely empty. They asked me if I could pay cash because they were taking the credit card receipts back down to Denver. I went past the first sign that said, Roads may be closed after November 1, and I said, Jeez, there's a story up here.

INTERVIEWER

What did you think of Stanley Kubrick's adaptation of the book?

KING

Too cold. No sense of emotional investment in the family whatsoever on his part. I felt that the treatment of Shelley Duvall as Wendy—I
mean, talk about insulting to women. She's basically a scream machine. There's no sense of her involvement in the family dynamic at
all. And Kubrick didn't seem to have any idea that Jack Nicholson was
playing the same motorcycle psycho that he played in all those biker
films he did—*Hells Angels on Wheels*, *The Wild Ride*, *The Rebel
Rousers*, and *Easy Rider*. The guy is crazy. So where is the tragedy if
the guy shows up for his job interview and he's already bonkers? No,
I hated what Kubrick did with that.

INTERVIEWER

Did you work with him on the movie?

KING

No. My screenplay for *The Shining* became the basis for the television miniseries later on. But I doubt Kubrick ever read it before making his film. He knew what he wanted to do with the story, and he
hired the novelist Diane Johnson to write a draft of the screenplay
based on what he wanted to emphasize. Then he redid it himself. I
was really disappointed.

It's certainly beautiful to look at: gorgeous sets, all those Steadicam
shots. I used to call it a Cadillac with no engine in it. You can't do anything with it except admire it as sculpture. You've taken away its primary purpose, which is to tell a story. The basic difference that tells
you all you need to know is the ending. Near the end of the novel, Jack
Torrance tells his son that he loves him, and then he blows up with
the hotel. It's a very passionate climax. In Kubrick's movie, he freezes
to death.

INTERVIEWER

Many of your earlier books ended with explosions, which allowed you to tie various plot strands together. But in recent stories and novels, like "Riding the Bullet" and *Cell*, you seem to have moved away from this. Your endings leave many questions unanswered.

KING

There is a pretty big bang at the end of *Cell*. But it's true, I get a lot of angry letters from readers about it. They want to know what happens next. My response now is to tell people, You guys sound like Teddy and Vern in *Stand by Me*, after Gordie tells them the story about Lardass and the pie-eating contest and how it was the best revenge a kid ever had. Teddy says, "Then what happened?" And Gordie says, "What do you mean, what happened? That's the end." And Teddy says, "Why don't you make it so that Lardass goes and he shoots his father, then he runs away and he joins the Texas Rangers?" Gordie says, "Ah, I don't know." So with *Cell*, the end is the end. But so many people wrote me about it that I finally had to write on my Web site, "It seems pretty obvious to me that things turned out well for Clay's son, Johnny." Actually, it never crossed my mind that Johnny wouldn't be OK.

INTERVIEWER

Really? I wasn't sure the kid was OK.

KING

Yeah, I actually believe that, man. I'm a fucking optimist!

INTERVIEWER

It's amazing that, in the introduction or afterword to many of your books, you regularly solicit feedback from your readers. Why do you ask for more letters?

KING

I'm always interested in what my readers think, and I'm aware that many of them want to participate in the story. I don't have a problem with that, just so long as they understand that what they think isn't necessarily going to change what I do. That is, I'm never going to say, I've got this story, here it is. Now here's a poll. How do you think I should end it?

INTERVIEWER

How important are your surroundings when you write?

KING

It's nice to have a desk, a comfortable chair so you're not shifting around all the time, and enough light. Wherever you write is supposed to be a little bit of a refuge, a place where you can get away from the world. The more closed in you are, the more you're forced back on your own imagination. I mean, if I were near a window, I'd be OK for a while, but then I'd be checking out the girls on the street and who's getting in and out of the cars and, you know, just the little street-side stories that are going on all the time: what's this one up to, what's that one selling?

My study is basically just a room where I work. I have a filing system. It's very complex, very orderly. With "Duma Key"—the novel I'm working on now—I've actually codified the notes to make sure I remember the different plot strands. I write down birth dates to figure out how old characters are at certain times. Remember to put a rose tattoo on this one's breast, remember to give Edgar a big workbench by the end of February. Because if I do something wrong now, it becomes such a pain in the ass to fix later.

INTERVIEWER

You mentioned wanting your study to feel like a refuge, but don't you also like to listen to loud music when you work?

KING

Not anymore. When I sit down to write, my job is to move the story. If there is such a thing as pace in writing, and if people read me because they're getting a story that's paced a certain way, it's because they sense I want to get to where I'm going. I don't want to dawdle around and look at the scenery. To achieve that pace I used to listen to music. But I was younger then, and frankly my brains used to work better than they do now. Now I'll only listen to music at the end of a day's work, when I roll back to the beginning of what I did that day and go over it on the screen. A lot of times the music will drive my wife crazy because it will be the same thing over and over and over again. I used to have a dance mix of that song "Mambo No. 5," by Lou Bega, that goes, "A little bit of Monica in my life, a little bit of Erica"—*deega, deega, deega*. It's a cheerful, calypso kind of thing, and my wife came upstairs one day and said, Steve, one more time . . . you die! So I'm not really listening to the music—it's just something there in the background.

But even more than place, I think it's important to try to work every day that you possibly can.

INTERVIEWER

Did you write this morning?

KING

I did. I wrote four pages. That's what it's come to. I used to write two thousand words a day and sometimes even more. But now it's just a paltry thousand words a day.

INTERVIEWER

You use a computer?

KING

Yes, but I've occasionally gone back to longhand—with *Dreamcatcher* and with *Bag of Bones*—because I wanted to see what would happen. It changed some things. Most of all, it made me slow down because it takes a long time. Every time I started to write something, some guy up here, some lazybones is saying, Aw, do we have to do that? I've still got a little bit of that scholar's bump on my finger from doing all that longhand. But it made the rewriting process a lot more felicitous. It seemed to me that my first draft was more polished, just because it wasn't possible to go so fast. You can only drive your hand along at a certain speed. It felt like the difference between, say, rolling along in a powered scooter and actually hiking the countryside.

INTERVIEWER

What do you do once you finish a first draft?

KING

It's good to give the thing at least six weeks to sit and breathe. But I don't always have that luxury. I didn't have it with *Cell*. The publisher had two manuscripts of mine. One of them was *Lisey's Story*, which I had been working on exclusively for a long time, and the other was *Cell*, which I had been thinking about for a long time, and it just sort of announced itself: It's time, you have to do it now. When that happens, you have to do it or let it go, so *Cell* was like my unplanned pregnancy.

INTERVIEWER

You mean you wrote *Cell* in the middle of writing *Lisey's Story*?

KING

I was carrying both of them at the same time for a while. I had finished a first draft of *Lisey*, so I revised it at night and worked on *Cell* during the day. I used to work that way when I was drinking. During the day I would work on whatever was fresh and new, and I was pretty much straight as an arrow. Hungover a lot of the time, but straight. At night I'd be looped, and that's when I would revise. It was fun, it was great, and it seemed to work for me for a long time, but I can't sustain that anymore.

I wanted to publish *Lisey* first, but Susan Moldow, Scribner's publisher, wanted to lead with *Cell* because she thought the attention it would receive would benefit the sale of *Lisey*. So they put *Cell* on a fast track, and I had to go right to work on the rewrite. This is one thing publishers can do now, which isn't always necessarily good for the book.

INTERVIEWER

Can't you tell them no?

KING

Yes, but in this case it was actually the right thing to do, and it was a huge success. *Cell* was an unusual case though. You know, Graham Greene used to talk about books that were novels and books that were entertainments. *Cell* was an entertainment. I don't want to say I didn't care, because I did—I care about anything that goes out with my name on it. If you're going to do the work and if someone is going to pay you for it, I think you ought to do the best job that you can. But after I finished the first draft of *Lisey*, I gave myself six weeks. When you return to a novel after that of time, it seems almost as if a different person wrote it. You're not quite as wedded to it. You find all sorts of horrible errors, but you also find passages that make you say, Jesus, that's good!

INTERVIEWER

Do you ever do extensive rewrites?

KING

One of the ways the computer has changed the way I work is that I have a much greater tendency to edit "in the camera"—to make changes on the screen. With *Cell* that's what I did. I read it over, I had editorial corrections, I was able to make my own corrections, and to me that's like ice skating. It's an OK way to do the work, but it isn't optimal. With *Lisey* I had the copy beside the computer and I created blank documents and retyped the whole thing. To me that's like swimming, and that's preferable. It's like you're writing the book over again. It is literally a rewriting.

Every book is different each time you revise it. Because when you finish the book, you say to yourself, This isn't what I meant to write at all. At some point, when you're actually writing the book, you realize that. But if you try to steer it, you're like a pitcher trying to steer a fastball, and you screw everything up. As the science-fiction writer Alfred Bester used to say, The book is the boss. You've got to let the book go where it wants to go, and you just follow along. If it doesn't do that, it's a bad book. And I've had bad books. I think *Rose Madder* fits in that category, because it never really took off. I felt like I had to force that one.

INTERVIEWER
Who edits your novels, and how much are they edited?

KING
Chuck Verrill has edited a lot of the books, and he can be a very hard editor. At Scribner, Nan Graham edited *Lisey*, and she gave me an entirely different look, partially because it's about a woman, and she's a woman, and also because she just came to the job fresh. She went over that book heavily. There's a scene late in the book where Lisey goes to visit her sister, Amanda, at a nuthouse where she's been committed. Originally there was a long scene in which Lisey stops at Amanda's house on her way there, and then Lisey ends up coming back later with her sister. Nan said, You need to reconfigure this section, you need to take out this first stop at Amanda's house because it slows down the narrative and it's not necessary.

I don't think it's me, I don't think it's a bestseller thing, I think it's a writer thing, and it goes across the board—it never changes—but my first thought was, She can't tell me that. She doesn't know. She's not a writer. She doesn't understand my genius! And then I say, Well, try it. And I say that especially loud, because I've reached a point in my career where I can have it any goddamn way I want to, if I want to. If you get popular enough, they give you all the rope you want. You can hang yourself in Times Square if you want to, and I've done it. Particularly in the days when I was doping and drinking all the time, I did what I wanted. And that included telling editors to go screw themselves.

INTERVIEWER

So if *Cell* is an entertainment, which of your books would you put in the other category?

KING

They should all be entertainments, you know. That is, in some ways, the nub of the problem. If a novel is not an entertainment, I don't think it's a successful book. But if you talk about the novels that work on more than one level, I would say *Misery*, *Dolores Claiborne*, and *It*. When I started to work on *It*, which bounces back and forth between the characters' lives as children and then as adults, I realized that I was writing about the way we use our imaginations at different points in our lives. I love that book, and it's one of those books that sells steadily. People really respond to it. I get a lot of letters from people who say, I wish there were more of it. And I say, Oh my God, it's so long as it is.

I think that *It* is the most Dickensian of my books because of its wide range of characters and intersecting stories. The novel manages a lot of complexity in an effortless way that I often wish I could rediscover. *Lisey's Story* is that way. It's very long. It has a number of interlocking stories that seem to be woven together effortlessly. But I'm shy talking about this, because I'm afraid people will laugh and say, Look at that barbarian trying to pretend he belongs in the palace. Whenever this subject comes up, I always cover up.

INTERVIEWER

When you accepted the National Book Award for Distinguished Contribution to American Letters, you gave a speech defending popular fiction, and you listed a number of authors who you felt were underappreciated by the literary establishment. Then Shirley Hazzard, that year's award winner in fiction, got on stage and dismissed your argument pretty flatly.

KING

What Shirley Hazzard said was, I don't think we need a reading list from you. If I had a chance to say anything in rebuttal, I would have said, With all due respect, we do. I think that Shirley, in a way, has proven my point. The keepers of the idea of serious literature have a short list of authors who are going to be allowed inside, and too often that list is drawn from people who know people, who go to certain schools, who come up through certain channels of literature. And that's a very bad idea—it's constraining for the growth of literature. This is a critical time for American letters because it's under attack from so many other media: TV, movies, the Internet, and all the different ways we have of getting nonprint input to feed the imagination. Books, that old way of transmitting stories, are under attack. So when someone like Shirley Hazzard says, I don't need a reading list, the door slams shut on writers like George Pelecanos or Dennis Lehane. And when that happens, when those people are left out in the cold, you are losing a whole area of imagination. Those people—and I'm not talking about James Patterson, we understand that—are doing important work.

So I'd say, yes, Shirley Hazzard does need a reading list. And the other thing Shirley Hazzard needs is for someone to say to her, Get busy. You have a short life span. You need to stop this crap about sitting there and talking about what we do, and actually do it. Because God gave you some talent, but he also gave you a certain number of years.

And one other thing. When you shut the door to serious popular fiction, you shut another door on people who are considered serious novelists. You say to them, You write popular, accessible fiction at your peril. So there aren't many writers who would take the chance that Philip Roth did when he wrote *The Plot Against America*. It was a risk for him to write that book because it's an accessible novel that can be read as entertainment. It is involving on a narrative level. That's a different book from Shirley Hazzard's *The Great Fire*—which, by the way, is a damn good book. But it's not the same thing at all.

INTERVIEWER

Is there really much of a difference, then, between serious popular fiction and literary fiction?

KING

The real breaking point comes when you ask whether a book engages you on an emotional level. And once those levers start to get pushed, many of the serious critics start to shake their heads and say, No. To me, it all goes back to this idea held by a lot of people who analyze literature for a living, who say, If we let the rabble in, then they'll see that anybody can do this, that it's accessible to anyone. And then what are *we* doing here?

INTERVIEWER

The use of brand names in your novels especially seems to irk some critics.

KING

I always knew people would have a problem with that. But I also knew that I was never going to stop doing it, and nobody was ever going to convince me that I was wrong to do it. Because every time I did it, what I felt inside was this little *bang!* like I nailed it dead square—like Michael Jordan on a fade-away jump shot. Sometimes the brand name is the perfect word, and it will crystallize a scene for me. When Jack Torrance is pumping down that Excedrin in *The Shining*, you know just what that is. I always want to ask these critics—some are novelists, some of them college literature professors—What the fuck do you do? Open your medicine cabinet and see empty gray bottles? Do you see generic shampoo, generic aspirin? When you go to the store and you get a six-pack, does it just say BEER? When you go down and you open your garage door, what's parked in there? A car? Just a car?

And then I say to myself, I bet they do. Some of these guys, the college professors—the guy, say, whose idea of literature really stopped with Henry James, but he'll get kind of a frozen smile on his face if you talk about Faulkner or Steinbeck—they're stupid about American fiction and they've turned their stupidity into a virtue. They don't know who Calder Willingham was. They don't know who Sloan Wilson was. They don't know who Grace Metalious was. They don't know who any of these people are, and they're fucking proud of it. And when they open their medicine cabinet door, I think maybe they do see generic bottles, and that's a failure of observation. And I think one of the things that I'm supposed to do is to say, It's a Pepsi, OK? It's not a soda. It's a Pepsi. It's a specific thing. Say what you mean. Say what you see. Make a photograph, if you can, for the reader.

INTERVIEWER

Do you ever feel typed by your reputation?

KING

If you mean, do I feel like I'm blocked in and I can't go where I want to go—not at all. No, I never did a bit. Other people will hang tags on me like the horrormeister, the schlockmeister, the fearmeister, the master of suspense, the master of horror. But I've never said what it is that I do, and I don't write letters complaining about these tags, because then it sounds like I'm trying to put on airs and make myself sound like something I'm not.

I remember having this conversation with Bill Thompson, my first editor, at Doubleday. They had just published *Carrie*, which was a big success, and they wanted a follow-up book. I gave him two other books I had already written: *'Salem's Lot* and *Roadwork*, which was later published under my pseudonym, Richard Bachman. I asked him which one he wanted to do first. He said, You're not going to like the answer. He said that *Roadwork* was a more honestly dealt novel—a novelist's novel, if you know what I mean—but that he wanted to do *'Salem's Lot*, because he thought it would have greater commercial success. But, he said to me, You'll get typed. And I said, Typed as what? He said, Typed as a horror writer. I just laughed. I thought, What? Like M. R. James and Edgar Allan Poe and Mary Shelley? I said, I don't care. It's nothing to me.

And they did type me as a horror writer, but I have been able to do all sorts of things within that framework. Only once in my entire career did I feel that it was a millstone, and that was when I did a book called *Needful Things*. I was in a sensitive place anyway, because it was the first thing that I'd written since I was sixteen without drinking or drugging. I was totally straight, except for cigarettes. When I finished the book, I thought, This is good. I've finally written something that's really funny. I thought that I'd written a satire of Reaganomics in America in the eighties. You know, people will buy anything and sell anything, even their souls. I always saw Leland Gaunt, the shop owner who buys souls, as the archetypal Ronald Reagan: charismatic, a little bit elderly, selling nothing but junk but it looks bright and shiny.

INTERVIEWER

Wait a minute. An autographed Sandy Koufax baseball card, nothing but junk? Come on.

KING

But that's not really what the kid's holding—it looks like a Sandy Koufax card, but it turns out it was somebody else's card entirely. And holy shit, was Sandy Koufax mad at me. Especially since the last thing the kid says is "Sandy Koufax sucks," and then, pow! He blows his head off. Koufax said that he had tried to be a role model for youth throughout his entire career as a pitcher, and that he was very angry about playing a part in a child suicide.

I tried to explain that the boy doesn't mean Sandy Koufax sucks, he means that Leland Gaunt and the shop and this whole business sucks. See, this is the only way that the character can say that this whole business of buying things and selling your soul is wrong. Koufax didn't understand. When they made the movie, they changed it to Mickey Mantle. Mantle didn't give a shit. He thought it was funny.

INTERVIEWER

What did you make of the negative reception of that book?

KING

The reviewers called it an unsuccessful horror novel, even though I had assumed everybody would see it as a satire. Over the years I've come to think that, well, maybe it just wasn't a very good book.

INTERVIEWER

Do you think a poorly received book gets a more serious critical response once it's made into a film?

KING

A movie tends to generate a lot more criticism, and frankly the criticism tends to be a little easier. It certainly happened for me with the adaptations of *Misery* and *Stand by Me*, and to a degree with *Dolores Claiborne*.

INTERVIEWER

You're something of a book collector. The book dealer Glenn Horowitz once told me that he sent you something by mistake and that when he apologized, you said you'd buy it anyway.

KING

I think that's true. I'm not a huge collector. I've probably got a dozen signed Faulkners and a lot of Theodore Dreiser. I've got *Reflections in a Golden Eye* by Carson McCullers. I love her. At home I've got one of those old-fashioned paperback racks they had in drugstores. And I have a lot of fifties paperbacks because I love the covers, and I've collected a certain amount of pornography from the sixties, paperback pornography that was done by people like Donald Westlake and Lawrence Block, just because it amuses me. You see little flashes of their style.

INTERVIEWER

What did you learn from writers like Faulkner, Dreiser, and McCullers?

KING

The voices. I'm reading *All the King's Men* again now, but I'm also listening to it on CD. And the guy who does it is a good reader. Willie Stark goes, "There is always something. . . . from the stink of the didie to the stench of the shroud. There is always something." You hear it and you say to yourself, Oh man, that's the voice! It just clicks in your head.

INTERVIEWER

You're rooted in a kind of American idiom. You're probably the most regional writer now writing.

KING

I've lived in Maine my whole life, and when I write about it, the dialect comes back to me. There are a number of good writers who are writing about that area, but they're not read a whole lot. There's Carolyn Chute, who wrote *The Beans of Egypt, Maine*, and John Gould, who wrote *The Greenleaf Fires*—but I'm the one that's widely read. In terms of regionalism, Grisham's a pretty good writer, and his book *A Painted House* is a terrific regional story about the South.

INTERVIEWER

You seem to go out of your way to promote other writers—giving favorable comments to new authors and referring to other contemporary authors throughout your novels. Are you really admiring of so many of them?

KING

When I read good stories, I get excited. I'm also aware of how small the market is. I've been fantastically fortunate, and I would like to spread some of that fortune around. Short stories are where I started. I came out of the story magazine market. Books themselves have become a niche market, short stories are an even smaller market, and so you want to make people as aware as possible that this stuff is out there.

INTERVIEWER

Now that you're editing next year's Best American Short Stories, are you considering stories from the kind of genre magazines that you read as a kid?

KING

Yes, I'm reading all the fantasy and science-fiction journals, especially *Ellery Queen Mystery Magazine* and *Alfred Hitchcock Mystery Magazine*, to see what's there. *Alfred Hitchcock* used to be a literary-quality magazine, but it's been subsumed by the same company that owns *Ellery Queen*, and the quality of stories has gone downhill. Editing Best American is a good project, but it's scary because there's so much out there. What haunts me is, what are we missing?

INTERVIEWER

When do you write your own short stories?

KING

I often write them between novel projects. When *Lisey* and *Cell* got done, I was flat. I tried to start another one, but I couldn't, so I wrote a couple of short stories. Then I began to read all these stories for Best American—a dozen, two dozen, three dozen, a hundred—and finally I got rolling on another novel. I mean, I've always got a couple of ideas for future stories whenever I'm working on something. But you can't think about what you're going to do next. You're like a married guy who's trying not to look at women in the street.

INTERVIEWER

Were you ever like the writer Mike Noonan in *Bag of Bones*, who would finish a novel and stash it because he had too many stocked up?

KING

There might have been a time in my life where I had two or three backed up. The inspiration for that detail in *Bag of Bones* came from a rumor I heard that Danielle Steel was writing three books a year and publishing two. And I was saying, If that's true over the last ten years, she must have a lot piled up. And there are other writers in the popular canon like that—Nora Roberts has published, my God, over a hundred and fifty books. And people think that I'm prolific.

You have used many different strategies to market your books—serialization, e-books, excerpting a forthcoming novel at the end of a new novel. Is there any kind of larger strategy at play?

KING

No, I'm just curious to see what happens, like a kid with a chemistry set: What if I pour these two together? The Internet publishing experiment was probably a way of saying to the publishers, You know, I don't necessarily need to go through you. I also wanted to break some trail for some other people. And it's a way of keeping things fresh.

Scribner asked me if I had a short story they could publish online. But their focus was never, in fact, the Internet. They were thinking more about these little gadgets that let you read a book in your hand, where you push a button to turn the page. I never liked the idea and most people don't. They want to have pages. We're like people who bought cars in the 1910s, and they would break down by the side of the road and people would yell, Get a horse! Now people yell, Get a book! It's the same deal. But all the excitement over online publication was interesting to me because people who had never talked to me before—business guys, suits—suddenly took notice. What are you doing? Can you do it all yourself? Are you going to be able to change publishing? It was always the bucks that were driving the interest. It was never about the stories.

This was at the very end of the dot-com bubble—the last big exciting thing that happened before the crash. Arthur C. Clarke had already sold a piece on the Internet—a six-page deal on broadcasts coming back from the stars—and I thought to myself, Jesus, this is like kissing your sister! It was a little essay that this guy probably flipped off in an afternoon when he couldn't take his nap.

INTERVIEWER

Since the Scribner story, "Riding the Bullet," was a big success, why did you stop publishing online? You ended your next online project, "The Plant," after just six installments.

KING

Many people thought that I didn't finish "The Plant" because the marketing strategy was unsuccessful. That's one of the few times that I felt a gentle but firm media push toward untruth. In fact, "The Plant" was very, very successful. And I published it on the honor system. With "Riding the Bullet" there was all this talk about people trying to hack the system to get it for free. And I thought, Well, yes, this is what these Internet people do. They don't do it because they want to steal it, they do it because they want to see if they *can* steal it. It's a game. And so I thought, Well, if you just say, look, here it is—it's like a newspaper honor rack. If you really want to be that much of a schmo, that much of a palooka, go ahead and steal it! Hope you feel good about yourself, turkey! And most people paid for what they took. I think some people still wanted to see if they could steal it, and then after that they paid.

I made almost two hundred thousand dollars, with no overhead. It was incredible when you think about it. All I did was write the stories and we set up a server. It was like a license to coin money, if I can be vulgar about it. But the story was just OK, and I ran out of inspiration. It remains unfinished.

INTERVIEWER

The relationship of your writing to money is now, I assume, beyond a sense of survival. Does it still mean anything to you?

KING

I think you should be paid for what you do. Every morning, I wake up to the alarm clock, do my leg exercises, and then sit down at the word processor. By noon my back aches and I'm tired out. I work as hard or harder than I used to, so I want to be paid. But basically, at this point, it's how you keep score.

One thing that I don't want to do anymore is take another monster advance. I've taken a couple of them. Certainly Tom Clancy has gotten his share of them. He boasts about them. John Grisham has gotten some big advances too. The big advance is the writer's way of saying, I want to get all the money up front and I'm never going to give a penny of it back when those books wind up on the remainder shelf. And the publishers go along because they would like to have a Stephen King or a Tom Clancy or a John Grisham. It draws attention to the rest of their list. Certainly the bookstore guys want those writers out there because they increase foot traffic into the store. The booksellers just about get down on their knees and worship John Grisham, not just because he sells as much as he does, but because he sells it when he does: he publishes in February, after the Christmas rush, when trade in the bookstores has a tendency to be totally dead.

I could get those big advances, but I can do just fine without them. I made a decision when I left Viking that I'd ask to be made a partner in the publishing. Give me a modest amount to bind the deal over, and then we'll split the profits. Why not? It's still a good deal for them. But if I were doing it just for the money I'd quit, because I've got enough.

INTERVIEWER

But did you ever feel you had to make as big a score as someone like Clancy or Danielle Steel?

KING

We're a competitive society, and I think I have a tendency to measure whether I'm as successful as one of these guys based on the amount of money that I can get. But the bottom line is always sales, and these guys outsell me. Grisham outsells me four to one. It's not a big deal to me anymore. Sometimes you look at the bestseller list in *The New York Times* and you say, Do I really want to bust my ass to be on this list along with Danielle Steel and David Baldacci and the born-again books?

INTERVIEWER

It's now been seven years since the accident. Are you still in pain?

KING

Yes. All the time. But I don't take anything for it anymore. I had to be hospitalized with pneumonia a couple of years ago, another operation, and after that it got to a point where I realized that I couldn't go on taking medication forever, because I'd have to be loading it on by the boxcar. At that time I'd been taking painkillers for five years. Percocet, OxyContin, all that stuff. I was addicted. If you're using it for pain and not using it to get high, it isn't terribly difficult to quit. The trouble is, you have to get used to living without it. You go through withdrawal. Mostly it's insomnia. But after a while your body says, Oh, all right!

INTERVIEWER

Do you still smoke cigarettes?

KING

Three a day, and never when I write. But when there's only three, they taste pretty good. My doctor says, You know, if you're going to have three you might as well have thirty, but I don't. I kicked booze, Valium, cocaine. Those were all the things that I was hooked on. The only thing that I could not kick was cigarettes. Usually I have one in the morning, one at night, one in the afternoon. I do enjoy my cigarettes. And I shouldn't. I know, I know. Smoking, bad! Health, good! But I sure do like to kick back with a good book and a cigarette. I was thinking this the other night. I came back from the ball game; the Red Sox won. And I was lying on the bed reading *The Quiet American* by Graham Greene. It's a terrific, terrific book. I'm smoking a cigarette, and I'm thinking, Who's got it better than me?

Cigarettes, all those addictive substances are part of the bad side of what we do. I think it's part of that obsessive deal that makes you a writer in the first place, that makes you want to write it all down. Booze, cigarettes, dope.

INTERVIEWER

Does that mean that writing is a kind of addiction?

KING

I think it is. For me, even when the writing is not going well, if I don't do it, the fact that I'm not doing it nags at me. Writing is a wonderful thing to be able to do. When it goes well, it's fantastic, and when it doesn't go so well, it's only OK, but it's still a great way to pass the time. And you have all these novels to show for it.

INTERVIEWER

Do you still go to AA?

KING

Yes. I try to go on a regular basis.

INTERVIEWER

How do you feel about the religious aspect of it?

KING

I don't have any problem with that at all. It says in the program if you don't believe, pretend that you do. Fake it till you make it, they say. And I know that a lot of people have problems with that, but I follow the program. So I get down on my knees in the morning and say, God help me to not think of drink and drugs. And I get down on my knees at night and say, Thank you that I didn't have to drink or use.

Whenever I speak about this, I tell people the story about that movie *Pink Flamingos* that John Waters made with Divine, this big fat female impersonator. There's a scene in *Pink Flamingos* where Divine eats a piece of dog excrement off the sidewalk. Waters was always asked about that particular scene. Finally, one time he exploded and said, Listen, it was just a little piece of dog shit and it made her a star! OK? As far as I'm concerned, the whole issue of God is a little piece of dog shit. But if you can swallow that part of the AA program, you don't have to drink and drug anymore.

INTERVIEWER

Have you ever been in therapy of any kind?

KING

When I was quitting drugs and alcohol, I went for a while to a counselor to see if I could find a way to get over that absence in my life. But if you're talking about real psychotherapy, I'd be afraid that it would put a hole in the bottom of my bucket, and then everything might go out the wrong way. I don't know if it would exactly destroy me as a writer, but I think it would take away a lot of the good stuff.

INTERVIEWER

Do you ever think about where your creations are coming from while you're in the process of writing?

KING

Once in a while, something will declare itself so obviously that it's inescapable. Take the psychotic nurse in *Misery*, which I wrote when I was having such a tough time with dope. I knew what I was writing about. There was never any question. Annie was my drug problem, and she was my number-one fan. God, she never wanted to leave. And at the same time, there was a funny side to all that. A lot of times those things will come up. I remember working on the end of *Black House*, the book I wrote with Peter Straub, and coming to a scene where one of the characters is talking about never being able to go back to this plane of existence—American life in the year 2001 or 2002—because this person would sicken and die if that happened. And I was thinking that it was an elegant way to describe where I was coming from at that time. I was in pain a lot of the time, but when I was writing, I felt fine, because I would be . . . wherever you go when you're making these things up. When I go there, I'm not physically aware of my body very much. And I was thinking, this is a pretty good analogue to the creative state. It's a place where you can go and feel well.

INTERVIEWER

At what point in the process of writing a story do you know whether any fantastic elements will come into play?

KING

It doesn't come because I want it to. I don't force it through that door. It just comes. Thing is, I love it. "Duma Key," the novel I'm writing now, is about a guy named Edgar Freemantle who has an accident and loses an arm. So right away I'm thinking, maybe there's some paranormal symptomatology with missing limbs. I knew that people who lose limbs have phantom sensations long after the accident.

So I Google "phantom limbs" to see how long the sensation lasts. I love Google. It turns out there are thousands of recorded instances, and the best one—and I put this in the book—is a guy who lost his hand in a baler. And he picked the hand up, wrapped it in a bandanna, took it home, and put it in a jar filled with alcohol. He put the jar in his cellar. Two years go by. The guy's fine. And then one day, in the winter, it's freezing cold at the end of his arm, where his hand used to be. He calls the doctor. He says, The hand is no longer there, but it's cold as hell at the end of my arm. The doctor says, What did you do with the hand? He says, I put it in a jar, it's down in the cellar. The doctor says, Go down and check it. So the guy goes downstairs. The jar was on a shelf and the window had broken and the cold wind was blowing in on the hand. So he moved the jar by the furnace and he was all right. This is a true story, apparently.

INTERVIEWER

Recently, and especially in *Lisey's Story*, it seems as if you're starting with a character instead of a situation. Do you think you're doing something differently?

KING

There might be a shift. It certainly wasn't the case with *Cell*, but *Cell* was an old idea. *Lisey*, on the other hand, is about character. I had the idea three or four years after my accident. I thought I was all better, but it turned out that the bottom part of my lung was still all crumpled up. I got pneumonia, and they ended up taking my lung right out of my chest in order to repair it. I almost died. It was really close. During this period, my wife decided that she was going to redo my study. When I came back from the hospital, everything had been pulled out, and I felt like a ghost. I thought, Maybe I died. This is what the study would look like after I died. So I started to write this story about a famous writer who died, and about his wife, Lisey, who is trying to get on with her life two years later.

Lisey just took off and went on its own. At some point it stopped being a book specifically about this woman's grieving process and it started to be a book about the way we hide things. From there it jumped into the idea that repression is creation, because when we repress we make up stories to replace the past.

INTERVIEWER

What does your wife think of the book?

KING

She never said that much about *Lisey's Story*, but then a lot of times she doesn't. A lot of times she'll just say, Good. I think anybody wants their wife to say, Oh, honey! This is great! And I love this part, and I love that part! But she's not that kind of person. "Good" is fine.

INTERVIEWER

Do you feel that *Lisey's Story* is a departure for you?

KING

Well, I am the wrong person to ask. I'm inside it, and to me it feels like a very special book. To the point where I don't want to let it out into the world. This is the only book I've ever written where I don't want to read the reviews, because there will be some people who are going to be ugly to this book. I couldn't stand that, the way you would hate people to be ugly to someone you love. And I love this book.

INTERVIEWER

Why do you think they'll be particularly ugly?

KING

Because it does try to do more than be a popular novel. It wants, on one level, to be taken more seriously than, let's say, a Mary Higgins Clark or a Jonathan Kellerman. When a writer spends a part of his life on a book, he has an obligation to ask himself, Why does it matter? And when I finished that book I thought to myself, Well, to some degree this is a book about myth, depression, and story making, but it's also about marriage and about faithfulness.

INTERVIEWER

Now that you've been published in *The New Yorker* and been honored with a National Book Award and other international awards, it seems pretty clear that you're taken more seriously than you were earlier in your career. Do you still feel a strong sense of exclusion from the literary establishment?

KING

It has changed a lot. You know what happens? If you have a little talent and you try to maximize it and you don't give in or settle, then you're taken more seriously. People who have grown up reading you become part of the literary establishment. They take you as part of the landscape that was there when they came along. In some ways you get a squarer shake. When Martin Levin from *The New York Times* reviewed *The Stand* he said it was "the plague novel goes to the devil" and he called it the "son of *Rosemary's Baby*." I thought, Oh my God, I worked on this book for three years to have this guy say that. As a writer, I've always been extremely conscious of my place. I've never tried to be highfalutin or to put myself on a level with my betters. I'm serious about what I do, but I never wanted to indicate to anybody that I was better than what I was.

The other major thing is that you get older. I'm pushing sixty now. I might have another ten creative years left, maybe fifteen. I say to myself,

I've got this amount of time, can I do something that's even better? I don't need the money. I don't need another movie based on one of my books. I don't need to write another screenplay. I don't need another big butt-ugly house to live in—I have this one. I'd like to write a book that's better than *Lisey's Story*, but I don't know if I ever will. Gosh, I'd like not to repeat myself. I'd like not to do shoddy work. But I'd like to keep working. I reject the idea that I've explored everything in the room.

Issue 178, 2006

Contributors

James Baldwin (1924–1987) was born in Harlem in New York City, where at age fourteen he became a preacher at a Pentecostal church. With the encouragement of Richard Wright and the painter Beauford Delaney he moved to Paris in 1948 to pursue a writing career. He remained in France for most of his life, though he returned to the United States to take part in the civil-rights movement. In 1953 he published his first novel, *Go Tell It on the Mountain*, to great acclaim. His best-known works include the collection of essays *Notes of a Native Son* (1953); the short story "Sonny's Blues" (1957); and the nonfiction book *The Fire Next Time* (1963). Baldwin won many prizes and honors, among them the George Polk Award for Journalism for his writings in *The New Yorker*, a Guggenheim Fellowship, a Partisan Review fellowship, and a Ford Foundation grant. He was made a Commander of the French Legion of Honor in 1986. **Jordan Elgrably,** formerly a Paris- and Madrid-based correspondent, is a writer whose work has appeared in numerous periodicals and anthologies. He is the author of the forthcoming novel *The Book of Love and Exile* and coeditor with Sholeh Wolpé of the anthology *Iconoclasts and Visionaries*. He is the founder and artistic director of Levantine Cultural Center in Los Angeles.
Harold Bloom was born in 1930 in New York City, the son of Russian and Polish immigrants. He graduated from Cornell University in 1951 and spent a year at Pembroke College, Cambridge, as a Research Fellow. After receiving a Ph.D. in English from Yale in 1955 he joined the Yale faculty and has remained there ever since. One of the most prolific critics in the English language, he has written more than twenty books, including *The Anxiety of Influence* (1973), *Ruin the Sacred Truths* (1989), *The Western Canon* (1994), and *Shakespeare: The Invention of the Human* (1998). He has received numerous awards, including a Fulbright Fellowship, a

Guggenheim Fellowship, a MacArthur Fellowship, the Zabel Prize from the American Institute of Arts and Letters, and the Christian Gauss Award. His most recent book is *The American Religion* (2006). **Antonio Weiss,** a former senior editor of *The Paris Review*, is managing director of the investment bank Lazard and a member of the board of directors of The Paris Review Foundation.

Peter Carey was born in Bacchus Marsh, Victoria, Australia, in 1943. He attended Monash University in Melbourne where he studied chemistry and zoology, but he left without completing his degree and went to work as a copywriter in an advertising company. He began writing fiction in 1964, and four years later he had written three novels, none of which were published. He left Australia to travel and settled for a short time in London, where he worked in advertising before returning home. Carey's first collection of stories, *The Fat Man in History*, was published in Australia in 1974 to critical acclaim. It was followed by a novel, *Bliss* (1981), which won two major Australian literary awards and was made into a feature film, for which Carey wrote the screenplay. His next novel, *Illywhacker* (1985), was short-listed for the Booker Prize, an award he won for *Oscar and Lucinda* (1988) and a second time for *True History of the Kelly Gang* (2000). His other critically acclaimed novels include *The Tax Inspector* (1991), *The Unusual Life of Tristan Smith* (1994), *Jack Maggs* (1997), *My Life as a Fake* (2003), and *Theft: A Love Story* (2006). **Radhika Jones** is the managing editor of *The Paris Review*.

William Faulkner (1897–1962) was born in New Albany, Mississippi, to a genteel Southern family and was awarded the Nobel Prize for Literature in 1949. He worked as a bank clerk, postmaster, roof painter, carpenter, and deckhand before becoming a full-time writer in 1925. He published his first novel, *Soldiers' Pay*, in 1926 but it was his fourth novel, *The Sound and the Fury* (1929), that proved to be his breakthrough. *As I Lay Dying* (1930), *Light in August* (1932), and *Absalom, Absalom!* (1936) established Faulkner as the preeminent voice of the American South. During the nineteen thirties and forties he wrote screenplays, first for Metro-Goldwyn-Mayer, then for several other studios. Among the best known are *To Have and Have Not* (1945), based on the novel by Ernest Hemingway, and *The Big Sleep* (1946), based on the novel by Dashiell Hammett. After receiving the Nobel Prize, Faulkner went on to win two National Book Awards, two Pulitzer Prizes, and a Gold Medal for Fiction from the National Institute of Arts and Letters. With his Nobel winnings, Faulkner established a fund to support new fiction writers, which ultimately became the PEN/Faulkner Award for Fiction. **Jean Stein** is an author and theater producer. She was editor and publisher of *Grand Street* magazine from 1990 to 2004.

William Gaddis (1922–1998) was born in New York City and raised by his mother in Massapequa, Long Island, after his parents separated in 1925. Gaddis matriculated at Harvard in 1941 but was asked to leave before finishing his degree on account of an incident of rowdiness. He worked as a fact-checker at *The New Yorker* for a year, then spent five years traveling around Central America, Europe, and Africa. In 1955 Gaddis published his first novel, *The Recognitions*, a reworking of the story of Faust, to mixed reviews. He did not publish another novel for twenty years. He supported his family by working in a public-relations position at the pharmaceutical company Pfizer, and he wrote scripts for promotional films for the United States Army. His second novel, *JR*, a satire of big business, won the 1976 National Book Award for Fiction. Gaddis was awarded a Guggenheim Fellowship in 1981 and MacArthur Fellowship in 1982, which enabled him to complete his third novel, *Carpenter's Gothic* (1985). He wrote two more novels in his lifetime, *A Frolic of His Own* (1994) and *Agapē, Agape* (2002), which was published after his death from prostate cancer in 1998. **Zoltán Abádi-Nagy** is a professor of English at the University of Debrecen, Hungary, and editor of the *Hungarian Journal of English and American Studies*. He is the author of numerous books, including a monograph study of Jonathan Swift and a book on entropy and comedy in the American novel of the sixties. He has translated the work of John Barth, Walker Percy, and many other American writers into Hungarian.

Gabriel García Márquez was born in 1928 in Aracataca, northern Colombia, and won the Nobel Prize for Literature in 1982. He began writing for newspapers while pursuing a law degree, and his first story, "The Third Resignation," was published in 1947 by the newspaper *El Espectador*. He abandoned his legal studies in 1950. Traveling in Europe and South America, he continued to write both short stories and journalistic pieces, collected in *Leaf Storm and Other Stories* (1955), *No One Writes to the Colonel and Other Stories* (1961), and *In Evil Hour*, among others. His novel *One Hundred Years of Solitude* (1967) established him as one of the greatest Latin American writers and the creator of magical realism. In 1985 he published *Love in the Time of Cholera* to critical acclaim; it was followed by *The General in His Labyrinth* (1990) and *Of Love and Other Demons* (1994). In 1999, García Márquez was diagnosed with lymphatic cancer, which encouraged him to begin work on a three-volume autobiography, the first part of which, *Living to Tell the Tale*, was published in 2002. A new work of fiction, *Memories of My Melancholy Whores*, was published in 2004. **Peter H. Stone** is the author of *Heist: Superlobbyist Jack Abramoff, His Republican Allies and the Buying of Washington*, published in 2006 by Farrar, Straus and Giroux. He has been a staff correspondent since 1992 for the magazine *National Journal*. Stone's articles have appeared in such publications as *The Washington Post*, *The New York Times*, *The Atlantic Monthly*, *Mother Jones*, *The American Prospect*, and *The Nation*.

John Gardner (1933–1982) was born in Batavia, New York, to a farmer and a schoolteacher who loved literature so much they quoted Shakespeare while milking the cows. When he was eleven, his six-year-old brother was killed in a farming accident in which Gardner was involved, an event that would figure prominently in his writing. He graduated from Washington University in St. Louis and received a Ph.D. in classical and medieval literature from what is now the University of Iowa. His fiction includes *Grendel* (1971), a retelling of *Beowulf* from the perspective of the monster, and *October Light* (1976), which won the National Book Critics Circle Award. He published several books of literary criticism, most notably the controversial *On Moral Fiction* (1978), an attack on what he perceived as the moral decrepitude of the contemporary novel. He was also the author of six books for children, three opera librettos, a translation of *Gilgamesh* (with John R. Maier), and a biography of Chaucer. He died in a motorcycle accident near his home in Susquehanna, Pennsylvania. **Paul Ferguson** (1943–2005) was an instructor in English at the State University of New York at Brockport and the author of the short story collection *Cleaning Up the Mess*. **John R. Maier** is a Distinguished Teaching Professor Emeritus of English at SUNY Brockport and is the author or coauthor of six books and more than fifty articles. He is working on a study of the ancient Iraq city of Uruk. He is also writing a book about the epic of *Gilgamesh* and editing a journal he kept in Syria and Jordan from 1979 to 1980. **Sara Matthiessen** is a graduate of Bennington College and has worked as a television journalist. **Frank McConnell** (1942–1999) was a professor of English, the author of a series of detective novels, including *Murder Among Friends* and *Liar's Poker*, and the media correspondent for the Catholic journal *Commonweal* for over fifteen years.

Graham Greene (1904–1991) was born in Hertfordshire, England, and educated at Balliol College, Oxford. He graduated in 1925 and published his first book of verse, *Babbling April*, the same year. In 1926 he converted to Roman Catholicism. Greene achieved some success with his first novel, *The Man Within* (1929), and continued to write prolifically through the start of World War II. He traveled widely in the 1930s, eventually spending time in the Far East, Latin America, and Africa, including a stint during the war as an MI6 agent in Sierra Leone. In 1941 Greene won the Hawthornden Prize for *The Power and the Glory*, and he went on to achieve further critical and popular success with novels such as *The Heart of the Matter* (1948) and *The End of the Affair* (1951). These explicitly Catholic works Greene distinguished from what he called his "entertainments," books written purely for the enjoyment of the narrative. Greene continued to publish novels until his death, also working extensively on nonfiction, drama, children's literature, and screenplays, including *The Third Man*. *Ways of Escape*, an autobiography, was published in 1980. **Simon Raven** (1927–2001) was an English novelist, dramatist, and essayist. He was the author of thirty-four books, including the ten-volume Alms for Oblivion series, and also wrote scripts for popular British television series such as *The Pallisers* and *Edward and Mrs. Simpson*. **Martin Shuttleworth** (1929–1999) was an English writer, filmmaker, and teacher. His translation of Diego Hurtado de Mendoza's *The War in Granada* was published in 1982. He held a number of teaching positions during his career, among them head of Liberal Studies at Leicester College, and tutor and librarian at the West Surrey College of Art and Design.

Stephen King was born in Portland, Maine, and has lived in Maine for most of his life. He attended the University of Maine at Orono, where he wrote a column for the campus newspaper. By the time he graduated in 1970 with a B.A. in English, he had already published his first story, "The Glass Floor," in *Startling Mystery Stories*. In 1971 King began teaching English at Hampden Academy, where he remained for two years until the runaway success of his first novel, *Carrie*. In the years that followed, King wrote *'Salem's Lot* (1975), *The Shining* (1977), and *The Stand* (1978) before taking a position as writer-in-residence at his alma mater. Among his many works are *Pet Sematary* (1983), *It* (1986), *Misery* (1987), *The Green Mile* (1996), *Lisey's Story* (2006), and the seven books of the Dark Tower series, as well as six novels published under the pen name Richard Bachman. King has won numerous Bram Stoker Awards from the Horror Writers Association as well as the O. Henry Prize. In 2003 he was awarded the National Book Foundation Medal for Distinguished Contribution to American Letters. **Christopher Lehmann-Haupt** was for four decades senior daily book reviewer then chief obituary writer for *The New York Times*. He is now editorial director of Delphinium Books. He is the author of a baseball memoir and two novels and is writing a memoir about Berlin. **Nathaniel Rich** is the senior editor of *The Paris Review* and the author of *San Francisco Noir*. His first novel, *The Mayor's Tongue*, is forthcoming from Riverhead.

Philip Larkin (1922–1985) was born in Coventry, England. He attended St John's College, Oxford, alongside Kingsley Amis, who was to become a lifelong friend. Exempt from military service because of his poor eyesight, he graduated in 1943 and became a librarian. In 1955 he was appointed librarian of the University of Hull's Brynmor Jones Library, a position he kept for the rest of his life. In 1945 ten of his poems were published in *Poetry from Oxford in Wartime*; they were later included in his first collection, *The North Ship*. In 1946 he published a novel, *Jill*; a second novel, *A Girl in Winter*, followed the next year. His next two collections of poems, *The Less Deceived* (1955) and *The Whitsun Weddings* (1964), secured his reputation as one of the foremost figures in twentieth-century poetry. *High Windows*, his last collection, was published in 1974. His lifelong love of jazz was immortalized in a collection of his monthly reviews of jazz recordings for the *Daily Telegraph*, titled *All What Jazz*. He received many awards for his contribution to writing, including the Queen's Gold Medal for Poetry, and was named a Commander of the British Empire in 1975. In 1984 he was offered the post of poet laureate but declined the honor. **Robert Phillips** is the author of thirty books of poetry, fiction, and nonfiction. He has contributed five interviews to *The Paris Review*. He is Moores Professor of English at the University of Houston.

Robert Lowell (1917–1977) was born into a wealthy Boston family that counted the poets James Russell and Amy Lowell among its ranks. Educated at St. Mark's School and briefly at Harvard, he began early in life to suffer bouts of psychological breakdown and violent temper that would plague him throughout his life. After dropping out of Harvard at age twenty, Lowell studied with John Crowe Ransom and Allen Tate at Kenyon College. He published his first book of poetry, *Land of Unlikeness*, in 1944, and two years later his second collection, *Lord Weary's Castle*, won the Pulitzer Prize. Lowell continued to publish poetry while traveling around Europe for several years. He returned to Boston in 1953, where he began work on *Life Studies* (1959), a free-verse sequence of poems that won the National Book Award. He followed up his next book, *For the Union Dead* (1964), with the trilogy of plays *The Old Glory* (1965), based on works by Nathaniel Hawthorne and Herman Melville. In 1974 he won his second Pulitzer Prize for *The Dolphin*, a book of unrhymed sonnets. **Frederick Seidel,** a former Paris editor of *The Paris Review*, is the author of twelve books of poems, of which the most recent is *Ooga-Booga* (2006).

Toni Morrison, who won the Nobel Prize for Literature in 1993, was born Chloe Anthony Wofford in Lorain, Ohio, in 1931. She received a B.A. in English from Howard University, becoming the first in her family to earn a college degree. She also holds an M.A. from Cornell University as well as more than fifteen honorary degrees. She published her first novel, *The Bluest Eye* (1970), while working as an editor at Random House. The novels *Sula* (1973), *Song of Solomon* (1977), and *Tar Baby* (1981) followed, and she won the Pulitzer Prize for *Beloved*, published in 1987. Her most recent novel is *Love* (2003). Her numerous awards include the American Book Award, the National Book Critics Circle Award, and the American Academy and Institute of Arts and Letters Award. Morrison recently retired from Princeton University, where she was the Robert F. Goheen Professor of Humanities for seventeen years. **Claudia Brodsky Lacour** is professor of comparative literature at Princeton University and author of *The Imposition of Form: Studies in Narrative Representation and Knowledge* (1987), *Lines of Thought: Discourse, Architectonics and the Origin of Modern Philosophy* (1996), and a forthcoming book titled *In the Place of Language*. She is the coeditor, with Toni Morrison, of *Birth of a Nation'hood* (1997). **Elissa Schappell,** a former senior editor of *The Paris Review*, is the author of *Use Me* and the editor, with Jenny Offill, of the anthologies *The Friend Who Got Away* and *Money Changes Everything*. She is cofounder and editor at large of *Tin House* magazine, a contributing editor to *Vanity Fair*, and a frequent contributor to *The New York Times Book Review*.

Alice Munro was born Alice Laidlaw in 1931 in Wingham, Ontario. Nearly all her fiction is set in the rural regions of her native southwestern Ontario. She published her first collection of stories when she was thirty-seven, and has since published eleven collections of short stories and one novel, *Lives of Girls and Women* (1971). Her first book, *Dance of the Happy Shades* (1968), won the Governor-General's Literary Award, Canada's highest literary prize; she won it again for *The Beggar Maid* (1978) and a third time for *The Progress of Love* (1986). She received the National Book Critics Circle Award for Fiction for *The Love of a Good Woman* (1998). Her most recent work is a collection of short stories, *The View from Castle Rock* (2006). **Jeanne McCulloch,** a former *Paris Review* editor, is a former editor of *Tin House* and the founding editorial director of Tin House Books. Her work has appeared in *Vogue*, *Tin House*, and *The New York Times Book Review*, among other publications. She is writing a memoir to be published by Bloomsbury USA, an excerpt of which appeared in the anthology *Money Changes Everything* (2007). **Mona Simpson,** a former senior editor of *The Paris Review*, is the author of four novels: *Anywhere But Here* (1987), *The Lost Father* (1992), *A Regular Guy* (1996), and *Off Keck Road* (2000), which was nominated for the PEN/Faulkner award.

Isaac Bashevis Singer (1904–1991), born Icek-Hersz Zynger in Leoncin, Poland, was awarded the Nobel Prize for Literature in 1978, the first and only primarily Yiddish writer to win the award. His father and grandfather were Hasidic rabbis, and at the age of seventeen Singer entered a rabbinical seminary in Warsaw but left within a year. Influenced by his older brother Israel Joshua, also a writer, he was introduced to the Warsaw Yiddish Writers' Club in 1923 and began working as a proofreader and translator. His first novel, *Satan in Goray*, was published in Yiddish in 1935. The same year he parted from his wife and son and followed his brother to New York. There he wrote for the Yiddish newspaper the *Forward*, which published many of his short stories. In 1950 he published a novel, *The Family Moskat*. Shortly thereafter, Irving Howe discovered Singer's work when he was selecting material for the anthology *A Treasury of Yiddish Stories*. Howe persuaded Saul Bellow to translate the story "Gimpel the Fool," and in 1953 it appeared in *Partisan Review*. Singer's stories were subsequently published in *The New Yorker*, *Harper's*, *Vogue*, and *Playboy*, translated into almost a dozen languages, and adapted for Broadway and the screen. After the mid-1960s he focused increasingly on his writing for children. **Harold Flender** (1924–1975) was a writer and filmmaker. His first novel, *Paris Blues*, became a successful motion picture starring Paul Newman and Sidney Poitier. He was also the author of *Rescue in Denmark*, the true story of the rescue of the Danish Jews during World War II, and *We Were Hooked*, a collection of interviews with former drug addicts.

James Thurber (1894–1961) was born in Columbus, Ohio. He entered Ohio State University in 1913 but left five years later without a degree. He worked as a code clerk for the U.S. State Department in Washington and later at the U.S. Embassy in Paris. Returning to Columbus in 1920, he joined *The Columbus Dispatch* as a reporter. In 1926 Thurber published his first short story, "Josephine Has Her Day," after his wife encouraged him to try writing fiction. His journalism career took him to France and then New York, where he joined the staff of *The New Yorker* alongside E. B. White, contributing short fiction, poems, drawings, nonfiction pieces, and photographs. *The Owl in the Attic*, a collection of his *New Yorker* stories and drawings, was published in 1931. He went on to publish several more collections of short stories and children's books even after years of deteriorating eyesight left him legally blind in 1951. Thurber died of pneumonia in 1961 in New York. **George Plimpton** was the editor of *The Paris Review* from its inaugural issue in 1953 until his death in 2003. He was the author of numerous books, including the bestselling works of participatory journalism *Paper Lion* (1966) and *Open Net* (1985). **Max Steele** (1922–2005) was a fiction writer and professor of English at the University of North Carolina at Chapel Hill, where he directed the creative writing program for twenty years. His books include *Debby*, *The Cat and the Coffee Drinkers*, and the story collections *Where She Brushed Her Hair* and *The Hat of My Mother*.

Eudora Welty (1909–2001) was born in Jackson, Mississippi. She received her B.A. from the University of Wisconsin in 1929 and attended the Columbia University Graduate School of Business. She returned to Mississippi in 1931 after her father's death, and from 1933 to 1936 she served as a publicity agent for the state office of the Works Progress Administration. She began publishing stories in the mid-1930s, including some of her most famous: "Death of a Traveling Salesman," "A Worn Path," "Lily Daw and the Three Ladies," and "Powerhouse," all of which concern the lives of rural Southerners during the Depression. After the war, with funding from a Guggenheim Fellowship, she traveled to France, Italy, Ireland, and England, where she held residencies at several universities. Welty's most notable works include *A Curtain of Green* (1941), *The Robber Bridegroom* (1942), *The Wide Net* (1943), *Delta Wedding* (1946), *The Golden Apples* (1949), and *The Optimist's Daughter* (1972). She was also an avid photographer, and five books of her photographs have been published, including *One Time, One Place* (1978). She was a member of the American Academy of Arts and Letters and won numerous literary prizes, including the O. Henry Prize (eight times), the Pulitzer Prize, the National Medal for Literature, the National Medal of Arts, and the PEN/Malamud Award for excellence in the short story. **Linda Kuehl** (1939–1978) was an editor, critic, and author. She interviewed Joan Didion for *The Paris Review* in 1978.

Acknowledgments

This book would not have been possible without the care and devotion of *The Paris Review*'s editorial team: Radhika Jones, Nathaniel Rich, Christopher Cox, Meghan O'Rourke, Charles Simic, and Sarah Stein, and a season of superb interns, Alexandra Andrews, Anjuli Davies, Perrin Drumm, and Benjamin O'Donnell.

Special thanks also to the generations of *Paris Review* editors who presided over the genesis of the interviews in this volume during the past half century.

Special thanks to Frances Coady, David Rogers, Eric Bliss, James Meader, and Tanya Farrell at Picador, and Jamie Byng and Anya Serota at Canongate.

Special thanks to the Wylie Agency.

James Baldwin manuscript page reprinted by permission of the James Baldwin Estate. Interview reprinted by permission of Jordan Elgrably and *The Paris Review*.

Harold Bloom manuscript page reprinted by permission of Harold Bloom. Interview reprinted by permission of Antonio Weiss and *The Paris Review*.

Peter Carey manuscript page reprinted by permission of Peter Carey. Interview reprinted by permission of Radhika Jones and *The Paris Review*.

William Faulkner manuscript page reprinted by permission of Random House, Inc. Interview reprinted by permission of Jean Stein and *The Paris Review*.

William Gaddis manuscript page reprinted by permission of the Estate of William Gaddis. Interview reprinted by permission of Zoltán Abádi-Nagy and *The Paris Review*.

Gabriel García Márquez manuscript page reprinted by permission of Gabriel García Márquez. Interview reprinted by permission of Peter H. Stone and *The Paris Review*.

John Gardner manuscript page reprinted by permission of the Estate of John Gardner. Interview reprinted by permission of Paul F. Ferguson, John R. Maier, and *The Paris Review*. A portion of this interview was taken, with permission, from a videotaped conversation with John Gardner conducted at the Brockport Writers Forum in October 1977 and copyrighted by the Brockport Writers Forum.

Graham Greene interview reprinted by permission of the Estate of Simon Raven and the Estate of Martin Shuttleworth and *The Paris Review*.

Stephen King manuscript page reprinted by permission of Stephen King. Interview reprinted by permission of Christopher Lehmann-Haupt and Nathaniel Rich and *The Paris Review*.

Philip Larkin manuscript page reprinted by permission of the Society of Authors and the Estate of Philip Larkin. Interview reprinted by permission of Robert Phillips and *The Paris Review*.

Robert Lowell manuscript page reprinted by permission of the Estate of Robert Lowell. Interview reprinted by permission of Frederick Seidel and *The Paris Review*.

Toni Morrison manuscript page reprinted by permission of Toni Morrison. Interview reprinted by permission of Claudia Brodsky Lacour and Elissa Schappell and *The Paris Review*.

Alice Munro manuscript page reprinted by permission of Alice Munro. Interview reprinted by permission of Jeanne McCulloch and Mona Simpson and *The Paris Review*.

Isaac Bashevis Singer manuscript page reprinted by permission of the Isaac Bashevis Singer Trust. Interview reprinted by permission of the Estate of Harold Flender and *The Paris Review*.

James Thurber manuscript page reprinted by permission of the Estate of James Thurber. Interview reprinted by permission of the Estate of George A. Plimpton and the Estate of Max Steele and *The Paris Review*.

Eudora Welty manuscript page reprinted by permission of the Estate of Eudora Welty. Interview reprinted by permission of *The Paris Review*.